'A wonderful store of gardening knowledge'
*Manchester Evening News*

'An excellent guide to any amateur gardener'
*The Yorkshire Post*

'Answers . . . almost every question the aspiring
vegetable gardener is likely to ask'
*Northern Echo*

'Describes everything from artichokes to
walnuts'
*Coventry Evening Telegraph*

'Packed with the detailed information one expects
from this writer . . . this book is particularly
welcome'
*The Field*

'Excellent for novice and expert. An investment
with rich dividends is how this book should be
regarded'
*Kingston Borough News*

Pears Encyclopaedia of Gardening
# Fruit and Vegetables

## Edited by Roy Genders

Mayflower

Granada Publishing Limited
Published in 1975 by Mayflower Books Ltd
Frogmore, St Albans, Herts AL2 2NF
Reprinted 1977

First published in Great Britain by
Pelham Books Ltd 1973
Copyright © Roy Genders 1973
Made and printed in Great Britain by
Richard Clay (The Chaucer Press) Ltd
Bungay, Suffolk
Set in Linotype Times

# List of Illustrations

# Line Drawings in Text

# General Entries

Entries in this encyclopaedia are arranged alphabetically, with cross references where a fruit or vegetable is known by more than one name. In addition, there are articles on the following subjects:

Crop rotation
Diseases (Fruit)
Diseases (Vegetable)
Fertilisers, Inorganic
Fertilisers, Organic
First Cross Hybrids
Fruit Trees in Pots and Tubs
Fruit Trees, Pruning
Fungicides

Green Manuring
Herbs
Hotbed
Insecticides
Lime
Manure, Liquid
Mulching
Pests
Sawdust

# Books Mentioned in this Encyclopædia

*Anatomy of Dessert* by Edward Bunyard, Published by Chatto & Windus, 1929.

*The Apple* by Robert Hogg, Published by Groombridge & Sons, 1859.

*Apples of England* by H. V. Taylor, Published by Crosby Lockwood, 1936.

*The Epicure's Companion* by Edward and Lorna Bunyard, Published by J. M. Dent & Sons, 1937.

*The Fruit Manual* by Robert Hogg, Published by *Journal of Horticulture,* 1845.

*The Gardener's Assistant* by Robert Thompson, Published by Blackie & Sons, 1859.

*Handbook of Hardy Fruits* by George Bunyard, Published by John Murray, 1920.

*Herball, or Historie of Plantes* by John Gerard, 1957.

*The Introduction to Natural System of Botany,* John Lindley, 1830.

*The Orchardist* by John Scott, Published by H. M. Pollett, 1872.

*Paradisi in Sole* (*Paradisus*) by John Parkinson, 1626.

*Profitable Culture of Vegetables* by Thomas Smith, Published by Longman Green, 1911.

# Metric Conversion

Temperatures in this encyclopaedia are given in both Fahrenheit and Celsius; the tables below give the linear, weight, area and volume metric equivalents.

LINEAR  1 inch = 2.54 centimetres   1 foot = 30.48 centimetres
3 feet = 1 yard = 91.44 centimetres

*Approximate equivalents*

| | |
|---|---|
| 1 in. = 2.5 cm | 3 ft. = 90 cm |
| 1½ in. = 3.5 cm | 4 ft. = 1.2 m |
| 2 in. = 5 cm | 5 ft. = 1.5 m |
| 2½ in. = 6.5 cm | 6 ft. = 1.8 m |
| 3 in. = 7.5 cm | 7 ft. = 2.1 m |
| 4 in. = 10 cm | 8 ft. = 2.4 m |
| 5 in. = 12.5 cm | 9 ft. = 2.7 m |
| 6 in. = 15 cm | 10 ft. = 3 m |
| 7 in. = 17.5 cm | 11 ft. = 3.4 m |
| 8 in. = 20 cm | 12 ft. = 3.7 m |
| 9 in. = 23 cm | 13 ft. = 4 m |
| 10 in. = 25 cm | 14 ft. = 4.3 m |
| 11 in. = 28 cm | 15 ft. = 4.6 m |
| 12 in. = 30 cm | 16 ft. = 4.9 m |
| 13 in. = 33 cm | 17 ft. = 5.2 m |
| 14 in. = 35 cm | 18 ft. = 5.5 m |
| 15 in. = 38 cm | 19 ft. = 5.8 m |
| 16 in. = 41 cm | 20 ft. = 6.1 m |
| 17 in. = 43 cm | 30 ft. = 9.1 m |
| 18 in. = 46 cm | 40 ft. = 12.2 m |
| 19 in. = 48 cm | 50 ft. = 15.2 m |
| 20 in. = 51 cm | 75 ft. = 22.9 m |
| 21 in. = 53 cm | 100 ft. = 30.5 m |
| 22 in. = 56 cm | 200 ft. = 61 m |
| 23 in. = 58 cm | 300 ft. = 91.5 m |
| 24 in. = 60 cm | |

**WEIGHT**

1 ounce = 28.35 grammes   16 ounces = 1 pound = 453.592 grammes
112 pounds = 1 hundredweight = 50.8 kilogrammes
20 hundredweights = 1 ton = 1016 kilogrammes

*Approximate equivalents*

| | |
|---|---|
| 2 oz. = 57 gm | 9 lb. = 4.1 kg |
| 1 oz. = 28 gm | 10 lb. = 4.5 kg |
| 3 oz. = 85 gm | 20 lb. = 9.1 kg |
| 4 oz. = 103 gm | $\frac{1}{4}$ cwt. = 12.7 kg |
| 8 oz. = 227 gm | $\frac{1}{2}$ cwt. = 25.4 kg |
| 12 oz. = 310 gm | $\frac{3}{4}$ cwt. = 38.1 kg |
| 1 lb. = 454 gm | 1 cwt. = 51 kg |
| 2 lb. = 908 gm | 2 cwt. = 102 kg |
| 3 lb. = 1.4 kg | 3 cwt. = 153 kg |
| 4 lb. = 1.8 kg | 4 cwt. = 203 kg |
| 5 lb. = 2.3 kg | 5 cwt. = 254 kg |
| 6 lb. = 2.7 kg | 10 cwt. = 508 kg |
| 7 lb. = 3.2 kg | 15 cwt. = 762 kg |
| 8 lb. = 3.6 kg | 1 ton = 1 tonne |

**AREA**

1 square foot = 92.9 square centimetres
1 square yard = 0.836 square metres
1 acre = 0.40 hectares

**VOLUME**

1 pint = 0.57 litres   8 pints = 1 gallon = 4.546 litres
8 gallons = 1 bushel = 36.37 litres

# APPLE

Apples are happiest planted in a soil that is well drained and is of a rich heavy loam, but not all gardens are fortunate in this respect; often the trees have to be planted in a cold, clay soil, especially where taking over new property. The commercial grower would select more suitable ground before embarking on his planting, selecting the land to suit the fruit. The amateur, however, must make the best use of what is available. But whilst pears require a warm soil, and cherries one of a chalky nature, there is a wide selection of apples suitable for most, and including the 'difficult' soils, with which the amateur gardener frequently has to contend. These will be:

(a) Soils of a limestone nature, which are generally shallow and likely to lack moisture during a dry period.

(b) Those of a cold, heavy nature.

(c) Those wet and badly drained.

(d) Those very light and sandy.

### APPLES FOR A LIMESTONE SOIL

The most difficult soils are those of a limestone nature, chiefly to be found in parts of Yorkshire, Derbyshire and across the south Midlands, and from Wiltshire, north Hampshire to Kent. Also, with the exception of Derbyshire, being in an area of low rainfall, lack of moisture about the roots is often experienced at a time when the fruit is maturing, and needs the necessary moisture to make a reasonable size. This is the reason for small, tasteless fruit.

The trouble may be partly overcome by manuring and by deep digging. The use of rape seed for green manuring, sowing the seed in April and digging in when several inches high will help to add fibrous humus to the shallow soil. The additional care with planting the trees will also help to ensure that the trees do not suffer from drought, but most important of all it is necessary to plant those varieties which have proved themselves capable of bearing a heavy crop in a chalky soil, for besides the question of moisture, some varieties show a liking for chalk, whilst others do not. Most important of these is Barnack Beauty, introduced in 1880 by Messrs Brown of Stamford, Lincolnshire. Yet this is an apple which has never become widely grown, because it is one of the few which is much happier in a dry, chalky soil than in a rich loam. If more amateurs knew of its merit when planted in chalk, many disappointments would be prevented, for in such a soil it bears heavily.

13

The tree is a strong grower and, like Worcester Pearmain, it is a tip bearer; that is, it bears its fruit on the tips of the twiggy wood, rather than forming close spurs as Cox's Orange. For this reason it is a tree for a good sized garden, and is not suitable for dwarf tree culture, e.g. cordons. It is a handsome fruit, greeny-yellow flushed bright crimson on the sunny side, and it will store until April. Indeed it is not at its best until March, when it is juicy and sweet.

Almost as good is Barnack Orange, the result of a cross from Barnack Beauty and Cox's Orange. It is at its best at Christmas, and like Barnack Beauty rarely crops well away from chalk. Another is St Everard, ready early in September, when it is one of the best of the early apples, but away from chalk it crops poorly, and makes only a small tree.

Making a tall, spreading tree – and, therefore, better for a large garden – is Gascoyne's Scarlet, raised in the chalk soils of Sittingbourne, Kent, and like Barnack Beauty, it crops well only on chalk. It bears a most handsome fruit, the skin being of palest cream, flushed with vivid scarlet, the sweet flesh also being coloured with scarlet. The fruit is equally good for cooking or for dessert. Another apple that crops well in shallow, chalky soils is Charles Ross, a delicious and most handsome apple, but it deteriorates if kept after November. It cooks well. The tree is of vigorous spreading habit, and so better in a country than a town garden.

APPLES FOR A CLAY SOIL

Soils of a cold, heavy nature, which are so often to be found in towns and in certain areas of the Midlands, will be quite unsuitable for Cox's Orange, and it is little use planting any variety which has not proved suitable under cold conditions. The same varieties should also be given preference for planting in cold, exposed northerly gardens and those situated in the north Midlands, and in parts of Scotland and Northern Ireland. Grow Cox's Orange in Dublin, Allington Pippin in Belfast.

Allington Pippin is a fine dual-purpose apple, widely grown in the Fens, Lincolnshire and East Yorkshire, but it blooms early and should not be planted in a frost pocket. Better, if a dessert apple is required, is Adam's Pearmain, possibly the hardiest of all dessert apples, and one of the very best for a cold, exposed garden. Lindley wrote, 'Its merit consists in it being a healthy, hardy sort, a particularly free bearer, extremely handsome, a good keeper ... acid and sugar being so intimately blended as to form the most perfect flavour.'* Added to this is its tolerance of cold, clay soils. The habit is compact, whilst the fruit is at its best after Christmas.

* John Lindley, Professor of Botany at University College in 1845 and Secretary to the (Royal) Horticultural Society; author of *The Introduction to Natural System of Botany.*

14

## Apple

For October, for a cold, heavy soil, King of the Pippins is an interesting apple. The fruit is oblong and of a bright orange colour, the flesh being hard, dry, aromatic and with a pleasant, almond flavour. It is hardy and is a heavy cropper.

For a culinary apple, ready in September, none is hardier than Pott's Seedling, raised in 1849 at Ashton-under-Lyne, Lancashire. It makes a compact tree and bears heavily. For late winter use, Newton Wonder, raised at King's Newton, Derbyshire, is as hardy as any apple and quite happy in a heavy clay soil. For size, shape and colour it is one of the most handsome of all apples and should be in every garden irrespective of soil and climate.

Another suitable variety is Herring's Pippin. Extremely hardy in a cold, clay soil, this apple will continue to crop well if never pruned, sprayed nor mulched. It is almost foolproof, and yet bears a large crop of handsome green and crimson fruit which possess a strong, spicy flavour, useful either for cooking or dessert. Like Newton Wonder, this too, should be in every garden, especially in the north, planted with Edward VII.

Something may be done to bring a clay soil into as satisfactory a planting condition as possible by incorporating drainage materials, such as grit, crushed brick and coarse sand, but first dig in deeply some caustic or unhydrated lime. This should be done during the early part of winter, the action of the lime as it decomposes also breaking up the clay particles in the soil. Then work in the drainage materials, and finally add some humus, such as straw, farmyard manure or straw decomposed by an activator, together with a small quantity of peat. Allow the soil to settle down and plant in March.

APPLES FOR A WET SOIL

Where land is wet and low lying, little can be done except to dig drains or trenches between the trees. Those varieties prone to scab should not be planted, but Lord Derby, Grenadier and Monarch, all excellent apples, are outstanding in their ability to tolerate a wet soil, and even cold conditions. Grenadier is the best of all pollinators for Bramley's Seedling, but whereas Bramley's Seedling will, like Grenadier, tolerate cold, heavy soils, it does not like wet, low-lying ground where it would also be susceptible to blossom frost damage.

Of dessert apples suitable for a wet soil, two will be found to be reliable croppers, Laxton's Superb, which makes only a small tree and comes quickly into heavy bearing, its handsome fruit being at its best in December; and Sam Young, a little-known variety of Irish origin and not mentioned in H. V. Taylor's comprehensive *Apples of England**. Robert Hogg in

* Published by Crosby Lockwood & Son Ltd., London, 1936.

15

his *Fruit Manual** describes it as being, 'a first-rate little dessert apple, in use from November until March.' It is a russet, cropping heavily in a damp soil, and though the fruit is small, it is one of the most richly flavoured of all apples.

APPLES FOR A SANDY SOIL

Light, sandy soils, which are generally well drained may be made more retentive of moisture by incorporating plenty of humus in the form of decayed stable manure, but they generally prove deficient in potash. The two best dessert apples for a light soil, yet not in an area of too heavy rainfall, are Worcester Pearmain and Ellison's Orange. Worcester Pearmain, introduced by Smith's of Worcester in 1873, is an indispensable apple to the commercial grower, an excellent pollinator for Cox's Orange, and is a heavy and reliable bearer, with its fruit of a rich crimson colour which sells on sight. Unfortunately for the amateur's garden, it is of vigorous habit and is a tip bearer, and so is not suitable in the dwarf forms. It is a gross feeder and requires plenty of room, and so is better suited to a large garden or small orchard.

For a small garden, Ellison's Orange, which comes quickly into bearing, its fruit maturing by October, will prove reliable in a sandy soil. It is a heavy and consistent cropper, and if it has a fault it is that its highly aromatic fruit takes on an aniseed flavour if stored too long. It should be consumed before November.

A long-keeping apple for a light soil, at one time widely planted throughout Sussex, is Forge, which Hogg describes as 'the cottager's apple *par excellence*.' It is a huge and consistent cropper, the greasy skinned fruits keeping well into the New Year. It makes a compact tree, is scab free and extremely resistant to frost.

SUMMARY

Apples for a limestone soil:
  Gascoyne's Scarlet, Barnack Beauty, Barnack Orange, Charles Ross, St. Everard.
Apples for a cold, clay soil:
  Allington Pippin, Adam's Pearmain, King of the Pippins, Pott's Seedling, Newton Wonder, Herring's Pippin.
Apples for a wet soil:
  Lord Derby, Grenadier, Monarch, Laxton's Superb, Sam Young.
Apples for a light, sandy soil:
  Worcester Pearmain, Ellison's Orange, Forge.

* Published by *Journal of Horticulture*, 1845.

# Apple

Apples like a soil containing both humus and nutrition. It is possible to give one without the other, with the result that a correctly balanced soil will not be obtained as where planting in a heavy soil when straw manure is dug in to prevent the soil particles becoming too compressed, which would deprive the roots of air, so necessary to bring about bacterial action of the soil, and without which the trees are unable to derive full benefit from manures. Humus is also necessary in both a light and shallow soil, but for a different reason. Here humus is provided to retain the maximum amount of moisture in the soil throughout summer, and though certain varieties will crop reasonably well in a light, poor soil, they will crop much better where both humus and a balanced diet is provided. Newton Wonder and Lord Derby will bear a heavy crop in light soil, but will only do so if humus and the requisite potash is present.

## TO CORRECT AN ACID SOIL

Besides the necessity for providing humus to counteract any deficiency in the soil, it is also important to ensure correct soil fertility. This means a balanced supply of the necessary foods to be made available to the trees over as long a period as possible, preferably for the lifetime of the tree.

As the soil of many town gardens is of an acid nature, due to deposits of soot and sulphur over a period of years, most town gardens will respond to a dressing of lime. This does not mean a heavy dressing unless certain varieties (e.g. Barnack Beauty and Gascoyne's Scarlet) are to be planted, which will benefit from a heavy application. As the apple requires magnesium in the soil, lime is best given in the form of magnesium limestone, or magnesium carbonate, and this should be applied in the early winter at the rate of 2 lb. per square yard. If planting a small orchard, the soil should be tested before applying the limestone, and this will only be necessary if the pH value shows an acid reaction below 6.0. Soil which is of an acid nature cannot fully convert the food content for the nourishment of the plants.

## CLIMATE AND SOIL FERTILITY

Fruit trees require food for them to grow, and to make new wood throughout the life of the trees. The trees also require a balanced diet to enable them to bear a heavy and consistent crop, but as to quantities of food required much depends upon soil, situation and variety. Apples growing in a light soil will require more potash than those in a heavy loam, whilst those growing in an area of high rainfall, which will tend to wash the minerals from the soil, will need heavier manuring and more careful attention to the plant's requirement in this respect. Variety too, plays an important part, for the most vigorous growers, e.g. Bramley's Seedling and Blenheim Orange, will become too vigorous and make an excess of wood and leaf if given the same amount of nitrogen needed for Sunset or Adam's Pearmain. In general, dessert apples require more nitrogen than the cookers, but as it is potash rather than nitrogen which gives colour to an apple, those noted for their high colour, e.g. Worcester Pearmain and Charles Ross, may be kept on a low nitrogen diet. Likewise those varieties which tend to be troubled by scab, for nitrogen tends to make excessive soft growth, and scab will be more prevalent.

Again, trees growing on the eastern side of Britain, where growth is much slower than on the west, will need additional nitrogen. It is therefore important to consider each tree and local climatic conditions before applying the manures, remembering that cooking apples will be of a more vivid green when given additional nitrogen, whilst dessert apples will show richer colourings of scarlet and orange if given liberal supplies of potash.

### HUMUS AND ORGANIC MANURES

When preparing the ground for planting new trees, dig in deeply some farmyard manure, or straw compost, possibly containing decayed vegetable waste, which has been rotted down with an activator. Possibly poultry or pig manure will have been incorporated. An average dressing is 10 tons to the acre, or roughly half a barrow load per square yard. This manure will contain nitrogen, potash and phosphates; it is slow-acting, which is advantageous to fruit trees, and it will also improve the structure of the soil. It is important to dig it deeply in and mix it well into the soil; manure, however, should not be packed around the roots of the trees.

Those who live near the coast could use seaweed as an alternative, or even fish waste. For those who live in the industrial north, shoddy, rich in nitrogen, and wood ash, rich in potash, may be used together and in place of farmyard manure. As apples also require small quantities of phosphorus, for otherwise the fruit will tend to remain small, 2 oz. per square yard of either bone meal, or steamed bone flour should also be worked in. To prevent waste, a square yard of ground should be marked out and prepared exactly where the trees are to be planted.

### GROWING IN GRASS

There is much controversy as to whether fruit trees should be planted into pasture (grass-covered ground), or into ground where the grass has been removed and which is possibly used for vegetable culture. Some growers compromise, by making large circles round the tree stems after planting.

It may be said that young trees will suffer serious nitrogen shortage if planted directly into grass, and older trees will be deprived of much valuable nitrogen, unless the grass is either grazed or kept cut short. Weed-infested grass, allowed to grow tall, will prove highly detrimental, especially in areas where growth is perhaps slower than normal. Grass which is grazed will use up little of the nitrogen in the soil and this will be replaced by the droppings of the animals. Grass which is constantly cut and left as a mulch will not only remove very little nitrogen, but will return valuable potash to the soil. Where grass is grazed, some additional potash will be necessary, quality and colour being the deciding factors.

A balanced diet is essential for fruit trees, nitrogen and potash requirements going hand-in-hand, an excess of one and shortage of the other proving detrimental to plant growth, whilst to a lesser extent phosphates and magnesium are also essential for a balanced diet. It should be said that, where being planted in grass which cannot be kept short, the trees will benefit from the removal of a large ring of turf from around the base, and over the exposed soil a mulch is given each year.

In districts of low rainfall, or where the soil is shallow, often overlying chalk, trees should never be planted in grass, for every drop of moisture will be needed by the trees. Here a mulch will prove most important, and if farmyard manure cannot be obtained, cover the ground with decayed leaves, peat or composted straw, and this should be applied in May, before the moisture evaporates from the soil. Fresh straw or sawdust should not be used, for this will utilise a considerable amount of nitrogen as it is undergoing the process of composting – nitrogen which is needed by the tree.

PROVIDING A BALANCED DIET

When the trees have been in their new quarters for two or three years, a check should be made on growth. If the trees are growing in an average loamy soil, and in a district of average rainfall, new, or extension growth, will be about 18 in. each season. If less than 12 in. of new growth is made, there will be need to provide a nitrogenous dressing, and the same may be said of established trees. Remember that certain varieties possess naturally a most vigorous habit, and these should be considered when determining nitrogenous requirements. The necessary nitrogen may be given by an application of sulphate of ammonia, raking round the tree about 2 oz. during late March when growth commences. More established trees may require double this amount, but it is much better to give a small quantity each year rather than a large amount one year, and none for several more years. Trees growing in long grass should be given from 3–4 oz., for here nitrogen deficiency will generally be greater.

A deficiency of potash, phosphorus and magnesium will not become apparent until the trees come into regular bearing, though lack of potash may be observed by the foliage turning brown and becoming crinkled at the edges. When the trees are bearing, the fruit will be small, of poor colour and will not keep as it should. There will also be a dearth of fruit buds, and so the crop will be small. Trees starved of potash will gradually become bare of foliage, and will die back. But potash must only be given where nitrogen is present, or with it, for it is essential to maintain a balanced diet. Potash in the soil will also release the necessary phosphates, so important for size of fruit, and thus it is only rarely that phosphates are artificially given by themselves.

Certain varieties show greater tolerance to potash deficiency than others. Worcester Pearmain is one which is very tolerant, whilst Lord Derby, Newton Wonder, Grenadier, Cox's Orange, Miller's Seedling and Beauty of Bath all require liberal potash supplies, especially on a light, sandy soil. It may be said that dessert apples require more potash than cookers, and most will require double the quantity on a light soil as those growing in a heavy loam.

Potash is best given in the form of sulphate of potash, using 1 oz. per tree, raked into the soil in spring. Too heavy applications must not be given for this will cause magnesium deficiency, now understood to be due to the use of excess potash. The trouble is frequently encountered where the soil is light and has received yearly potash applications. A tree deficient of magnesium will be observed where the foliage turns pale green, with purple blotches appearing about the centre ribs. In addition the new wood will shed its foliage too soon, before the end of summer. If left uncorrected, the trees become stunted and bear small crops.

The trouble may be prevented by an occasional dressing with magnesium limestone, especially where the soil tends to be sour, but a more rapid corrective will be to spray the foliage in midsummer (June), with a solution of magnesium sulphate (Epsom Salts) made by dissolving 1 lb. to 5 gall. of water, the magnesium being absorbed through the leaves.

An excellent method of maintaining the health of a young plantation is to lightly fork fish manure around each tree in December. This contains a high percentage of nitrogen, potash and phosphates, in addition to being of an organic nature. Farmyard manure is then used as a summer mulch.

PLANTING

The trenches or holes to take the plants should be made before the trees are taken from where they have been heeled in, or kept covered from frost, so that the roots are not unduly exposed to the air, and especially to a drying wind so often experienced in early spring. As a general rule, trees for a light, chalky soil should be planted during November to December. Those for a heavy, cold soil are best planted in March. Equally important is depth of planting.

Failure for the tree to bear well over a long period is so often due to either too shallow or too deep planting, and both contribute equally to the various causes of failure. Too shallow planting will cause the roots to dry out during a period of prolonged drought, and especially where the soil lies over a chalk subsoil. It may also cause the trees, where Type MIX rootstock (*see Rootstocks, below*) is being used, to fall over even when fully established, and especially where planted in an exposed garden.

Too deep planting, on the other hand, will mean that the roots will be in the cold, less fertile subsoil, cut off from air and the sun's warmth, whilst it will mean that the scion, at which point the graft has been made on to the rootstock, will be buried and may take root. This will mean that the characteristics of the rootstock will play little part on the habit of the tree.

When buying and planting fruit trees, bear in mind that the roots are as important to the tree, more so in fact, than its shape, and for this reason the younger the tree the more readily is it transplanted. Where planting an orchard, however small, maiden trees, one year old, are not only less expensive, but are also more readily established and may be trained and pruned to the requirements of the grower. And as with all trees, the younger they are, the more readily will they transplant, though in this respect the exception is the pear, which will transplant up to twenty years of age. After the hole or trench has been made to the correct depth, so that the level of the soil will be at a point just above the top of the roots, as near as possible to the same level as the tree was planted at the nursery, a spadeful of a mixture of sand and peat, to encourage the formation of new fibrous roots as quickly as possible, should be spread about the hole. To enable the roots to be spread out correctly, a small mound of soil should be made at the bottom of the hole.

The old gardeners would place a flat stone on the top of this mound to prevent the formation of a tap root. This may have its devotees, but the shortening of any large tap root with a sharp knife just before planting should be all that is necessary, at the same time removing any damaged roots, or shortening any unduly long roots. Here again, the experienced nurseryman whose reputation is built upon the success of the trees sent out, will see that the trees are lifted as carefully as possible, with the the roots in no way damaged. All too often those 'bargain parcels' arrive almost rootless and take years to become re-established.

The roots should be spread out so that each one is comfortable. All too often trees are planted in holes which are made far too small, with the result that they are bunched up, and compete with each other for nourishment. A tree badly planted can never prove satisfactory.

When the roots have been spread out, scatter more peat and sand about them, then commence to pack the soil around them. This is best done by holding the tree straight, or at the required angle in the case of cordons, which should be fastened to the wires before the soil is filled in. By pushing in the soil with the feet, a strong pair of boots being the best guarantee of correct planting, the job may be performed by one person. As the soil is pushed into the hole it is trodden firmly about the roots so that there will be no air pockets, which would cause the roots to dry out. Tread the soil in little by little so that a thorough job is done, rather than fill up the hole and tread down afterwards. Where planting against a wall it is advisable to incorporate additional humus materials, as the soil is being placed in the hole to retain the maximum of moisture about the roots. The same may also be done where planting in a light, sandy soil. The planting of a few trees may be much more thoroughly done than where planting in an orchard, and the work should not in any way be hastily carried out. If there can be two people to do the planting, so much the better.

## ROOTSTOCKS

The question of rootstocks is one of the utmost importance, for the habit of each variety will greatly depend upon the planting of a certain rootstock. These rootstocks, upon which the grafts or buds are made, may be divided into four main types:

    (a) Those of very dwarf habit.
    (b) Those of less dwarf habit.
    (c) Those more vigorous.
    (d) Those of robust habit.

Upon which stock is being used will depend the planting distances and ultimate weight of the crop.

## VERY DWARF ROOTSTOCKS

On the very dwarf rootstock, Malling IX, the trees will come more quickly into heavy bearing than on any other rootstock. It is that often

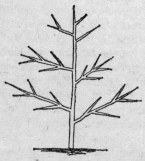

FIG. 1 *A dwarf pyramid tree*

used for cordon and pyramid trees which are required to be of less vigorous habit than bush and standards, but it may also be used for bush trees, which are required for a small garden and which are expected to remain reasonably dwarf and yet come early into bearing. Trees on this rootstock fruit abundantly at the expense of making wood, though they have a tendency to burn themselves out after thirty years fruiting, unless carefully tended throughout their life. This means:

(a) Regular attention to pruning, though this will not present much of a problem with those trees making little new wood.

(b) Care in keeping the ground clean.

(c) Providing a regular balanced diet.

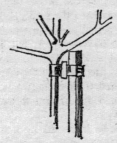

FIG. 2 *The correct way to tie a standard tree*

They also need careful staking during the first years after planting, for their root action, as may be expected, is not vigorous, and the trees easily blow over.

Bush trees on this rootstock should be planted from 10–12 ft. apart, pyramids 6–8 ft. and cordons 2 ft. apart, but much depends upon the natural habit of each variety. Beauty of Bath, for example, makes a spreading tree and should be given wider spacing than Adam's Pearmain; whilst the more vigorous varieties such as Bramley's Seedling, Blenheim Orange and Miller's Seedling should never be planted on this dwarf rootstock, for weight of foliage and fruit would most likely prove too much.

Trees on Malling IX, which are planted closer than those of other rootstocks, and as they come into heavy bearing sooner than any other type, will ensure the largest weight of fruit from a small garden, in the quickest possible time. But it must be said that these trees will never yield more than a bushel of fruit (40 lb.) at whatever age they reach, whereas Bramley's Seedling and Newton Wonder, on Malling II will yield up to 10 bushels when in full bearing, and Blenheim Orange and Worcester Pearmain about half that weight.

A more recent dwarfing rootstock is the Malling-Merton, MM 104, which has so far shown a greater resistance to woolly aphid than Type

IX, and has also given heavier crops, especially with Cox's Orange Pippin and Ellison's Orange. In trials of the East Malling Research Station in Kent, eleven year old Cox's Orange produced 461 lb. per acre on this rootstock compared with 382 lb. on Type MIV, which is similar to MIX.

Another rootstock MM 106 gave in comparison only 257 lb. on the same trees, planted in the same heavy loam, but this stock has proved a heavier bearer when used in light, sandy soil. With its much better anchorage, and being a more satisfactory propagator for the nurseryman, MM 104 looks as if it will supersede all other dwarf rootstocks.

SEMI-DWARF ROOTSTOCKS

Malling IV has for some time been the recognised rootstock with a semi-dwarfing habit, and over a period of the first twenty-five years, trees will bear larger crops than with any rootstock, but like MIX the trees root badly and need to be well staked. This rootstock suits Cox's Orange better than any other and is used entirely for this purpose, but it is safer to plant in a position sheltered from strong winds. From the latest results of the new MM 104 it would appear that this rootstock will eventually supersede both MIX and MIV.

Planting distances should be increased by 2 ft. for bush trees where using MIV, as in their first ten to twelve years, the trees will make rather more growth than on MIX. Apart from the same need to stake securely they will prove more suitable for orchard culture, not requiring quite such detailed attention as those on MIX.

MORE VIGOROUS ROOTSTOCKS

For large garden or orchard planting, MI and II have been most successful during the past twenty years. Trees on MI will come more quickly into bearing than those on MII, and it has been observed that MI is better suited for planting in a district of high rainfall and soil moisture, and so has been propagated considerably by West Country nurserymen. It does not suit Cox's Orange and with many varieties in a dry soil it has not resulted in such heavy crops as from trees on MII, which may be said to be the most successful of all rootstocks for commercial planting. It produces a tree of good size which it builds up gradually, at the same time increasing its cropping so that there is a balanced, long-lived tree, which over fifty years or more will bear a heavier weight of fruit than from any other rootstock.

As the trees, especially of the most vigorous varieties, will require a spacing of 20 ft. where the soil is of a heavy loam, this is not a suitable rootstock for a small garden, but much depends upon whether one wishes to enjoy a heavy crop during the first twenty to twenty-five years of the tree's life with diminishing crops later, or more regular bearing over fifty years or more.

Trees on MII root deeply and rarely require staking, and being able to search widely for their nourishment are good orchard trees, able to withstand drought, and do not require such meticulous attention as to feeding and upkeep. They will however, require more attention as to their pruning. Certain varieties, such as Winston and Sunset, which are of only semi-vigorous habit in comparison with Blenheim Orange or Newton Wonder, would find MM 104 more suitable, for these less vigorous varieties will give a greater yield per acre on a less robust tree, and planted half the distance apart of that allowed for MII rootstocks. The amateur can draw his own conclusion, possibly planting six trees 10 ft. apart on MIX or MM 104, or on the same area of ground, three trees 20 ft. apart of MII or the new rootstock MMIII. But whereas the six dwarf trees may yield around 150 bushels of fruit over the first thirty years of their life, the three trees on the vigorous stock should yield 300 bushels, though the greater weight will be given between twenty to thirty years of age. For an orchard or large garden, the more vigorous rootstock is to be recommended; for a small garden, the more dwarfing rootstocks.

The new MMIII in the East Malling Trials has cropped more heavily than MII, a combination of Cox's Orange, Jonathan and Ellison's Orange yielding an average of 348 lb. from eleven-year-old trees, compared with 273 lb. on MII, and with there being little difference in the size of tree, it would appear that MMIII will become widely used in future years. It is also remarkably free from woolly aphid.

MOST ROBUST ROOTSTOCKS

The two most vigorous rootstocks yet produced are the old MXVI and the new MM 109, the latter however may be said to come somewhere between this and the previous groups of rootstocks for vigour. Both make large trees, as bush or standards, and require planting between 20–30 ft. apart. This stock is generally used for standard orchard trees and will take from fifteen to twenty years before coming into heavy bearing. At from ten to twelve years of age, it bears only half the crop produced by MIX or MM 104 at the same age, much less than given by MMIII or MII. These robust rootstocks are of little use for the amateur's garden, but they may be used for those culinary varieties which make rather sparse growth, e.g. Lord Derby and Grenadier, and they will respond favourably to the additional vigour.

MM 109 has so far shown a high resistance to drought, more so than either MII or MMIII, and for this reason is being planted in East Anglia, also where the soil is shallow and overlying chalk, often a dry soil. No comment can be made on Barnack Beauty or Gascoyne's Scarlet, used on

MM 109, but one would imagine this rootstock to give heavy crops planted in a dry, chalky soil.

A new rootstock of great vigour, MXXV has shown that trees will come into heavier bearing at an earlier age than those on MXVI or MM 109, in spite of it making a large tree, but it has been troubled by woolly aphid, and it is early yet to acclaim it as being an advance over others of robust habit.

All this may, to the amateur, sound most complicated, but it is advisable to consider the part played by each rootstock, not only on the weight of crop, but on the habit of each variety, so that the correct choice may be made for the size of one's garden. To put it more clearly:

(a) Very Dwarf Rootstocks – MIX, MM 104.

(b) Semi-Dwarf Rootstocks – MIV.

(c) More Vigorous Rootstocks – MI, MII, MMIII.

(d) Most Robust Rootstocks – MXVI, MXXV, MM 109.

## POLLINATION

When planting new fruit trees there is a great tendency to neglect the pollinating factor, with the result that, although the stock may be of the best and have been planted with care, nothing but disappointment will be the result. Certain varieties are self-fertile and so will, up to a point, set their own fruit; some are partially self-fertile, and so will set a partial crop without a pollinator. These are the diploids. Others, called triploids, are almost sterile and so must be given a suitable pollinator to help them set fruit. The question of providing a suitable pollinator is not easily worked out, and yet to obtain heavy crops it is essential. It is of little use rushing to post off your order for Cox's Orange Pippins, your favourite apple, in the hope that they will bear plenty of fruit without a suitable pollinator. They will not.

### POLLINATION OF COX'S ORANGE PIPPIN

It was Messrs. Backhouse and Crane, of the John Innes Institute, who discovered that Cox's Orange Pippin would not set its own pollen, a fact still not realised by many gardeners, who continue to plant this variety by itself in the expectation of a good crop. Research has shown that even where the blossoms of certain varieties open at the same time as the Cox's Orange, it does not mean that a successful pollination will result, for it has been shown that the pollen of such varieties as Stirling Castle, Merton Worcester, Worcester Pearmain, James Grieve and Egremont Russet ensures a setting for fruit more than twice as high as that of most other varieties.

One interesting tree, a Cox's Orange which had been crossed with

Sturmer Pippin, had one half covered in fruit, whilst the other half, self-pollinated, set only two small fruits. Experiments carried out at the John Innes Institute by the two fruit experts, resulted in the interesting information that of 11,949 flowers of Cox's Orange self-pollinated, only 92 flowers or 0.76 per cent set any fruit. Yet crossed or pollinated with Egremont Russet 13.4 per cent set fruit; with St Edmund's Russet, 14.4 per cent; and with Stirling Castle 15.5 per cent. Where Ellison's Orange, Worcester Pearmain and Sturmer Pippin were used separately as pollinators, the set was just 8.0 per cent. The results also clearly show that not only is Cox's Orange a poor pollinator for most other varieties, but also where Cox's has been used as a parent. For instance, crossed with St Everard, of which Cox's Orange is a parent, the percentage of fruit set showed only 3.3 per cent, though St Everard crossed with Beauty of Bath gave a setting of 10.8 per cent. Of all the tests carried out at the John Innes Institute, the average fertility from cross-pollination showed that 10 blooms set fruit out of every 100, yet where varieties were self-pollinated the average of fruit set was only 2.5 per cent.

Plant both the self- and partially-fertile varieties, and another which will be in flower at the same period, planted as near as possible, so that the bees, and other insects, are able to transfer one lot of pollen to the other without having to travel long distances. For example, with Royal Jubilee, which blooms late and so misses late frosts, plant the equally late flowering Crawley Beauty or Edward VII, or Lane's Prince Albert, which has a prolonged flowering season. It is interesting that, where several trees of Royal Jubilee have been planted together, they set only .09 per cent of fruit, yet planted with Lane's Prince Albert the percentage was as much as 16 per cent. Gardeners of former times got over the trouble by planting dozens of varieties together, but then they had large gardens in which to do so.

BIENNIAL BEARING

Again, the question of biennial bearing must be considered. Ellison's Orange, a useful pollinator for Cox's, tends to biennial cropping, and if this apple is used as a pollinator, another, possibly Worcester Pearmain, to take over on its 'off' season, should be planted with it. The following apples also tend to biennial planting:

Allington Pippin, Bramley's Seedling, D'Arcy Spice, Miller's Seedling, and Newton Wonder.

The choice must also be governed by climatic conditions; James Grieve is not suitable for planting in the moist west of England, and so Worcester Pearmain may be used in that region, and James Grieve confined to the drier Midlands, parts of Scotland, and the south-east. Cox's Orange should also be planted in these parts:

There is also the question of lime-sulphur spraying to combat scab and mildew. Here certain varieties are sulphur shy, and leaf and fruit drop are often the result. It will, therefore, be essential to plant together only those apples which are unharmed by lime-sulphur. St Cecilia, Beauty of Bath, Newton Wonder and Lane's Prince Albert are all fairly sulphur shy, and Newton Wonder, a really grand quality apple, is also inclined to biennial bearing, so it would be advisable to plant several of these apples together. Or plant Newton Wonder with Lord Derby, which, although tolerant of lime-sulphur, is extremely resistant to scab and mildew, and no spraying may, in any case, be necessary. The two are also excellent pollinators.

## TRIPLOID VARIETIES

In many years connected with orchards, I have found that three suitable varieties planted together will give the largest set of fruit. This is certainly true when planting biennial croppers and the triploid varieties, those which will not cross-pollinate with each other, and which are not very good pollinators for others. They must be planted with diploid varieties, which fortunately most apples are, and with those which bloom at the same time and are not given to biennial cropping. It is, therefore, wise to use two diploid pollinators, for there also may be the additional loss of the blossom of one variety through frost damage; also, the diploids will pollinate each other. The popular Bramley's Seedling is a triploid variety, and should be planted with Grenadier, an early cooking apple, and with James Grieve or Lord Lambourne, for providing dessert.

Those three fine dessert apples, Blenheim Orange, Gravenstein and Ribston Pippin, are all triploids, and should never be planted together. With Ribston Pippin and Gravenstein, plant Lord Lambourne; and with Blenheim Orange, plant Egremont Russet, they will give no trouble, for neither pollinator tends towards biennial bearing. Beauty of Bath is also a suitable pollinator for Ribston Pippin and Gravenstein, but it is sulphur shy, which the others are not. To fertilise the pollinator itself, it is advisable to plant another similar-flowering diploid, as previously explained.

## BUILDING UP THE COLLECTION

When commencing with apples, most wish to begin with Cox's Orange, the best eater, and with Bramley's Seedling, renowned as the best cooker. Then plant with them James Grieve, which will pollinate both, and add Grenadier, another good cooker, as a second line of defence, for this will also pollinate both. These will then be an early and a late apple for both cooking and for dessert. Others can be added by degrees. Laxton's Advance, a grand early apple, is also a Cox's pollinator, though not so good as James Grieve, but, as it will also pollinate Bramley's Seedling, it may be a much better proposition in wet districts. Then add Laxton's Superb, also a reasonably good Cox's pollinator, but which inclines to biennial cropping, and so should be assisted with Laxton's Advance, or with Worcester Pearmain, or Fortune. And so on.

Of those that are very self-fertile, such as Laxton's Exquisite, and Epicure, Worcester Pearmain, St Everard, Chrimas Pearmain and Rev. W. Wilks, two only with the same flowering period need be planted together, and one would be assured of a satisfactory pollen setting, but even though each is self-fertile, it is inadvisable to plant on their own, for only a proportion of the expected maximum crop will be the result.

FLOWERING TIMES

Flowering times are interesting, for whereas Ribston Pippin and Wagener flower early in the season, they are classed as late-maturing apples. And in bloom at the same time, Gladstone and Beauty of Bath are the first apples to mature; in the West Country, they are ready for use late July. The average length of time for apple trees to bloom is about fifteen days, spread over a period of about thirty days, the very early-flowering varieties being in bloom for the first fourteen to fifteen days or so, whilst the mid-season-blooming varieties partially overlap the last few days of the early-flowering apples, e.g. Edward VII, Royal Jubilee and Crawley Beauty, do not come into bloom until the last of the mid-season varieties have finished flowering, with the exception of the very long-blooming Lane's Prince Albert. In selecting suitable pollinators one must be governed by the flowering period of the trees, and not by their maturity.

These apples bloom early, depending upon climatic and seasonal conditions, and will pollinate each other:

(*Note:* T. = Triploid; P.S.F. = Partly Self-Fertile;
  S.F. = Self-Fertile; S.S. = Self-Sterile.)

| | |
|---|---|
| Beauty of Bath | (P.S.F.) |
| Bismark | (P.S.F.) |
| Gladstone | (S.F.) |
| Gravenstein | (T., S.S.) |
| Keswick Codlin | (P.S.F.) |
| Laxton's Advance | (P.S.F.) |
| Laxton's Exquisite | P.S.F.) |
| Laxton's Fortune | (P.S.F.) |
| Lord Lambourne | P.S.F.) |
| Miller's Seedling | (P.S.F.) |
| Rev. W. Wilks | (S.F.) |
| Ribston Pippin | (T., S.S.) |

| | |
|---|---|
| St Edmund's Russet | (P.S.F.) |
| Wagener | (P.S.F.) |

These apples bloom early mid-season:

| | |
|---|---|
| Allington Pippin | (P.S.F.) |
| Annie Elizabeth | (P.S.F.) |
| Arthur Turner | (P.S.F.) |
| Bramley's Seedling | (T., S.S.) |
| Cox's Orange Pippin | (P.S.F.) |
| Egremont Russet | (P.S.F.) |
| Ellison's Orange | (P.S.F.) |
| Grenadier | (P.S.F.) |
| James Grieve | (P.S.F.) |
| King of the Pippins | (P.S.F.) |
| Laxton's Epicure | (P.S.F.) |
| Mother | (P.S.F.) |
| Orleans Reinette | (P.S.F.) |
| Peasgood's Nonsuch | (P.S.F.) |
| Stirling Castle | (P.S.F.) |
| Sturmer Pippin | (P.S.F.) |
| Tydeman's Early Worcester | (P.S.F.) |
| Worcester Pearmain | (P.S.F.) |

These apples bloom late mid-season:

| | |
|---|---|
| Blenheim Orange | (T., S.S.) |
| Charles Ross | (P.S.F.) |
| Claygate Pearmain | (S.S.) |
| D'Arcy Spice | (S.S.) |
| Early Victoria | (P.S.F.) |
| Howgate Wonder | (P.S.F.) |
| Lady Sudeley | (P.S.F.) |
| Lane's Prince Albert | (P.S.F.) |
| Laxton's Superb | (P.S.F.) |
| Lord Derby | (P.S.F.) |
| Monarch | (P.S.F.) |
| Newton Wonder | (P.S.F.) |
| Rival | (P.S.F.) |
| Sunset | (S.F.) |
| Warner's King | (T., S.S.) |
| Winston | (S.F.) |

These apples bloom very late:

| | |
|---|---|
| Court Pendu Plat | (P.S.F.) |
| Crawley Beauty | (S.F.) |
| Edward VII | (P.S.F.) |
| Royal Jubilee | (P.S.F.) |

As a general rule varieties from each section should be planted together to obtain the best results from pollination, though many will overlap, such as Lane's Prince Albert, which has a very long flowering period, about twenty-one days, with Edward VII and Crawley Beauty.

When ready for use:
To mature July – August: (c = Culinary.)

Beauty of Bath
Duchess of Oldenbury
Early Victoria (c)
Elton Beauty
George Cave

Gladstone
Irish Peach
Lady Sudeley
Laxton's Advance
White Transparent

To mature September:

Arthur Turner (c)
Celia
Ellison's Orange
Grenadier (c)
Hereford Cross
James Grieve
Laxton's Epicure

Laxton's Exquisite
Laxton's Favourite
Laxton's Fortune
Miller's Seedling
Pott's Seedling (c)
Tydeman's Early Worcester
Worcester Pearmain

To mature October – Early November:

Allington Pippin
Charles Ross (c)
Egremont Russet
Herring's Pippin
Kidd's Orange
King of the Pippins
Lord Derby (c)
Lord Lambourne
Merton Worcester
Michaelmas Red

Monarch (c)
Mother
Peasgood's Nonsuch (c)
Rev. W. Wilks (c)
Rival
St Edmund's Russet
Shaw's Pippin
Taunton Cross
Wealthy (c)

To mature December:

Acme
Blenheim Orange
Christmas Pearmain
Claygate Pearmain
Cockle's Pippin
Cornish Aromatic
Cox's Orange Pippin
D'Arcy Spice
Forge
Gascoyne's Scarlet
Golden Noble (c)

Gravenstein
Howgate Wonder (c)
Laxton's Superb
Margil
Merton Prolific
Orleans Reinette
Pearl
Ribston Pippin
Rosemary Russet
Sunset

## Apple

To mature (use) January – February:

| | |
|---|---|
| Adam's Pearmain | Newton Wonder (c) |
| Barnack Beauty | Northern Greening (c) |
| Belle de Boskoop | Opalescent |
| Bramley's Seedling (c) | Sam Young |
| Brownlee's Russet | Wagener |
| Golden Russet | Woolbrook Pippin |
| Lane's Prince Albert (c) | |

To use March – June:

| | |
|---|---|
| Annie Elizabeth (c) | May Queen |
| Crawley Beauty | Sturmer Pippin |
| Easter Orange | Tydeman's Late Orange |
| Edward VII | Upton Pyne |
| Laxton's Rearguard | Winston |

### VARIETIES

ACME. Of all the dessert apples introduced over the past decade, this gives promise of being the most outstanding, and has been named accordingly. Raised by W. Seabrook & Sons Ltd, of Chelmsford, this is the first apple to crop on its own roots, setting its fruit freely, even in the nursery rows the second season after planting.

It is later than Cox's Orange, of which it is the nearest in flavour of any apple, the bright yellow skin being flushed and striped bright crimson on the sunny side. The flesh is yellow, firm and juicy. If gathered mid-November, it will keep through winter.

ADAM'S PEARMAIN. For the period Christmas to mid-March, there is no better apple for the small garden, and Lindley (see footnote on p. 14). writing in 1830, said that this apple possessed the finest flavour of any dessert variety. It makes a small tree and is extremely hardy, cropping well even in clay soils. The yellow russeted fruit is particularly handsome, the yellow flesh being rich and juicy.

ALLINGTON PIPPIN. Those who enjoy a brisk, acidy apple, as does the author, will find this a welcome change from the rather sweet, earlier-maturing varieties. It is inclined to biennial bearing, and makes a large spreading tree. Growth is more restricted in poor soils, those of a dry, sandy nature for which it is most suitable. This could be said to be a dual-purpose apple, for like all those possessing a tart flavour, it cooks well.

ANNIE ELIZABETH. Raised by Messrs Harrisons of Leicester, this apple may be considered one of the very best for a small garden. It makes a healthy, compact tree, and comes quickly into bearing; the fruit, if harvested at the end of November, keeping until Early Victoria is available in early July. Valuable in the north in that it blooms late, it bears a handsome ribbed fruit which is popular on show bench.

ARTHUR TURNER. A vigorous but upright grower, bearing handsome blossom and a large handsome fruit, the polished green skin having an orange flush. The fruit should be used from the tree, but it hangs well and may be removed when required, from late August until November. For this reason it is extremely useful for the small garden.

BARNACK BEAUTY. For a chalk soil this is the best of all dessert apples, but only on such soil does it crop abundantly. It was originally a seedling found in the village of Barnack, near Stamford in 1900. It is a tip bearer, and makes a large, spreading tree. The fruit is very handsome, being of beautiful shape and of a deep golden colour, heavily flushed with crimson. The flesh is yellow, juicy and extremely sweet, at its best during January and February.

BEAUTY OF BATH. Introduced about a century ago by Messrs Coolings of Bath. It makes a vigorous, spreading tree and has been widely planted until recently on account of there being no similar variety, bearing highly coloured fruit so early. In Somerset orchards, this variety is ready by late July when it should be used, otherwise the fruit will become dry and flavourless. It would appear that George Cave and Laxton's Advance would replace it for commercial planting. It blooms early and may prove useless in a frosty garden, whilst it is tip bearing and self-sterile. Plant Laxton's Advance as a pollinator.

BELLE DE BOSKOOP. A native of the Low Countries, where it is widely planted, this makes a strong-growing tree and takes a year or two to come into bearing, but the fruit is so valuable for Christmas use that it could well be more widely planted. That it is not is because its bright yellow fruit with its grey russeting is none too attractive. This however, will not deter the amateur, for it makes delicious eating either as dessert or when cooked.

BLENHEIM ORANGE. One of the great apples of England in every sense of the word. It makes a huge tree, bears a tremendous crop and one of the largest of dessert fruits. It is at its best from mid-November until early January, useful both for dessert and for cooking, like eating sweet Brazil nuts. It was discovered at Woodstock, near Blenheim, Oxfordshire, about 1820, and as long ago as 1822 was awarded the Banksian Silver Medal by the then London Horticultural Society. It has however, two disadvantages. One is that it is a triploid and although being pollinated by James Grieve, Ellison's Orange, etc, it is not able to pollinate them in return. Another is that it takes ten years to come into heavy bearing, and is therefore little planted in private gardens. And like its culinary counterpart, Bramley's Seedling, its blossom is most susceptible to frost.

BRAMLEY'S SEEDLING. One of the richest apples in vitamin C content, making a huge orchard tree and bearing heavily, where the blossom is not worried by frosts, and where the soil is a well-drained loam. It also takes several years to come into heavy bearing, and it is a triploid, requiring a pollinator and yet being of little use itself for pollination. This is not a variety for an amateur's garden, for it is also a biennial cropper. Against all this, it bears the finest of all cooking apples, which should be used from Christmas until Easter.

BROWNLEE'S RUSSET. Another fine apple which retains its olive green colour when mature. Its flavour is brisk and aromatic, and it keeps in condition right until early spring without its skin shrivelling. The tree is extremely hardy, of compact upright habit, is very fertile and almost completely devoid of disease. Where the soil is cold and none too well drained this is an indispensable keeping apple. I have seen trees standing in water for weeks without any ultimate loss of crop. Its blossom is amongst the most beautiful, being of a rich cerise-pink colour.

CELIA. Raised by Mr N. Barritt of Chester, it is proving a valuable late mid-season apple. It was raised from Langley Pippin × Worcester Pearmain, bearing a heavy crop of fruit which stores until early December. This is an apple of beautiful shape, with a glossy green skin, mottled and striped reddish-brown, and is ready for eating in early September. The flesh is sweet and crisp, and the fruit is well able to stand up to adverse weather. Like Mr Barritt's other introduction, Elton Beauty, this apple is free from mildew, and able to withstand lime-sulphur spraying.

CHARLES ROSS. A handsome apple of large proportions, the flesh being crisp and refreshing, the skin deep green, heavily flushed scarlet on the sunny side. That it is not a strong grower except where suited, has detracted from its popularity of recent years, but it always does well in a chalky soil. It is also somewhat sensitive to lime-sulphur, and for this reason is not now planted commercially. Nor does it keep well, becoming rather dry, but taken from the tree in mid-October and used before 1 December, there is none better as a dual-purpose apple. It is pollinated by most mid-season flowering varieties, especially Grenadier, Ellison's Orange and James Grieve.

CHRISTMAS PEARMAIN. Like Claygate Pearmain, it makes a neat, upright tree, is extremely hardy, does well in a cold, clay soil, and crops heavily. For an exposed garden it should be included, but though its flesh is crisp and juicy, it cannot compare in flavour to the others of this section.

CLAYGATE PEARMAIN. Found growing in a hedge at Claygate in Surrey about 1820, this is one of the very finest of all dessert apples. Anyone who has gathered the green and grey russeted fruit, covered with frost on a late December morning, will have tasted the English apple at its very best. The flesh is also green, deliciously sweet and crisp, and very aromatic. It makes a neat, compact tree, ideal for a small garden, for which it should be a first choice. Few know it because the vividly-coloured imported apples attract most attention today.

CORNISH AROMATIC. Its handsome fruit of orange and red, is marked with russet and possesses a nut-like aromatic flavour. This is a neat, hardy variety, excellent both for cooking and dessert. It is not a heavy cropper, but is so resistant to scab and canker in wet districts that it is still valuable for these areas.

COURT PENDU PLAT. One of the oldest apples in the world, widely planted in Tudor gardens, and which is still a valuable variety. Its hard, yellow flesh is pleasantly aromatic, much like Cox's Orange, but unlike that variety, it blooms very late and so misses late frosts. For this reason it was known to Stuart gardeners as the Wise Apple. Though making only a very small tree, it bears heavily, a handsome, highly-coloured apple.

COX'S ORANGE PIPPIN. Raised from a pip of Ribston Pippin, which accounts for its quality, by Mr W. Cox, a brewer at Colnbrook, Buckinghamshire, and introduced in 1850 by Charles Turner, who gave us that excellent cooker Arthur Turner. Cox's Orange not only possesses superb flavour, but is of arresting appearance, which accounts for its popularity. It does however, possess a wide variety of adverse points, which make it one of the most difficult to crop well. The blossom is susceptible to frost, the tree may be termed a weak grower, and is very frequently troubled by scab, mildew and canker in cold soils. It is sensitive both to lime-sulphur and copper sprays. Yet the fruit carries a more subtle blending of fragrance and aromatic flavour than any apple, and nothing has yet been found to take its place.

CRAWLEY BEAUTY. Found growing in a Sussex garden and introduced by Messrs Cheal & Co of Crawley, Sussex, this is a superb apple and quite indispensable in a garden troubled by late frosts, being in bloom the first days of June. The fruit should be allowed to hang until mid-November, when carefully stored it will keep until April. The skin is deep green, striped and spotted with crimson, the flesh is soft and sweet. The tree is resistant to the usual apple diseases and is of upright habit, making it most suitable for a small garden.

D'ARCY SPICE. At its best in eastern England, for it does best in a sandy soil and in dry areas. It tends to biennial cropping and its fruit is nobbly, not nearly so attractive as the others mentioned, but it is the nearest apple to nut-like eating, and is sweet and aromatic, a grand amateur's apple, at its best during December.

EARLY VICTORIA. Also known as Emneth Early, for it was discovered at Emneth, Cambridgeshire, and introduced by Messrs Cross of Wisbech, at the turn of the century. The bright green, irregular-shaped fruit is borne in such profusion that in some seasons it may require thinning. The tree is compact, and comes early into bearing.

EASTER ORANGE. This is an excellent apple introduced by Hilliers of Winchester, the fruit, orange-flushed with scarlet and russet, being at its best for Easter, the creamy flesh being crisp and sweet. The tree is of quite vigorous growth, but like Claygate Pearmain, is of neat habit.

EDWARD VII. This dual-purpose apple is one of the very best of all. Like Crawley Beauty, it blooms late and makes a neat, upright tree. It is the result of a Blenheim Orange X Golden Noble, two splendid apples.

Though usually listed as a cooker, Edward VII makes delicious eating if kept until Easter, and it will store until the first July apples are ready. It will then be golden skinned and possess a rich, subtle flavour.

EGREMONT RUSSET. For the small garden or orchard, this is an ideal variety, for it makes a small, upright tree, and crops heavily in all seasons. It also makes a fine cordon. It is at its best a little earlier than most russets, in November, and does not need storing to bring out its flavour and abundant juice. With its round, even-shaped fruit, it is one of the most handsome of all the russets, and one of the most delicious for late October dessert.

ELLISON'S ORANGE. Valuable in that it quickly comes into heavy bearing, the large, handsome fruit is of Cox-like appearance, but must be eaten early September, just before it is ripe. If over-ripe, the flesh is soft and has a peculiar aniseed flavour. It is a good Cox pollinator and extremely resistant to scab, mildew and canker.

ELTON BEAUTY. This is a handsome fruit certain to become a favourite on the show bench. It is the result of a cross between James Grieve and Worcester Pearmain, bearing the better qualities of these two prolific cropping apples. Its green skin is flushed and striped bright scarlet, with an attractive green ring round the centre. This is possibly the best-flavoured of all early apples, maturing at the end of August, and yet keeping until early December, the only long-keeping, early apple. Just right for the late summer shows, and for the late seaside trade. Where it is grown for profit, this is one of the best of all early apples.

FORGE. Where the garden is in a frost pocket, or is troubled by cold winds, or where space is limited, plant this variety. It makes a small, compact tree, comes quickly into bearing, and its fruit, with its pale yellow skin and pleasing perfume, will keep from late October until late in January. Hogg wrote, 'a great and constant bearer'.*

GASCOYNE'S SCARLET. Also strong-growing, but only in a soil heavily laden with chalk. This variety is one of the best of all apples for planting on a thin, chalky soil. The aromatic flesh makes pleasant eating in early November, whilst it is also delicious and soft when cooked. It is a handsome apple with a skin of palest yellow, heavily splashed with scarlet.

GEORGE CAVE. Is this the long-awaited apple to replace Beauty of Bath, with its spreading habit and inability to hold its fruit until fully mature? It matures a week before Beauty of Bath and has quite exceptional fertility, its bloom being resistant to frost. The skin is almost as highly coloured as

---

* Robert Hogg, Vice-President of the British Pomological Society, and the greatest authority on fruit growing in the nineteenth century. Author of *The Fruit Manual*, 1845 and *The Apple*, 1859.

a ripe Worcester Pearmain, the flesh being white, firm, sweet and juicy, with almost no core. The next generation of gardeners will plant this abundantly.

GLADSTONE. This is the first of all apples to mature, being ready for eating mid-July in a sheltered garden. It makes a large, spreading tree and is a tip bearer; it bears very large fruit, highly-coloured, which must be used just before they mature or they will become soft and flavourless. The variety was found growing in Worcestershire, and was introduced about the same time as Beauty of Bath.

GOLDEN NOBLE. This fine old Norfolk apple may be used between mid-October and Christmas, its soft yellow flesh being soft and juicy, and delicious when baked. It makes a compact tree, ideal for small gardens, its fruit being amongst the most handsome of all, with its orange-yellow skin slightly speckled with grey and brown.

GOLDEN RUSSET. Of all the dessert apples which yield well year after year, none is more reliable than Golden Russet, of which H. V. Taylor in his famous *Apples of England* dismissed in three lines, but of which Dr Hogg wrote in his *Fruit Manual* published over 100 years ago as being 'a first rate apple in use from December to March, crisp, rich and aromatic' – a perfect description. It has a handsome skin completely covered with golden russet. It is an exceedingly hardy variety, and if it has a fault it is that it bears too heavily and should be thinned.

GRAVENSTEIN. This apple is ready for eating at the end of October. It will, however, keep until Christmas, and is of such superb quality that it is a sacrilege to use it before. To enjoy its honey-like flavour to the full, one needs to be able to sit in front of a log fire entirely at ease. It is an old German variety of poor appearance, which conceals its soft, juicy, creamy flesh with its subtle aroma. It makes a huge, spreading tree, requires plenty of room and should be given a warm soil. Not for north-country gardens.

GRENADIER. If only its massive, exhibition quality fruit would keep even a few weeks, this would be one of the finest of all apples, for not only does it make a small, well-shaped tree able to withstand any amount of moisture at the roots, but it is a tremendous cropper in all parts, and is used for pollinating a wide range of apples, including Bramley's Seedling, Laxton's Superb, Cox's Orange, Ellison's Orange, and others too numerous to mention. A fine apple in the West Country, it is highly resistant to scab and canker, its fruit amongst the best of all for baking, and yet it will not keep. It must be used from the trees. But for this, no other apple would be grown for cooking.

HEREFORD CROSS. Not having grown this variety I can offer few remarks, but in the West Country it is being fairly widely planted. Raised by Mr Spinks at the Long Ashton Research Station, Bristol, it has Cox's Orange as a parent, the fruit having the same crisp, orange flavour, and is of similar appearance. It is ready for eating at the end of September.

HERRING'S PIPPIN. Introduced by Messrs Pearsons of Nottingham, at the beginning of the century, and a most reliable apple for a cold, heavy soil, cropping freely even if entirely neglected. The deep green fruit, flushed crimson on the sunny side, possesses a strong aromatic perfume and spicy flavour. Should be used through November, there being no better apple for this month, yet it still remains neglected.

HOWGATE WONDER. This is a new cooking apple, now being widely planted commercially. It was raised in the Isle of Wight, but is thoroughly hardy, the fruit being ready mid-October and keeping until early February. The large apples are of a handsome green colour, striped scarlet. An excellent exhibition variety.

IRISH PEACH. A tip bearer and a vigorous grower, and although not suitable for cordons it bears an apple of such delicious flavour, that it should be grown wherever space permits. The fruit, with its crisp, aromatic flesh, is ripe the first week of August, and should be eaten during that month. The fruit is of conical shape, pale green, mottled and flushed with crimson.

JAMES GRIEVE. Except in the warm, moist districts of the west, where it cankers badly, this is one of the most reliable of all apples. It should not be over-fed with nitrogenous manures, or it will make excessive growth and crop less freely. It is early to bloom, and should not be planted where late frosts persist. Gladstone or Laxton's Epicure are suitable pollinators, whilst James Grieve is an excellent pollinator for Cox's Orange. Though it is of vigorous habit, it is of upright growth, and as it is a spur bearer it proves suitable for all but the smallest gardens. It crops well and regularly, the fruit being of a rich flavour from the tree early in September, or stored for 3–4 weeks. One of the few apples introduced from Scotland, and valuable in every way.

KIDD'S ORANGE. Raised in New Zealand, it may be said to be the most highly-coloured of all late apples, and is being extensively planted commercially. It has the same high colour as Worcester Pearmain, and possesses even better keeping qualities than Cox's Orange; moreover, it is one of those valuable varieties which, like Herring's Pippin, will crop well with the very minimum of attention. In Essex, where it is most successful, it is a great success when grafted on to cookers. It is resistant to scab and makes a neat, upright tree.

KING OF THE PIPPINS. This is a hardy variety, which at one time was widely planted commercially. It makes a small, upright tree and bears heavy crops, the orange-coloured fruit possessing a distinct almond flavour, the flesh being firm and nutty, like a russet. James Grieve, Beauty of Bath or Grenadier, would be good pollinators. The fruit should be used during November.

LADY HENNIKER. Raised at Thornham Hall in 1850, this old Suffolk apple now seems to have taken a back seat. It is a fine cooking apple for December, and makes pleasant eating in the New Year as dessert when the fruit has lost some of its acidity. It makes a large spreading tree and crops heavily, the fruit being of large, uneven shape and keeping well into the New Year.

LADY SUDELEY. Like all early apples this one is extremely highly coloured, being of a rich golden colour, vividly striped with scarlet. This makes the best tree of any for a tub or pot. It bears heavily and remains free from disease. It comes into use early in August, but must be gathered just before fully ripe to obtain its best flavour. Flowering late, it is a valuable early apple for a frosty garden, and especially in the north.

LANE'S PRINCE ALBERT. Raised at Berkhamsted in 1871, this makes a dwarf, yet spreading tree, with drooping branches, and is most sensitive to lime-sulphur. It requires a rich, deep loam, when it will bear profusely a handsome apple with white, juicy flesh.

LAXTON'S ADVANCE. Ripe in mid-August, when it should be eaten, and not left to become dried by the sun, this is a delicious apple of large, handsome appearance, and possessing the crisp texture of Cox's Orange Pippin. The fruit is coloured a rich crimson, and may be said to be the sweetest of all apples, too sweet for some.

LAXTON'S EPICURE. Like Fortune, this is another apple of excellent qualities from the Cox's Orange × Wealthy stable, and a winner of the Bunyard Cup for the best seedling apple. It is ripe by, and should be used during September, when it will be found to possess the juicy sweet flavour of Cox's Orange. Like Fortune it is self-sterile, and needs James Grieve or Worcester Pearmain as a pollinator.

LAXTON'S EXQUISITE. A handsome dual-purpose apple, the result of Cox's Orange × Celleni Pippin (the latter an old variety no longer grown). It follows Worcester Pearmain, ready at the end of September. It is a vigorous upright grower, the fruit being highly-coloured and of rich flavour, but has only a short season before it goes soft and dry.

LAXTON'S FAVOURITE. This new apple, with its high colouring and crisp, sweet flesh is ready for eating towards the end of September. It is a vigorous, but upright grower, and so is suitable for a small garden. It crops regularly, the fruit being of an even size and well shaped.

LAXTON'S FORTUNE. Rightly given an Award of Merit by the R.H.S., this is one of the best apples ever introduced, the result of a Cox's Orange × Wealthy. It is early to bloom and is self-sterile, and must be planted with Lord Lambourne, or Laxton's Exquisite. The fruit is at its best during October, when it should be used for it will not keep. It is a strong and regular cropper, the bright yellow fruit being profusely striped with red.

LAXTON'S REARGUARD. This is the longest-keeping of all dessert apples, only Edward VII, which may be termed a dual-purpose apple, keeping longer. It is an extremely hardy variety, with the same characteristics as its parents Court Pendu Plat and Ribston Pippin, both being hardy and of compact habit. The fruit, which has a slightly russeted appearance, is similar to Cox's Orange, but is of a more flattened shape. It should be allowed to hang on the trees until early December, and is not at its best until March. It will keep until June.

LAXTON'S SUPERB. Like James Grieve and Worcester Pearmain, this is a grand all-round apple, making delicious Christmas and New Year eating. It is extremely hardy, much better than Cox's Orange, for a northern garden, and much easier anywhere, and yet it has the flavour and high quality of Cox's Orange, its other parent. Though widely planted as an orchard tree, it crops abundantly in the cordon form, and makes a compact bush tree, ideal for any garden. It is a tremendous cropper, the fruit being slightly larger than Cox's Orange, of similar colouring but with pure white, nutty flesh. Carefully stored it will keep until March. Pollinated by Rival, Worcester Pearmain and others. Like all huge croppers, it often requires a rest season, and is inclined to biennial bearing.

LEMON PIPPIN. This strangely-shaped variety makes a small, compact tree and bears a huge crop of medium-green fruits, which are quite oblong, almost lemon-shaped. But do not be put off by this for its fruits hang until Christmas, and it will store until Easter, its rich, sharp flavour being excellent for cooking and reasonable for dessert.

LORD DERBY. Another excellent Lancashire culinary apple, raised at Stockport; like all the early cookers, it should be used from the trees. It makes a tree of vigorous growth though of upright habit, and bears heavily in all seasons and in all soils. Like Grenadier, it always does well in a wet, clay soil. It bears an irregular green apple, and the flesh cooks to an attractive, deep-claret colour, and is especially delicious sweetened with brown sugar.

LORD LAMBOURNE. Raised by Messrs Laxton Bros and awarded the R.H.S. Cup for the best seedling apple of 1921, it has since been widely planted commercially. It makes a good-sized tree and does especially well in standard form. It is self-fertile and is a heavy cropper, but is best away from damp districts, like James Grieve, from which it was evolved, and being of similar colour. It is ripe mid-October and remains sweet, crisp and juicy until late in November. A grand apple for a large garden, and should be in every collection.

MARGIL. A very old apple, which Edward Bunyard includes in his best 'selection' for Christmas. It makes a very small tree and bears heavily in all districts. It is not popular for its small, flattish fruit is not in any way handsome, being yellow and crimson and covered with splashes of russet, but this matters little, it is what is inside that counts, and the crisp yellow flesh is sweet and juicy and strongly perfumed. With a light sherry this fragrance is brought out to the full, but use it by the early New Year.

Robert Thompson suggests that it should be grown in wind-swept gardens on account of its dwarf habit.*

MAY QUEEN. Raised near Worcester, this is an ideal apple for a small garden, making a very small, compact tree, immune to scab, yet cropping heavily. The fruit, with its crisp, nutty flavour, is at its best if kept until May.

MERTON PROLIFIC. This a late-maturing apple, raised by the John Innes Institute. It is a regular and heavy cropper, the almost olive-green skin having a striking carmine-red flush which becomes brighter with keeping. It has Cox's Orange Pippin and the excellent dwarf late cooker, Northern Greening, as parents. It makes a neat, upright tree, The fruit should be gathered in mid-November, and will keep until the end of February.

MERTON WORCESTER. Raised by Mr M. B. Crane at the John Innes Institute, the result of a Cox's Orange × Worcester Pearmain, it ripens a week later than Worcester Pearmain, is a better keeper, but has the appearance of Cox's Orange, a yellow skin, flushed with scarlet and russet. The creamy-yellow flesh is crisp and aromatic. Does best in the drier districts, and is being widely planted in East Anglia.

MICHAELMAS RED. Raised by Mr H. Tydeman at the East Malling Research Station. The fruit is almost a replica of its parent Worcester Pearmain, having the same shiny crimson skin, and matures about a fortnight later. For a small garden this is a better variety than its parent, for it is of less vigorous habit, and is not a tip bearer, so may be grown as a cordon.

MILLER'S SEEDLING. Raised by James Miller of Newbury, Berkshire, this is an excellent early-September apple, at its best just before Worcester Pearmain. It makes a large tree, yet comes quickly into bearing and crops so heavily that it tends to biennial bearing, requiring a season of rest after one of plenty. It is a handsome apple with pale yellow skin, striped scarlet, with the fruit on the small side and no outstanding flavour. It will prove reliable in all soils, including a chalky soil.

MONARCH. Though often used in late November as harvested, this apple will keep, if stored carefully, until April. It was introduced by Messrs Seabrooks of Boreham, Essex, in 1913, and is a useful Cox's pollinator. The blooms are extremely resistant to frost, but the tree often suffers from brittle wood, requiring its lower branches to be supported. A most handsome apple with its olive green and pink flushed skin, it is delicious when cooked.

MOTHER. An American variety introduced by Messrs Rivers of Sawbridgeworth, Hertfordshire. The yellow and crimson fruits with their pinky flesh possess rich, aromatic flavour, and are exceptionally sweet and

---

* Robert Thomson, Keeper of the Royal Horticultural Society's Gardens, Chiswick, Author of *The Gardener's Assistant*, Blackie & Son, 1859.

juicy. The tree makes slow growth though cropping heavily, and it is an excellent variety for a northern garden.

NEWTON WONDER. With its highly-coloured fruit, at its best when grown in grass, its pale green skin flushed and striped with scarlet, this is one of the very best cookers for storing. It makes a large, spreading tree, and is definitely biennial, but it blooms late and misses late frosts. Plant with Lady Sudeley, Charles Ross or Early Victoria. Raised at King's Newton near Derby in 1887, the particularly handsome fruit keeps well until Easter.

NORTHERN GREENING. A grand cooker for small gardens, keeping well until mid-April, It makes only a dwarf, upright tree, yet crops abundantly, the fruit being of a rich, glossy green colour. Ideal for a cold garden, its only fault is that the fruit is small, but against this, it never shrivels when stored.

OPALESCENT. A fine all-round apple of American origin, its glossy, almost purple-crimson skin and its large size make it one of the most handsome of all apples. Used for dessert during December, it is rich and juicy and will remain so until mid-March. It is also, in my opinion, second only to Bramley's Seedling as a cooking apple. Add to this its hardiness and its large and regular cropping habit, it must be an apple with a distinct future. Grown well, the fruits reach huge proportions without in any way becoming coarse, nor do they require thinning. Yet, strange as it may seem, there seems to be only one firm which stocks this variety.

ORLEANS REINETTE. This is possibly the most richly flavoured and sweetest apple in cultivation, grown at least for 200 years, and originating from the Low Countries, where it has for long been popular. The fruit is flat and of a beautiful golden colour, shaded crimson with a large open eye, rather like a small Blenheim Orange. It is at its best over Christmas: 'as a background for an old port it stands unapproachable', says Edward Bunyard in his *Anatomy of Dessert*.* It makes a compact tree and is extremely hardy, and like all russets is rarely troubled by disease.

PEARL. A really good dessert apple for the Christmas period, like Rival, one of the parents (with Worcester Pearmain), of this new apple. Pearl blooms reasonably late, and is extremely frost-resistant, although it is tip bearing and is of vigorous habit. It is a heavy cropper, the conical fruit hanging well and ripening to a deep red colour by late September, the flesh being yellow and with almost a Cox's Orange flavour. It will keep well until the end of January, the flavour improving with storing. One of the best of all apples for the festive season.

PEASGOOD'S NONSUCH. Yet another famous apple from the Stamford district of Lincolnshire. It makes a dwarf garden tree, yet bears a reasonable, though not enormous crop of handsome, golden fruit, with a bright

* Published by Chatto & Windus, 1929.

crimson cheek. The tree is very hardy, though it crops well only in a deep, well-drained loam.

POTT'S SEEDLING. Raised in Lancashire, home of so many cookers, this is a very hardy variety of excellent culinary value, but its great value lies in its hardiness and ability to crop well in poor soils.

REV. W. WILKS. Yet another famous offspring of Ribston Pippin, introduced about 1900, and what a handsome apple it is, making large size and being a universal winner on the show bench. The skin is primrose-yellow, thinly striped with scarlet, the flesh is creamy and juicy and quite sweet. Fruits will frequently weigh more than 2 lb. each. The tree is of neat habit and is a tremendous cropper, but the fruit must be used by the end of November.

RIBSTON PIPPIN. Though almost past its best by Christmas, being suitable for November and early December, this magnificent old apple, found in the garden at Ribston Hall, Knaresborough, Yorkshire, about the year 1750, has achieved fame as the parent of Cox's Orange, as well as for its own delicate flavour. It makes a spreading tree and crops regularly, though sometimes lightly, and must have plenty of moisture at its roots. The fruit is most handsome, being of an olive-green, striped and flushed scarlet. It is still grown commercially throughout the world, but is now strangely neglected by the amateur. Do not forget it is a triploid.

RIVAL. This is one of the best of all apples for November, being of outstanding flavour, no apple being more juicy. It makes a large, spreading tree and crops well in the north, the handsome fruit having an olive-green skin, flushed bright scarlet on the sunny side. May be eaten from the tree mid-October to mid-November, or may be stored until Christmas.

ROSEMARY RUSSET. 'Very juicy, sugary and highly aromatic', is the description given to this fine late apple by Robert Hogg (see footnote on page 36). Its skin is golden, tinged with green and red, and covered with brown russet. It was widely planted at the beginning of the nineteenth century, when it was regarded as the best of all New Year apples. It is a hardy variety, and makes a small tree.

SAM YOUNG. For cold, clay soils, this is a most reliable apple, at its best from November until mid-February. Its bright yellow skin is russeted with grey, and spotted with brown, the flesh being green and especially rich and juicy. Introduced from Ireland about 1771, it is also known as Irish Russet.

SHAW'S PIPPIN. This is an apple of unknown parentage, found in a garden near to the late George Bernard Shaw's home at Ayot St Lawrence in Hertfordshire. It makes a large apple, of rich colouring, and possesses the flavour of Blenheim Orange. It is ready for gathering in mid-October, and will keep in condition until the year end. The tree comes more quickly into bearing than Blenheim Orange and is a more suitable variety for a small garden. Although the fruit is large, no thinning is necessary.

SOWMAN'S SEEDLING. For mid-August, this is a useful variety; raised in Lancashire, where it crops well, the fruit being very large and round, and of excellent quality when cooked.

ST EDMUND'S RUSSET. Raised in Suffolk where it seems to make more growth than in the west, it is a tip bearer, and a strong grower. It is early flowering and pollinated by Beauty of Bath. To many it is the best flavoured of all October apples, almost equal to a Cox's being juicy and sweet. The skin is bright orange, shaded with russet. Only in size and appearance have russets any bad marks against them, in all other respects they are the most hardy and easily managed of all top fruits, and no apples make for better dessert.

STURMER PIPPIN. It is so late to mature that it should only be planted where the fruit receives the maximum of late autumn sunshine, and it always seems to do best south of Birmingham. It was raised at Haverhill in Suffolk, about a century ago, from a seed of Ribston Pippin (surely the best and most prolific parent of all apples). Though a green apple, the fruit is handsome, being covered with dark brown russet, the flesh being firm and having a gooseberry-like flavour. The fruit will keep until June, and is only at its best early the following summer.

SUNSET. With its sweet, yellow flesh and orange russeted skin, this is an excellent substitute where Cox's Orange proves a poor grower. Raised in Kent in 1920, Sunset has all the good points of Cox's Orange, and none of its bad ones, and whereas Cox's likes a sandy soil, Sunset likes a heavy loam. The tree is strong-growing without being too vigorous, the blossom is very fertile, whilst it bears heavily from an early age. It also blooms late and so misses late frosts. Making top quality dessert for November and December, this is an apple with a future.

TAUNTON CROSS. Also raised by Mr Spinks at Long Ashton, this is a mid-October-maturing apple of most handsome appearance, very similar to Charles Ross, although the fruit is flatter and its green skin has a bright crimson flush. The flesh tinged with pink, and is particularly sweet. Of dwarf habit, the tree is extremely resistant to scab and crops particularly well in wet districts.

TYDEMAN'S EARLY WORCESTER. Raised at East Malling, the fruit is mature about ten days before Worcester Pearmain, and has the same glossy crimson skin. The round, medium-sized fruit is at its best about the first week of September.

TYDEMAN'S LATE ORANGE. Also raised by Mr Tydeman at East Malling, this variety may be described as a late-keeping Cox's Orange, storing until April, and being of similar flavour, with dark crimson-russeted skin. It is pollinated by Grenadier or Charles Ross. It would appear to crop heaviest and remain more free from scab in the drier districts.

UPTON PYNE. Bearing heavy crops in the worst seasons and making a large apple of exhibition quality, Upton Pyne was raised by Mr George Pyne of Topsham in Devon. The skin is of a pale primrose, striped with pink, and the fruit will keep well until Easter. The flesh is crisp and sweet, and it makes possibly the best baked apple of any, Bramley's included. It should also be planted for beautiful blossom.

WAGENER. Like a number of the dual-purpose apples, this is an American variety and an instance of a variety known for more than 150 years that is only now becoming popular. It makes a small, compact tree, and is an abundant bearer, the fruit being the best keeping of all apples; if taken from storage as late as mid-April, they will not contain a single wrinkle, and will be still firm and juicy. The bright glossy green skin, flushed with scarlet, makes this a most handsome exhibition apple. It needs a pollinator to crop abundantly, preferably Egremont Russet or Lord Lambourne.

WEALTHY. A dual-purpose American apple of handsome appearance which is cropping well in Britain. It is not a new apple, but one which is only becoming popular. It bears a most attractive fruit with a yellow skin, flushed and striped scarlet and russet. The flesh is juicy and refreshing, and is delicious eaten from the tree in November; or it is equally useful for cooking, breaking down beautifully when baked. At its best in November.

WINSTON. This is a fine, late-keeping apple, raised in Surrey, in which county and in Sussex it crops extremely well. It is also valuable for a northern garden, for it blooms quite late, missing all but the latest frosts. The fruit is one of the richest coloured of all apples, being bright orange profusely streaked with scarlet, the flesh being sweet and having a strong aromatic flavour. It makes a compact tree, is immune to disease and bears consistently well. It is, in fact, one of the best apples now grown commerically, and should be more widely planted in private gardens.

WOOLBROOK PIPPIN. Introduced in 1920 by Messrs Stevens of Sidmouth, Devon, this is a splendid dual-purpose apple for January to February use. It may be used for cooking until Christmas, but afterwards its juicy and aromatic fruits with their yellow-and-red russeted skin are so delicious as to be worthy of best dessert. It is a vigorous but upright grower, and bears especially well in light soils.

WORCESTER PEARMAIN. Unlike the equally highly-coloured Gladstone, this apple is generally picked all too soon or as soon as it colours. The quality will be greatly improved if allowed to hang for several weeks, when it will be as crisp and juicy as the best of dessert apples. It may be said to be the best apple of its period, and is widely used as a Cox's pollinator, but it is a tip bearer and makes a large tree, and so should be omitted from the smallest gardens, even though it may be said to be the best all-round apple ever introduced, good in all soils, completely hardy, a regular cropper and free from disease.

# APRICOT

To crop well, the apricot requires a high rainfall and grows well in the western parts of the British Isles and as far north as Glasgow. It requires a soil with a high lime content and should be given the shelter of a sunny wall, against which it is grown as a fan-shaped tree. The apricot suffers from Die Back or Brown Rot which will cause long-established shoots to die back entirely and flowering early, the blossom is frequently harmed by frost, against which protection may be given by planting against a southerly wall to provide the warmth necessary to ripen the new wood; or by planting against the higher wall of a lean-to greenhouse.

Plant in autumn, spacing fan-shaped trees about 18 ft. apart for they make long shoots and fruit on short spurs. The stems of the fan should be allowed to grow on without branching as far as space permits, pinching back the side shoots in summer to about 1 in.

Though apricots are self-fertile, there will be a better set of fruit if the flowers are hand pollinated. This is done with a camelhair brush, with which the flowers are dusted in turn as they open. This is a necessary procedure where growing indoors.

When the fruits have set and are beginning to swell, thin them three to a cluster and again to about 4 in. apart as they begin to ripen. Allow the fruit to become fully ripe before removing it when dry and place on a layer of cotton wool to prevent bruising.

## PRUNING

Pruning for replacement wood is done as described for Peaches. The apricot also fruits on the preceding season's growth, and when the old spurs have borne fruit for two seasons they should be removed to make way for newly-formed spurs.

## VARIETIES

EARLY MOORPARK. It makes a large oval fruit of pale apricot colouring, the flesh being orange and is the first to mature, ripening towards the end of July.

HEMSKERK. The best variety, bearing large crops outdoors and in pots under glass, the conical fruits being of orange-yellow, marked with red and of delicious flavour.

MOORPARK. One of the latest to ripen, and one of the best, the large round fruits of orange-red being borne in quantity. Introduced by Admiral Lord Anson in 1760.

POWELL'S LATE. A heavy cropper, it is the latest to ripen, its deep golden-yellow fruits being flushed with red.

SHIPLEY'S BLENHEIM. A mid-season variety, it is the hardiest apricot and is a most abundant cropper, the small oval fruits being of deepest orange and of rich flavour. It is the variety most grown for canning.

## ARTICHOKE, GLOBE

Valuable in that the globular heads are rich in vitamins and natural salts, the Globe artichoke should be far more widely grown. That is may not be altogether hardy in a heavy soil or in an exposed garden, may go against its popularity, but simple precautions will make it long-lived, and a welcome change from the usual summer vegetables. Established plants will bear their mature heads in midsummer, and suckers planted and rooted in November in the south, and in April in the north, will come into bearing early in autumn. If suckers, which appear in spring from around the neck of the plants, are rooted each year, the older plants may be dug up and destroyed after four years, for they then tend to make small heads.

The suckers, which are the chief means of propagation, are removed when 8 in. high, using a knife to sever them from the parent plant. Where possible ensure that each has a small piece of root attached to help it to a good start. Suckers are removed and planted in late autumn in the south, for they will root before any severe weather sets in, but north of Birmingham it is better to wait until April. They should be planted into prepared beds, a crop of lettuce or some other quick-maturing vegetable being grown between the suckers for the first few months whilst they are making growth.

Plant 3 ft. apart each way, for they will make large, bushy clumps during their second year. The shoots should be set 4 in. deep into a friable soil, well enriched with decayed compost and, like asparagus and beetroot, they revel in seaweed and a light, sandy soil. If the soil is of a heavy nature it must first be lightened with grit, boiler ashes, coarse sand or peat, or perhaps a little of each. Then work in the manure. This plant likes cow manure, though any humus-forming manure is suitable, and for those who live near the coast, seaweed is cheap and effective. The plants should also be given a top dressing with strawy manure every November after the foliage has died down. This will also give protection, during winter, but in the north soil should be heaped over the roots as well, and a covering of bracken or wood shavings held in place by more soil should ensure complete immunity to frost during the severest of winters. Where the soil is of a heavy nature, boiler ash or sand would be better used to cover the roots during winter, heavy soil retaining too much moisture.

Between May and early August, the plants will appreciate an application of manure water every week, and during summer a mulch of lawn mowings will also help to conserve moisture around the roots. In most soils this is sufficient to ensure succulent heads without artificial watering, except during a dry summer. A $\frac{1}{2}$ oz. per plant application of sodium nitrate sprinkled around the roots during a damp day in spring will help the plants to get a good start. Above all, see that the ground is clear of all perennial weeds, and keep the hoe moving during summer.

The heads should be removed when young and tender, at the same time cutting the stem half-way back. A guide to when to cut is when the heads have attained a good size, but have not commenced to open. Use at once, steaming for a full hour, then remove the centre and fill with chopped mushrooms, egg, tomatoes or anything available, and serve with tomato sauce.

Where the suckers can be obtained, the Green variety is more tender and of superior flavour to the Purple Globe. This plant is troubled neither by pest nor disease.

## ARTICHOKE, JERUSALEM

The white-skinned artichoke is a nourishing and pleasant vegetable. It differs from the Globe artichoke in that it grows under the soil, the tubers being formed in clusters, like potatoes. The reason for such a valuable vegetable being so neglected by gardeners must be because their rough, nobbly skin proves rather difficult to clean, and shortage of kitchen staff does not help matters.

No vegetable could be easier to grow, but this is its undoing. It will grow almost anywhere, but it will grow better and prove of superior quality if grown well. Though it prefers a dry soil, some decayed manure should be incorporated, being deeply dug in. Just before planting, work in 2 oz. of potash, and the same of superphosphate.

As the tubers begin to grow early, they should be in the ground by 1 March in the south and by the month end in the north. Small tubers are the best to use, rather larger than a walnut, and they should be planted in V-shaped drills about 5 in. deep. Allow 16 in. between the tubers in the rows and 30 in. between the rows. Watering with liquid manure through early summer will help to increase the yield, and so will earthing up the rows early in May, after the manner of potatoes.

The roots are carefully lifted as soon as the tops die down towards the end of October, and they should be stored in dry sand in a frost-proof room. But as the roots are of better flavour used as soon as they are lifted, they should be lifted from mid-September, those not used being lifted and stored in October.

## ASPARAGUS

Early April is the best time to make up a new asparagus bed, and the secret of success is to allow the plants plenty of room. This is a vegetable all enjoy yet few grow it, and of those who do, so few grow it successfully. When making up the beds which remain in prolific bearing for many years, the plants should be set 3–4 ft. apart each way. The French allow more room. As it is, the male plants that crop most freely, for the females concentrate most of their vigour on producing seeds; females should be replaced by males wherever possible; or the females should be prevented from seeding.

The asparagus is a maritime plant, enjoying a warm, sandy soil, similar to the conditions provided by the Mediterranean sea-shore, where it grows wild. As thorough drainage is essential, a raised bed should be made, and to make for ease in cutting the stalks this should be made no more than 6 ft. wide. This will allow three rows with almost 3 ft. between each.

Trenches should be taken out 9 in. deep and a liberal amount of well-rotted stable manure incorporated with the bottom soil. If the soil is at all heavy, sand or boiler ash must be added. Two-year roots should be purchased and, to keep them fresh and as moist as possible, the trenches should be prepared in advance, as soon as the soil permits for easy working. The spider-like roots, which should be spread out over small mounds of soil and manure, are placed at 3 ft. intervals in the trench. Before replacing the soil, add some coarse sand around the crowns, which should be about 4 in. below the level of the trench top. Then carefully fill in the prepared soil, to which has been incorporated a 2 oz. per square yard dressing of superphosphate and 1 oz. per square yard of sulphate of potash. Take care to see that all perennial weeds have been removed before the soil preparations commence, for the beds soon become a mass of root growth and any cleaning, except that of surface weeds, will be impossible. It is also important to see that the roots are not allowed to become dried by cold winds when being planted. Plant and cover in one trench at a time. For the first year after planting, 'catch' crops can be grown between the rows, but this is not advisable afterwards.

By mid-May plant growth will be observed, but no sticks should be cut. It is necessary to build up a strong plant, and in early June a 1 oz. per square yard (35g. per square metre) dressing of common salt should be given, followed by a repeat a month later. As soon as the seeds begin to form they should be removed, not only to conserve the energies of the plant, but also to prevent the seeds from ripening and falling when they will germinate and fill the ground with a mass of young plants. When the foliage turns brown in early autumn it should be cut down almost to ground level and the beds should be given a mulch. This treatment is also to be given to established beds.

Another method is to give a thick covering of seaweed, which the plants love and which encourages those thick, succulent sticks the following season. A keen gardener in the Midlands believes it worth while to send a lorry to the coast to collect a load of seaweed every October, and his asparagus beds are outstanding.

All annual weeds and any docks or dandelions should be removed before giving a mulch. If seaweed cannot be obtained, cover the beds with rotted manure or compost straw and decayed leaves. In early April, all long litter should be removed and a 2 oz. per square yard dressing of nitrate of soda should be carefully raked into the top soil. To obtain sticks of exhibition quality, feed once each week from early May with liquid manure water, and keep this up until late in July.

For the first seasons after planting only few sticks should be cut; this may be increased with each year, but over-cutting of even established beds will cause exhaustion, and no sticks should be cut later than the third week of June in the south, and early July in the north, where cutting begins later.

Asparagus may easily be raised from seed sown in drills in April. A well nourished seed bed should be prepared and the seeds should be spaced 1 in. apart in the rows. Germination takes about a month. Throughout summer it is important to see that the seedlings do not suffer from lack of water. Thin out any plants that become congested and keep the hoe going between the rows. If the seeds have been planted individually they will require no transplanting, but the following spring may be moved to permanent beds as soon as growth commences in April. To prevent the formation of seeds, cut off the tops of the foliage in autumn.

Two of the best varieties are Connover's Colossal and Sutton's Perfection, both of which bear very large sticks. Also excellent is Early Argenteuil, which is earlier than the others and of excellent flavour, although not so robust; Bedenham's Purple, widely grown in the Evesham district, is also good.

## AUBERGINE

Commonly known as the Egg Plant, it may be grown with the minimum of heat. All that is required is a temperature of 52°F. (11°C.) when the seed is sown early January. Use the John Innes compost and only just cover the seed. To hasten germination, cover with a sheet of glass. When the seedlings are large enough to handle, move to small pots containing the J.I. Potting Compost and to larger pots after 3–4 weeks. Then nip out the growing point to make for a bushy plant. By late April, artificial warmth should be discontinued and, on warm days, ventilation given. Keep the plants as near to the glass as possible for they love the sunlight.

When once the fruit has set, feeding with liquid manure will increase the size of the egg-shaped fruit, attractive in their purple hue, and each plant will yield a dozen or more.

The fruits are removed as soon as they are ripe, and to serve, cut them into halves, remove the seeds and grill in salad oil and butter; alternatively, they can be eaten raw.

To grow outdoors, sow them in early March under glass, – a sunny window will be suitable – and prick out the seedlings to small pots when they are large enough to handle. The plants will require hardening in a cold frame or under barn cloches before planting out early in June when fear of frost has diminished. Plant in well-manured ground, 15 in. apart, and keep well watered during dry weather.

Early Long Purple is the best variety. It crops well outside and under glass, and bears large oval fruits of darkest purple with firm and richly-coloured flesh.

## BEAN, BROAD

Broad beans like a deeply-worked soil, and one which has been well manured for a previous crop. If not, work in a quantity of decayed manure (they particularly like old mushroom-bed compost). In a sheltered garden a double row may be sown in early November and left unprotected through winter. Make the rows 9 in. apart, allowing the same distance between the beans in the rows, though if the soil is of a heavy nature and the garden is in any way exposed, it is better to sow the seeds at half the distance apart, and to remove alternate plants in spring if there should be no winter losses. Plant the seeds 2 in. deep. A second sowing should be made in March, to mature when the earlier crop is reaching its end.

Most varieties will require supporting, as the plants make growth in spring. This is done by placing stout stakes at regular intervals along the rows, to which is fastened strong twine when the plants are 12 in. above soil level, and again when they reach a height of 2 ft.

VARIETIES

DREAMLIGHT. It received an Award of Merit at the R.H.S. trials in 1966, and for quality it is outstanding, bearing eight or nine seeds per pod.

LONGFELLOW. Raised by Unwins, the pods are of great length and each contains nine or ten beans. The cropping powers are tremendous.

RED EPICURE. For flavour there is no broad bean to equal this; the variety is so named because the beans are of an unusual rich chestnut colour, and because they possess much of the flavour of the chestnut when cooked. The plant is hardy in all districts and is a heavy cropper.

THE MIDGET. Similar to The Sutton in habit, it is, nevertheless, quite unlike any other broad bean, for it makes a bush only 15 in. tall and 18 in. across, each stem bearing several 6 in. pods containing five to six seeds in each. The best for a small garden, it crops well even in poor soils.

THE SUTTON. Receiving an Award of Merit in 1952, this bean grows only 12 in. and yet crops abundantly. A characteristic of the plant is its branched, bushy habit. It is hardy, and the white-seeded pods mature early.


PESTS

*Black Fly*. This is the menace with the broad bean and, as in all things prevention is better than cure, it is advisable to pinch out the tops of the plants as soon as a fair crop has set. This discourages the fly and also makes for early maturity. From early May, the plants should be sprayed once a week with a liquid Derris preparation, which will also keep the pest under control. Apart from this trouble and the drawing up of the soil along the rows as the plants make growth, the broad bean will look after itself.

*Slugs*. As with all beans, slugs can prove almost devastating. Water the ground just after the seeds have been planted with the new liquid Slugit, which will prove lethal to these pests as soon as they reach soil so treated. A second application to soil and plants should be given when the plants are making the first leaves. All types of beans should be treated in this way.


## BEAN, DWARF OR FRENCH

To enjoy a succession from early summer until late autumn, it is necessary to make several sowings over a period of three to four months. The first sowing is made under barn-type cloches in early April or in the most favourable districts, early March. A second sowing will take place mid-May in the open, for the plants will not appear until risk of frost has departed. Another sowing should follow at the end of June or early in July, using a quick-maturing variety. This sowing will continue the succession through autumn, or until the first hard frosts. For the first sowing, use an early-maturing variety such as Sutton's Premier or Masterpiece, and for the main crop sowing in May, sow any or all of those mentioned. The commercial grower would be advised to concentrate on the more orthodox varieties, whilst those of more unusual form and colour can be planted in the home garden.

Where no cloches are available, it will be possible to enjoy a reasonably early crop if a sowing is made in a sheltered, sunny bed, between maturing lettuce. The seed is sown about 1 May, and, if no late spring frosts are experienced that year, an early crop will be obtained. The risk is worth taking, with a second sowing being made towards the end of the month for succession and as a safeguard against failure of the first sowing.

As far as culture is concerned, dwarf beans present no difficulties. They like a rich soil, one containing nitrogen and humus, and decayed farmyard manure will supply both. This should be deeply dug into the ground during winter, but, with the main sowing not being done until well into May, French beans generally follow a crop of lettuce or late-maturing brocoli, for which the ground has been well manured in autumn. This being the case, no further manure will be necessary, a 1 oz. per sq. yd. dressing of superphosphate, and $\frac{1}{2}$ oz. of potash being forked in just before planting time.

When sowing under barn cloches it is usual to sow a double row and a single row, spacing the seeds 6 in. apart in the rows. To allow for any misses, it is advisable to sow two seeds together, removing one seedling if two seeds germinate. If sowing at the end of April instead of early in the month, the seed could be sown at 3 in. intervals, and every alternate plant transplanted to the open ground at the end of May. This is a more satisfactory method than sowing directly into the open, where slugs prove troublesome. Or, again, seed may be sown in deep fish boxes in a cold frame, or directly into the frame in a friable compost, sowing in early May immediately after vegetable and flower plants have been hardened and removed. The bean plants are set out into the open, 6 in. apart early in June, after hardening. Then the plants will require no further attention other than to keep the hoe moving between the rows and to provide a regular spraying if the soil is dry.

The beans should be removed when they reach a reasonable size, when they are fresh and succulent. If allowed to remain on the plants too long they will not only become tough and stringy, but will also lose their flavour, and the weight of the crop will be greatly reduced. From the end of July until late September it is advisable to go over the plants daily.

VARIETIES

BROWN BEAUTY. So called because of the seeds, for the almost straight pods are pale yellow, attractive against the dark leaves of the plant. A tremendous cropper in all soils.

CANADIAN WONDER. An old favourite which is not quite so heavy a cropper as the other orthodox varieties. The beans are of excellent flavour.

CHEROKEE. May be described as being in appearance somewhere between the Golden Butter and Pencil Pod Wax bean, and possessing the good qualities of both.

CHOCOLATE SPLASHED BEAN. The pale green beans are attractively splashed with chocolate brown, and in shape and appearance are fine for exhibition. They are produced in abundance over a long period, and possess a delicious, sweet flavour.

EARLIGREEN. A fast-maturing bush bean which comes ten days earlier than any other. It is a heavy cropper, with straight pods measuring up to 6 in. long.

FULLCROP. For canning and preserving, the stringless, fleshy pods, no more than 6 in. long are the most suitable of all varieties. This variety is early to mature, and should be gathered before the beans become too large.

GOLDEN BUTTER. The golden pods are borne in great profusion. Stewed in margarine, and then covered in cheese sauce and placed under the grill for a few minutes to be eaten with brown bread, there is no more tasty dish.

GREEN SNAP BEAN. This to my knowledge is the smallest of all. The tiny, curved beans are produced in great profusion, and are of a deep green colour, quite stringless. They should be cooked whole.

GREENFEAST. One of the best of the dwarf beans, bearing a profusion of smooth, stringless pods of deepest green and excellent flavour.

KEENEY'S STRINGLESS REFUGEE. No vegetable has a more romantic name, but it is a heavy cropper and, if sown in mid-June, it will continue to crop until early November, when all other varieties have finished.

MASTERPIECE. One of the orthodox dwarf beans, and one of the best ever introduced. The long, straight, dark-green pods are extremely tender and are borne in quantity. Reliable in all soils.

MEXICAN BLACK. It is the seeds that are black; dried and used in sauces they give a flavour very similar to a matured field mushroom. The same flavour but not so pronounced is enjoyed from slicing and cooking the beans in the usual way.

MONT D'OR WAXPOD. A well-known golden bean, renowned for its heavy cropping and perfectly-formed beans.

PENCIL POD WAX BEAN. Making a large, bushy plant and bearing huge quantities of round, yellow-podded beans, of pencil size and shape, this is one of the best of all dwarf beans, extremely valuable in that it yields from the end of July until early October.

PURPLE PODDED. In appearance the beans are almost the colour of the Blue Coco bean, though are of better shape and more freely produced.

ROYALTY. A dwarf form of the Blue Coco bean growing 15 in. tall, and bearing long, stringless pods of brightest blue, which turn dark green when cooked.

SHELLEASY. An early-maturing variety which bears attractively mottled seed pods and bright, rose-coloured beans, which are valuable dried and used as haricot beans during winter.

SUTTON'S PREMIER. Valuable in that the beans, broad and long and very tender, are the first to mature under cloches.

THE PRINCE. An immense cropper and quick to mature. The pods are thick and fleshy, and often up to 12in. long. A fine exhibition variety.

### CLIMBING FRENCH BEANS

Where a sunny wall is available and a small garden is used for flowers and fruits, the climbing version of the dwarf French bean will yield a heavier crop than dwarf beans planted in the same amount of ground. These beans are best when allowed to climb up bushy pea sticks, rather than up canes and wooden laths, as is the custom for runner beans. The best variety is Tender and True. It is also known as the Guernsey Runner, for it is generally cultivated in the Channel Isles instead of the true runner bean. Another valuable variety is Kentucky Wonder, introduced from America. The round, fleshy pods are borne in clusters, and are most prolific. It is hardy and better than Tender and True for a Northern garden.

Also good is the new Amateur's Pride, introduced by Messrs Suttons. It is a climbing form of dwarf bean, The Prince, and it possesses all this variety's good points and is even more prolific. It is suggested that those who prefer the milder flavour of the climbing French bean should grow Amateur's Pride in preference to the runner.

Apart from the staking, which is done as soon as the plants have formed their first leaves after shedding the bean pod, the climbing varieties require the same culture as the dwarf beans, trenching not being done as is usual for the scarlet runners.

### HARICOT BEANS

These are grown chiefly for their beans, which should be dried, first by allowing the pods to hang until the weather loses its summer look, which may be mid-September, or, in a good year, almost the end of October. If the pods have to be gathered before being fully ripe, they should be spread out in a dry, sunny room to finish ripening. They will then remove easily from the pods, and should be stored in a clean cardboard box, not a tin, for they may tend to sweat and will then deteriorate. It is the white and pale-coloured seeded varieties that should be used for drying; those with black and brown seeds, although valuable for sauces, are too hard to make good haricot beans. Amongst the best are:

CHINESE YELLOW. Used either as a French bean, or for drying, the flavour is distinct and savoury. The green pods, with their attractive yellow seeds, are produced in abundance.

COMTESSE DE CHAMBORD. This is the best variety for drying; although the seed is small in comparison with other varieties, the skin is exceedingly thin. The flavour is excellent and the crop most prolific. Owing to the small size of the seed, only ½ pint is required to sow a 15 yd. row, compared with double the quantity required for the French beans.

Dried haricot beans should be soaked in water for upwards of two hours before cooking. They are extremely valuable for use through winter and spring.


UNDER GLASS

A valuable crop of dwarf beans may be raised under glass, provided that a temperature of 60°F. (16°C.) can be maintained in the coldest weather. Sow the seed mid-August, several to a 48 pot, in a compost made up of two parts fibrous loam; one part each decayed manure and coarse sand. Sow 1 in. deep, and place the pots in a frame or under barn cloches until early October, when the beans will have grown 8 in. tall and should be supported by twigs. Move them to a warm greenhouse and syringe them frequently to get the flowers to set, and to prevent an attack of red spider. A too humid atmosphere should not be given, and the ventilators should be opened on mild days.

The plants will crop during the early New Year, and if a second sowing is made in January, there will be a succession of beans until mid-May. Black Prince and Masterpiece are two of the most satisfactory varieties to crop under glass.


## BEAN, RUNNER OR CLIMBING

Runner beans come later into bearing, they may even be classed as a late-summer and autumn crop. They are valuable for prolonging the summer vegetable season, but it cannot be said that they can take the place of the succulent French varieties. True, they possess a stronger flavour, but they are less tender, and if not gathered whilst reasonably young, they become tough and stringy. Again, they require staking, and a matured crop being heavy and having to withstand winds in the autumn, the scarlet runner requires more attention than the climbing French bean.

For exhibition they are always popular, for, like the vegetable marrow, they may be grown to an enormous size – flavour and quality mattering but little in these circumstances.

The runner bean is rather less hardy than the dwarf bean, and so must not be sown until the end of May.

The plants make a large amount of foliage and are heavy bearers; they are also gross feeders, and should be trenched. About 12 in. of soil is removed, and into the bottom of the trench is placed a quantity of garden refuse, decaying cabbage and broccoli leaves, and anything that will decompose readily. Over this, place a layer of soil and some well-decayed manure. This is allowed to settle down, and the trench is then topped up with soil to which is added 1 oz. of superphosphate and $\frac{1}{2}$ oz. of potash per yd.

After making up the trench, erect the stakes. Fish netting is suitable if neither canes nor wood laths are available, but whatever is used it must be made strong enough to hold a heavy weight of foliage. Stout poles should be deeply inserted into the ground at intervals of 10 ft.

The seeds should be planted with a trowel on either side of the netting, or one seed to each cane, and they should be spaced 8 in. apart in the row. After planting, a number of seeds should be sown in a frame, or in a small seed bed, for use if there are any misses in the row.

As soon as the plants are beginning to form their first beans, you should feed them with manure water each week, if possible given during a rainy period, and early in August the plants will benefit from a mulch of strawy manure.

Beans must not be allowed to suffer from lack of moisture at the roots, and regular spraying of the foliage will help the flowers to set, and will keep the plants fresh and free from red spider.


UNUSUAL VARIETIES

BLUE COCO BEAN. This plant is well worth growing about the garden, if only for its striking foliage, the leaves and stem of the plant being of a bright shade of purple-blue. The long-podded beans are also of the same colour, yet, when cooked, they are indistinguishable from ordinary runner beans, except that they have a distinct flavour. The plant makes rather more foliage than the orthodox runners, whilst the beans are borne in clusters at regular intervals. The plants are as hardy as the other varieties, but do not crop over so extended a period as the others.

The sliced beans should be steamed, not boiled, covering them in margarine and simmering for an hour when the flavour will be quite outstanding. The beans are free from stringiness if gathered young.

PEA BEAN. Although until recently it had almost passed out of cultivation, many epicures consider this to be the most richly-flavoured bean of all. It grows to satisfaction only in a light, sandy soil, and in the warm south-west, where it crops heavily. It is really a true bean in spite of its name, but the beans are round, like peas, and can be seen through the pod – hence its name. It is tall-growing, and requires the same culture as for Scarlet Runners.

THE BLUE LAKE BEAN. An American bean, the small, round, stringless pods are ideal for canning. Its habit and white flowers would suggest a climbing French Bean, likewise the size of the pods. It is quick to mature, and bears a heavy crop.

THE ROBIN BEAN. The numerous small pods are of a vivid cerise colour when ready for gathering, the seeds being pale pink, spotted crimson, exactly like a robin's egg, so it is well-named. The plant makes a wonderful wall decoration, being trained up canes which are wired together at 3 ft. intervals, so that the foliage and beans may dangle over the wires. They will attain a height of 10 ft. if grown against a sunny wall, and in a sandy soil enriched with humus.

SCARLET RUNNERS

ACHIEVEMENT. A super bean, the pods being long, straight and of refined appearance, making it one of the best for exhibition. It makes mild, tender eating.

CRUSADER. A recent introduction, and one of the best of all scarlet runners. Unlike many of the others it does not drop its buds, and it bears an abundance of large, fleshy pods in all soils. The average-sized pods are in no way coarse.

GIRAFFE. So named because it is the tallest growing of all runner beans, and in comparison it is an extremely heavy cropper, bearing to the end of October, with pods attaining a length of 20 in. – although they are best used when smaller.

LONG AS YOUR ARM. One of the few beans to have gained an Award of Merit from the R.H.S. (in 1964), it is a heavy cropper, bearing straight pods up to 18 in. long, and of outstanding quality and flavour.

PRINCEPS. Just as there are 'climbing' dwarf beans, so are there 'dwarf' runners, and for those who do not wish to erect stakes, this is the best bean to grow. It is a scarlet runner, naturally early to mature, and it will come into bearing a fortnight before the ordinary runners. Under cloches, sown in mid-April, it will begin to crop early in July, and will prove extremely profitable. Sow the seeds 12 in. apart in single rows, and when the plants have made sufficient growth to fill the cloches nip out the growing point. This will bring them into bearing even earlier. To keep the beans off the soil – where they are often attacked by slugs – small twiggy sticks should be inserted about mid-June.

RAJAH. A unique bean, in that the pods are only 8 in. long, yet more than 1 in. wide, being meaty and yet quite stringless, and produced in profusion.

STREAMLINE. A grand bean for heavy soils, borne in large trusses, the pods being up to 18 in. long, and straight and narrow, which makes it a good exhibition variety.

YARDSTICK. Introduced by Dobie's of Chester, it is without equal for kitchen and exhibition, combining length and straightness of pod with outstanding quality. It bears a large crop of succulent, stringless beans.

PRESERVING BEANS

To enjoy all these runner beans through the winter, a quantity of each should be salted down. But do not wait until the end of the season when the beans tend to become tough and stringy. Salt them when they are still young, and they will remain delicious for two years, if necessary.

The method is to slice the beans, placing a layer in an earthenware jar (the modern large glass jars with screw tops are equally as good), and cover the first layer with salt, then add another layer of beans and so on, salting and filling up the jar as the season advances.

When required for use, a quantity of the beans are removed, washed free of the salt, and allowed to soak for an hour or so before cooking. They will be just as green and fresh as beans gathered from the plants, and will have lost all trace of the salt.

BEET, PERPETUAL

Perpetual beet is also known as Spinach Beet, on account of the similarity of its top foliage to spinach when cooked. It is a root crop, but the root is never used, only the tops, which are able to withstand hard frost, and may be sown both in spring for summer use, and again at the beginning of July for use until Christmas. As it is required to produce an abundance of leaf, a soil rich in nitrogen should be used. Dig in plenty of decayed manure, particularly shoddy, if it can be obtained and sow the seed in drills 18 in. apart, thinning the plants to 9 in. in the rows. The leaves, if gathered when young, possess a richer and less earthy taste than ordinary spinach.

Sea Kale, or Silver Beet, as it is sometimes called, is rarely seen today in the cottage garden, although at one time it was a firm favourite. Unlike the Spinach Beet, it will crop well in a poorly-manured soil if the soil is of a heavy nature, and it will retain summer moisture. This may be helped by working in a small quantity of peat.

As it is of such vigorous habit, the plants should be thinned out to 12 in. in the rows, which should be 18 in. apart. The seed is sown in late May, so that the plants will make plenty of leaf by autumn, when it is most wanted.

As with all beet – except the non-bleeding beetroot – the Sea Kale Beet should have its leaves removed by twisting, and should not be cut. The succulent stems are either stewed or steamed, the leaf part being cooked like spinach. Like the Spinach Beet, under average conditions the leaves will remain green until Christmas.

# BEETROOT

This is a universal favourite, and has lost none of its popularity over the years. For bottling, the new Non-Bleeding Beet should be used, for, unlike the ordinary beets, it does not lose its crimson colour when sliced and bottled, no matter how long it is kept. It should be preserved in malt vinegar.

The red beetroot is a vegetable that was first enjoyed during the late-Tudor period. Parkinson tells us that the beet described by Gerard in his *Herball* was the Great Red Beet given to Gerard by 'Master Lete, a merchant of London' who received it from southern Europe.* The beetroot is a maritime plant, liking a sandy soil, and like the asparagus enjoys salt in its diet, the soil being dressed with 1 oz. per sq. yd. of common salt before the seed is sown. At the same time, rake in the same amount of superphosphate and of sulphate of potash, no other manures being necessary if the crop is grown in a friable soil manured for a previous crop.

Beetroot is not quite hardy and should not be sown until the middle of April in the south or early May in the north. Sow in drills 1 in. deep and 15 in. apart and thin out the plants to 8 in. in the rows. An ounce of seed will sow a 20-yd. row. This is a crop which must never be allowed to suffer from lack of moisture, or the roots will become coarse and bitter and the plants may run up to seed. They will appreciate a peat mulch given between the rows in July, which will also help to retain summer moisture and keep down weeds.

From an early summer sowing, the roots may be used as they reach tennis-ball size for summer salads and with meats, having first been pickled in vinegar. A second sowing should be made in early June, both of the non-bleeding and ordinary varieties, to mature in autumn. This is pickled as lifted or it may also be stored in boxes of dry sand in a dry, airy room for using in salads and for pickling through the early winter.

The greatest care should be taken when lifting beet, for the smallest cut will cause bleeding of the ordinary varieties. Before storing or before the freshly-lifted roots are to be boiled, the leaves should be twisted off at the point where they join the root. They should not be cut off with a knife for only twisting will prevent bleeding.

The beet for exhibition is one of the few vegetables to be judged for quality rather than size. The long beet should have an evenly-tapered root; the globe type should be spherical with a small tap root. Both should have clear smooth skins and be of uniform crimson colouring.

* John Parkinson (1567–1650) wrote the *Paradisus*, published in 1629. He later became Botanist to King Charles I, and dedicated his great work to Queen Henrietta Maria, John Gerard (1545–1612) looked after Lord Burghley's garden in the Strand and later had his own garden in Holborn. His *Herball* was published in 1597.

VARIETIES

BOLTARDY. Of Detroit type, it forms a large globe of deepest red and will not run to seed during a long period of dry weather.

CHELTENHAM GREENTOP. A long-rooted variety of first-rate flavour, being sweet and succulent, and extremely tender when boiled and used in salads.

CRIMSON GLOBE. A long-established variety of merit, bearing a round, smooth-skinned root of dark blood-red. It retains its colour after cooking.

DETROIT GLOBE. Possibly the best round beet, of perfect globular shape for exhibition and free from any 'rings' when cooked. The flesh is crisp and sweet.

EXHIBITION CRIMSON. This is a long beet and though not now as popular as the round varieties, it is of exceptional quality with a delicious flavour.

FELTHAM INTERMEDIATE. A short, stump rooted variety, very early to mature which should be used for early sowing.

NEW NON-BLEEDING. Retaining its crimson colour after boiling even if cut in half, this is excellent for pickling. The roots are of good shape and of excellent quality when boiled.


# BLACKBERRY

Blackberries may be grown in unwanted ground where, provided they are supplied with humus and kept free of dead wood, they will continue to bear fruit for many years. In much the same way the plants of the more vigorous varieties such as Himalaya Giant may be planted either as a hedge or a windbreak. Loganberries are not suited to this purpose, for their wood is brittle and liable to be cut back by cold winds. Planted 8–10 ft. apart and trained along stout galvanised wires, blackberries will form a most valuable windbreak, at the same time yielding large crops.

Where used for a windbreak, the plants will be grown in rows and trained along wires. This method is also to be recommended for field and garden culture where growing as a specialised crop. Or the plants may be grown up stout poles like rambler roses. Where growing up poles, planting may be closer, allowing about 6 ft. apart.


SOIL REQUIREMENTS

As all the hybrid berries require an abundance of humus to encourage them to bear a large, juicy berry, and as nitrogen is continually required to make new growth, large quantities of shoddy or farmyard manure should be incorporated into the soil. Lawn mowings, seaweed, and peat all have value in supplying humus and this should be augmented with farmyard manure, old mushroom-bed compost, hop manure or shoddy. A heavy loam suits the hybrid berries best, for it is more retentive of moisture, and where a sandy soil is to be made suitable, additional humus must be provided. In a starved soil the berries will be small, seedy and lacking in juice. The plants will also make little new growth, becoming a mass of dead wood and by degrees the plants will die back. With blackberries the formation of new wood is important to maintain the health of the plant, but with loganberries the production of new wood is vital for a heavy crop the following year.

An April, each plant should be given ½ oz. of sulphate of potash, raked into the soil around the stems, followed by a mulch with strawy manure in early May. This is necessary to control the moisture, for it must be remembered that the fruits swell during the driest period of the year. A heavy mulch of decayed manure, will add several pounds (kilos) of fruit per plant. Like all the soft fruits, blackberries and the hybrids make an abundance of active surface roots, which supply the greater part of the moisture and nourishment needed by the plant. The surface roots will also be harmed if cultivations are taken too close, so for smothering weeds a mulch possesses an additional value.

PLANTING AND PROPAGATION

Neither blackberries nor the hybrid berries should be planted too deeply. Almost any time during the winter months will be suitable, but with a heavy soil it is preferable to plant in November, or in March when moisture conditions permit. The stakes and wires should be in position before the plants are set out, the stakes having been creosoted well in advance so that the fumes have dispersed before planting. Immediately after planting, the shoots are cut back before being tied to the wires, and spaced evenly to prevent overcrowding.

Alternatively, rooted 'tips' may be planted. These are obtained from canes which have been bent over and the tips planted beneath soil level and made secure. If this is done during July and early August, using the new season's canes, rooting will have taken place by early November. The rooted 'tips' are then severed from the parent but left in position until March, when they are used either to make fresh plantings or to replace decayed plants in the fruiting rows. A special bed can be made where every new shoot is tip-rooted and used for making additional plantings for fruit production. This will ensure that every cane formed is used only for fruiting.

Pruning of blackberries is done by cutting out dead wood and excess growth that will interfere with ripening and picking.

COVERING WALL

Almost every house has a bare wall somewhere, which, if covered, would greatly enhance the property. But rather than plant ivy or Virginia creeper, which tend to damage the property if neglected, why not let these bare walls produce some fruit? One of the best plants is the Japanese Wineberry. It is one of the most handsome of all wall plants, for its canes quickly make considerable growth, attaining 10 ft. or more in a season, and not only do they remain a rich crimson through winter, but also the berries (which make delicious jam) are long-lasting and of a vivid amber colour. There is no better plant for covering a trellis. With the possible exception of the loganberry, most of the hybrid berries are so hardy that they will prove suitable for a cold, northerly wall.

Rather than being fastened to the wall by nails into the mortar, the canes should be trained against wire fixed permanently to the wall. In this way the old fruiting canes may easily be removed and the new canes fastened to the wires.

EARLY-FRUITING VARIETIES

BEDFORD GIANT. This, together with Himalaya Giant, is considered the best for canning and freezing. It is one of the earliest varieties, ripening towards the end of July. The fruit is large, juicy and sweet, but it is not such a generally reliable cropper as Himalaya Giant.

EDWARD LANGLEY. This is a wild blackberry, specially selected by Mr E. Langley for its vigour, freedom from disease, and fruit of exceptional flavour. The fruit is ripe by early August; the plants carry a good crop of medium-sized fruit.

MERTON EARLY. A variety from the John Innes Institute, which ripens its fruit towards the end of July and bears a heavy crop. The fruit is large, of exceptional flavour and contains few seeds. It is the only variety propagated from seed which is sown in a cold frame in March. The seedlings are transferred to nursery beds, planting 6 in. apart, in July. They are moved to their fruiting quarters the following April. This variety resembles a loganberry in that the fruit cane dies after fruiting, next season's crop being grown on the new canes. It is of dwarf, compact habit and should be planted 6 ft. apart in the rows. It is an ideal variety for a small garden.

MID-SEASON FRUITING

ASHTON CROSS. Introduced at Long Ashton in 1937, but though a hardy, vigorous variety has never become popular. It is strongly resistant to virus and could therefore be grown with advantage in virus-troubled areas. It is an early mid-season variety, bearing a large, round berry.

HIMALAYA GIANT. Raised in Germany from seed brought from the Himalayas and introduced to Britain in 1900. One of the most popular varieties with the canner, it is widely planted commercially owing to its hardiness and ability to bear fruit on the old wood as well as the new, thus giving an immense crop. It is a wonderful variety for providing a windbreak or hedge, but is so vigorous that when grown in a small garden it must be kept under strict control.

KING'S ACRE BERRY. This early mid-season variety should be in every garden. It is a strong grower though not so rampant as most blackberries. It bears delicious fruit which parts from the core like a raspberry, making it exceptionally suitable for dessert and culinary purposes.

MERTON THORNLESS. Neither a strong grower nor a heavy cropper, but in Kent and where given good cultivation it is proving a commercial success, and has become popular for canning. The canes are entirely thornless, so the plant is popular with the pickers and with amateur gardeners.

PARSLEY-LEAVED. This is a variety with attractively serrated leaves which turn to the most arresting colours in autumn. An arch of the parsley-leaved blackberry makes an imposing sight and also bears a heavy crop of aromatic fruit.

LATE-FRUITING

JOHN INNES. Raised by Sir Daniel Hall and Mr Crane at the Institute and introduced in 1923. Cane growth is vigorous whilst, like Himalaya Giant, it fruits well on the old canes. But it crops abundantly only in the warm south-west; in the north, fruiting is generally so late as to be almost useless.

LOWBERRY. A hybrid of American origin, it is a magnificent berry, being a cross between a loganberry and a blackberry and combining the better qualities of both parents. It bears true loganberry-shaped fruit, quite 2 in. long, but of a shining, jet-black colour with the sweet flavour and delicious aroma of the blackberry.

# BLACKCURRANT

Though not usually grown as a dessert fruit, the blackcurrant is much in demand for making fruit drinks, jams and flans, and with the extended cropping season of new varieties and greater control of disease, the fruit is now widely planted.

SOIL REQUIREMENTS

Of all soft fruits, blackcurrants favour a heavy soil, one enriched with nitrogenous humus and capable of retaining an abundance of moisture throughout summer. Only one variety, Baldwin, does well on a light soil and in general a shallow soil is quite incapable of producing a heavy crop. The plants have a vigorous rooting system which not only penetrates to a great depth but also forms masses of fibrous roots just beneath the surface of the soil. Thus, whilst a deeply-worked soil is important, a mulch each year will greatly increase the amount of new wood produced, and it is on both the new and the old wood that the fruit is borne. As much new wood as possible should therefore be encouraged; indeed a profitable plantation will depend upon the amount of new wood produced, for the fruit buds are borne along the whole length of the branches. These branches appear from buds which are below the surface of the soil, and it is important to guard against damage to these buds, and to the surface roots, by avoiding cultivations too close to the plants. Hence the importance of planting into clean ground, whilst a yearly mulch of strawy farmyard manure will suppress annual weeds.

Because the formation of new wood is of primary importance and the plants will, where possible, be growing in a heavy soil, nitrogen is of greater importance than potash. Blackcurrants like a heavy soil and a warm climate; gooseberries prefer a light soil, plenty of potash and cool conditions. Their likes and dislikes are completely opposite, and whereas gooseberries will crop well given the partial shade of orchard trees, blackcurrants must have full sun. They do, however, require a position protected from strong winds, for these not only cause bud dropping but lead to unsatisfactory pollination by insects, and of all fruits ample pollination is essential to set a good crop of blackcurrants. Though an open, sunny position is preferred, protection must be given from prevailing winds by erecting wattle-hurdles, or by planting a hedge of blackberries. The plants also suffer from frost, and those which bloom early should, especially, be planted away from low-lying, frost-troubled ground. Where late frosts persist, pieces of muslin should be placed over the bushes at nightfall. And whilst this fruit does best in a heavy soil, this does not mean a badly-drained soil which will encourage disease. A well-drained heavy loam is ideal for the blackcurrant and before planting incorporate as much farmyard manure or other nitrogenous humus materials as possible. Shoddy is excellent for this fruit, and hop manure, peat, leaf mould and straw which has been composed with an activator will all prove of value for the amateur. An ideal compost may be made by composting straw and poultry manure which has been kept dry and is rich in nitrogen. Heavy crops of blackcurrants may always be expected where there are poultry, this being the best of all fruits for the poultry farmer to grow. The amateur should give each plant a handful of bone meal, slow to release its nitrogen, at planting time.

Those who live near the coast will find fish waste, fish manure and chopped seaweed all suitable for supplying the necessary nitrogen over a long period. As much as 20 tons of farmyard manure or composted straw to the acre is not excessive, but of shoddy 5 tons will be sufficient as it has a higher nitrogen content than farmyard manure. Feathers and hoof and horn meal, both of which will release their nitrogen slowly, are also of value. But whilst nitrogen is so essential for this fruit, a satisfactory crop will not be obtained where nitrogenous artificials are used, and where humus in quantity is not present in the soil, for it is vital to provide the plants with moisture.

A soil that dries out quickly is of no use to the blackcurrant. A light soil may be made more retentive of moisture by incorporating additional quantities of humus and by giving an extra heavy mulch in summer, preferably of strawy farmyard manure or of composted straw. This may be given towards the end of May at the same time as for gooseberries and for strawberries, where a straw mulch is used instead of peat. The mulch is then dug into the ground in autumn when the crop has been cleared. In addition to this, established plantations will benefit from a 2 oz. per sq. yd. dressing of sulphate of ammonia or nitro-chalk applied in April, given during a rainy day. But to obtain the maximum benefit from artificials, humus must be present in the soil. An additional application of nitro-chalk, given at the rate of 2 cwt. per acre, or 1 oz. per plant, during early autumn, will give a greatly increased crop the following season and this is now widely practised by growers.

PLANTING

Planting distances will depend upon the vigour of the variety. Those making a more compact plant, for example, Amos Black and Westwick Choice, may be planted 5 ft. apart each way, without fear of overcrowding. Both are suitable varieties for a small garden. Those of more vigorous, yet of upright habit, such as Westwick Triumph, should be allowed 6 ft. whilst those of vigorous, spreading habit, for example Wellington XXX, are best allowed an extra foot between the plants.

A method of planting that is now followed is to allow an extra 2 ft. between the rows, and to plant closer together in the rows. The advantage is that cultivation can be done between the rows more easily with a mechanical implement and with less risk of harming the roots, although with closer planting there is less risk of damage either by frost or from cold winds. This method may be followed when planting in exposed ground, and is most suited to those varieties having a less vigorous and more upright habit. Those with a spreading habit may require the removal of alternate plants when five to six years old. Blackcurrants do not grow on a leg like gooseberries or red currants. A two-year-old plant is the most satisfactory.

As with all soft fruit, plants infected by disease will never prove profitable and with blackcurrants it is important to obtain stock guaranteed free from 'reversion' or 'big bud', caused by the Gall Mite. Where present, the flower buds fail to open and little fruit is obtained. All the specialist growers and well-known suppliers of fruit trees supply guaranteed plants at no extra cost.

Planting may take place at any time between early November and the end of March, but where possible, and where the ground is well drained, early winter planting is the best. However, as the shoots should be cut back to about 3 in. of the base upon planting and, like the raspberry, will produce no crop the first season, it matters little when planting is done, the state of the ground being the governing factor. If the ground is prepared during October, planting is done in November. The shoots are untouched until mid-March, when they are cut back to stimulate the formation of plenty of new growth, no mulching being done during the first summer. Firm planting is essential, re-treading the plants when they are pruned back after winter frosts.

Pruning consists of the removal of the older shoots as the plants make excessive growth, but little pruning will be necessary for the first two to three years. Overcrowded shoots should be cut back right to the base during October when the shoots are removed for propagation. Also several shoots which have made excessive growth could, with advantage, be cut back to a 'break' and the younger shoot grown on. This will keep the plant free from too much old wood. Varieties with a spreading habit should be kept in reasonable shape to facilitate picking and cultivation.

PROPAGATION

Blackcurrants are the easiest of all soft fruits to propagate, for they make plenty of wood and root with few losses; hence the reasonable price of the plants. Provided that the plants remain free from disease, they may be readily increased by removing, in early October, the shoots formed during the previous season. These shoots are shortened to about 12 in. long, but as no 'leg' is required, all the buds are allowed to form shoots.

The severed shoots are inserted in trenches of peat and coarse sand, 3 in. apart, with the rows 9 in. apart. They are made quite firm by carefully treading and will require no further attention until the following summer, by when they will have rooted. During summer the rows should be mulched, either with peat or strawy manure, and the plants kept moist. They are then carefully lifted in early October twelve months after being inserted, and are planted out, cutting back as described. The following season they will come into fruit and will continue to bear for as long as twenty years or more, if carefully pruned and mulched. This is important in stimulating a constant flow of fresh wood.

## Blackcurrant

BOSKOOP GIANT. Raised in Holland and introduced to England in 1895. It makes a bush of vigorous, spreading habit, the fruit truss being long, the berries large and sweet. It is however intolerant of cold winds and highly susceptible to frost damage. At the 1948 Trials at the East Malling Research Station, in a year of late frosts, this variety set the lowest proportion of fruit of any variety, 23 per cent, compared with 51 per cent of Seabrook's Black and Mendip Cross.

LAXTON'S GIANT. Rarely has any currant created such enthusiasm as Laxton's Giant, for it heralds quite a new break in this fruit. It is a genuine dessert variety. Bearing fruit the size of a black Early Rivers cherry (and even larger in gardens where it enjoys a cool, heavy, loamy soil) it may be eaten like a dessert gooseberry, being both sweet and juicy. It bottles well and is delicious in a tart or flan. It makes a large bush, bears a heavy crop, and in some districts reaches maturity as early as the end of June. It is both frost- and disease-resistant, and is able to hold its ripened fruit on the bush for at least a month. For the exhibitor's table, it is unrivalled.

MENDIP CROSS. Raised at Long Ashton, Somerset, the result of a Baldwin-Boskoop cross. It possesses all the good qualities of the latter and none of its defects. It is of more compact habit, is extremely frost-resistant and bears a heavy crop, the fruit being sweet, juicy and of medium size. The best early currant for an exposed garden.

THE RAVEN. Like Mendip Cross, it is the result of a Boskoop-Baldwin cross, raised and introduced by Laxton Bros in 1925, but is not so tolerant of frost as Mendip Cross, not does it crop so heavily. It makes a spreading bush and bears a long fruit truss; the berries are large, thin-skinned and of exceptional flavour.

WELLINGTON XXX. With Mendip Cross this is possibly the best all-round blackcurrant, for it crops heavily in all districts, especially on the dry, eastern side of England. It also has Boskoop and Baldwin for parents, and was introduced by Captain Wellington at East Malling in 1913, yet is only now being widely planted. It is of vigorous, spreading habit, bud burst being late, and so is a valuable variety for a frost district. It bears a heavy crop of large, thick-skinned fruit, which mature after the earlies and before the mid-season varieties. The fruit travels well and is valuable for freezing.

MID-SEASON VARIETIES

BLACKSMITH. Raised by Laxton Bros and introduced in 1916. It is such a heavy and reliable cropper that, but for a tendency for reversion, it would be much more widely grown. Bud burst is late, which makes it suitable for frost areas. The fruit is large and borne in long double trusses.

With Baldwin it is one of the few blackcurrants to crop well in light soils. It is noted for its high Vitamin C content.

MATCHLESS. Raised by Mr H. Jones of 'Market Drayton, Shropshire, its neat upright habit commends it to the small garden, though not for a frosty district, as bud burst is early. It bears a heavy crop, the berries being sweet and thin-skinned.

SEABROOK'S BLACK. This is an excellent variety for the amateur's garden, for it makes a compact bush of upright habit. Though it bursts its buds early they are very resistant to frost. The trusses are borne in twos and threes, the berries being large and rather acid but in great demand for canning and jam making. It is very resistant to 'big bud'.

WESTWICK TRIUMPH. To follow Wellington XXX, this would be the choice, especially for a small garden, for it makes a compact bush of upright habit. Though a mid-season variety, bud burst is so late as to make it immune to frost damage. The fruit is large and borne in long trusses. It is sulphur-shy.

LATE VARIETIES

AMOS BLACK. Raised at East Malling from a Baldwin cross, the plant possesses the same compact habit of the parent; the shoots being slender and upright, make it an ideal small garden variety and allow closer-than-usual planting where it is grown commercially. It blooms later than any variety and matures its fruit in September. The medium-sized berry possess a tough skin, which makes it a good traveller.

BALDWIN. An old favourite, the Hilltop Strain being the best. Like Leveller gooseberry, it is exacting as to soils and climate, requiring large quantities of nitrogen and warm conditions, and so is generally confined to the south. Its value to the large fruit grower lies in its ability to hold its fruit after becoming fully ripe, whilst for the amateur it is a compact grower. The favourite of the juice extractors.

COTSWOLD CROSS. A new variety from Long Ashton having the same parentage as Amos Black and the same good qualities. At East Malling it has proved the heaviest cropper during the past few years, and it would seem to crop well in all parts of Britain. The berries are large and borne in short clusters.

DANIELS' SEPTEMBER. Introduced by Messrs Daniels of Norwich in 1923. It makes a large, spreading bush and, with bud burst being early, it does best in a warm district where frosts are not troublesome and where there is ample pollination. The berries are large, thick-skinned and valuable for canning.

LALEHAM BEAUTY. Raised by Mr R. Salter of Laleham, Middlesex, it received an Award of Merit in 1951. It is the latest of all varieties, it holds its berries until early October, thus prolonging the season considerably. The berries are thick-skinned, sweet and juicy.

MALVERN CROSS. May be classed as a late mid-season variety. Raised at Long Ashton. It makes a neat bush with upright growth. Bud burst is late, the berries being large, thick skinned and juicy.

WESTWICK CHOICE. Following Blacksmith, it may be described as a late mid-season variety. Like that variety, it is much in demand, together with Baldwin, for the fruit trade. Bud burst is much earlier than with Blacksmith, and so cultivation should be restricted to favourable districts. Like Wellington XXX, this variety bears especially heavy crops down the eastern side of England. The fruit is large and juicy, and has a high Vitamin C content.

# BLUEBERRY

The cultivated blueberry is a form of the bilberry or wortleberry, which may be found growing about the moors of Derbyshire, Yorkshire, Devon and parts of Scotland, forming low bushes about 12 in. high. Because of lack of suitable strains and growing conditions, these bear only lightly, and except for home use, and a limited local sale, are uneconomic to pick and market.

It was Dr Colville of the U.S. Department of Agriculture, who pioneered the cultivation of a selected form of the bilberry, *Vaccinium corymbosum*, which would appear to have cranberry 'blood' in it and is known as the blueberry. Two of the most vigorous varieties are Rubel and Jersey, which laid the foundations of the industry in America, and have also proved successful in Britain. The species *V. corymbosum* has for long been culti- vated in private gardens in this country, not for its fruit but for its foliage, which takes on tintings of crimson, bronze and yellow in autumn. It requires the same soil conditions as the rhododendron and azalea – an acid soil of a peaty nature with a pH value of about 4.5. Here in partial shade, and in a soil in which no other fruits would grow, *V. corymbosum* will make a bush almost 5 ft. tall, possibly more than 6 ft. in a mild, damp climate. Protected from cold winds, which the blueberry does not enjoy any more than the blackcurrant, it will bear a heavy crop of large, juicy, richly-flavoured fruits, which are very much easier to pick at this height than from the low bushes of the wild species. It is an ideal plant for the country estate to provide cover for game, or for providing colour and fruit from land which normally would give neither. It is also valuable for planting in wet, nor-too-well-drained land, for the blueberry responds best to a moist climate and a soil which retains summer moisture. If the soil is of a sandy nature, then work in quantities of a cheap grade, acid peat to retain the requisite moisture, or the berries will remain small and lack juice. They also respond well to a mulching of decayed, strawy manure given during early summer. The nitrogen in the manure will encourage the formation of new growth, which is apt to be slow in a district of low rainfall or where the soil dries out rapidly. But concerning manuring, much still remains to be done before the most suitable soil conditions are known. The American growers provide a balanced fertiliser of chiefly potash and phosphates each April, and in certain districts some growers have obtained up to 20 lb. of choice fruit per plant from plantations as large as 50 acres in area, though the average yield is about 14 lb. per plant from the age of four years. In Britain, where planted on a small scale commercially, the yield has been about 7 lb. per established plant.

PLANTING

The plants are expensive to purchase, costing as they do about 50p each, but they will bear fruit for thirty or more years. They are set out 3–4 ft. apart, with the rows 8 ft. apart where planting commercially, in the style of the 'hedge' system for blackcurrants. Where planting for game cover, or about the shrubbery, allow 6 ft. between the plants. To give shelter from cold winds, especially if the position is at all exposed, the plants should be set out slightly closer; but it must be remembered that they make thick, round, bushy plants, and too close planting will deprive them of sunlight and air, and the resultant brittle, twiggy wood will decay and die back.

Plant deeper than is usual for fruit bushes, for this will encourage the formation of sucker-like shoots (like blackcurrants) below soil level and build up a large plant as quickly as possible. The use of nitrogenous manures greatly increases such production of new shoots.

March is the best time to plant, although as with all deciduous shrubs, there is no reason why planting in well-drained ground should not be done any time from November until early April.

The plants come into flower early in May, bearing, sprays of bell-shaped, pale pink flowers, like lily of the valley. They remain several weeks in bloom, and the first fruit ripens early in August, continuing until late October.

CULTIVATION

Apart from providing a mulch in early summer, it is essential to keep the plants free from the weeds which tend to choke young plants and rob mature ones of the soil moisture needed to swell the fruit. This is borne in profusion on the slender sprays which remain in an upright position, simplifying picking.

Where growing on a small scale, there may be some loss of fruit through birds, although, being black, on nothing like so large a scale as with red currants. Where planting a few bushes for home use or in an ordinary soil, large amounts of cheap-grade peat should be placed round the roots at planting time. It is advisable to place netting, removed from the red currants or strawberries, over the plants early in August.

PROPAGATION

The plants may be increased in several ways, hence it is difficult to understand why they remain expensive. Seed may be sown in shallow drills as soon as ripe in early October. Germination will take place the following spring, and the young plants may be moved to special beds for growing on in early autumn. At no time should the seedlings be allowed to suffer from lack of moisture.

Alternatively, the plants may be increased by layering shoots in autumn, bending them down until they reach the soil, then partially splitting the stem. This is inserted in the ground and held in position by a layering pin, in the same way as when layering carnations. Rooting will have taken place by early the following summer, when the rooted portion is severed from the parent and transplanted. Again, suckers may be removed and grown on; or shoots of the new season's wood, 6 in. long, are removed early in August, and inserted into a peat and sand mixture under a glass bell-jar or cloche. Rooting will have taken place by the winter, and the plants are moved to beds the following spring for growing on.

BROCCOLI, GREEN SPROUTING, *see* Calabrese

BROCCOLI, LARGE-HEADED

To withstand a severe winter, broccoli must be well grown from the time that the seed is sown. The plants attain maturity in exactly twelve months, therefore those required for March cutting should have the seed sown the previous March, a succession being sown until mid-May of those varieties suitable for maturing from March until June.

As with all seeds it is important to obtain the best strains, and particularly with broccoli, for the plants must not only withstand the winter but also, at the end of it, have formed a compact head, uniform in size, if grading for market is to be done. The same standards are required by the home grower, for it is disappointing to have to wait a full year for the plant to reach maturity if a poor head is the result.

Having to stand through the winter means that the plants must be grown 'hard', and yet must receive enough nitrogen to make a large head.

This means providing a soil rich in humus, and one in which the manure releases its nitrogen slowly, over the longest possible period. The ideal is a soil which has been heavily manured for a previous crop and which has been augmented by a small quantity of strawy manure and 2 oz. per sq. yd. of hoof or horn meal just previous to planting. The soil should also be given a 1 oz. per sq. yd. dressing with potash at planting time. A firm seed bed is an absolute necessity as with sprouts. The plants are set out 2 ft. apart each way.

## SOWING THE SEED

Raising the plants is of equal importance to the preparation of the land. To withstand the winter, short, sturdy plants are essential, and this means a strong plant from the beginning. The seed must be thinly sown, and the plants thinned out should any appear too close. Plants which become drawn and 'leggy' will never recover.

It is advisable, where seed is sown over a hot bed, to transplant into a cold frame, otherwise the plants may make too much growth and become drawn before they can be planted out.

## VARIETIES

DOBIE'S ROYAL OAK. Should be grown instead of June Market where space is limited. It matures at the same time and makes a more dwarf, compact plant.

JUNE MARKET. Should be sown late in spring, the large heads maturing in May and early June the following year. A vigorous grower which should be planted 2 ft. each way.

LEAMINGTON. A top-quality broccoli, ready for cutting during April. The heads are large and of firm texture.

METHUEN'S JUNE. The last of all to mature, but should be sown in April as it requires a longer season than most. The huge, white heads will be ready for cutting in June and even into July in the colder parts.

MICHAELMAS WHITE. This is the first to mature, ready to cut in September from an autumn sowing. The heads are pure white, very large and of firm texture.

SUTTON'S EXTRA EARLY ROSCOFF. One of a range introduced by Messrs Sutton and Sons, primarily raised for the Cornish growers. Roscoff 1 to 5 provide a succession of heads from November, when Extra Early Roscoff is mature. Extra Early is a good variety for all districts, forming huge white heads in December.

SUTTON'S SAFEGUARD PROTECTING. One of the hardiest vegetables in existence, being uninjured in the severest weather, the medium-sized heads of excellent shape being at their best during February and March.

SUTTON'S WHITE BEAUTY. The large, well-protected heads are ready early in the New Year from an autumn sowing. It is hardy in all districts.

## BROCCOLI, SPROUTING

In cold, exposed districts this vegetable, with the Brussels sprout, should be first choice. As all varieties of the sprouting broccoli will occupy the ground for a long season, several continuing to bear their shoots for two years or more, they must not only be planted into a rich soil but also into one in which the nitrogen content is released slowly. Clean ground and a soil similar to that prepared for the cauliflower-headed broccoli will be suitable, and it is advisable to give the plants a mulch of strawy manure in winter. This is forked in during early spring, taking care not to work too close to the plants and, to help the plants to continue to produce their sprouts through summer, give occasional waterings with liquid manure.

As the sprouting broccoli is a tall-growing plant, a position of some shelter should be provided, where they will not be blown over by strong winds early in spring. You should also provide a firm soil and ensure that, throughout the winter, the plants are made firm after frost and wind.

Seed is sown in April, sowing thinly so that the plants do not become drawn. Plant out 2 ft. apart in May, and keep the soil stirred through the summer. The shoots will be ready for using from December onwards, the Nine-Star Perennial being at its best through early summer, with the Calabrese providing the supply through autumn and early winter. The shoots are cooked whole, braised and served with sauce – either mushroom or cheese sauce being a most happy combination with broccoli.

Though the various sprouting broccolis are not generally grown for sale, nor for exhibition, they should be in every garden where a vegetable of rich flavour is appreciated in the home. It should be said that the shoots or sprouts (not to be confused with the Brussels sprout), should be removed when young and tender. They will also run to seed if left ungathered, especially with the advent of the warmer weather of late spring.

### VARIETIES

EARLY PURPLE SPROUTING. Should be sown early in April, and it will be ready for using from the following March.

LATE PURPLE SPROUTING. Coming into use in April, it will continue to bear a profusion of richly-flavoured shoots up to July, when peas and beans demand attention.

NINE-STAR PERENNIAL. Well-named, for it is a perennial, and if given a regular mulch it will bear its pure white shoots, like tiny cauliflowers, for four to five years during spring and early summer, producing nine or ten heads from every plant. A wonderful substitute for those exposed gardens where late broccoli or early cauliflowers often fail. As it grows tall, it should be planted against a fence, or in an out-of-the-way part of the garden where it can be left undisturbed.


## BRUSSELS SPROUT

The most important of all winter vegetables and if there is room in the garden to produce only one winter crop, it must be this on account of its hardiness and prolonged cropping. But rather than grow those large, almost cabbage-like sprouts which lack the qualities which make up a vegetable of refinement, aim at those hard little sprouts of walnut size which make for crisp eating. Steam them in a little butter or margarine, rather than boiling them in water, for this makes a delicacy out of an ordinary vegetable.

Tight sprouts are obtained by planting in a compact soil, and the plants will not bear a heavy crop unless the soil is made rich. Brussels sprouts occupy the ground for a long period, eighteen months from the time the seed is sown until the plants are removed, and the nitrogen they require must be slowly released over long period. The ground should be prepared in winter, digging in some compost, either artificially prepared, or farmyard manure, and giving the soil a generous application of lime. In early spring 4 oz. per sq. yd. of hoof or horn meal should be forked in. This will release its nitrogen over the entire life of the crop, and will not cause the plants to form the excessive leaf and large, coarse sprouts which will be formed with an excess of nitrogenous artificials. Soot, raked into the soil before planting, will also release its nitrogen content over a long period. In addition to these supplies of nitrogen, the soil should be given a dressing of 2 oz. per sq. yd. superphosphate and potash and planting time. Firm planting is essential, and to prevent the rather tall, heavy plants from being blown about, tread round each plant regularly.

This attention to detail with this crop might be considered excessive, but cropping is heavy from October until April, with almost daily gatherings of sprouts, yielding at a rate of 4 tons per acre, which is 1 lb. per plant at 2 ft. apart each way. In the amateur's garden, the yield may be more than double.


SOWING THE SEED

Sprouts enjoy a long season in which to grow, so make two sowings, one in late August to come into bearing in September the following year; another in March, or if a frame is available, sow in February, to begin bearing at Christmas when those sown earlier are coming to an end. Sow thinly so that transplanting is not necessary. The plants should be set out 2 ft. apart in March, and early in May.

The prize-winning sprout should be solid and tight and of medium size; those large, open sprouts, generally field-grown, being of little use either on the show bench or for cooking.

Sprouts, like so many winter vegetables, are at their best following light frost, which makes them crisp and brings out their flavour, and they should be gathered just before being used. Always gather the lower sprouts first, as these are the first to mature, and keep the plants free of decayed leaves as they turn yellow.

VARIETIES

CAMBRIDGE No 1. Tall-growing, the sprouts are produced right down the stem. The first to mature and should be sown in early autumn.

CAMBRIDGE No. 5. Very late to mature, the solid sprouts remaining firm until the New Year, when they should be used – not before.

HARRISON'S XXX. A new sprout of excellent qualities. The plants are of medium size, the sprouts large, but tightly closed and of exceptional flavour.

PEER GYNT. A valuable F.1 Hybrid, early to mature for use mid-October until Christmas. It makes a compact plant, tightly-packed with smooth, solid sprouts, each being of large size, smooth and jade green. They are excellent for freezing, and mild when cooked.

RUBINE. This is the first red sprout. It is a vegetable which crops heavily, even in the north. It requires exactly the same culture as the ordinary sprout and it bears a tight, small sprout which is of a bright crimson colour. To enjoy a really delicious vegetable, half cook the sprouts, adding a little vinegar to preserve the colour, then drain off all moisture and steam in a casserole with a little butter or margarine. Serve piping hot, and, if it is desired to put on a really good colour scheme, cook a quantity of preserved beans in the same way and serve together.

THE ARISTOCRAT. A wonderful new introduction bearing an abundance of medium-sized sprouts, firm and weighty, over a long period. The best all-purpose variety.

THE WROXTON. A grand sprout for a small garden on account of its dwarf, compact habit. Extremely hardy, it is best sown in spring to mature late.

BULLACE

A species of wild plum which possesses extreme hardiness and grows well in areas of high rainfall as experienced down the western part of Britain. The Damson is a variety of the Bullace, and both are valuable for planting as windbreaks. Both extend the fruiting season until almost the year end, the plums often hanging until Christmas.

The Bullace bears fruit somewhere in size between the garden plums and damsons, whilst it is more rounded in form. It is less acrid than the damson and sloe. It grows well in a thin soil, especially over chalk.

VARIETIES

ESSEX BULLACE. The fruits are round, about 1 in. diameter and are deep green until ripe, when they turn yellow, resembling the Greengage. The flavour is rich and juicy. This variety is excellent in the pyramid form.

LANGLEY BULLACE. Making a compact, upright tree, it ripens its fruit later than the damson, as do all the bullaces, and makes tough, thorny wood, ideal for hedgerow planting. This is a more recent introduction and possesses the true damson flavour. It is extremely hardy and ripens its fruit in November, but the fruit will hang until almost the month end.

NEW BLACK BULLACE. This is an improvement on the old Black variety, well known to Tudor gardeners. It makes a neat, upright tree, is hardy and bears a tremendous crop of juicy, but acrid fruit, best used for jam.

ROYAL BULLACE. It is ripe by mid-October and makes a fruit of 2 in. diameter, being bright green, mottled with red and when ripe covered in a grey 'bloom'. It crops heavily.

SHEPHERD'S BULLACE. Valuable for a cold garden, in that it blooms late and bears a heavy crop at the beginning of October, the fruit being grass green when ripe.

# CABBAGE

It is one of the most important of vegetables, for the crop may be cut during those sparse late-spring and early-summer months when there is little else available. The plants never attain those large proportions of the winter varieties, and so never become coarse and strongly flavoured.

With spring cabbage timing the plants calls for care, for they have to be large and strong enough to withstand severe winter weather, yet must not be grown too quickly. If so, they grow 'soft' and are liable to be damaged by hard frosts. Again, if too advanced, there would be a tendency for them to 'bolt' if the spring is dry and warm.

In the south, where the autumn is generally milder and plant growth continues until November, a sowing should be made early in August; in the north, sow a month earlier. Sow in a prepared seed bed, very thinly, and in shallow drills 9 in. apart. Keep free from weeds, and water if dry conditions prevail.

The plants should be set out at the end of August in the north, a month later in more favourable areas, the ground having been previously well manured and deeply worked, and allowed time to consolidate before planting. A 2 oz. per sq. yd. dressing with basic slag should be raked in at planting time. As spring cabbages never attain a large size, the plants may be set out 16 to 18 in. apart each way. Except for keeping the hoe moving between the rows, they will require no more attention other than a $\frac{1}{2}$ oz. per sq. yd. dressing with nitrate of soda given during a rainy day, as soon as growth commences again in early spring.

When removing the heads, cut them off, rather than uproot the plants. This enables the roots to produce a succession of succulent, small heads from the point where the cabbages have been removed. Steamed in butter they are delicious, very different from those large stringy winter cabbages boiled (and served) in water.

Owing to the frequency of Club Root disease amongst members of the brassica family, cabbages and all other 'greens' should be given fresh ground every year on a four-year rotation.

VARIETIES FOR SPRING AND SUMMER

EMERALD CROSS. A F.1 Hybrid to sow for succession to mature late summer and autumn. It forms ball-like heads of emerald green and shows great uniformity.

FLOWER OF SPRING. Matures early and makes a good-sized plant, compact and pointed.

GREYHOUND. The first of the pointed cabbages to mature, this being a valuable variety to bridge the gap between the spring- and summer-maturing cabbages. A dwarf, compact variety with few outer leaves.

MYATT'S EARLY OFFENHAM. Early to mature, uniform in size and shape and. making few outer leaves, this is an old favourite still unsurpassed.

STONEHEAD. A F.1 Hybrid, making compact heads 6in. across which remain firm for several weeks to be used when required. The flavour is mild and sweet.

UNWIN'S FOREMOST. This is a new variety rapidly becoming a favourite for its firm, dark-green heads and delicate, tender flavour.

VARIETIES FOR AUTUMN USE

To continue the supplies when the spring cabbage finish in June, there are several excellent varieties which will make plants little larger than the spring varieties, and which for mildness and tender eating are superior to those that are grown for winter use. They may be said to come somewhere between the two in habit of growth.

The seed is sown in early September, the young plants remaining in the seed bed through winter, protected during severe weather by bracken and short twiggy sticks, which will allow the air to reach the plants but will keep off excessive frost.

At the end of March the plants are set out exactly as for spring cabbage and, if kept moist, will have formed small, well-hearted heads by early mid-March to mature in September.

AUTUMN QUEEN. A new variety which should be sown in March, for September to October cutting. It bridges the gap until the winter cabbages are ready in November, and makes a small, ball-like head.

GOLDEN ACRE. Like Primo, it is early to mature and makes a compact ball-shaped head which sits on the ground like a football.

PRIMO. If makes a dwarf, ball-like head of delicate flavour and tenderness. A fine market variety, as it is an ideal cabbage for a small family. May be planted 15 in. apart.

VARIETIES FOR WINTER USE

The year end should see the cabbage give way to the savoy, for, with its crinkled leaves which allow moisture to drain away, the savoy does not decay as readily as do cabbages during a spell of prolonged rain. For maturing November to the early New Year sow in early April, and when planting out allow 18 in. in and between the rows, for the winter varieties make much larger heads than others. Town garden soils which tend to be of an acid nature should be given a 4 oz. per sq. yd. dressing of nitrochalk before planting, and for winter cabbages a liberal quantity of farmyard manure should be incorporated, small amounts being augmented by hoof or horn meal, or wool shoddy. Like all brassicas, winter cabbages enjoy a soil containing plenty of nitrogen.

ENKHUIZEN GLORY. A continental variety of value, making large solid heads, which stand for a considerable time after hearting.

JANUARY KING. Almost like a savoy, the leaves being crinkled and large. The most frost-resistant of all cabbages, standing through January.

WINNIGSTADT. A very fine cabbage for late autumn use, making solid, pointed hearts which do well in all soils.

WINTER WHITE. Sown in April, it will produce enormous round heads for cutting in November, when those heads not required for immediate use may be stored in a shed or cellar for several weeks.

CABBAGE, CHINESE

Distinct from the ordinary cabbage, it is little grown in Britain. It originates from China and the Far East, and it is a dual-purpose vegetable: the leaves may be eaten in a salad up to Christmas as a substitute for lettuce, or they may be steamed, and served with meats. They are delicious either way, having a mild flavour.

The Chinese or Pe-tsai cabbage should be given the same treatment as the endive, a not-too-rich soil, but one containing some moisture-holding humus. As the plants readily run to seed, do not sow until early July, the seedlings being thinned out, those remaining being left where they are to mature as it does not transplant well. Keep the hoe moving between the rows, and water during dry periods.

The best variety is Wong-Bok, which is hardy, the leaves being crisp and tender.

Of different habit, making a larger head and growing taller, is Chihili, the formation of the dark green leaves being like those of a large cos lettuce. It requires the same treatment.


## CABBAGE, RED

The secret of success with this cabbage is that it must be given a long growing season. The seed is sown early in September, and the plants remain in the rows through winter. In March they are planted into a soil enriched with liberal quantities of manure, and which has been well limed during winter. Plant 2 ft. apart, making the plants quite firm. A 2 oz. per sq. yd. dressing of superphosphate and sulphate of potash should be raked in at planting time. Through summer keep the hoe moving, and give a sprinkling of sulphate of ammonia around the plants during a rainy period at the end of April. The plants will be ready for cutting in late autumn.

Red cabbage is also delicious used in a winter salad, cut into shreds, using only the tender portions. Season with salt, vinegar and mayonnaise, and serve with sliced onion, grated Hamburg parsley or anything that can be found for the winter salad.


VARIETIES

EARL BLOOD RED. This is the best variety for northern gardens where the growing season is shorter than the south. It is deep crimson in colour, and makes a small, compact head.

STOCKLEY'S GIANT. Makes a huge head, tender and sweet and of a rich, blood-red colour.


DISEASE

*Club Root.* All members of the brassica family suffer from this disease, if planted in an acid soil. Its presence is noticed by the appearance of swollen nodules about the roots, causing the plants to become stunted. Thorough liming of the soil will prevent any serious outbreak, but as a precaution members of the family should not be planted in the same part of the garden for three years.

PESTS

*Cabbage Caterpillar.* If this pest is troublesome, whole fields may be destroyed. Dusting at fortnightly intervals with Lindex will keep plants free from the trouble. There should be no need to continue after the beginning of August for winter greens.

*Cabbage Root Fly.* This pest is often troublesome, its larvae attacking the roots below soil level, causing wilting or stunting. It may be prevented by dusting Aldrin around the plants, or 4 per cent Calomel.

# CALABRESE

This is somewhere between a cauliflower and sprouting broccoli, with a flavour all its own. The small heads, which are produced like those of the perennial broccoli, are pale green, and the plant is also known as the Green Sprouting Broccoli. Around a central green head, like a small cauliflower, numerous small heads continue to form in autumn and until the year end. It should be used before the Brussels sprouts are at their best, and before the hard frosts, for it is not as hardy as the ordinary sprouting broccoli.

The calabrese likes a soil rich in nitrogen, particularly manures of an organic nature which release their nitrogen slowly, and at the same time provide the soil with humus, though it is an accommodating vegetable which will grow almost anywhere, and crops well in a town garden. It will, however, respond to liberal manuring, the ground being dug over during winter, at the same time incorporating as much farmyard manure, shoddy, hops or artificially-composted manure as can be spared. Early in the year the ground should be given a liberal dressing with lime.

The seed is sown in drills in the open, either in late September or in mid-March. Sow thinly, allowing 9 in. between the drills, so that the hoe may be taken between. No transplanting is necessary, the plants being set out during April 2 ft. apart each way into a well-firmed soil. The plants require little attention, apart from keeping the ground free from weeds.

Late in July the first heads will be ready for cutting, and, from then until Christmas, the side shoots will appear as fast as they can be cut.

They should be steamed for half an hour and served with butter, like asparagus.


## CARDOON

This plant, the Spanish Cardoon, is a close relation to the Globe artichoke, and is handsome with its silver fern-like foliage. But whereas the Globe artichoke is generally propagated from shoots or suckers, the cardoon is raised from seed, and it is the succulent stems of the cardoon which are used, like celery, rather than the heads, as with the Globe artichoke. The cardoon requires the same culture as given for celery: a deep trench, at the bottom of which is mixed some decayed compost. Like the celery, the cardoon requires a moist, rich soil, preferably a heavy loam which will be retentive of moisture.

There are various methods of raising plants. Either the seed may be sown early in April in the trench, placing two or three seeds at 12 in. intervals and thinning out the plants when large enough to handle. To hasten germination, cover them with a cloche or plant pot. Alternatively the plants may be raised over a gentle hot bed, sown in mid-March, and planted in the trenches towards the end of May. They may also be sown in a heated greenhouse.

The plants are not quite hardy, and if planted out before the end of May they should be given protection from frost. The cardoon needs a long growing season, but should not be frosted, the rows being covered with bracken and the plants used before the more severe weather which generally begins about the year end.

Through summer the plants must be kept moist, and the regular use of liquid manure water will help to build up a large, succulent plant.

By the end of September the plants will be ready for blanching, but not before, for they will continue to grow until then. The method is to tie together the top of the fern-like foliage with raffia, neither too tight nor too loose. Then the soil is heaped up along the rows, the plants covered with bracken, and more soil is thrown over the bracken to keep it in place. By early November the plants will have blanched, and be ready to use.


## CARROT

When sown over a mild hot bed in February, the roots will be ready for use early in May, a time of scarcity in vegetables. If a frame is not available, a sowing may be made over a hot bed in a sheltered, sunny corner in early March, when the roots will be ready towards the end of May.

## Carrot

The seed is best sown broadcast into a finely-screened soil, radishes being sown at the same time for an early crop, for they will be removed before the carrots mature. If the carrot seedlings are overcrowded they must be thinned, although if used when young they will not need as much space to mature in as will maincrop varieties. The bed should be kept comfortably moist, the frames being closed during cold weather, with as much air as possible being admitted when milder.

Later-sown seed, sown early in April for the maincrop, should be sown in drills, preferably with radish seed. A soil previously manured for an earlier crop, and a fine seed bed is essential for carrots. Fresh manure or stony ground will cause them to become fanged.

### PEST

*Carrot Fly.* A pest which troubles almost all root crops, particularly turnips, swedes, carrots and parsnips. The flies lay their eggs in the soil, the yellow larvae burrowing down to the roots of young plants which they attack and can cause considerable damage. Dusting with Lindex as soon as the seedlings appear, and again a fortnight later, should keep the fly under control.

### VARIETIES

AMSTERDAM FORCING. Excellent for frames, for the variety makes little foliage. The cylindrical roots are free of core and of good flavour.

CHANTENAY RED CORED. A stump-rooted early maincrop carrot of rich colouring, with the core the same red colour as the flesh.

EARLY NANTES. For early forcing this is one of the best. It has a long stump root, almost free of any core. The flavour is mild and sweet, and rich in Carotene.

GOLD SPIRE. An ideal exhibition variety, the long tapering roots have a smooth outer skin and are almost devoid of any core.

JAMES' SCARLET INTERMEDIATE. A first-rate carrot of renown, the handsome root tapering to a point. A main crop variety.

PARIS FORCING. Possibly the best all-round carrot, bearing bright orange roots the size of a tennis ball. It forces well and may be sown for succession throughout the year.

SCARLET PERFECTION. The roots are long and stump-rooted, and of the same colouring right through. This variety is a heavy cropper, and an excellent keeper.

SUTTON'S FAVOURITE. A fine carrot for all purposes, but never better than when sown for an early summer crop in the open, and again for using young in autumn. It is also a handsome exhibition variety with its long stump roots.

# CAULIFLOWER

For an early summer crop, seed should be sown in a cold frame in September, the young plants being pricked off into a frame 4 in. apart. The soil should not be too rich and must not lack lime. Like stocks, cauliflower plants damp off so readily that they should be watered as little as possible after the seed has germinated. After sowing and at regular intervals thereafter, water them with Cheshunt Compound made by dissolving 1 oz. to 2 gal. of water.

The plants remain in the frames through winter, and almost no water is given from Christmas until the end of February. They are then set out in March in the south, early April in the north; or where barn cloches are used to cover them, the plants can be moved a month earlier. Seed may also be raised on a mild hot bed in early March, to be planted out in April, the plants maturing only a few days later than those sown in autumn. Plants raised under glass should be hardened off before planting.

Where no glass is available and to give a succession of heads, seed may be sown outdoors in a prepared bed early in April. Sow thinly so that transplanting will not be necessary. The plants may be set out into permanent quarters early in May, planting 2 ft. apart. Those set out early in spring will mature during July, followed by hot-bed sown plants early in August. Those sown in the open will mature towards the end of summer, the later varieties being used in the autumn, with Veitch's Self-protecting sown in early May being sufficiently hardy in sheltered gardens to stand out during November and into December, thus providing five months of cauliflowers with five months of broccoli to follow in the new year.

PREPARATION OF THE SOIL

Cauliflowers will not form a large compact head if grown on a soil lacking manure. The plants require plenty of moisture and, for this reason, must be given a soil rich in humus. They also require an abundance of nitrogen, which is best given in the form of decayed farmyard manure, old mushroom-bed compost, wool shoddy, or compost prepared from straw and garden refuse. Besides supplying nitrogen, these materials will also provide moisture-holding humus. The land must also be limed.

To make compact heads, the plants also require potash, which should be given together with a dressing of superphosphate at planting time, at the rate of 2 oz. per sq. yd. Should the spring be cold and the plants are slow to grow away, dust around each a small quantity of nitrate of soda given during wet weather.

In dry weather, the plants should be thoroughly watered at regular intervals, for otherwise the heads will be small, and will run to seed almost as quickly as they mature.

As the heads will not hold for long, it is advisable to plan for succession, rather than to make large-scale plantings. Home users should commence cutting the heads the moment they become of a reasonable size, otherwise those left until later may have passed their best.

For exhibition, the heads must be solid, symmetrical and perfectly white. Those beginning to open, however slightly, or showing signs of yellowing are not required. They should be cut with just the pale green inner leaves surrounding the head, making the white part most attractive with the touch of bright green.

VARIETIES

ALL THE YEAR ROUND. Ideal for autumn sowing or for sowing under glass in early spring. It holds for a long period without going to seed.

CAMBRIDGE EARLY ALLHEAD. A new variety of promise, maturing early from a spring sowing. Of dwarf, compact habit, the heads are of fine texture.

DEAN'S EARLY SNOWBALL. Early and quick to mature from a spring sowing under glass.

DWARF MONARCH. A compact variety suitable for a small garden, and forming medium-sized heads of exceptional quality. At its best in October from a May sowing.

HARBINGER. The first of all to mature from an autumn or hot-bed sowing. Produces large, compact heads.

ROCKET. An early summer variety, forming a large, deep head, which stands well during hot, dry weather and is of mild flavour when cooked.

SNOWDRIFT. A second early and a fine exhibition variety, bearing a large snow-white head well-protected by its leaves. Stands well without running to seed.

SUTTON'S POLARIS. The largest-headed of the early-maturing varieties, the leaves affording good protection for the pure white curds.

SUTTON'S SUPERLATIVE PROTECTING. A superb variety very late to mature, being at its best late in November. The incurving foliage affords the head complete protection from frost.

VEITCH'S AUTUMN GIANT. An old favourite, still popular for late-October. The heads are large, firm and beautifully white.

VEITCH'S SELF-PROTECTING. The incurved leaves afford protection to the large, well-shaped heads until the year end, it being the hardiest of all varieties, and in a sheltered place it may be left until January, to bridge the gap until the earliest broccoli is ready.

WHITE KING. A new variety, and very fine for autumn sowing. The heads are large, compact and of purest white.

It should be said that those varieties which are not self-protecting and are required to stand out from late autumn should have their head covered by partially breaking and bending over the leaves. A head caught by hard frost will turn brown.

## CELERIAC

Where celery proves difficult to manage, celeriac should be grown instead, for it grows readily if given a long season. This means raising the plants over a gentle hot bed early in spring. The seed should be sown early in March, keeping the frame closed, and admitting air only if the spring sun is powerful. The seed should be kept comfortably moist, when it will germinate by the month end, and be ready for transplanting into a cold frame in April. The young plants must never be allowed to lack moisture; they must be grown on until it is time to plant out – which will be during the last days of May.

Celeriac is planted on the flat, there being nothing like as much labour attached to its culture as with celery. It requires no blanching, no earthing up, not so rich a soil nor so much moisture, but it does like a deeply-dug soil to which is added some humus such as peat and decayed manure. It enjoys a friable loam, for although it does need some moisture, it does not need the copious amounts required by the celery.

The plants should be set out 1 ft. apart each way, with the slight bulbous-like root just sitting on the top of the soil. Watering will be necessary to start the plants, then, apart from keeping the ground free from weeds and the soil away from the root which will grow half-out of the ground, it will need little more attention. Towards the end of September, all soil should be scraped away from the roots, and any lateral shoots removed with a sharp knife.

In the south the roots may be left in the ground throughout the winter and used when required. In this way they will retain their strong celery flavour and nuttiness. In the north the roots should be lifted early in November, the tops being removed and the roots trimmed. They will store through winter in boxes of sand in any shed or building.

The roots may be grated and used in a winter salad, or the sliced roots may be fried in butter. Or again, they may be stewed and served with cheese or parsley sauce. The roots should be peeled before cooking. The best variety is Giant Prague.

## CELERY

Make two sowings of celery, that of the delicious self-blanching to use from the latter weeks of summer until late autumn; another of the ordinary white or pink celery to use through winter. Those who are put off by the necessity for blanching the more orthodox varieties should grow only the self-blanching.

### SELF-BLANCHING

It requires different cultural treatment and is grown on the flat, in a soil enriched with well-decayed manure, and does best in a heavy loam.

Set out the plants early in June about 10 in. apart, for they are of more compact habit than the orthodox varieties. Plant firmly, and never allow them to suffer from lack of water. At the end of August the first 'sticks' may be lifted and used as soon as possible afterwards. Used raw or stewed, the self-blanching celery is a delicious vegetable.

### VARIETY

GOLDEN SELF-BLANCHING is the best variety, the heart being self-folding, pure white and tender. Where the 'sticks' are required for eating raw, they will be more succulent and sweeter if cardboard is tied round the stems for about three weeks before using. This takes only a few minutes, if the paper is cut beforehand. It is tied top and bottom of the stems with raffia, but no earthing is necessary. Or, if planted only 8 in. apart in the beds, the plants will blanch themselves.

### NON SELF-BLANCHING

It requires a heavy loam and it needs blanching, so it must be grown in trenches containing some decayed manure. Well-rotted farmyard manure is best, but where in short supply it may be augmented by lawn mowings or material from the compost heap. It must be covered with soil and firmly trodden down. Celery is planted in June and should follow an early crop of lettuce, for which the soil will have been liberally manured. Where the trench can be made of sufficient width, a double row should be planted, to obtain the most economical use of the compost.

Raising the plants demands attention. If the seed is sown too early the seedlings will be ready for planting out before the frosts have finished. If kept too long without transplanting, the plants will become 'hard', then, should the midsummer weather be dry, they will run to seed. Taking three to four weeks to germinate, the seed must also be sown early enough to have made good-sized plants by the time they are wanted for planting out in June. This means sowing over a frame hot-bed about mid-March. The seed is sown thinly, and must be germinated quickly, which means care with watering and ventilation. This is especially important after the seed has germinated, and whilst the young plants are growing on. To allow the soil to dry out or the plants to endure stuffy conditions will mean that they will either run to seed in August, or will be found to have hollow stalks when lifted in autumn.

The young plants should be gradually hardened off so that they will be ready, having made good-sized plants, for planting in June. Plant them on a showery day, and give them a thorough soaking before they are moved. They must be kept damp in the trenches by giving repeated soakings, whilst regular watering with diluted manure water will help in the formation of plants of exhibition quality. Where planting in a double row, set them 10 in. apart each way, allowing 12 in. for the most vigorous varieties such as Lancashire Prize Red.

BLANCHING

Blanching also calls for care. In the first place, so many go wrong with celery by blanching too soon, before the planting has fully matured. Certainly the plants will appreciate a little earthing up late in July when they are about 12 in. high, and this should be done as for potatoes, but full blanching should not be done until much later. A second earthing will be given towards the end of August, then again about 1 October, when the soil is still dry and friable. In this case the tops of the plants are tied together with strong twine, looping this around the plants right along the rows without cutting the twine. This will prevent the soil from reaching the hearts, as it is earthed right up to the top of the foliage.

By early November the plants should be thoroughly blanched and ready for lifting as required, frost ensuring the crisp nuttiness that is the hallmark of good celery.

Care should be taken in lifting, so that the soil does not reach the heart, when it will prove difficult to clean. Always begin at one end of a row and lift the roots as you come to them, first pulling away the soil, but taking care not to damage the plants. The roots should be trimmed off, and the plants washed free of soil.

Unlike most vegetables, when size generally stands for coarseness, with celery a large root is generally taken to mean one with tender stalks. So, in this case, the exhibitor's standard should also satisfy the epicure. For the show bench, plants should have thick, solid, brittle and well-blanched stems, and be free from pest damage.

Although celery is relatively free from disease, the plants may occasionally be attacked by Leaf-Spot. Seed should be obtained which has been treated for the fungus, as recommended by the Ministry of Agriculture.

VARIETIES

AMERICAN GREEN. Extensively grown in South America without blanching, it is eaten green, the flavour and tenderness being the equal of blanched celery.

BIBBY'S DEFIANCE. Probably the best white. Although making a large root, the sticks are crisp and sweet when grown well.

LANCASHIRE PRIZE RED. Makes a solid plant of noble proportions, and possesses exquisite flavour.

RYDER'S EXHIBITION PINK. The best pink variety, the stalks being tall and free of any stringiness.

SANDRINGHAM DWARF WHITE. A reliable white celery of very compact habit; tender and nutty.

# CHERRY

The cherry, unless planted for its blossom, as well it might be, is rarely grown in the amateur's garden, for it succeeds only as a standard, or half-standard, and in this form will take almost ten years to come into reasonable bearing. None of the sweet cherries are able to set any fruit with their own pollen, but it is not enough to plant together several varieties which bloom at the same time, in the expectation that they will pollinate each other, for only certain varieties are capable of pollinating each other. Again, a cherry in the standard form makes such a large tree, that it tends to crowd out other trees growing near, and then again, the birds are a constant worry, for even if the trees do set a good crop, half the fruit might be taken by them. By all means plant a cherry, or a number of them where space permits, for they remain in bloom longer than any other fruit and provide a charming display during the spring. Also by planting a wide selection of fruits and beginning with the first of the plums, and ending with the latest flowering apples such as Crawley Beauty and Edward VII, a display of blossom may be enjoyed from the end of March until early June.

If cherries in the standard form prove too unproductive for the ground they occupy, then the small grower might have room for two or three trees in the fan-shape form, planting them against a wall. It is not suggested that they should be grown instead of pears or plums in this way, although where several outbuildings are available for wall planting, then sweet cherries – the earliest fruit to mature – may be enjoyed in addition to the other fruits. For the formation and care of wall trees, see under Plums.

## SOIL REQUIREMENTS

Cherries like exactly the opposite conditions to the plum, although both are stone fruits. Whereas the plum depends upon a heavy moist soil and copious quantities of nitrogen to crop well, requiring almost no potash and very little lime, the cherry likes a dry soil, preferably a light loam over chalk, a dry, sunny climate, like that of Worcestershire and Kent, and plenty of potash. It does not require nitrogen in more than average amounts. In the cold districts of the north, and in the warm, but moist climate of the south-west, cherries do not crop well, and a too-rich soil will also cause excessive gumming, which will eventually weaken the constitution of the tree.

Lime and potash are its primary needs, and where planting in a soil deficient in lime, incorporate plenty of lime rubble at planting time. The planting of both plums and cherries is best done during November. When planting, take great care to ensure that the bark of the tree is in no way damaged, otherwise it will permit Bacterial Canker or Silver Leaf Disease to enter the wound – plums and cherries being highly susceptible to both diseases. No manure should be given at planting time, nitrogenous manure would only encourage an excess of lush growth, but 1 oz. per tree of sulphate of potash should be given in early April each year. Wood ash, rich in potash may be incorporated at planting time. If planting standard trees, allow 20–25 ft. between them, for they form large, spreading heads.

As to pruning, the same remarks apply to the cherry as to the plum, cut out during late spring any dead wood, and leave it at that.

ROOTSTOCKS

For centuries, cherries have always been grown on the wild cherry stock, and propagated by layering. A form, specially selected by the East Malling Research Station, to give greater uniformity of performance, is now being used by nurserymen. Propagation is by budding, as described for the plum.

POLLINATION

The correct pollination of cherries is complicated, only certain groups being able to pollinate each other, and the research done in recent years to determine the most suitable pollinators would have revolutionised cherry growing, if other conditions were also in favour of their being more widely grown.

It has been carefully noted that each variety has a flowering period of 18 days, almost twice that of the plum, whilst the time from the first to bloom until the latest has finished flowering is 24 days, again almost twice the flowering period of the plum. Except for the very earliest and latest to bloom, all the cherries overlap with their flowering times on account of their long period of bloom, and yet, contrary to expectations, this plays little or no part in their pollination. The sweet cherries will not pollinate each other, but the following table gives a guide:

| Variety | Pollinators |
|---|---|
| Amber Heart | Bigarreau Napoleon, Governor Wood, Roundel Heart, Waterloo. |
| Bigarreau Napoleon | Bradbourne Black, Florence, Roundel Heart, Waterloo. |
| Bradbourne Black | Bigarreau Napoleon, Roundel Heart. |
| Emperor Francis | Bigarreau de Schreken, Early Rivers, Frogmore, |
| Florence | Waterloo. |
| | Bigarreau Napoleon. |
| Governor Wood | Early Rivers, Emperor Francis. |
| | Waterloo. |
| Knight's Early Black | Amber Heart, Bigarreau Napoleon, Bradbourne Black, Governor Wood, Waterloo. |
| Roundel Heart | Amber Heart, Bigarreau Napoleon, Florence, |
| Waterloo | Roundel Heart. |

FLOWERING TIMES

V.E. = Very early.          V.L. = Very late.

**Early**

Early Rivers (V.E.)          Merton Premier
Emperor Francis (V.E.)          Notberry Black (V.E.)
Merton Bigarreau          Waterloo

**Mid-Season**

Elton Heart          Knight's Early Black
Frogmore          Merton Heart
Governor Wood          Gaucher

**Late**

Amber Heart          Florence Heart (V.L.)
Bigarreau Napoleon          Roundel Heart
Bradbourne Black (V.L.)          Noble (V.L.)

These are the most reliable pollinators:

Bigarreau Napoleon          Waterloo
Roundel Heart          Early Rivers
Waterloo          Emperor Francis

These will not pollinate each other:

Early Rivers with Knight's Early Black
Elton Heart with Governor Wood
Frogmore with Waterloo
Noble with Florence Heart

91

VARIETIES

AMBER HEART. Pollinated by Waterloo and ready in mid-July. This is the best all-round cherry in cultivation, being hardy, a consistent cropper, and doing well as a standard or fan-trained tree. It is widely used by the canners. The attractive yellow fruits are flushed red; this is also the popular White Heart sold by the barrow boys.

BIGARREAU NAPOLEON. Pollinated by Waterloo and also by Roundel Heart, this is a delicious cherry for dessert, being large, very sweet and vivid red in colour. It is ready by the end of July.

BRADBOURNE BLACK. Plant in a large garden or orchard, for it makes a large, spreading tree. It is a heavy cropper, the huge crimson-black fruit being of delicious flavour. Excellent for a frosty garden planted with Napoleon and Roundel Heart, for they pollinate each other and all bloom late.

EARLY RIVERS. This is the earliest variety to fruit, ready mid-June and bears huge, jet-black fruit in profusion. It is a hardy variety, and the tree has enormous vigour.

EMPEROR FRANCIS. Grown with Early Rivers (or Waterloo), this variety would ensure a crop in June and another (Emperor Francis) in late August. It is a fine all-round variety, the large, dark crimson fruits being of excellent flavour. It is also the first cherry to flower, and the last dessert cherry to fruit.

FLORENCE. Another bright-red cherry which does well when planted with Napoleon, cropping about ten days later. A heavy cropper in either the standard or fan-trained form.

FROGMORE. Useful for a small garden in that it makes a compact, upright tree. It crops heavily and comes into bearing earlier than most cherries, bearing large yellow and red fruit.

GOVERNOR WOOD. It makes a large, spreading tree and, pollinated with right tree. It chops heavily and comes into bearing earlier than most cherries, bearing large yellow and red fruit.

KNIGHT'S EARLY BLACK. Of compact habit and useful for a small garden, it bears a heavy crop of large, jet-black fruit of excellent flavour.

MERTON HEART. This new cherry is now widely planted to follow Early Rivers and Waterloo. It is a heavy and consistent cropper, and bears a large, deep-crimson fruit of rich flavour. It should be grown with Emperor Francis or Early Rivers as pollinators.

ROUNDEL HEART. This variety may also be planted with Waterloo, as they pollinate each other. It produces very large, deep-purple fruit, which is ready for picking in early July.

WATERLOO. Early to mid-season flowering, and a suitable pollinator for Early Rivers, Emperor Francis, etc. It makes a compact tree, but bears less regularly than most cherries, though its fruit, deep-crimson coloured, is sweet and juicy.

CHERRIES IN ORDER OF RIPENING THEIR FRUIT

Early Rivers – Mid-June
Governor Wood – Late June
Knight's Early Black – Early July
Frogmore – Early July
Roundel Heart – Early July
Merton Heart – Mid-July
Waterloo – Late July
Amber Heart – Late July
Bigarreau Napoleon – Early August
Florence – Mid-August
Bradbourne Black – Mid-August
Emperor Francis – Late August

## DISEASES

*Canker.* Just as it affects the plum, so does the disease affect the cherry, entering wounds of the tree over the autumn and winter months when gumming does not act as a deterrent. Pruning should take place early in summer and, prevention being better than cure, the whole tree should be sprayed during early winter with a solution of Bordeaux Mixture.

*Leaf Scorch.* When the leaves change to a mottled green and yellow colour and remain on the trees long after the period when they should have fallen, leaf scorch disease will be the cause. Luckily cherries will tolerate Bordeaux Mixture, and an application should be given just before the buds open. The same treatment will also rid the tree of the spores of Brown Rot Blossom Wilt disease, which can cause serious damage to the culinary or acid cherries.

## PESTS

*Black Fly.* The tiny black eggs winter on the twigs, and if not killed by a January tar-oil spray, will hatch out minute grubs early in summer, which will devour not only the leaves, but also much new growth.

*Winter Moth.* This pest lives in the soil beneath the trees and will crawl up the trunk during the early winter months to lay their eggs on the twigs and branches. Grease band the trees at the end of October as for apples.

To protect the fruit from birds, close-mesh fish netting should be hung over the trees as soon as the fruit has set, and this may also be used for covering the heads of young standard trees until they become too large. Some protection for the fruit may then be given by fastening tobacco tin lids together and suspending them amongst the trees, to clatter in the wind.

# CHERVIL

This annual herb, *Scandix cerefolium*, will not transplant for, if this is attempted, it runs to seed at once. Where the soil is well-drained, and fresh, seed should be sown in autumn, for the plants are hardy. It grows 18 in. tall, although in its wild form it will grow taller. Its leaves possess what may be described as a sweet, caraway flavour, and are widely used on the continent for flavouring stews and salads.

# CHICORY

Expensive to buy, but easy to grow. Once again it is the blanching which may put people off, although nothing could be easier. And taking it right through from the moment that the seed is sown, no vegetable is more easily managed.

The seed is sown in a rich soil early in June, not before, or the plants will run to seed in a dry, hot summer. Sow them in rows 18 in. apart, and thin out the plants to 10 in. apart when large enough. Being deep-rooting plants, a deeply-dug bed, to which considerable quantities of decayed compost and manure are dug in, is essential. Throughout summer the plants must be kept free from weeds and comfortably moist. So far, so good.

By the beginning of November the foliage will have died down, and the roots – which by then will be about as thick as a man's wrist – may be dug up with care, trimmed of any small shoots and forced – a process which presents no trouble. A cellar, cupboard, garden shed or barn are all suitable places for the forcing or blanching, but very slight warmth is desirable to bring on the shoots in two to three weeks. An excellent method is to fill a large orange box with freshly-composted manure to a depth of 6 in. and over this is placed a 6 in. layer of fine loam. Remove all leaves just above the crowns and set the roots close together. Water thoroughly, and place in a completely darkened room. Or cover with sacking to exclude the light. With the slight heat from the compost the shoots will be ready for use in a fortnight, being broken off when 8–9 in. long, the roots being left undisturbed to bear a second lot of smaller shoots, equally succulent. If the roots are to be forced in a kitchen cupboard, the manure will not be necessary, but the other requirements will be the same.

The shoots should not be removed until actually required for cooking, for they require but a few minutes to prepare. The only variety to grow for cooking and use in salads is Giant Witloof, which is tender and white when forced.

CHIVE, *see* Onion, Bunch

## COBNUT (HAZEL)

The Hazel and Filbert, of the genus *Corylus*, may be distinguished from each other by the length of husk; the Hazel having nuts with husks shorter than themselves; the Filbert with husks longer than the nuts. Both require similar culture which includes shelter from cold winds and a well drained gravelly soil. Plant in November, 12 ft. apart, and they make attractive hedgerow trees. It will take four to five years to build up a tree and bring it into bearing. After planting, cut back the main stem to 3 buds and do so each year until the trees reach a height of 5–6 ft. by which time they will begin to crop.

The trees will require only the minimum of pruning, and none at all until after they have finished flowering in March, for the female flowers are borne on the old wood, and the male (the catkins) on the young or previous season's wood. They are fertilised by wind, thus relying on dry weather during early springtime for a good set of pollen and a heavy crop of nuts. Cut back vigorous shoots which have borne fruit the previous year, to three buds. At the same time, remove any suckers.

The plants will respond to a dressing with decayed manure or shoddy given early in January and in March, a 2 oz. per tree application of sulphate of potash. This will greatly increase the nut size.

Allow the nuts to remain on the tree until quite ripe, which will be early October, by which time the husks will have turned brown. If gathered too soon, whilst still green, the nuts will become mouldy in storage.

VARIETIES

COSFORD. It originated in Suffolk and is most prolific in its catkins whilst the shoots are covered in glandular hairs. It makes a large, oval nut with a thin shell, and is sweet and juicy.

DUKE OF EDINBURGH. The nut is round and tapering with the husk drawn tightly around it. The catkins are plentiful, and the crop heavy and of excellent flavour.

KENTISH COB. Since its introduction in 1830, it has been the most widely planted variety, for its catkins appear late and so miss the worst of the late winter weather. The nuts are large and are completely covered by the husk, and it is a heavy bearer of excellent flavour.

PEARSON'S PROLIFIC. Introduced by Pearsons of Chilwell, Nottinghamshire, it has a dwarf habit but bears heavy crops, the nuts being large, and sweet and juicy.

# CORIANDER

*Coriandum sativum* is an attractive plant growing 3–4 ft. tall with glossy, dark-green leaves, and bearing small, pale-mauve flowers. While its leaves have some value for flavouring soups, stews and curries, it is the small round seeds that are most in demand, to cover with sugar in making sweets. The seeds should be removed on the point of ripening and dried in a warm room.

A hardy annual, the seed is sown in well-drained soil in September for it requires a long season to ripen its seeds, fully twelve months. Sow in drills 8 in. apart, and thin to 4 in. apart in the rows.

# CORN SALAD

Lamb's Lettuce is the more popular name of the Corn Salad because it is at its best during the latter part of winter, at the start of the lambing season. In France and the Low Countries the vegetable is much appreciated as a winter salad, the large rounded leaves being grown on a considerable scale around Paris.

Unlike most salad crops, the Lamb's Lettuce likes a sunny position and a dry, sandy soil. Only to help the seed to germinate is artificial watering necessary. Not even the most severe of winter weather will kill the foliage, a few leaves being removed from each plant as required. The seed is sown in drills 9 in. apart early in August to supply a large amount of green through winter, and a second sowing is made towards the middle of September to supply the late-winter and spring green. The plants should be thinned to 8 in. apart when large enough to handle.

The pleasantly-flavoured leaves are delicious used with grated Black and China Rose radishes, and with celery and the strongly-flavoured Hamburg Parsley, both grated raw. American Land Cress grown under glass may also be used, and the aromatic celeriac, the whole dish being rich in vitamin content and most appetising.

# CORN, SWEET

Maize, Indian Corn or Corn-on-the-Cob is a vegetable which was little eaten or grown in Britain before the war. It became popular with the arrival of the American forces but the old strains were unsuited to our climate, and much work has had to be done by British and continental hybridists to introduce a sweet corn which will mature in the short summer of northern Europe.

As it is necessary to give the plants as long a season as possible in which to mature, the seed should be sown over a well-made hot bed at the end of March. If the seed can be sown in a warm greenhouse, so much the better. Otherwise make up a hot bed, turning the manure with care so that it has not lost any heat before the bed is made up. Add some poultry manure to encourage a really high temperature then place in a frame, tread firmly and cover with 3 in. of fine soil. It is preferable to sow one seed in a 2½ in. pot containing the John Innes Sowing Compost, and to plunge these almost to their rims in the hot bed, keeping the compost comfortably moist and the frames closed. To retain the maximum of heat, it is advisable to bank soil around the outside of the frame. Sowing may also be done in the soil over the hot bed, later transplanting the seedlings to individual pots, but with sweet corn the minimum of root disturbance the better, for any check, however slight, is to be avoided.

The young plants should not be hardened off too soon; mid-May is early enough to begin the process so that the plants will be ready for setting out during the first days of June – about 7 June in the north. Where barn cloches are employed, and this is an excellent crop for that form of glass, the plants may be planted out early in May, from a mid-March sowing, having been hardened off partially at the beginning of May. The great value of barn cloches is in providing shelter from cold winds, which the Sweet Corn will not tolerate, for the glass sides may be kept in position long after the plants have reached the top glass, which is removed early in June. The use of barn cloches will almost certainly ensure success with this crop, the cobs ripening by the end of July, early August in the north, a full month earlier than those planted out without protection.

PREPARATION OF THE SOIL

Sweet Corn must be given a rich soil and a sunny position, but one where the plants will be protected from strong winds. If no glass is used it is as well to erect a row of wattle hurdles or corrugated iron sheeting on the northern side, or against that of the prevailing wind. The plants detest winds even more than they do frost.

Having selected a position, commence soil preparations early in spring, digging in as much humus as possible. Sweet Corn thrives on wool shoddy, whilst spent hops are also of value. Decayed strawy manure, or that from old mushroom beds is particularly suitable, so is bone meal. Indian Corn is a form of grass, and like all grasses it must have nitrogen to grow well. Peat may also be used, but in addition to the manure, whilst the soil should be liberally supplied with lime.

Where barn cloches are being used, or where tent cloches are available, it is advisable to place the glass over the ground ten days before planting, to warm the soil so that there will be no check to growth. The cloches may later be turned on their sides around the plants to give protection from cold winds when they have commenced growing. The soil should be friable and fairly dry when the plants are set out.

They should be set out 18 in. apart when planting in the open, 12 in. under cloches, a double row being planted under a 2 ft. wide barn cloche. Water the plants well after planting, and from early July give copious waterings with liquid manure twice each week until the cobs have finished swelling. Keep the hoe moving between the rows and give a mulch of strawy manure at the beginning of July, for the roots must never suffer from drought.

POLLINATION

Pollination is interesting. The plants produce the male flower at the top. In appearance it is almost like that of an astilbe, but the flowers which are to form the cob, the females, develop from the leaf joints at the bottom of the plant, the silky tassels catching the grains of pollen as they fall from above. Though the plants should not be unduly cramped when set out, the closer they are planted, the better will the cob-forming flowers be pollinated. It is therefore best to compromise and plant about 18 in. apart, and in beds rather than in rows for the same reason.

When the cobs are ready for gathering will call for some care. On no account must the seeds be allowed to become too hard in the cob. The seeds must have matured, be firm and yet still be juicy, the cobs being almost like a short ridge-cucumber in size. Where they have been grown in the open quite unprotected, the cobs should be ready for removing at the beginning of September, but if the summer has lacked warmth, they may have to depend on a good autumn to mature.

By then the plants will have made considerable height, so it will be advisable to fix stakes at the ends of the rows during August, and to pass strong twine down each row. This will prevent the weight of foliage and fruit from breaking the stem.

The cobs may be served in numerous ways. They are at their best with young chicken, served either with white sauce or melted butter; or they may be eaten on their own with cheese sauce. But first the husk is removed, then the corn is boiled for fifteen minutes, no longer, for this vegetable is the exception to the rule that the more it is boiled the more tender it becomes; actually it becomes less tender.

VARIETIES

The F.1 hybrid varieties have been raised especially for the British climate and are hardier and earlier to mature than the older strains.

EARLY KING. The earliest to mature, it forms a broad cob 8 in. long, well filled and of excellent flavour.

HURST'S HONEYDEW. Early to mature, it has exceptional vigour and cropping powers, bearing uniform cobs 7 in. long, tightly filled with pale yellow corn.

KELVEDON GLORY. The best variety for southern gardens, it follows Early King, bearing pale yellow cobs 8 in. long and is of delicious flavour.

NORTH STAR. The best for northern gardens, it received an Award of Merit at the Royal Horticultural Society trials in 1969. It will mature even in a cold summer, and bears large broad cobs 8 in. long, packed with golden corn.

## CRESS

Mustard and cress present few difficulties, being grown in a frame or in boxes indoors for winter salads, or in a small outdoor bed of finely sifted soil throughout summer. The cress, being slower to mature, should be sown four days before the mustard, merely pressing the seed into the soil. The double, or curled, cress should be sown in preference to the ordinary variety, for it has a richer flavour. The commercial grower uses rape seed, which produces that rich green foliage, to be obtained throughout the year in those small punnets. It is cheaper, quicker to mature, and less trouble than mustard and cress.

## CRESS, AMERICAN LAND

It is an excellent substitute for watercress for it needs no water, and is not so much trouble to grow. It is perennial, and the best way is to make up a bed in a partially-shaded position, where the plants may be kept cool and shielded from the sun in summer. The bed should be divided into two parts, one for cutting in summer, the other for late autumn and winter use.

The seed is sown in a cold frame or under cloches in a soil containing plenty of humus, March being the best time to sow. When large enough to handle, the plants should be moved to the prepared bed, being spaced 8 in. apart and well watered in. The bed should have been deeply dug, and have had liberal quantities of well-decayed manure incorporated. Like all salad crops, Land Cress likes a well-nourished soil so that the shoots will be mild and succulent. The seed may also be sown in early August and wintered in a frame, setting out the plants in spring.

If the soil is kept moist the first shoots will be ready for cutting towards the end of summer. They are almost exactly like those of watercress, being of a deep green and possessing a strong flavour, and are not only delicious in salads through the year, but are also equally enjoyable between brown bread which has been spread with farm butter and cream cheese.

To enjoy the green sprigs through winter, half the bed should be covered with a garden light, having first erected boards around the part to be covered. Admit plenty of air on all suitable days, but should the weather be severe close up the frame and cover with sacking. Only limited supplies of water should be given. The frame should be removed early in spring, and the beds given a mulch with decayed manure and leaf mould.

## CROP ROTATION

Crop rotation applies especially to vegetables, but cut flower crops such as gladioli and narcissi will also benefit, for not only is disease much reduced by giving the crop a frequent change of soil, it is also possible for each crop in turn to make the most economical use of the various plant foods present in the soil. Nor does the soil build up a preponderance of one plant food, thus destroying the balance of the soil.

Where space is limited, it may not be possible to change the crop more than in alternate years, but for vegetables, where a four-course rotation can be planned, this will enable the plants to obtain the maximum value from the soil in addition to producing healthy crops. Taking each crop in turn, peas require a well-limed soil containing plenty of humus. They possess the ability to convert nitrogen in the air and to release it in the soil through their roots which should never be removed. After cropping, remove and burn the haulm after cutting it away at ground level. In this way, the soil is given free nitrogen which, with a high lime content, will be in condition for a brassica (greens) crop to follow. Then follow with root crops – turnips, parsnips or carrots – which require no liming but a well-nourished soil brought to a fine tilth. Then potatoes, which prefer a lime-free soil but plenty of farmyard manure or garden compost. This will leave the soil in a clean friable condition for a crop of peas or beans, which will, once again, begin the rotation.

## CUCUMBER

Where a cold frame or barn-type cloches are available, the Frame cucumbers may be grown; where there is no glass then one may have summer cucumbers by growing the Ridge varieties. These are the hardiest of all, whilst those for frames are also suitable for growing in a heated greenhouse. For flavour and tenderness the frame varieties are the equal of greenhouse cucumbers and, as they are most prolific and easily grown, they should be more widely cultivated. They may be grown quite cold in a well-manured bed, although growing over a gentle hot bed will bring on the crop much earlier, and give an additional month's fruiting.

SOWING THE SEED

Make the hot bed at the end of March, the compost being placed 18 in. deep in the frames and covered with 6 in. of soil. When the bed temperature has fallen to below 80° F. (27°C.) sow the seed. As cucumbers are intolerant of root disturbance, the seed is sown where the plants are to grow rather than in pots as for marrows. Where there are two lights, the frame will accommodate three plants, two seeds being sown close together in three parts of the frame, the strongest plant in each group being retained.

If no hot bed is used, then the soil should be thoroughly enriched to a depth of 8 in. with well-decayed strawy manure. The seed is sown early in April and, being slower to germinate owing to lack of bottom heat, the plants will fruit a month later. If two frames are available it is better to delay planting this seed until early May, so that the plants will be bearing their largest number of fruits when the hot bed plants have passed their peak.

After sowing the seed, which should be planted into soil made damp, cover with the lights, placing sacking over them at night to retain as much heat as possible, Keep the frames closed to maintain a warm, humid atmosphere until the seed has germinated. The sacking should be placed over the lights each night until the end of May, for hard frosts are often experienced until then. Should the temperature of the frame fall due to the hot bed losing heat, fresh compost should be placed round the frame boards to give additional warmth, especially at night.

Keep the plants comfortably moist but not wet, and use slightly warm water for spraying and watering. Until the end of May, damping down should be done before mid-day, so that the moisture will dry off the plants before the cooler temperature of night. Regular spraying must be done to keep down red spider, and cucumbers must be given a humid atmosphere and a high degree of moisture at their roots. If the plants are too dry they will not be a success. Attention should be given to watering throughout the life of the crop.

BRINGING ON THE CROP

As the plants grow they should be trained about the frame, spacing out the shoots and pegging them down so that each has room to develop. The laterals should be stopped at the second leaf, the sub-laterals being grown on, and if the frame tends to become crowded, excess growths should be removed altogether. It is important to remove the fruits before they become too large, for they will not only lose texture and flavour, but will crowd the frames, at the same time taking too much out of the plants. Ventilate freely whenever the day is warm.

Pollination of the flowers is not necessary, and before the frame becomes too filled with plant growth it is advisable to give a light top dressing around the roots, using finely-sifted loam to which has been added a small quantity of decayed manure. This will provide the surface roots with nourishment, and will act as a mulch in keeping the roots cool and moist. Some peat may also be added or used instead of the manure.

Watering with dilute liquid manure when the first fruits begin to form will also increase the vigour of the plants and result in a heavy crop. As the fruits have a tendency to decay if they come into contact with the soil and may also grow slightly misshapen, each fruit should be placed on a piece of wood until it has matured and been removed. Glass is also used for this purpose, but it tends to hold moisture; the fruits may rot on the side nearest the glass, especially if the weather is dull and the fruits slow to mature.

For exhibition the fruits must be fresh and pale green, straight, and of uniform thickness. Yellow, crooked fruits with long necks are not required, and the same may be said for those fruits that are being marketed. Single-layer cucumber trays are used to market the fruit.

They should be lined with blue tissue paper with the fruits placed close together, the noses pointing in the same direction.

GROWING UNDER CLOCHES

Cucumbers do well under barn-type cloches. Ground the width of the glass should be enriched with decayed manure dug in to a depth of 12 in. This should be done during March, the glass being placed in position for a full week before the seeds are sown at the end of April. They are planted 3–4 ft. apart. The plants, from the seedling stage, should be well watered, a humid atmosphere being created exactly the same as when growing in frames.

The plants should be stopped at the fourth leaf, two laterals only being allowed to develop. These in turn should be stopped at the fifth leaf. A mulch of peat and soil, regular syringing during hot weather, and placing narrow pieces of wood beneath the fruit to mature, should be done during the life of the crop. If the plants make too much foliage as the season advances, defoliation should be done with care and by degrees, so as not to upset the balance of the plant.

VARIETIES

BUTCHER'S DISEASE RESISTING. Very hardy and of vigorous constitution. Possibly the best variety for the north.

CONQUEROR. A splendid cucumber for a cold frame, long and of even shape, with a handsome, dark green skin. Best given hot bed cultivation.

EVERY DAY. A valuable variety in that it will set its fruits well in a dull summer. The fruits have a smooth dark green skin and are of excellent flavour. Unsurpassed for exhibition.

FEMINA. An F.1 Hybrid, producing almost all-female flowers and so crops heavily. The long, smooth fruits are free from bitterness.

LOCKIE'S PERFECTION. Not so well known as it should be. With its black spine it is a handsome cucumber, of rich flavour.

ROCHFORD'S MARKET. Excellent for cold frame culture. The fruit is large and extremely prolific, and has a spiny skin.

TOPNOTCH. An F.1 Hybrid bearing a large crop of slender, dark green cucumbers. The skin is thin, the flesh white and of excellent mild flavour. Suitable for a greenhouse or frame, with or without heat.

RIDGE CUCUMBER

Where there are neither frames nor cloches available, the Ridge Cucumber should be grown, for it is perfectly hardy and in an average season will grow well in the north. No plant is more prolific, and it will be necessary to look over the plants almost daily, so quickly do the fruits form.

Select a sunny, open position, but one where the plants may be given some protection from strong winds. In a walled garden they crop abundantly and are as richly-flavoured as the frame varieties. On the balcony of a flat they will prove most attractive with their handsome foliage. All that is required is a box filled with decayed manure and loam, the seed being germinated by covering the box with a sheet of clean glass.

This is also the method by which the seed is germinated outdoors; if no cloche is available construct a miniature frame with bricks, and cover with a sheet of glass. A miniature hot bed may also be made by removing soil and filling this to a depth of 8 in. with prepared manure. This is covered with 3 in. of soil which is made level with the surrounding soil. Similar hot beds can be made at intervals of 3–4 ft., keeping them in line to help with cultivations. Bricks are placed round each, two seeds sown, 1 in. deep, the weaker of the two plants being removed.

Should the garden be exposed, the plants should be grown between ridges which will provide protection from cold winds, but if water collects in the trenches, stem rot may result. Neither should planting be done on the top of the ridges, for in a dry summer the plants would lack moisture at the roots.

Sow the seed at the end of May in the north; mid-May in the south.

When the plants have formed two or three leaves they should be stopped to encourage the formation of the lateral shoots which will carry the crop. No further restriction will be necessary, but to ensure a heavy crop give a mulch around the roots either of decayed lawn mowings, or decayed manure and do not allow the plants to lack moisture. During a dry period and where growing in a light soil, copious amounts of water will be required daily.


VARIETIES

BEDFORDSHIRE PRIZE RIDGE. Long-fruited and a heavy cropper, it is hardy and crops well in all soils.

BURPEE HYBRID. A fine hybrid from America bearing handsome, dark green fruits in great abundance and in all seasons. The skin is smooth and thin, the flesh crisp and white.

HAMPSHIRE GIANT. A splendid hardy cucumber. The fruits are more than 12 in. long, the skin pale green, the flesh never coarse, even when left too long on the plant.

KING OF THE RIDGE. A well-grown plant will bear fruit up to 15 in., almost free of spines and of exceptional flavour. Possibly not quite as hardy as Stockwood Ridge, but otherwise one of the best.

STOCKWOOD RIDGE. Hardy and prolific, bearing long, well-shaped fruits.

SUTTON'S PROLIFIC. Hardy and of compact habit, making it popular for small gardens. The medium sized fruit possesses excellent flavour.


MORE HARDY CUCUMBERS OF VALUE

THE GHERKIN. A ridge cucumber which bears short, spiny fruits which, if removed, before they become too large, are excellent for pickling. They have a tender skin and are also delicious eaten fresh, especially if allowed to become slightly more mature.

The fruit is borne in profusion, and should be gathered every day when at the height of the season. The plants require the same conditions as for other ridge cucumbers, but where manure is scarce they will also crop abundantly if planted in friable soil, which has been well manured for a previous crop. Work in small quantities of manure and after giving the plants a mulch as the season advances, give frequent applications of manure water.

THE WEST INDIAN GHERKIN. Too tender to be grown in the north, but in the south it bears an abundance of prickly fruits, about the size of a golf ball and possessing so rich a flavour that they should be used all the year round, either fresh or preserved. They require the same culture as the ordinary ridge varieties.

JAPANESE CLIMBING. A valuable variety which may be classed somewhere between the frame and ridge type, and where space is limited may be grown in an upright position, a trellis being ideal. Or it may be grown up strong wires against the side of a sunny wall. It is of the same hardiness as the other Ridge cucumbers, and bears fruit about 9 in. long and of even thickness. The plants will continue to fruit as long as there is no frost, but where growing against a wall it is imperative to give the foliage a daily syringe to guard against red spider. The roots will also require watering copiously every day, for there is little moisture beneath the eaves of a house. Frequent mulchings with strawy manure and lawn mowings will help to keep the roots moist.

APPLE CUCUMBER. Of all cucumbers this, in the opinion of connoisseurs of good food, is the most delicious. But it is listed by few seedsmen, and rarely found growing in any gardens.

The fruits are like pale yellow apples, oval in shape and should be gathered and used when they have reached the size of small apples, for the plants bear abundantly, and over a long period. Whilst the fruits possess the true refreshing cucumber flavour, they are much more juicy and yet the flesh is crisp.

THE WHITE CUCUMBER. Possessing almost the same delicate flavour and juiciness of the Apple Cucumber, it is surprising that this excellent variety has never become popular. It makes a handsome table decoration, with red tomatoes and green salads. The fruits are equal to the best Ridge varieties, long and evenly shaped, the skin being of a bright creamy-white colour. On the Continent they are greatly prized, and with the Apple Cucumber are eaten to the almost complete exclusion of the green varieties. For marketing they have never been popular, but might be tried again on a small scale. As with all vegetables, size is the criterion of a good vegetable with the British public, and so these delicately-flavoured cucumbers remain in obscurity. For those who suffer from indigestion, this is the cucumber to eat. The flavour is delicate and the flesh so juicy that this variety is always the choice of discerning salad eaters, even where other types are available.

The habit of the plant being more compact than for other Ridge cucumbers, it is an excellent variety for a small garden. The plants should be given the same treatment and culture as for the ordinary Ridge varieties, but it is noticeable that the Apple Cucumber is happier in a cold frame in the north where it should be given hot bed or cold frame treatment. In the south it is hardy and quick to mature, but the plant is able to acquit itself to both frame and open ground culture. The fruits are peeled and cut into slices, but to preserve the crisp, juiciness, serve the fruits whole, to be cut the moment they are eaten with salad. Or peel and stew, and serve with white sauce.

GREENHOUSE CUCUMBER

It is grown up the greenhouse roof, and although heat is necessary for an early crop, tulips or French beans may be forced on the bench at the same time. To have the crop beginning to mature early in June with the arrival of warm weather, seed must be sown, one to a 3 in. pot, early in the new year. But this means employing a minimum temperature of 68°F. (20°C.) during the coldest weather.

The sowing compost should be made up of two parts fibrous loam, one part each peat and sand, and to each barrowful of the mixture is added 2 oz. superphosphate of lime to encourage root action. Plant the seed 1 in. deep, on its side. Water thoroughly and raise the temperature to 75°F. (24°C.) to hasten germination. Covering the pots with glass or plastic sheeting will also help with germination. In three weeks, the seedlings should be large enough to move to 60 size pots containing a compost made up of fibrous loam, peat, decayed manure and sand in equal parts by bulk. Do not make the compost too compact. Reduce the temperature to 68°F. (20°C.) and keep the compost comfortably moist. By mid-March, move them to larger pots in which the plants will fruit and into a similar compost. As the plants make growth, fasten to wires stretched across the greenhouse roof at intervals of 9 in. and maintain a moist atmosphere by frequent syringing and damping down. It may not be necessary to admit ventilation until the fruits have formed, and then only on mild days. Allow the main stem to grow up the roof but 'stop' the laterals at the second leaf, also any sub-laterals. It is here that the fruits are formed, any flowers being removed from the main stem. Give a top dressing of decayed manure, or feed with liquid manure from early June, once every three weeks.

VARIETIES

FEMINEX. As all the flowers are female, all bear fruit, consequently yielding enormous crops. Extremely disease-resistant, the fruits are long and straight, and entirely free from bitterness.

PEPIMEX. An F.1 Hybrid, it bears a heavy crop of dark green fruits of medium size and which is highly resistant to Spot disease. The fruit is of mildest flavour and the long, straight fruits make it a valuable market variety.

SIMEX. An F.1 Hybrid and like Feminex, bears few male flowers and so crops heavily. Highly resistant to Spot disease, the fruit has a mild flavour and a thin skin.

TELEGRAPH. For years, one of the most widely grown for it crops heavily, the fruits being deep green and even in size and shape.

DAMSON

With the exception of the counties of north-west England, from the borders of Shropshire and Cheshire to Scotland, damsons are not grown on any considerable scale. The Damson, which is a variety of Bullace and is prolific around Damascus (hence its name), remains comparatively neglected in Britain. Yet it is so hardy that it could well be used much more for providing a shelter or windbreak for fruit trees in an exposed district. Or these hardy fruits may be planted as a substitute for the earlier-flowering plums. As to soil, they will crop abundantly in a thin soil, provided that they are planted in an area of excessive rainfall, such as the western side of Britain, for damsons flourish in abundant moisture, as do plums. They should also be given a nitrogenous dressing each year, preferably in spring. Damsons bloom later than plums and the strongest of cold winds do not trouble them. Retaining their foliage right through autumn, they provide valuable protection for other fruit trees.

Possessing a flavour and fragrance all their own, delicious used for tarts and pies, and for making jam, also bottling to perfection and retaining their flavour for several years if necessary, the damsons are one of the most valuable fruits for an exposed garden. The modern generation, as with Claygate Pearmain apple, does not realise what it is missing!

With the exception of Farleigh Prolific, all damsons will set fruit with their own pollen, but as with most fruits, where two or more varieties, possibly for succession, are planted together, heavier crops result.

These hardy fruits may be planted about the garden where others would not grow well, or they may be planted in a hedgerow, or as a shelter belt, their silver-grey blossom being most ornamental, and their fruit most attractive throughout autumn.


VARIETIES

BRADLEY'S KING. The best variety for a northern garden, for it is extremely hardy, blooms late and is a heavy bearer, besides making a vigorous tree, the wood not being brittle. It bears its fruit in mid-September and is almost as large and richly flavoured as the Shropshire Prune, being of an attractive, dark crimson colour, whilst the foliage takes on the autumnal tints usually associated with the pear.

FARLEIGH PROLIFIC. Found growing in Kent at the beginning of the nineteenth century, this is the most prolific bearer of all, if given a pollinator, e.g. Bradley's King. Known also as Crittenden's or The Cluster Damson, its fruit hang in huge clusters, and it is the first of the autumn damson to mature, ready for use early September. Its small, coal-black tapering fruits make superb jam. It forms a small, compact tree, and is generally planted in South-East England and East Anglia.

MERRYWEATHER. With its large, round blue-black fruit, it may easily be mistaken for a plum, yet it possesses the rich flavour and fragrance of a true damson. It makes a large, spreading tree and blooms quite early, so should be planted where late frost are not troublesome. Yet it is extremely hardy and bears a heavy crop, which will hang through October. It was introduced by Merryweather & Sons of Southwell, Nottinghamshire.

RIVER'S EARLY. The only summer fruiting damson, being ready for use early in August. It blooms very early and should not be planted where frosts are troublesome. In more favourable gardens it sets a heavy crop, and makes a compact tree.

SHROPSHIRE PRUNE. Though for flavour its fruit is the most outstanding of all, it makes but a small, slender tree, and crops only lightly unless planted in a heavy loam, and well supplied with nitrogen. It bears a large, oval fruit at the end of September, which is suitable to use as dessert when fully ripe. Also known as the Westmorland damson.

## DANDELION

Its leaves are valuable for early salads, and the seed may be sown in any odd corner of the garden, even in almost full shade, sowing in clumps 18 in. apart. Some humus should be added to the soil in the form of leaf mould and a small quantity of manure. Sow in April, using an improved form which will make larger and more succulent leaves. As the leaves should be blanched before use for otherwise they tend to be bitter, four or five plants should be allowed to remain in each clump to be covered with a rhubarb forcing pot, or with a deep box or large plant pot. All light must be excluded. The first plants will be ready for blanching twelve months from sowing the seed, ten days being required for complete blanching. The clumps may be blanched at intervals as required and no blanching should be done after the beginning of June, to enable the plants to recover, and to build up their strength for the following year. The almost pure-white leaves are cut off at soil level, and they should be chopped and added to a bowl of spring lettuce. It is advisable to give the roots a mulch of compost as soon as blanching has finished.

## DILL

Like fennel in that it grows 3–4 ft. high, *Anethum graveolens* is an annual with attractive feathery foliage and it bears yellow flowers. It is a very old herb and received its name from the Saxon word *dilla*, to lull, for its seeds were used to lull children to sleep. Today it is the leaves which are most used, to flavour salads and for sauces to serve with fish, again very much like fennel. In ancient times the plant was to be found in every cottage garden for it was believed to have powers to safeguard the home against witchcraft. The leaves, with their spicy taste, may be used to boil with new potatoes and with peas, but as the flavour is strong it should only be used sparingly.

Sow in April in a light, sandy soil in drills 9 in. apart, and thin to 9 in. in the rows.


# DISEASES (FRUIT)


### AMERICAN GOOSEBERRY MILDEW
It attacks chiefly the gooseberry (occasionally black and red currants), and appears in summer as a white, mycelium-like growth on the new shoots and on the fruit. Later it turns brown and, during winter, it peels off the shoots and falls to the ground, where it remains to begin its activity again in spring. Any affected shoots must be cut away and destroyed, but it is important to ensure that the plants do not receive an excess of nitrogen, which will encourage 'soft' growth. Give each plant a $\frac{1}{4}$ oz. dressing of sulphate of potash in spring each year, which will do much to build up resistance.

To prevent an outbreak, spray or dust the plants in May with Karathane, repeating just before the fruits set. Or use colloidal sulphur; or a solution made up of 4 lb. washing soda and 1 lb. soft soap dissolved in 25 gal. of water. The latter preparation is recommended as an alternative to lime-sulphur on sulphur-shy varieties. These are the yellow varieties, e.g. Leveller and Cousen's Seedling, which will drop their leaves and fruits if in contact with sulphur preparations.


### BACTERIAL CANKER
This is a disease of cherries, affecting mostly the 'black' varieties. The yellow Amber Heart and Governor Wood are resistant. On others, the disease appears first as yellow circular spots on the leaves which curl at the edges, turn brown and fall. The fungus will spread along the branches causing large areas to die back, and here it will remain over winter. As the disease is highly destructive it is advisable to give cherries a routine spraying in late autumn each year with Bordeaux Mixture, at a strength of 1 lb. copper sulphate and $\frac{3}{4}$ lb. slaked lime to 6 gal. of water. Repeat early in spring before the buds open.


### BLACK CURRANT REVERSION
A characteristic of black currants caused by a virus and believed to be introduced by the 'Big Bud' mite, which is controlled by spraying with two

per cent lime sulphur. Where attacked by the virus, the leaves appear long and narrow, and the plant will not set fruit. Like the leaves, the flower trusses appear long and thin. It may be that only one or two branches are affected, and these must be removed at once and burnt. Keeping the plants free from Big Bud' mite and other pests will ensure clean stock.

BROWN ROT

It attacks apples and plums, appearing on the spurs as buff-coloured spores, and causing them to die back. The fungus also grows along the wood, causing it to decay, the apple variety Lord Derby being particularly susceptible. Fruit from a tree attacked by Brown Rot will also be affected, turning brown in storage, although possibly appearing quite healthy at picking time. Diseased fruits must never be allowed to remain on the ground or on the tree, for in spring the spores will be dispersed by wind and may affect healthy trees. Spraying with lime-sulphur whilst the flower buds are green will give control.

BROWN ROT BLOSSOM WILT

This is caused by the Brown Rot fungus *Sclerotina laxa,* and it attacks the blossom of apples, pears, cherries and plums (in another form), causing it to turn brown and die back. The fungus will then work down the flower steams on to the spurs and the branches, causing them to die back as well. A petroleum-oil wash in January, followed by a one per cent lime-sulphur wash just before the blossom opens (using Orthocide for the sulphur-shy varieties) should give control. With cherries, spray with Bordeaux Mixture just before the blossoms open.

CANE BLIGHT

The fungus attacks raspberry canes at ground level after wintering in the soil. It causes large purple cankers to form, which later may encircle the stem and cause it to die back or to break off at the point of infection. When this occurs, the spores formed on the surface are released and may infect nearby canes. There is no known cure, although spraying with Bordeaux Mixture as for Cane Spot has usually prevented an outbreak.

CANE SPOT

It attacks raspberries, loganberries and blackberries as purple-brown spots on the leaves and, if unchecked, it will spread to the canes, especially in cold, wet weather. Any affected canes should be cut out and burnt to prevent the disease from reaching new canes and, as routine, complete control can be obtained by spraying in spring (before the flowers open) with weak Bordeaux Mixture followed by a colloidal copper preparation as used for Raspberry Beetle.

### CANKER

This occurs on apples, pears, plums and cherries, usually where growing on badly-drained land, and takes the form of red-coloured bodies which will often encircle a branch, clustering together, causing the branch to die back above the point of attack. Bramley's Seedling, Gladstone and Grenadier apples are highly-resistant. To control, cut away the cankered part and apply a dressing of 'Medo', which will destroy any remaining fungus spores. With plums, Myrobolan B. rootstock has proved to be resistant.

Plums and cherries which have been pruned in autumn or winter may be troubled by canker which enters where the trees have been cut for at this time, gumming does not act as a deterrent. This fruits should be pruned early in summer, as for Silver Leaf.

### CHLOROSIS

It may affect all top fruits, the leaves taking on a yellowing due to lack of iron in the soil. It is a common trouble of fruits growing in a limestone soil, but it will rarely be experienced where the trees are growing in grass-land. It should be corrected without delay, for otherwise the leaves cannot carry out their proper functions, and the quality and quantity of the fruit will rapidly deteriorate. The gardeners of old used to drive an iron nail through the trunk of the tree; but the modern gardener will spray the foliage with ferrous sulphate during midsummer.

### CLUSTER CUP RUST

This fungus occurs on plum leaves, as well as on the foliage of *Anemone coronaria* and *A. fulgens*, infecting the underside of the leaves with clusters of bright orange cups, with tiny black dots appearing on the upper surface. Diseased plants seldom flower, and should be dug up and destroyed. It is, therefore, not advisable to plant anemones beneath or near plum trees, as there is no known cure for the disease.

### GREY MOULD (*Botrytis*)

A troublesome disease of strawberries and gooseberries, also of dahlias and anemones and of tomatoes, peas and brassicas, especially those growing under glass or outdoors under humid conditions. With gooseberries it attacks the new shoots, leaves and fruit, and the affected branch will wilt and die. It is important to remove any affected shoots as soon as the disease is observed, and strawberry and tomato plants must be dug up and burnt. Succulent and soft-wooded plants growing under glass will also be troubled if not given sufficient ventilation or if carelessly watered, and the splashing of soil will encourage the disease. It will rarely attack those plants growing outdoors which have been well supplied with potash, but an outbreak may occur where excessive nitrogen has been used and which will make for soft growth.

With soft fruits, it may be prevented by dusting with Orthocide as the flowers open, and again 10 to 12 days later. But fruits used for canning or bottling should not be treated. For tomatoes, spraying with Shirlan AG as routine will prevent an outbreak.

### LEAF BLOTCH

Also known as Cercospora Spot, it attacks the leaves of melons and cucumbers, first as pale yellow spots, later turning brown, and continually spreading in size to cover large areas of leaf. The disease is most troublesome where growing in a heated house and, because of this, cucumber Butcher's Disease Resisting and the F.1 hybrid Femina are now the most widely grown indoor varieties. Should the greenhouse have grown an infected crop, it should be sterilised with formaldehyde before growing another crop of melons or cucumbers.

### LEAF CURL

This affects peaches, apricots and nectarines, as well as cherries, and causes the leaves to crinkle and curl up at the edges, and take on a crimson coloration. The leaves die before their time, causing the trees to lose vitality.

The disease may also attack the shoots, causing them to become swollen and die back, and it is here that the disease spores pass the winter, to attack the new leaves in spring. To prevent an attack, spray the trees early in February with Orthocide or Copper Fungicide, and spray them again in autumn, after the foliage has fallen. Spray cherries with weak Bordeaux Mixture at bud burst.

### LEAF SCORCH

This disease causes the leaves of apples and pears to turn brown at the margins and curl up, or, with cherries, they take on a mottled green and yellow appearance. The trouble may be due to potash deficiency, and may be corrected by feeding 2 oz. of muriate of potash per tree. Trees troubled by Leaf Scorch will bear small fruits, completely lacking in flavour.

But similar trouble may be caused by magnesium deficiency, which may be corrected by spraying the tree in foliage with two per cent solution of magnesium sulphate. With cherries, spray with Bordeaux Mixture just before the blossoms open.

### SCAB (APPLE)

Scab attacks apples, often where growing on land which has been given an excess of nitrogen. It attacks the leaves and fruits and also the wood; Worcester Pearmain apple and Comice and Durandeau pears being most susceptible. On leaves and fruits, the disease appears as pale green spots; on the wood as black blisters. The fungus winters on fallen leaves, fruits and prunings, which should be collected and burnt. It is most active during a cold, wet spring, and in early summer. Fruit which has been attacked by the disease may not show the symptoms (brown at the centre) until in storage.

To control, spray with two per cent lime-sulphur or with Orthocide at the green-bud, and again, a month later, at the pink-bud stage. Those apples susceptible to lime-sulphur (for example, Beauty of Bath, Cox's Orange, Egremont Russet and Newton Wonder) and Doyenne du Comice pear should be sprayed with Orthocide only, after the green-bud stage. These varieties however, are highly-resistant to scab.

### SCAB (PEAR)

This disease is similar to Apple Scab, although one cannot affect the other, both being biologically different. It affects the shoots as large black blisters. The disease later attacks the fruits, making them unsuitable for storing and marketing. Pears do not take kindly to lime-sulphur spraying as do apples, but they are tolerant of Bordeaux Mixture, which may be used both at bud-burst and when the blossom has opened.

### SILVER LEAF

The most dreaded of plum and cherry diseases, it enters the tree through a cut or break and, if this occurs between October and March, the tree will exude no gummy substance to heal the wound and prevent fungus spores from entering. A Ministry of Agriculture order makes it compulsory to complete all pruning by mid-July to allow the tree time to 'gum' before mid-September. Where breakages occur at other times, treat the wound with white-lead paint as a precaution against the disease.

The symptoms of Silver Leaf infection are readily observed. The foliage takes on a silver-like appearance and wilts, and this is followed, eventually, by the death of the tree. All prunings must be removed and burnt without delay. Czar and Victoria are the two most susceptible varieties; the Pershores and the Gages being most resistant.

FRUIT DISEASES – SUMMARY

| | | |
|---|---|---|
| Apple | *Podosphaera leucotricha*<br>APPLE MILDEW | Spray with two per cent lime-sulphur at green bud. |
| | *Sclerotinia fructigena*<br>BROWN ROT | Spray with two per cent lime-sulphur at green bud. |
| | *Venturia inaequalis*<br>SCAB | Spray with two per cent lime-sulphur or Orthocide. |
| Cherry | *Gnomoria erythrostoma*<br>LEAF SCORCH | Spray with Bordeaux Mixture before blossoms open. |
| | *Pseudomonus mors-prunorum*<br>BACTERIAL CANKER | Spray with Bordeaux Mixture in October. |
| | *Sclerotinia laxa*<br>BROWN ROT BLOSSOM WILT | Spray with tar-oil when dormant and with Bordeaux Mixture before blossoms open. |
| | *Taphrina deformans*<br>LEAF CURL | Spray with Bordeaux Mixture at bud burst. |
| Currants | *Cronartium ribicola*<br>RUST | Spray with Bordeaux Mixture after fruit is gathered. |
| | *Pseudopeziza ribis*<br>LEAF SPOT | Spray with Bordeaux Mixture after fruit is gathered. |
| Gooseberry | *Puccinia pringsheimiana*<br>CLUSTER CUP RUST | No known cure |
| | *Spaerotheca mors-uvae*<br>AMERICAN GOOSEBERRY MILDEW | Spray with one per cent lime sulphur before and after flowering. |
| Peach | *Taphrina deformans*<br>LEAF CURL | Spray with Bordeaux Mixture at bud burst. |
| Pear | *Venturia pirina*<br>PEAR SCAB | Spray with Bordeaux Mixture before blossom. |

| | | |
|---|---|---|
| Plum | *Pseudomonus mors-prunorum*<br>BACTERIAL CANKER | Spray with Bordeaux<br>Mixture at bud burst. |
| | *Sclerotinia laxa*<br>BROWN ROT | Pre-blossom spraying<br>with Bordeaux Mixture. |
| | *Stereum purpureum*<br>SILVER LEAF | No known cure. |
| Raspberry | *Elsinoe veneta*<br>CANE SPOT | Spray with two and a<br>half per cent Bordeaux<br>Mixture at bud break. |
| | *Leptosphaeria coniothyrium*<br>CANE BLIGHT | No known cure. |
| Strawberry | *Botrytis cinerea*<br>GREY MOULD | Dust with Orthocide. |
| | *Sphaerotheca humuli*<br>MILDEW | Spray with one per cent<br>lime-sulphur. |

## DISEASES (VEGETABLE)

### BLIGHT

Blight is a disease of the potato and of the tomato, and is recognised by dark brown patches on the leaves. If the weather is warm and damp, the stems turn black and decay, and, at the same time, give off an unpleasant odour. With potatoes, the tuber is also affected, turning brown and decaying. Early varieties are usually most troubled by the disease, though Epicure is virtually immune. To keep the disease at bay, the tubers should be either planted out, or be in the sprouting trays early in spring. Spraying or dusting with Bordeaux or Burgundy Mixture during the early days of July, and again three weeks later, should prevent any serious outbreak. Burgundy Mixture is also suitable to use on tomatoes.

### BLOSSOM-END ROT

A non-parasitic trouble of tomatoes which occurs as a brown circular patch of decay at the blossom end of the fruit. It is a disorder attributed to careless watering, when the plants may suffer from lack of moisture at an important stage of their development. Lack of moisture retaining humus in the soil may, also be a cause. It is important to ensure that the plants are kept steadily growing from the time that the seed is sown. Lack of moisture at a crucial period in their growth will bring about functional disorders that may affect the crop-yield.

BLACK HEART

A condition rather than a disease, but similar to Hollow Heart. It occurs in potatoes which have been stored in a room which is so badly ventilated that the tubers do not receive sufficient oxygen. They should be stored and sprouted in a frost-free room but the temperature should not exceed 40°F. (4°C.). A damp, humid atmosphere will cause Black Heart, and it cannot be detected at planting time unless the tubers are cut.

BROWN PLASTER MOULD

A trouble disease of mushroom beds, first appearing as a white mould on the surface of the compost, later turning brown. It usually appears in wet, badly-prepared compost, and will make its way into the casing soil at a later date. It may be prevented from spreading by treating the infected area with a two per cent formalin solution, after which the affected area is removed and replaced with clean soil. Care must be taken in removing the mould, for, under a microscope, the fruiting body appears as a minute bulb capable of dispersing millions of reproductive spores.

BUBBLES

The most dreaded of all mushroom bed diseases, and the most prevalent, present in most unsterilised soils used for casing the beds. The mushrooms affected will take on the most grotesque shapes, becoming puffed up, like large bubbles, and exude a brown, evil-smelling liquid.

Affected mushrooms must be removed at once and burnt, and the hands washed in disinfectant. But mushrooms beds cased with lime and peat will rarely be troubled, likewise those where the soil has been sterilised. Where unsterilised soil is used, the beds should be dusted as routine with Zibimate every two weeks, using 3 oz. per 1,000 sq. ft. of bed space.

To control an outbreak, spray the beds with Bordeaux Mixture, which will also control *Verticillium*. High temperatures will encourage *Mycogone perniciosa* (Bubbles).

CLUB ROOT

Also known as Finger and Toe, it attacks all plants of the *Cruciferae* family, but more especially the brassicas, the roots becoming swollen and knobbly. It is caused by a Slime Fungus, which lives in decayed vegetable matter, and is most troublesome in badly-drained soil. The diseased roots contain the spores, which later pass into the soil, and later attack other *Cruciferae*. Well-limed land will rarely support the disease, and Calomel dust applied to the soil before seed is sown and to the roots of brassica seedlings before they are planted out will prevent an attack. Plants of stunted growth should be lifted and burnt, for the cause of stunting will most likely be Club Root.

### FOOT ROT

A parasitic organism which attacks the base of the stem of cucumbers, marrows and melons, causing the plants to collapse. The stem becomes soft and black, and this condition is usually brought about by a too-wet condition of the soil. When watering the plants it is advisable to do so at some distance from the stems. If caught in its early stages, Foot Rot may be controlled by rubbing the stem with a powder made up of one part flowers of sulphur; one part copper sulphate (finely ground); and three parts hydrated lime.

### FRENCH BEAN BLACK SPOT

This disease attacks dwarf beans, appearing as dark, circular craters on the pods, also on the leaves. From the pod it will also attack the seeds, and it is most troublesome during cold, wet weather outdoors, or where beans are grown under glass and lack sufficient ventilation. Where an attack is serious, large areas of the pods will be covered in black spots. Spraying with liver of sulphur (1 oz. to 4 gal. of water) if the disease is noticed on the foliage, and continuing until the pods have formed will give control.

### FUSARIUM WILT

One of the most troublesome diseases attacking the pea, it causes the roots to turn brown, and then the stem, which later becomes black, when the plant collapses and dies. It is caused by *Fusarium solani martii*, which enters the roots where they are weakened by poor drainage. There is no known cure, but good cultivation and growing wilt-resistant varieties – for example Topcrop, Everbearing and Kelvedon Wonder – on ground known to be troublesome, will ensure clean crops.

### GREEN BACK

A disorder of tomatoes, whereby the fruit, even though fully-ripe, show green on the top. Lack of potash may be a cause, although most of the Hybrid varieties are immune to Green Back, and it would appear to be a trouble bred into the strain. A commercial variety not troubled is Witham Cross, whilst the older Moneymaker is usually without Green Back.

GUMMOSIS

A fungoid disease caused by *Cladosporium cucumerinum*, which produces dark, sunken spots to appear on the young fruits, and from which a gum-like liquid exudes. It attacks cucumbers and marrows, usually where growing under glass in a high temperature, and causes them to fall or to grow sickle-shaped. Dusting the plants as routine with green flowers of sulphur from planting time and at fortnightly intervals should give control or, if this has not been done, spray with colloidal sulphur.

HEART ROT

An uncommon disease of celery which may be prevalent in wet weather, when the centre of the plant becomes a slimy mass. The disease enters the plant through wounds made by slugs or other pests, or by careless earthing up, which should be done when the plants are dry. Routine dusting with lime and weathered sulphur will do much to prevent an outbreak.

HOLLOW HEART

This is not a disease, but a condition of potatoes, and it usually troubles those varieties which form large tubers. Outwardly they show no sign of the trouble, but when cut, they reveal a black, shrunken area at the centre. This is usually due to slow growth during a cold spring and early summer, so that, under such conditions, it is necessary to stimulate the plants by the careful use of artificial fertilisers, keeping them growing slowly from start to finish of a crop.

LEAF-DROP STREAK

A virus disease of potatoes, causing small brown spots to appear on the leaves and on the underside of the leaves – a brown discoloration of the veins which later spreads down the leaf stalks and main stem to enter the tubers. If used for another year, the tubers produce stunted plants and a low yield. There is no cure, and all diseased plants should be lifted and destroyed as soon as the virus is observed.

LEAF ROLL

A virus disease of potatoes, which is believed to enter the plant through the puncturing of the leaves by aphis attack. It is usually in the second season of planting that the virus makes its presence known, when the leaves curl up at the edges and become limp to the touch. The plant grows stunted, and the crop is greatly reduced. There is no known cure, but any infected plants should be dug up and burnt. The disease is rare in potatoes purchased as 'seed' from Scotland or Ireland, which are grown on fresh ground each year and regularly inspected for virus.

### LEAF SPOT

This is a disease of celery, caused by the fungus *Septoria apii*, which first appears as small brown spots on the leaves. The spots rapidly increase in size in a wet summer and, upon magnifying, they will be seen to be covered with blackish dots. These are the fruiting bodies, and soon the entire foliage will turn brown and die. As the fungus is carried by the seed, it is advisable to immerse it in weak formalin solution (and then to dry) before sowing. Spraying the plants with weak Bordeaux Mixture shortly after being set out and again before earthing up will keep them free from leaf spot.

### MARSH SPOT

A non-parasitic disease of peas, whereby they turn black at the centre. It is believed to occur through magnesium deficiency of the soil, and is prevented by watering the ground around the plants when in flower with a solution of 1 oz. magnesium sulphate dissolved in 10 gal. of water.

### MOSAIC

This disease affects tomatoes, peas, potatoes, and causes alternate dark and green mottling of the leaves. It is a virus disease, perhaps originally introduced by aphis puncturing the leaves, but it is also introduced by tobacco smokers, who should be excluded from greenhouses growing tomatoes. It may be passed on to the plants by a tobacco smoker attending to the plants, or by throwing away cigar or cigarette ends about the greenhouse. It is a dreaded disease, present in tobacco, and it can destroy an entire house of plants, causing them to collapse, often when they are ripening the first fruit. There is no cure. Diseased plants should be removed and burnt, and conditions of absolute cleanliness should be obeyed whenever growing tomatoes.

### ONION MILDEW

A common disease of onions, caused by the parasitic fungus *Peronospora schleideniana*, and most troublesome in a wet summer. It first appears as light-brown spots on the leaves, and these spread, to affect the whole leaf. The plant may heel over and die, and the bulbs make no further growth. Spraying as routine with Bordeaux Dust or Mixture, will give control, but where using onion 'sets,' plant only clean stock, and burn all leaves when removed from the bulbs, for the fungus is able to survive the winter on diseased leaves. The disease can also occur on spinach, if it does, dust with green sulphur.

PEA MILDEW

This attacks the foliage of peas, covering the leaves and stems with a white powder. Mostly, it attacks early peas, and it is most troublesome during dry weather in June, when it may affect an entire row and greatly reduce the yield. To control it, spray with Bordeaux Mixture or use as a dust, repeating after three weeks.

SCAB (POTATO)

A common disease of potatoes, causing scab-like markings to appear on the skin of the tubers and, in bad outbreaks, the whole surface may be covered with unsightly markings. The crops most troubled by the disease have often been grown in soil devoid of humus, or in soil of a high lime-content. Flowers of sulphur dug in at a rate of 2 oz. per sq. yd., or about 5 cwt. to the acre, will usually prevent any serious outbreak.

SMUT

Although not common, Smut is a notifiable disease of onions and leeks. It appears on young plants as dark brown blisters on both the leaves and bulb, and it is caused by a parasitic fungus, the blisters eventually splitting to release black, powder-like spores, which fall to the ground and contaminate later plantings.

There is no cure, and infected ground should not be planted with onions or leeks for three to four years; or before the soil is treated with formaldehyde, which must be repeated for each crop.

STEM ROT

This attacks the stem of tomatoes, usually at soil level, causing the tissues to turn brown and, later, the plant to collapse. There is no known cure, but plants raised in sterilised soil and treated with Cheshunt Compound are rarely troubled. Remove any affected plants and burn, taking care not to cause unnecessary movement which would disperse the spores on to nearby plants. After burning, wash the hands in mild disinfectant.

TOMATO LEAF MOULD

Also known as *Cladosporium*, after the name of the fungus which causes the mould; or Leaf Spot. Until the arrival of mould-resisting varieties from Canada, and the introduction of L.M.R.I. during the mid-1950s, Leaf Mould was a dreaded disease amongst greenhouse tomato growers. Now, however, a range of new mould-resistant varieties has brought new hope to commercial growers. Also, the modern multi-light greenhouse has greatly improved growing conditions by permitting a better circulation of air.

The disease appears as a mould which first attacks the leaves, as small yellow spots. Later, it spreads over the whole of the leaf, and becomes a mass of brown mould. The fruits will also be affected, falling off without ripening. If unchecked, the disease spreads with such rapidity that an entire house may be wiped out. To prevent an outbreak, spray with Mildew Specific from the time of planting, and at 14-day intervals.

TRUFFLE

A parasitic fungus which feeds on growing mushroom spawn, killing it completely and reducing the compost to a sticky mass with a most unpleasant smell. It normally appears towards the latter part of the crop, increasing in its intensity as the bed becomes more acid. It may be prevented by the addition of copper sulphate in the compost, as for vert-de-gris.

VERT-DE-GRIS

A mushroom disease, also known as Mat Disease, it causes a thick yellowish-green mat of mycelium-like threads between the compost and casing soil, often so dense as to prevent the spawn growing from the compost to the casing layer. The addition of 2 lb. of ground copper sulphate per ton of manure will usually prevent its appearance and will also prevent an outbreak of Truffle.

WART

Wart or Black Scab disease of potatoes is a notifiable disease for which there is no known cure, although many varieties show complete immunity to the disease. Only these varieties should be grown on land which has, in the past, grown infected potatoes. The tubers, upon lifting, show small cauliflower-like growths which may also appear on the stems. The potatoes will have become mummified and will be unfit to use.

WHITE PLASTER MOULD

A mushroom bed disease which is most active in a too-alkaline compost, appearing as a white mould first in the compost, later entering the casing.

The use of gypsum (calcium sulphate) in the compost will help to neutralise a too-alkaline condition whilst correct humidity, and will help to prevent an outbreak. The disease may be controlled by removing the affected area and filling in the cavity with peat saturated in a solution of one part acetic acid to seven parts water.


WHITE ROT

A disease of onions, often present during cold, wet weather and in badly-drained soil, when it will attack the bulb, covering it with fluffy black sclerotia and causing it to decay. The first sign is the yellowing of the foliage, when the plant should be dug up and inspected and destroyed. There is no known cure and infected ground should not be planted with onions for at least three years, or sterilised with formaldehyde before planting again. White Spanish is highly resistant; Ailsa Craig is susceptible.


VEGETABLE DISEASES — SUMMARY

| | | |
|---|---|---|
| Asparagus | *Puccinia asparagi* RUST | Spray with Bordeaux Mixture. |
| Beetroot | *Cercospora beticola* LEAF SPOT | Spray with Boreaux Mixture. |
| | *Perenospora schachtii* DOWNY MILDEW | Spray with Bordeaux Mixture. |
| Brussels Sprouts, Cabbage, Cauliflower Savoy | *Perenospora parasitica* DOWNY MILDEW | Dust plants with lime and sulphur. |
| | *Plasmodiophora brassicae* CLUB ROOT | Dust soil with Calomel. |
| Celery | *Bacterium carotovorum* HEART ROT | Dust with lime and sulphur. |
| | *Septoria apii* LEAF SPOT | Spray with Bordeaux Mixture. |
| Cucumber, Marrow | *Bacterium carotovorum* FOOT ROT | Rub stem with sulphur, copper sulphate and lime mixture. |
| | *Cercospora melonis* LEAF BLOTCH | Sterilise soil. |
| | *Cladosporium cucumerinum* GUMMOSIS | Dust with flowers of sulphur. |
| Dwarf Bean | *Colletotrichum lindemuthianum* BLACK SPOT | Spray with liver of sulphur. |

| | | |
|---|---|---|
| Mushrooms | *Diehliomyces microsporus* <br> TRUFFLE | Add copper sulphate to compost. |
| | *Myceliophthora* <br> VERT-DE-GRIS | Add copper sulphate to compost. |
| | *Mycogone perniciosa* <br> BUBBLES | Treat with Bordeaux Mixture. |
| | *Papulaspora byssina* <br> BROWN PLASTER MOULD | |
| | *Scopulariopsis fimicola* <br> WHITE PLASTER MOULD | Treat with acetic acid. |
| Onion | *Perenospora schleideniuna* <br> ONION MILDEW | Spray with Bordeaux Mixture. |
| | *Sclerotium cepirorum* <br> WHITE ROT | Sterilise soil. |
| | *Urocystis cepulae* <br> SMUT | No known cure. |
| Pea | *Erysiphe polygoni* <br> PEA MILDEW | Spray or dust with Bordeaux Mixture. |
| | *Fusarium solani marii* <br> FUSARIUM WILT | No known cure. |
| | *Pythium sph.* <br> DAMPING OFF | Treat soil with organo-mercury dressing. |
| Potato | *Actinomyces scabies* <br> SCAB | Dig in flowers of sulphur. |
| | *Fusarium coeruleum* <br> DRY ROT | No cure. |
| | *Phytophthora infestans* <br> BLIGHT | Spray with Bordeaux Mixture. |
| | *Synchytrium endobioticum* <br> WART | No cure. |
| Spinach | *Perenospora effusa* <br> DOWNY MILDEW | Dust with flowers of sulphur. |
| Tomato | *Botrytis cinerea* <br> GREY MOULD | Spray with Shirlan AG. |
| | *Cladesporium fulvum* <br> LEAF MOULD | Spray with Mildew Specific. |
| | *Didymella lycopersici* <br> STEM ROT | Water with Cheshunt Compound. |
| | *Phytophthora infestans* <br> BLIGHT | Spray or dust with Bordeaux Mixture. |

| | |
|---|---|
| *Phytophthora parasitica* DAMPING OFF | Water with Cheshunt Compound. |
| *Verticillium albo-atrum* WILT | Water with Cheshunt Compound. |

EGG PLANT, *see* Aubergine

## ENDIVE

Endive grows best sown where it is to mature and without the check of transplanting. Sow thinly in drills 1 in. deep and 15 in. apart, and in July. If sown before, the young plants are liable to 'bolt' during a period of dry weather, but from July sowings the plants will mature in the cooler conditions of early autumn. It demands soil enriched by the addition of some well-rotted manure and peat. No vegetable appreciates humus more than endive, and peat should be given in quantity. If manure is scarce, use hops and decayed leaves. Humus is essential where growing in light, sandy soils, which tend to dry out quickly. For this reason endive makes a more robust plant in a heavy soil. It also likes a firm seed bed. After sowing, the bed should be beaten down with the back of a spade, or if the soil is not too wet, treading will not be too drastic.

The seed will germinate quickly if kept moist and, as soon as the seedlings are large enough to handle, they should be thinned to 8 in. apart in the rows. The thinnings should not be discarded; they may be planted again in a prepared bed. If the weather is hot they may 'bolt', but if moved whilst small and not allowed to suffer from lack of moisture, this tendency will be reduced. If possible, select a position away from strong sunlight and drying winds, one facing north or east is ideal, for here the soil will not become baked. When reaching maturity the plants will respond to weekly applications of dilute manure water, and the ground should be constantly stirred up with the hoe. If sown in two batches, endive may be kept into winter, for the plants will stand several degrees of frost, and by covering with barn cloches it is possible to enjoy endive until Christmas. Should the weather be severe, straw is placed around the cloches, when it will be found that the plants will stand up to prolonged frost. If a very late crop is grown and the land is of a heavy nature, it will be advisable to sow on slightly raised beds, for although the endive loves a moist soil, this does not mean it will be happy in waterlogged ground.

Blanching is the most important part of the culture of this plant. Tie raffia round the tops as soon as the plants have reached maturity; this should be done on a day when they are dry. Handle with care so as not to cut through the leaves. After three weeks they will be blanched and ready for use. Endive must be one of the healthiest of all plants, only mildew may occasionally prove troublesome, and this may be controlled by regular dusting with sulphur.

The variety to grow is Batavian White, which is tender and crisp, and has the best flavour of all. It is hardy, too, able to withstand the early autumn frosts, whereas the Green and Moss Curled varieties are less hardy and less easily blanched.

When sowing endive seed, do not sow too thickly, in order to use up the seed, for it will germinate even if ten years old.

## FENNEL

Because of its hay-like smell, the Romans gave it the name *foeniculum*, and it is one of the oldest of cultivated plants, steeped in history. The seed is used to flavour gin, the leaves to consume with fish, either boiled with the fish, or to make sauce. It was Falstaff in *Henry IV* who said, 'And a'plays at quoits well, and eats conger and fennel', for the qualities of the herb had a similar appreciation in Shakespeare's time. It grows to a height of nearly 6 ft. and bears yellow flowers in June, while its feathery leaves take on a bronze tint which makes it a handsome garden plant. It grows in any soil, but likes plenty of sun to ripen its seeds. The leaves are used throughout summer as required, while the water from which the seed has been steeped is excellent for stomach disorders.

## FERTILISERS, INORGANIC

Inorganic fertilisers supply no humus but are mostly quick-acting and are used to redress the balance of many organic fertilisers, also where it is desired to provide the plants with a particular food as quickly as possible. Inorganics should be used in conjunction with humus-forming manures for most satisfactory results, for the inorganic fertilisers supply the plants with the necessary food from the time they are set out until the organics, which release their food more slowly, have taken over. Releasing their plant food more quickly, the inorganics will correct, in the quickest possible time, any tendency for a plant to be lacking in a particular food. During a cold spring, artificial manures rich in nitrogen will stimulate the plants into growth with the minimum of delay, and whilst few organic manures, with the exception of guano and poultry manure, are rich in potash, this is readily supplied as sulphate of potash and in other inorganics of steady and continuous action. Systematic rotation of cropping will enable the plants to take advantage of all the foods available in the soil, so that the soil does not build up an excess of one plant food – which would require correcting, often expensively, before future crop yields could be expected to be satisfactory. The content of some inorganic fertilisers is given in the following table.

| FERTILISER | ACTION | NITROGEN CONTENT | PHOSPHORUS CONTENT | POTASH CONTENT |
|---|---|---|---|---|
| Basic Slag | Slow | – | 12% | – |
| Calcium Cyanamide | Slow | 20% | – | – |
| Kainit | Medium | – | – | 14% |
| Muriate of Potash | Quick | – | – | 50% |
| Nitrate of Potash | Quick | 14% | – | 44% |
| Nitrate of Soda | Quick | 16% | – | – |
| Nitro-Chalk | Medium | 15% | – | – |
| Phosphate of Potash | Quick | – | 50% | 35% |
| Sulphate of Ammonia | Medium | 21% | – | – |
| Sulphate of Potash | Medium | – | – | 48% |
| Superphosphate of Lime | Slow | – | 15% | – |

To describe each in turn:-

### BASIC SLAG

A useful fertiliser for acid soils, for it has a high lime content. It is rich in phosphorus, which it releases slowly, and is used as a base dressing in autumn and winter, at the rate of 4 oz. per sq. yd. It is especially valuable for roots and legumes. Stimulating root activity, it may be used as an alternative to superphosphate of lime.

### CALCIUM CYDNAMIDE

One of the few inorganic manures that is slow acting. It is usually applied to the soil in spring fourteen days before planting, and is especially valuable for lettuce, for not only does it release its nitrogen slowly but also, being dark-coloured, increases the warming of the soil at this time. Use at the rate of 1 oz. per sq. yd. and dig into the soil. It is also valuable as a composting agent for straw and garden refuse.

### KAINIT

A slow-acting fertiliser with a valuable potash content but is best used on light soils. In heavy soils, its high 50 per cent salt content may cause it to set hard, and so to deprive the soil of bacterial activity. It should be used in winter, scattered over the surface and worked in, and is especially useful for maritime crops, for example, beetroot and asparagus. Use at the rate of 1 oz. per sq. yd.

MURIATE OF POTASH

It is applied in autumn and winter, and should be used sparingly as otherwise it is liable to cause damage to young roots. Of high potash content, it has also a 15 per cent salt content. It is generally used as a compound fertiliser for vegetable crops, at a rate of 1 oz. per sq. yd.

NITRATE OF POTASH

As it contains both nitrogen and potash it is a valuable dual-purpose fertiliser, but it is expensive, and is used mostly as a top dressing or liquid feed for indoor pot plants, $\frac{1}{2}$ oz. being dissolved into 1 gal. of water. It is applied whilst the plants are making growth early in summer.

NITRATE OF SODA

Invaluable for starting plants into growth in a period of cold winds, or when the soil fails to heat up, it will also release potash in the soil. It is used as a top dressing in spring at the rate of $\frac{1}{2}$ oz. per sq. yd., and should be applied during wet weather, taking care not to use in excess otherwise it will prove detrimental. It must also be kept away from direct contact with plant foliage, for it is slightly caustic and may cause burning.

NITRO-CHALK

Applied to the surface of the ground in spring to start plants into growth after a period of inactivity, and it is especially useful for an acid soil owing to its high lime content (50 per cent). Use at the rate of 2 oz. per sq. yd., taking care not to bring into contact with plant foliage.

PHOSPHATE OF POTASH

It contains both phosphoric acid (50 per cent) and potash, and being expensive, it is used mostly as a liquid fertiliser for indoor pot plants, $\frac{1}{2}$ oz. dissolved in 1 gal. of water, and used sparingly as the plants make growth.

SULPHATE OF AMMONIA

Used in spring as an alternative to Nitrate of Soda or Nitro-Chalk though has an acid reaction and should be used with care. It may be applied to the surface of the ground just before planting, raking it in or as a top dressing to stimulate plant growth. It is best used with phosphatic and potash fertilisers, at a rate of $\frac{1}{2}$ oz. per sq. yd.

SULPHATE OF POTASH

The purest form of potash available as a general fertiliser, it has a steady and continuous action. It is used to increase the colour and quality of crops, and it will build up a hardy plant. It is applied in spring (usually before planting) and early summer, scattered over the surface and worked in at the rate of 1 oz. per sq. yd., being wasteful to use in excess. It is used in the base formula of the John Innes potting compost.

SUPERPHOSPHATE OF LIME

Like Basic Slag, it provides the necessary phosphoric acid to promote vigorous root action. It is mostly used with compounds of nitrogen and potash as a balanced fertiliser, to be scattered over the surface and worked into the ground before spring planting. Use at the rate of 2–3 oz. per sq. yd. It is also an ingredient of the John Innes sowing and potting composts.

| Fertiliser | Crop | Strength | Application |
|---|---|---|---|
| Kainit<br>Superphosphate of Lime | Asparagus | 6 oz. sq. yd.<br>2 oz. sq. yd. | Early spring |
| Kainit<br>Superphosphate of Lime | Onions | 1 oz. sq. yd.<br>2 oz. sq. yd. | Early spring |
| Kainit (or Muriate of Potash<br>Superphosphate of Lime<br>Sulphate of Ammonia | Potatoes | 1 oz. sq. yd.<br>2 oz. sq. yd.<br>1 oz. sq. yd. | Early spring |
| Nitrate of Soda | Cabbage<br>Lettuce | ½ oz. sq. yd. | Summer (four week intervals) |
| Nitrate of Potash | Gooseberries | ½ oz. in 1 gall. | As they bloom |
| Superphosphate of Lime<br>Sulphate of Ammonia | Young brassicas | ½ oz. sq. yd.<br>½ oz. sq. yd. | Early spring |
| Superphosphate of Lime<br>Sulphate of Ammonia<br>Sulphate of Potash | Gooseberries<br>Strawberries<br>Vines | ½ oz. sq. yd.<br>½ oz. sq. yd.<br>½ oz. sq. yd. | Early spring |
| Basic Slag | Turnips, Swedes | 2 oz. sq. yd. | Winter |

# FERTILISERS, ORGANIC

The value of organic fertilisers is that they supply the soil with humus and release their manurial value slowly. Thus it is particularly valuable for those plants maturing over a long period and for all permanent plants such as fruit trees and those of the shrubbery and herbaceous border. The manurial content of the chief organic fertilisers is set out in the following table:

| FERTILISER | ACTION | NITROGEN CONTENT | PHOSPHATIC CONTENT | POTASH CONTENT |
|---|---|---|---|---|
| Bone Meal | Slow | 5% | 20% | – |
| Dried Blood | Medium | 10% | – | – |
| Farmyard Manure | Slow | 0.5% | 0.25% | 0.5% |
| Feathers | Slow | 8% | – | – |
| Fish Meal | Medium | 10% | 8% | 7% |
| Guano | Quick | 15% | 10% | 5% |
| Hoof and Horn Meal | Slow | 15% | 10% | – |
| Poultry Manure | Medium | 3% | 2% | 6% |
| Rape Meal | Slow | 5% | 2% | 1% |
| Seaweed | Slow | 0.5% | – | 1.5% |
| Sewage | Slow | 1% | 2% | – |
| Shoddy | Slow | 12% | – | – |
| Soot | Medium | 5% | – | – |
| Spent Hops | Slow | 4% | 2% | – |
| Steamed Bone Flour | Slow | 1% | 20% | – |
| Wood Ash | Medium | – | – | 10% |

The organic manures supplying the most balanced diet are those made up by composting straw with guano or poultry droppings. They will also supply valuable humus. Fish manure or fish meal will be available to those living close to the sea, and it should be augmented by chopped seaweed, which is a valuable source of humus though of limited manurial value. Hop manure or used hops from a brewery, which contain nitrogen and phosphatic compounds, should be used with wood ash, which is rich in potash and should be kept dry; for, if subjected to heavy rain, the potash content will be quickly washed away.

Nitrogen is required to promote plant growth, but too much will cause the formation of excessive leaf at the expense of fruit. Phosphates are required to bring a crop to maturity. A cauliflower lacking phosphates will form only a small seedy head but plenty of leaf. Phosphates are also necessary to stimulate root action, and are used in seed and potting composts. Potash is essential for all crops. It makes a plant 'hard', able to withstand severe weather and gives it resistance to disease. It also improves flavour and colour in fruit and colour in flowers. As most organic manures are deficient in potash, this should be given as wood ash, or by adding nitrate or sulphate of potash, both of which are inorganic and should be used sparingly.

The most inexpensive way of using organic manure is to obtain that which is available locally. Those living in Lancashire and Yorkshire will utilise wool or cotton waste, known as shoddy. It is rich in nitrogen and supplies valuable humus. Feathers and poultry manure are readily obtainable from most poultrymen and may be used as obtained, or for composting straw to increase its bulk, adding humus-forming peat during the composting. Old mushroom-bed compost, rich in phosphates, will also provide humus and, being fine and clean to handle, it is valuable for pot plants. To take each in turn:

#### BONE MEAL

A slow-acting fertiliser, particularly rich in phosphorous, which is so valuable for seedlings and young plants in stimulating root action, it will bring vegetable crops to profitable maturity. It is given as a base dressing for seed sowing composts, used at the rate of 4 oz. per bushel of compost, and in the preparation of the soil outside, using 4–6 oz. per sq. yd.

#### DRIED BLOOD

Rich in nitrogen, which it releases over a long period, it is used as a top dressing during plant growth, mostly for greenhouse tomatoes and cucumbers. It is usually applied to the surface soil of pots or border and watered in. Use at the rate of 2 oz. per sq. yd.

#### FARMYARD MANURE

It contains traces of nitrogen, phosphorus and potash, which it releases slowly, but its chief value is to improve the texture of the soil, creating bacterial activity. It is used to dig into the soil when the ground is prepared in autumn and winter; it is also used as a mulch in spring and summer, for roses, ornamental trees and shrubs and soft fruits. Dried cow manure is valuable to use for most bulbs, either indoors or in the open.

#### FEATHERS

Very slow-acting, feathers are used as a base dressing in the preparation of outdoor soil and though of little manurial value, they provide humus and are especially valuable in lightening a heavy soil. Feathers may be used with poultry manure as a more balanced fertiliser.

FISH MEAL

A complete fertiliser with medium-quick action, it is used as a base or top dressing, scattered over the surface and worked in. It is usually applied in spring or early summer, and is widely used with fruits and vegetables.

GUANO

The dung of seabirds which is imported from Chile and Peru. It is a complete fertiliser, and is quick-acting. It is used for fruit trees and soft fruits such as gooseberries, and is applied during spring and early summer at 2 oz. per sq. yd. Or it may be used to compost straw, as a substitute for farmyard manure.

HOOF AND HORN MEAL

It may be used in potting composts (also in John Innes), or as a general fertiliser, applied in spring at the rate of 1 oz. per sq. yd., and augmented with wood ash or sulphate of potash for a balanced fertiliser. It may be applied as a base dressing, or scattered over the surface and dug in.

HOP MANURE

Used hops from a brewery have a useful nitrogen content and traces of phosphorus. There are several proprietary brands which also contain inorganic fertilisers to make up a balanced diet. Hop manure is clean and easy to handle and in addition to its food value, provides valuable humus. It is useful for lightening a heavy soil. It should be scattered over the surface, preferably in spring and worked into the ground during the season. It may also be used as a mulch in early summer.

MUSHROOM-BED COMPOST

The used compost (see page 204) will have a valuable nitrogen and phosphatic content. When removed from the beds, it will be clean to handle and be well broken down. It is a valuable fertiliser for bowling and golf greens and may be used for potting and for bulb bowls, also for mulching. It will provide valuable humus as it is worked into the soil.

POULTRY MANURE

Used for composting straw, it provides a balanced diet and humus, although it is not so rich in the chief plant foods as Peruvian guano. Bulk may be increased by the addition of farmyard manure or peat. It is medium-acting, but is continuous over a long period. It is usually applied in spring or early summer, to the surface to be worked in during the season, or in autumn, when it is worked in as the soil is prepared. An excess given in concentrated form should be avoided. Like guano, it should be stored under cover and used dry.

RAPE MEAL

A balanced, slow-acting fertiliser used as a top dressing for fruit and vegetable crops. It is applied in spring and is worked into the soil as the season advances.

SEAWEED

Slow-acting, it contains traces of the chief plant foods but as a basal dressing, provides humus. Bladderwrack is richest in plant food. It should be worked into the ground in autumn and augmented by inorganic fertilisers in spring.

SEWAGE

Its nitrogen and phosphatic content varies greatly, and it usually contains unwanted seed and other refuse, although where readily obtainable it is cheap for use in quantity, working it into the ground as it is prepared in autumn. Sewage manure usually has a high lime content and should be used with peat.

SHODDY

Slow-acting, it supplies both nitrogen and humus, and may be dug into the soil in place of farmyard manure and garden compost when the ground is prepared in autumn. Its nitrogenous content varies considerably.

SOOT

Used as a top dressing in spring or early summer, not only as a source of nitrogen but also for darkening the soil, soot causes it to attract and retain the sun's warmth, which results in earlier crops. Use at the rate of 6–8 oz. per sq. yd., scattered over the surface.

Soot water has a beneficial effect on plants if used during spring when starting into growth. Besides its small nitrogenous value, it also contains many trace elements which are beneficial to chrysanthemums and roses. It is made by filling a sack with fresh soot and immersing it in a tank of rain water for two weeks. After removing the sack, fill up the tank with clean water and use as required.

## STEAMED BONE FLOUR

It is slow-acting and has a similar phosphatic content to bone meal, though less nitrogen. It is used as a 'drier' in compound fertilisers, in potting composts at 4 oz. per bushel, or as a top dressing for outdoor crops (6 oz. per sq. yd.) and worked into the soil.

## WOOD ASH

It has a high potash content but only if stored dry. After leaves and thinnings from trees and shrubs have been burned, the ash should be removed under cover and used in spring by scattering it over the surface of the soil and raking in. It will release its potash almost at once.

# FIG

The fig is hardier than is generally believed, and as a wall plant it grows and crops well in East Anglia and as far north as Lincolnshire, Along the western side of Britain it can be grown as far north as Ayrshire, where it will ripen its fruit in an average summer. It is said that figs crop well where growing close to the sea and where the roots are restricted. They also grow well over a chalky subsoil, and to restrict root growth it is advisable to plant over a stone or brick base made compact by ramming. This will prevent the plant from forming tap roots to the detriment of fruit.

## PLANTING

Select a south or west wall and remove the soil to about 2 ft. from the wall and to a depth of 18 in. At the bottom, place a 6 in. layer of crushed brick or stone which is made firm. The base will be more efficient if a small quantity of sand and cement are mixed together and poured over the base to percolate amongst the stones. It should be allowed to set hard before planting and filling in the soil.

Figs are lime lovers and if the soil is deficient, mix in some lime rubble but no manure, otherwise the plant will make an excess of rank growth at the expense of fruit. Late autumn is the correct time to plant, making the soil compact about the roots. To restrict the roots still further, obtain pot-grown plants and plant in the pots, burying them just below soil level.

Throughout summer water copiously. A mulch of decayed compost given early in June, will help to retain moisture in the soil.

Figs crop most abundantly when trained in the horizontal form; they also do well in the fan-shape as for plums and peaches.

The fruits should be harvested when they begin to split, not before. They should be spaced out (not touching each other) in trays, and may be kept for some little time in a cool but frost-proof room.

PRUNING

As the fruit is borne on the new season's wood, the only pruning to be given an established tree is to limit the shoots which will be produced from each fruit bud. The replacement shoot is stopped at the fourth leaf, and this is done at the end of July. Too early stopping will upset the balance of the tree, as the fruit expected to mature the following summer will form too quickly at the expense of new wood. Yet, at the same time, if the shoot is not pinched back, the fruit will not develop, turning yellow and falling.

The fruits are formed at the axils of the leaves, where they begin to swell the following spring. If the extension shoots are pinched back towards the end of July, new fruitlets will form at the axil of each leaf and these will be next season's crop.

Much of the old wood and its extension shoots may remain each year, but if the tree becomes overcrowded some of the wood that carried the previous season's fruit will need removing. The size of the area to be covered and the vigour of the tree will decide the wood to be retained.

Should the plant make excessive growth, root pruning will be necessary, otherwise fruiting will be reduced. To keep a plant in check it may be necessary to prune the roots in alternate years. First remove the soil 3 ft. from the stem and to a depth of 18 in., severing the larger roots with a sharp knife. Then place some lime rubble in the trench and ram it well down. If planted in its pot, root pruning may not be necessary, although after three to four years the roots will usually have burst through the pots.

Figs growing under glass where gentle heat is used may be made to bear two crops each year. The fruits formed the previous season will begin to swell early in spring if the extension shoots are stopped at the fourth leaf. Whilst the first fruit is reaching maturity early May, the fruit formed in spring will ripen by late August. Again, the shoots formed during the later weeks of summer will be those on which the fruitlets will form for the crop the following spring.

PROPAGATION

Figs are increased by (a) cuttings; (b) layers; and (c) suckers – the first method being that usually adopted for indoor plants. A dormant and well ripened 8 in. long shoot is removed in January and inserted in a small pot containing a sandy compost. It should be placed in a propagating frame or on the greenhouse bench where it can be given brisk bottom heat. It will root in three to four months, and in April or May should be moved to a sunny situation outdoors to ripen.

Outdoor figs are increased from suckers detached with their roots in autumn, when they may be replanted into their fruiting quarters. Or young low shoots may be layered early in summer and detached and planted in a permanent site late in autumn by which time they should be well rooted.

### VARIETIES

BLACK ISCHIA. Hardy for outdoor planting in the British Isles, the medium-sized, purple-black fruits with crimson flesh are sweet and juicy, and are borne in profusion.

BROWN TURKEY. The best all-round fig, good under glass and hardy outdoors, bearing large, purple-brown fruits of excellent flavour. It makes moderate growth and is very fertile.

BRUNSWICK. Excellent under glass and sufficiently hardy for the more favourable parts outdoors, the large pale green fruits with their white flesh being sweet and juicy.

ST JOHN'S. One of the most delicious figs and a prolific bearer under glass, its large, white-fleshed fruits being sweet and juicy.

WHITE MARSEILLES. Prolific under glass and sufficiently hardy for outdoor culture, it bears large, yellowish-green fruits with white flesh, and they are sweet and juicy.

FILBERT, *see* Cobnut

## FIRST CROSS HYBRIDS

F. 1 hybrid seed is obtained by the crossing of two distinct parent strains by carefully-controlled hand pollination. The result is to transmit the special qualities of the parents to the first generation progeny. These qualities may be earliness to bloom; compactness of habit; or size of bloom and freedom of flowering. Since 1950, the hybridists of America and Japan have worked especially with the petunia, antirrhinum and marigold, and have improved them out of all recognition from those previously known.

In Britain and Holland, the experimental stations have concentrated on

135

food crops, especially tomatoes and cucumbers, and have discovered that certain varieties at the first generation crossing produced qualities which appear to have become lost in later generations, when trying to 'fix' the results of the original cross. These desirable qualities are earlier fruiting; a longer season; heavier crops and greater freedom from disease. One of the first of the hybrid tomatoes was Ware Cross, which had as its parents Potentate and E.S.1, the latter being the seed bearer. The result was a tomato maturing early like Potentate and setting heavy first trusses, but in addition, producing the same heavy weight of top trusses as E.S.1. A great all-round vigour has ensured Ware Cross greater immunity from disease.

Being hybrids and not coming true from their own seed, it is necessary to carry out the crossing of two selected varieties each time seed is to be saved, and not only have special varieties to be selected, but also special strains which show no deterioration in the original quality and habit. Also, to ensure that cross-pollination does not occur, the two parents used in pollination are grown in separate houses, one acting as the seed-bearing parent, the other as the pollinator.

## FRUIT TREES, IN POTS AND TUBS

Where space is at a minimum, apples, pear and plums may be grown in large pots or tubs. Whilst it is possible to grow choice fruit round the walls of a tiny courtyard, it is also possible to enjoy fresh fruit on a terrace or veranda, provided that the trees receive some shelter from wind and get a liberal amount of sunshine. Apples and pears are more easily managed under these conditions of restricted planting than plums and gages, and where town culture is required, then apples would prove more reliable and dessert apples more so than cookers, on account of their size.

### METHOD OF GROWING

It is usual to grow in pots in the single cordon system, for in this way the maximum number of different varieties may be grown. This will help with pollination where bees and insects are generally few, besides providing the maximum weight of fruit in the minimum of space. The cordons should be supported by stout canes which, when growing against a wall, will be held in position by strong wires looped round each cane and fastened to the wall at 7–8 ft. intervals by a strong nail.

Where a wall, especially a sunny wall can be provided, this will prove ideal for all fruits, for not only will the trees be protected from winds, but also the fruit will ripen and colour better than it would where growing in the open ground. If a wall cannot be provided and the plants are to be unprotected, it will be better to grow several dwarf pyramids in tubs, for they will be better able to withstand strong winds.

Both the horizontal form for pears and the fan-shaped tree for plums may be used against a wall, whilst pears and apples may be grown in the single or double cordon form. Besides the need for particular care to be taken in the selection of suitable pollinators, the most suitable trees will be those which form close spurs, rather than those which bear fruit on the tips of the wood, and are of less compact habit.

MOISTURE REQUIREMENTS

A matter of importance is to provide sufficient moisture, lack of which is the one chief cause of failure with fruit trees in pots or tubs. Lack of moisture will prevent the fruit from reaching its normal size, without which it will lack flavour and may not store well, whilst the fruit may also fall long before it is mature.

Any plant growing in a pot or tub will dry out at the roots during the period June to September more quickly than will a tree growing in the open ground, which may be provided with a mulch to retain moisture in the soil, as well as being able to search more freely for its food and moisture. It must also be remembered that a tree in a pot or tub will have its roots subjected to the almost unprotected rays of the hot summer sun. It is therefore imperative that the maximum of protection is provided for the plants, and during May straw, strawy manure or sacking should be packed around the pots and kept always damp. This will protect the rays of the sun from the pots and prevent a too rapid loss of moisture from the soil.

An even better method is to fix a 10 in. board along, and 18 in. from the base of the wall. This will form a trough which is to take the pots, the space around each pot being filled in with peat. This is clean to use and may be kept continually more moist than straw, or boiler ashes may be used. The pots should be placed on a 3 in. layer of ashes or peat, which may also be placed over the soil of the pots to act as a mulch. An alternative mulch for those living in or near the country is one of strawy farmyard or stable manure, though this will not be so clean to handle as peat.

Throughout the summer months the roots must be constantly supplied with moisture, a thorough watering being given almost daily, so that the moisture may reach the roots at the very bottom of the pot. The peat or straw around the pots must also be kept moist. To allow the soil in the pots to dry out for only a short period will be to cause irreparable damage for that season.

APPLES AND PEARS FOR POTS AND TUBS

Here is a selection of dessert apples and pears suitable for pot or tub culture:

## APPLES

| | |
|---|---|
| Duchess of Oldenburg | August |
| Lady Sudeley* | August |
| Ellison's Orange | September |
| Michaelmas Red | September |
| Egremont Russet | October |
| Sunset | November |
| King of the Pippins | November |
| Adam's Pearmain | December to January |
| Claygate Pearmain | December to March |
| May Queen | April to June |

## PEARS

| | |
|---|---|
| Laxton's Superb | August |
| Beurré Bedford | September |
| Gorham | September |
| Conference | October |
| Louise Bonne | November |
| Glou Morceau | December |
| Roosevelt | December to January |
| Winter Nelis | December to February |
| Santa Claus | December to February |
| Bergamotte d'Esperen | February to March |

*Though Lady Sudeley is a tip bearer, it bears its fruit on very short twigs or shoots, and may be said to come somewhere between the tip and spur bearers and is suitable for pot culture.

PLANTING

A large pot or small tub should be used, so that the roots are not unduly restricted and the plants may be able to obtain the maximum of food from the compost. Crocks or broken brick should be placed at the bottom of each so that the drainage holes are kept open, and over them is placed a small quantity of fresh turf loam. Do not use the ordinary soil to be found in a town garden, which will generally be sour and lacking in nutriment.

Carefully remove the tap root and trim off any unduly large roots before placing the trees in the pots, spreading out the roots.

The compost should consist of turf loam to which has been added a small quantity of old mushroom-bed manure, or well-decayed farmyard manure, but not too much, for an excess of nitrogen must be guarded against, otherwise the trees will make too much wood and foliage. But potash is important, $\frac{1}{4}$ oz. of sulphate of potash being allowed for each pot and which must be thoroughly worked into the compost. This should be friable so that it may be carefully packed around the roots and the pot filled to within 1 in. of the rim. The cane is then placed into position and immediately fixed to the wall.

It is not necessary to wait for the ending of the usual winter frosts before planting if the compost is made up indoors (a cellar or shed); planting may be done at any time from mid-November until mid-March, but the six weeks preceding Christmas is the best time. This will enable the trees to become thoroughly settled in their new quarters before coming into bloom late in spring.

## CULTURE

The care of the trees will be carried out on the same lines as for other trees in the artificial form, but help should be given with the setting of the blossom by dusting the individual blooms with a camel hair brush during a dry day, and on several occasions during flowering time. If suitable pollinators are also planted together, there should then be a heavy set of fruit.

Help may also be given the trees to satisfy their moisture requirements by frequent syringing of the foliage, from early June onwards, but if this is done whilst the trees are in bloom, it must be done in time for the moisture to have dried off before nightfall, as damage might be done by late frosts if the blooms are damp.

The trees will also benefit from feeding once each week with diluted liquid manure water (obtainable in bottles from any sundriesman), from early July when the fruit is beginning to swell. This should be continued until the end of September, for the trees will benefit in addition to the fruit.

Where growing in a sheltered position, the fruit may be allowed to hang almost until Christmas, being removed as it is required, and only that of the very late-maturing varieties will need to be stored for use in the New Year. This should be removed by the third week of December, when the trees growing in pots should be re-potted in alternate years into a completely freshly-made-up compost. Trees in tubs, which will contain a larger quantity of compost and provide more nourishment, may be allowed to remain without re-potting for a number of years, if systematically fed and never allowed to suffer lack of moisture. During winter the trees will require no artificial watering, but this may be necessary in April, possibly following a long period of frost and drying winds.

# FRUIT TREES, PRUNING

The care of a neglected orchard which the purchaser of an old property so frequently comes up against will be the first consideration. Here the trees may be anything from twenty to a hundred years of age. First it will be necessary to see them fruiting so that the numerous varieties may be given the individual treatment they need. Should the varieties not be known, send some of the fruit to an apple specialist for identification, so that each variety can be treated individually when its name is known. With an old orchard, where the trees have grown tall, a ladder will be necessary to reach most of the branches. But first look at the orchard as a whole, then the individual trees. Do not take the saw and cut away branches here and there just because the trees look untidy. Consider exactly what treatment can be given to each to increase its efficiency.

FIG. 3 *Long-arm pruners for fruit tree pruning*

CUTTING OUT DEAD WOOD

The first operation will be to cut out all dead and decayed wood which is playing no part in the life of the tree and which it will be better without, for the greatest source of disease will then be removed. Then look at each tree again, and where one branch is possibly growing into another tree, obstructing light and the flow of air around each tree, cut this away also, but when removing any wood, whether decayed or green, make the cut right up to the main trunk, and in the same way if decayed or surplus wood is to be removed from a small branch. It is often observed that a branch has been removed an inch or even several inches away from the main trunk or branch, with the result that the remaining wood gradually decays and falls a victim to pest and disease, especially Brown Rot desease, which will attack the remaining parts of the tree and also the fruit.

When removing a large branch it is advisable to give it some support whilst the cut is being made, to take off much of the weight and so prevent the branch from tearing away from the stem, which would cause damage to the bark. It will be found that a cut made close to the bark will quickly heal over and will be closed against disease. But with an old orchard certain branches might have been carelessly removed, or may have snapped off leaving several inches of wood which will have decayed and have fallen away, leaving an unhealthy-looking cavity on the main trunk or on a large branch.

To prevent further decay, this cavity should be filled with cement or if only a small opening, with putty; if it is left there will be the chance that disease may enter.

The pruning and de-branching of an old tree must be done by degrees. The first winter, possibly no more than decayed wood and a few small branches overlapping each other will be removed. The following winter more unwanted wood may be cut away, then later, if the tree has become excessively tall and straggling, it may be advisable to cut back the main branches to a sturdy young shoot and build up once again the lower part of the tree so that it will, in time, be capable of bearing a heavy crop. The rejuvenation of an old, neglected tree must be done gradually. If you take out the saw and pruners and cut away right and left during the first winter there may be nothing but dying trees left. When a tree has been allowed to fall into neglect the temptation to restore its vigour at once is great, but it must be resisted. It may take four years to renovate an orchard, or even longer if the trees are very old.

PRUNING YOUNG TREES

When pruning neglected young trees, large branches will not need to be cut away. Instead, thinning and cutting back laterals to form vigorous buds will be all that is necessary. First remove any overlapping wood, taking care to cut back to an outward bud, for the centre of the tree must be kept as open as possible to let in sun-light and air. Then take a look at the laterals, which are the shoots growing out from the main stems and on which the fruiting buds are formed. Each season, additional wood is formed and also buds, but if not kept pruned the laterals will become longer and longer and, at the same time, the buds will become weaker and weaker. Instead of allowing them to remain unchecked, with the result that the fruit will be small, they should be cut back to two or three fruiting buds. Into these the energies of the plant will be diverted, with the result that the fruit will develop to a good size.

Cutting back the unpruned laterals to two or three buds should be done before the buds begin to swell, before the end of March, in order that when the sap commences to flow it can be directed at once to the fruiting buds. Also, there will be a danger of knocking off the buds if pruning is done when they have started to swell. Vigorous varieties, such as Bramleys Seedling and Newton Wonder, would be able to develop

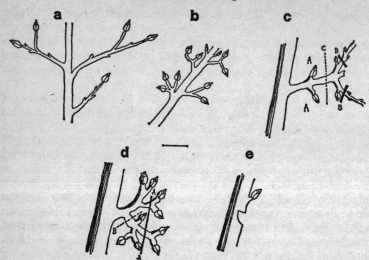

FIG. 4 (*a*) *Fruiting buds of tip bearer* (*b*) *Buds of spur bearer*
(*c*) *Forming a spur* (*d*) *Treatment of an established spur*
(*e*) *Notch to retard bud*

four or five buds, and too drastic pruning will increase the vigour of the
tree to the detriment of fruit.

RESTRICTING THE VIGOROUS TREE

Very strong-growing varieties such as Worcester Pearmain and Blenheim
Orange will require very little pruning, for they do not need stimulation
to make fresh growth. Their growth may, of course, be regulated by planting a known root-stock of dwarfing habit, but this is known only where
a new tree is being planted. To prune the vigorous varieties without
knowing which they are, will cause only disappointment by increasing
their wood to the detriment of fruit. Thus no orchard should be touched
except to cut away decayed wood without first seeing the trees in fruit.

As hard pruning of a vigorous-growing tree will make it more vigorous,
an over-crowded tree of this nature should have a branch or two completely cut away. This will allow the extra light to reach the buds without
increasing its vigour. or it may be restricted by either root or bark pruning.
Usually, a strong-growing tree will form less fruit buds than will a slow-
growing tree, and so with the vigorous growers some method of restricting growth may be necessary. For this reason, when planting new trees
of vigorous varieties, place a flat stone beneath the tap root to prevent it

growing away unrestricted, and becoming more difficult to prune in later years.

November is the best time to root prune, and if the tap root is thus checked it will be an easy matter to make a trench 3–4 ft. away from the trunk and to sever the strongest roots, spreading out the remaining roots before filling in the trench. The same rule of careful pruning, doing only a little at a time, apertains equally to the roots as it does to the branches, particularly where old trees are concerned. It is advisable to root prune only one side the first year, the other side the next year. Where standard trees are being grown it is not advisable to remove the tap root which is the tree's anchor. If a stone is placed under the main root at planting time the tree will concentrate on strong secondary roots, which may, if necessary, be restricted by root pruning.

It should also be remembered that root pruning should be consistent with the removal of wood, to retain the balance of the functions of both roots and foliage. In the case of vigorous growers, the removal of a branch or of unwanted wood should correspond to the restriction of roots. In dealing with old wall trees which are being root pruned in order to bring them into full bearing once again, the general practice is to prune back the fruiting spurs at the same time as the roots are cut back, and this will ensure quality rather than quantity of fruits. Thus will the connection between roots and foliage be maintained.

## BARK PRUNING

Bark pruning or ringing is done to curb the flow of sap, with the result that more fruiting buds are formed instead of wood growth. As there is danger that too much bark may be cut away which would not heal over in a reasonable time, ringing should only be done when root pruning has no effect, but it is worth trying it with a tree which refuses to crop, and is continually making fresh wood even when every known method of restriction has been tried. Instead of making a complete circle round the stem, it is safer to make two half circles, allowing 6 in. of bark between each. Cutting should be done with a short knife; a pruning knife is best, and immediately the cuts have been made and about three-quarters of an inch of bark has been removed, tape should be bound securely round the place where the cuts were made. Early May is the best time to do this, and choose a calm day so that the tissue of the tree at the exposed place is not open to drying winds. Cover with tape immediately each tree has been treated.

## PEARS

Everything that has been said about apple trees may be done for pears, but here again we should discover the name of each tree and learn something of its habits before taking up the pruners. Pears are divided into two sections, those with a vigorous upright habit, and those of a weaker and semi-weeping habit. In the former group are Comice and Durondeau and Clapp's Favourite; those of slender habit are Louise Bonne and Beurré d'Amanlis. The importance is in pruning, for the upright growers should have their buds facing outwards, whilst the slender, weeping growers must be pruned so that the buds, as far as possible, face in an upward direction. Most of the weepers are tip bearers and should be pruned, but only a little, for they make only a few fruiting buds; but those of vigorous, upright habit may need to have their spurs reduced to obtain fruit of size and quality. The remarks for the tip bearers in pears also concerns the tip bearers of apples, for example, Worcester Pearmain, St Edmund's Russet and Grenadier, which will require but little pruning. But every variety should be treated on its merits. Do not over-prune any tree, first try the lightest possible pruning, then wait for the results. Never prune for pruning's sake, and a little at a time is better, especially with established trees, than being drastic. First look at your trees then try to imagine them in fruit and remember that the aim is a healthy, well-balanced tree, one able to bear the maximum amount of the best quality fruit, and over as many years as possible.

It should be noticed that each shoot or lateral will form both fruiting and wood or foliage buds, the former being easily distinguished by their habit of appearing on short, woody stems, whilst the wood-making buds lie flat along the stem and are smaller and of a pointed nature.

In the correct treatment and care of a young fruit tree lies its ultimate cropping powers – which include its health, vigour, shape and ability to bear a heavy crop of quality fruit as soon as possible and over as long a period as possible. There is a wide choice of types of tree available; the bush form, standards, cordon, fan-shaped and horizontal-trained, and each demands rather different treatment not only in its establishment, but also in its subsequent care when established.

So, firstly, we are concerned with the care of the young tree after it has been formed. It must be remembered that, in its early years, a young tree should not be expected to bear excess fruit at the expense of making a healthy frame; at the beginning, the formation of wood is more important than fruit, for a solid and lasting foundation must be formed.

George Bunyard of Kent said that a newly-planted tree, which would be between two and five years old, should be allowed to grow away for a full season entirely untouched.* This was to allow it to form ample new wood whilst the new roots were forming, and so the balance of the tree was maintained. There was then no fear of excessive pruning interfering with the functions of the rooting system whilst settling in.

* George Bunyard, *Handbook of Hardy Fruits, Vol I & II*, published in 1920 by John Murray.

The following winter, pruning may commence, and by then one should have formed an idea as to the system to follow. It will be one of three alternatives:

(a) The Established Spur System, generally carried out for the more artificially-trained trees of apples and pears.

(b) The Regulated System, which requires the minimum of pruning and is generally carried out on trees with a vigorous habit.

(c) The Renewal System, which simplified, means keeping the tree in continuous growth.

## THE ESTABLISHED SPUR SYSTEM

The great difference between this system and the older, indiscriminate cutting, is to allow the tree a greater freedom of growth with the formation of fruiting spurs along the main branches. Wood formed during the summer is cut back during winter to four buds. During the following summer the two top buds will make new growth, whilst the lower spurs will develop into fruiting buds. From the place above the top buds where the cut has been made, two laterals will have formed during the second season, which in turn are cut back to two buds. This method will ensure that whilst the tree is concentrating its energies on the formation of fruiting spurs, the balance of the tree is being maintained, with the spurs forming fruiting buds without having to form new growth themselves.

During the third winter, the fruiting spurs being now correctly formed, the previous year's wood is cut back, for its functions are now complete and the energies of the tree can concentrate on the production of fruit at the spurs. Again to encourage the building up of a strong fruiting spur, the laterals should be pinched back during mid-summer, reducing them by about a third. In this way a tree is built up to its full fruit-bearing capacities in the quickest possible time, bearing in mind the affinity between the rooting system and the formation of foliage – both necessary to maintain the vigour and health of the tree. When once the tree is established, little pruning will be necessary other than to remove any overcrowded branches and to cut out overcrowded spurs. This method is suitable only for the spur-bearing varieties such as Cox's Orange Pippin, Christmas Pearmain, etc., and it is the trained forms which best respond to this method.

A word should be said about the necessity to thin out the spurs when once the trees have become established, when they are about ten years old, and those taking over a garden with trees of this age should remember that, if no spur thinning is done, the tree may soon exhaust itself by forming excess fruit, too much for it to carry in comparison with new growth. Most gardeners are shy at removing fruiting buds, but too many will cause a reduction in the size and quality of the fruit.

**THE REGULATED SYSTEM**

This system is more suitable for the tip bearers and for bush and standard trees of all apples and pears, for these are the most natural forms of fruiting trees. By using vigorous rootstocks like Malling II for apples and Quince A for pears, the tree will not come into bearing as quickly as if the dwarfing rootstocks are used, but it will retain its vigour and its fruiting capacities over a much longer period. With the tip bearers any excessive pruning will cause greatly diminished cropping, for the buds are borne at the end of the laterals and not in clusters, as with the spur bearers. So under this system cut away as much over-crossing and centre wood as will keep the tree 'open', and also remove all 'in-growing' laterals as they are observed each season. Any strongly-growing branches which appear to be growing away too quickly should be cut back, or de-horned as it is called, to a lateral growing out in a manner that will encourage the shape of the tree. The spur bearers should have their spurs thinned out in the way previously described, and although this will not be so essential as with those trees growing on a dwarf rootstock or in artificial forms, overcrowded spurs should be regularly thinned. This system demands just as constant attention in the pruning programme, and a little cutting back should be done each year, rather than the removal of excessive wood in alternate years. Those varieties which are excessively strong-growing should be root pruned every three or four years, for if too much de-horning is done this may only increase the vigour, and too much wood will be the result, to the detriment of fruit.

When forming new fruit trees, the less pruning the better until the fruiting buds have started to form, for pruning tends to encourage excess wood at the expense of fruiting buds. So allow the trees a full year's growth before pruning, then commence with the bush and standard forms by shortening back the new season's wood of the leaders by a third at the end of every season. Then as the tree begins to take shape the leaders will require only tipping each year and possibly occasional de-horning if growth is too vigorous. For spur bearers the laterals, too, will require cutting back as described, the tip bearers being left untouched until the time when they become excessive and some wood may have to be cut away.

**THE RENEWAL SYSTEM**

It is the continual renewal of old wood by new, thus retaining the vigour of the tree over a very long period without making too much old wood. The idea is to maintain a balance between the production of new wood and fruit buds, and so it is necessary to build up an open tree with well-spaced, erect branches, for it is on these that the new wood is continually formed. Suitable erect growing shoots or leaders which form on these branches are pruned back to form replacement branches, which in due course will take the place of the older branches. The same method takes place with side shoots. These are left to fruit unpruned. They are then cut back to within two buds of the base, which will then produce two more shoots. Again, these are left unpruned and allowed to fruit. In turn, each of the two shoots are pruned back to two buds after fruiting, and so the process of the continual replacement of new wood for old goes on. The proportion of shoots pruned and left untouched will be governed by the vigour of the variety. For Bramley's Seedling a better balance will be maintained if a greater proportion of shoots are left unpruned, for stimulation is not required. But much will depend on the general health and vigour of the variety or tree. If the tree seems to be making heavy weather of life, it will require more pruning of side growths to provide the necessary stimulation. Where a tree is healthy and vigorous a large number of the shoots may be left unpruned for as long as three or four years, thus maintaining a balance between fruit and wood.

BIENNIAL CROPPING

With apples there is a tendency for certain varieties, e.g. Blenheim Orange, Miller's Seedling and Newton Wonder, to form an extremely heavy crop in alternate seasons, and some form of regulated pruning is necessary to limit the blossom during the 'on' year so that the fruit will retain its size and to encourage the tree to bear a certain amount the following, or 'off' year. All spurs should be reduced to two buds, and all maiden wood must be left unpruned. This will ensure that blossom buds will be numerous for the following season, whilst during the 'on' year much of the vigour of the tree will be utilised in the formation of new buds, rather than on the concentration of those already formed. Where severe frost has damaged the blossom for one year it frequently happens that the tree will produce an excessive amount of fruit the following year, and this may be followed by a lean year. But by employing these methods a more regular crop will be assured.

A variety expected to make a good-sized fruit very early in the season, such as Grenadier and Emneth Early apples; and pear Doyenné d'Eté, it will be necessary to cut back their laterals more than is normally done. Instead of cutting back a third of the wood, as much as two-thirds will ensure a more rapid maturing of the fruit, even if the quantity may not be so high as when given normal treatment.

BRANCH BENDING

Where a tree is making such excessive growth that there is a fear that further pruning will only stimulate more wood, branch or shoot bending will help to halt this, and by restricting the flow of sap will also help to form fruit buds at the expense of new wood. It is the lower branches which are more easily bent, and they may be either tied at their tips to the stem of the tree or may be weighted down with strong stones or bricks fastened with cord to their tips. Whilst this does not really come under the title of pruning it does restrict growth of fresh wood, and will also cause these bent branches to bear a heavy crop of fruit. In this way, old fruiting shoots can be constantly replaced by new wood.

NOTCHING AND NICKING

It often happens that a certain bud is required to be restricted in its growth whilst another may refuse to break and so may cause the tree to become mis-shapen. To encourage a bud to break, a notch should be made above it and to retard a bud, a notch should be made on the stem immediately beneath it shaving off a small piece of bark.

In general it is found that the most vigorous buds are those towards the top of a stem or branch, the vigour diminishing with the buds at the centre and being less vigorous at the lowest point. It may therefore be necessary to stimulate those at the lowest point by notching, and this would even out the formation of branches.

Nicking of the stem has a similar effect. It is generally done where restriction of the extension of lateral growth is required. In addition to the cutting back of the stem, the prevention of an extension by the top bud will ensure that those buds lower down the branch will make more growth, which may be the object when building up a bush or standard tree. The cut or nick should be made with a sharp knife.

There is no more interesting occupation than in training and building up a young fruit tree, so that it will bear a heavy crop on branches formed in a way that the tree will prove most economical in the position in which it is to be planted. In a small garden – possibly one enclosed by a wall – wall-trained trees may be formed so that they will bear a useful crop of quality fruit without occupying more than a few feet of space. These are varieties suitable for growing against a north wall such as Lord Derby and James Grieve apple or Pitmaston Duchess pear and, of course, almost all will be happy against a south wall.

Then there is the horizontal-trained tree, so valuable for planting along a path or around a lawn, whilst the cordon is ideal for the very small garden, bearing a heavy crop in a restricted space and coming quickly into bearing. But those of more natural form will require just as careful handling throughout and will need to be trained for both health, vigour, and cropping capabilities in the same way. The various types may be divided into sections all needing different treatment in the formation of the tree, but all responding to similar methods of pruning when established. There are:

    (a) Bush and standard forms.
    (b) Dwarf Pyramids.
    (c) Cordons.
    (d) Espalier or horizontal forms.
    (e) Fan-shaped.

### BUSH AND STANDARD FORMS

The Bush and Standard forms will require much the same treatment and present few difficulties. Apples in the bush form should always be purchased as 'maiden' trees, which are simply one year old. They may, then, be brought along as it is desired right from the infant stage. For a standard, what is called a two-year feathered tree should be obtained, for besides its quickness to become established, it may be trained to the length of stem required. 'Feathers' are the small lateral shoots on the main stem or trunk. The tree should be allowed to grow away without any check or pruning, then when the standard has reached its desired height it should have its 'feathers' removed and the head is then built up in the same way as for a bush tree.

Formation will consist of two methods:

    (a) The Open Centre form.
    (b) The Delayed Open Centre.

It is the Open Centre form which is generally employed and this is obtained by removing the main lateral or stem possibly to as much as 18 in. From just below this cut, sturdy laterals are formed, and these will become the main branches of the tree. They should be allowed to grow away for two years, when they may be tipped to persuade them to 'break' along the stems. Any laterals or feathers which may appear down the lower portion of the stem should be cut back half way each year, and finally removed altogether as soon as the head has taken shape.

The Delayed Open Centre tree is formed by removing only the very

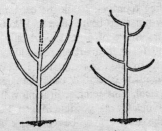

FIG. 5 *Open, and delayed open centre forms*

top 4–6 in. of the main stem. Then buds are formed down the whole length, and it is from these that the tree is built up. So as not to interfere with the laterals which will grow from the top two buds, the two immediately beneath should be removed. This will prevent the centre from becoming crowded. With this form it is the spacing that is all important, and to see that the shoots are facing in the right direction on all sides of the tree rather than too many appearing together.

Remember that those trees with a dwarf rootstock and of weaker habit will require more vigorous pruning of the laterals than those varieties of more vigorous habit. The tree is then subjected to one of the systems outlined in the previous chapter.

DWARF PYRAMIDS

This is a form of great value in the small garden, and can be built up into a heavy cropping tree in a very short period. As it is desired to make as much growth as possible at the beginning and the tree to be brought into bearing early, bud growth must be stimulated. This is done by making a cut in the bark just above each of the buds on the main stem, taking care to select buds suitably spaced. These shoots may be pruned back to half the new season's growth each year so as to stimulate the formation of fruiting buds, and all blossom buds forming on the leader should also be removed. The dwarfing East Malling rootstock Type II should be selected and vigorous trees should not be chosen for dwarfing forms. When once the tree comes into bearing it should be thinned out as for other forms by using one of the proven systems of pruning. Throughout its early life and until thoroughly established the main or central extension shoot must be constantly pruned back, so that the tree can concentrate its energies on the formation of branches.

CORDONS

It is the single-stemmed cordon that is most frequently used, and it should be planted at an oblique angle so as to limit its tendency to grow away. Once again, a dwarfing rootstock should be used, and neither a vigorous tree like the Bramley nor a tip bearer like the Worcester Pearmain. Likewise the upright spur bearers of pears should only be used. The maiden trees should be planted 3–4 ft. apart and should be fastened to wires at an angle of 45°. The extension or main stem is never pruned, and in the early years pruning consists of cutting back the laterals during August to 6 in. from the main stem. This summer pruning will ensure the formation of fruiting spurs as quickly as possible. When the tree has made the necessary growth, the leader may be cut back so that the tree can concentrate on the formation of fruit rather than on extending its form.

Henceforth the tree may be kept healthy and the fruit of a high quality by the careful elimination of surplus spurs, and a tree with excessive vigour may be curbed with root pruning done every three years. But by keeping the stem at an oblique angle this will also retard the formation of too much new wood.

Besides the Single or Oblique cordon, the U-shaped form, or Double cordon should be understood, as this is occasionally required. Though growing in an upwards direction as against the angle of the single cordon, the bend at the bottom will act as a check to vigorous growth. The U-cordon will be grown against a wire frame, as in the case of espaliers and single cordons. Its formation is in fact very similar to that of the horizontal-trained tree, the maiden being cut back to 12 in. of stem to two buds facing in opposite directions. These are allowed to grow un-pruned throughout the year, being fastened to canes against the wires, first at an angle, then gradually to a vertical position.

Pruning consists of cutting back the leaders each autumn to one-third of their new season's growth and of pinching out any side growth during August. These side shoots may be further cut back in November to two buds which will form the fruiting spurs. A variety showing excessive vigour may be root pruned in alternate years. Should either of the buds fail to form an arm, notching or nicking immediately above will have the desired stimulating effect.

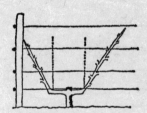

FIG. 6 *Forming a double cordon*

ESPALIER OR HORIZONTAL FORMS

Trained horizontally along the wires in a similar position as for cordons, there is no more satisfying way of growing apples and pears adaptable to this form. A maiden should always be planted, the stem being shortened to about 18 in. above soil level and to a point where there are two buds close together, one on either side of the stem. It is a simple matter to train the tree, the laterals formed by the two buds being tied to the wires to the right and to the left, whilst the extension shoot is allowed to grow away unchecked until sufficient growth has been made for it to be cut back to two more buds similarly placed and spaced about 15 to 18 in. above the first to form. To encourage more rapid growth, the laterals should first be fastened at the angle of 45° and only placed in the horizontal position at the end of the first year's growth. Small canes should be used to train it at this angle, otherwise there will be fear of damage by strong winds.

A new tier may be formed each season and when the first has been formed, to encourage it to make fruiting spurs, all shoots formed on these branches should be pruned back in summer to within 5 in. of the main stem. This will encourage the plant to form fruiting buds instead of new wood. The work should be done towards the end of July. This is followed by cutting back still further during winter in the usual way. Treatment then consists of thinning out the established spurs, and root pruning if the tree is inclined to make excessive growth. As the side arms continue to make wood, this new wood should be shortened back to a half of the newly-formed wood each winter, again making certain to cut to a bud which is to form the extension shoot. This may continue for a number of years, and until the branches reach the required number. To make for ease in picking and pruning, it is general to allow five pairs of arms or tiers to form the top at a height of about 7 ft., the reach of the average person.

It sometimes happens that a bud will fail to 'break', which would mean the loss of an arm and a badly-balanced plant. In order to persuade the bud into growth, a notch should be made immediately above the bud, a small piece of bark being removed. This will stimulate the bud into growth.

## FAN-SHAPED (see under PLUMS, page 245)

## FUNGICIDES

### BORDEAUX MIXTURE

Made by mixing together 1 lb. hydrated lime; and 1 lb. copper sulphate and dissolving them in 12 gal. of water. Do not use a metal container when mixing or storing the mixture and do not use an excess for fear of scorching the foliage. It may be used on most fruit trees as well as on gooseberries, currants, raspberries, vines, tomatoes and potatoes to control potato blight; vine mildew; raspberry cane spot; peach leaf-curl; blackcurrant leaf spot. Do not use on Cox's Orange.

### BURGUNDY MIXTURE

Made by mixing 1 lb. copper sulphate; 1¼ lb. washing soda and dissolving in 10 gal. of water. It may be used on peaches for leaf curl and to prevent gooseberry mildew and should be applied as a spray just before the buds begin to 'break'. An excess will cause leaf scorch.

### CALOMEL

Used as a dust to control club root of brassicas, dusting the roots before planting. It is non-poisonous and is clean and easy to use in puffer packs.

### CAPTAN

It controls strawberry botrytis and other moulds, and may be used either as a spray or dust. It is used in hormone rooting powders to give cuttings protection against mildew whilst rooting.

### CHESHUNT COMPOUND

Made by mixing 11 parts of ammonium carbonate and 2 parts copper sulphate which must be kept in air-tight containers until ready to use. It will prevent damping off in seedlings and is used at a strength of 1 oz. dissolved in 2 gal. of water, with which the compost is soaked both before and after sowing the seed. It is especially valuable to control the dreaded damping off disease.

### FORMALDEHYDE

The most effective preparation to prevent soil 'sickness' or glasshouse and mushroom house sickness, when the soil becomes 'tired' after the production of a number of crops, and the yield gradually diminishes. It may also be used for celery leaf spot and for root rots, to be used at a strength of 1 pint to 50 pints of water, at which concentration it may be used to sterilise soil. Seed drills may also be treated (1 part in 300) before sowing the seed. It should be used with care, for the gas given off is poisonous and greenhouses and mushroom houses should be sealed up immediately fumigation has taken place and after 24 hours should be allowed to remain open to the air for several weeks until the fumes have entirely dispersed. Soil sterilised by formaldehyde should not be used until completely free of the fumes, which will take about four weeks.

### FUNGEX

A copper sulphate preparation, used to correct rust and leaf spot. Used in liquid form at a strength of 1 pint to 50 gal. of water, the plants being sprayed at three-weekly intervals.

#### KARATHANE

The registered trade name of a preparation by Rohm and Haas Co of Philadelphia U.S.A., it may be used either as a spray or a dust for the control of powdery mildew on roses, chrysanthemums, begonias, michaelmas daisies and gooseberries. It should be applied as soon as the disease appears, and should be repeated at ten-day intervals.

#### LIME-SULPHUR

Used on apples, pears, plums, peaches, currants, gooseberries, raspberries to control mildew, scab, big bud, brown rot, 1 pint to 4 gal. of water and applied as a spray just before they come into bloom and with a second application after the petals fall. Sulphur-shy varieties should not be treated with it, and instead, should be dusted with copper-lime.

#### MERCURIC CHLORIDE

Also known as Corrosive Sublimate, it is used to control club root on brassicas and turnips. Before planting, soak the ground with 1 oz. dissolved in 12 gal. of water; also the ground where seed is to be sown. It is extremely poisonous and must be handled and used with care.

#### ORGANO-MERCURY DUSTS

These prevent root rot and storage rot in bulbs, and a damping off and common scab in potatoes; they may also be used on bulbs, corms and tubers whilst dormant and in storage. Dusting is done at monthly intervals. The dusts are non-poisonous.

#### ORTHOCIDE

Containing Captan, it is the registered trade name of The Chevron Chemical Co of San Francisco and controls a wide range of diseases. It may be used as a spray or dust to control black spot on roses; scab on apples and pears; grey mould on strawberries; damping off; corm rot of gladioli, tulips and begonias. It should be mixed with a spreading agent and may be obtained as orthocide wettable. It should be used in spring and every 14 days after, at a strength of $\frac{1}{4}$ lb. dissolved in 10 gal. of water, or as a dust.

#### SULPHUR

Flowers of sulphur, in the green or yellow form, is invaluable to prevent outbreaks of mildew amongst cuttings whilst rooting. Safe, inexpensive and easy to handle, it should be used at monthly intervals when the cuttings have been removed and are rooting. It may be dusted on potatoes to prevent an oubreak of scab.

**THIRAM**

Tetramethylthiuram disulphide is a non-poisonous fungicide, harmless to foliage. It should be used at a strength of 1 lb. dissolved in 30 gallons of water and applied to combat mildew on vines and chrysanthemums; rust and black spot on roses; rust on antirrhinums; and leaf mould of tomato and cucumber. It must not come in contact with hydrangeas.

## GAGE, *see* Plum

## GARLIC

Garlic requires a light sandy soil, a position of full sun, and neither humus nor manure. Two plantings are made, one in the south towards the end of October; another in March, this being the most suitable time for planting in the north. The cloves or bulbs should be separated and planted in clean ground, setting them out in drills 12 in. wide and spacing the cloves 6 in. apart in the rows. They should be planted 2 in. deep in a loose soil, this being one of the few plants that likes a soil which is not too compact.

Cloves planted in October will, in a favourable district, be ready for lifting late in July the following year, or before if it is required; those planted in March, being ready in the autumn. The plants should be lifted as soon as the leaves turn yellow, the bulbs being dried on the ground if the soil is dry, or in an open shed. They are then strung together and hung up in a dry, frost-proof room for use when required.

## GHERKIN, *see* Cucumber

## GOOD KING HARRY, *see* Mercury

## GOOSEBERRY

The gooseberry is at its best in a cool climate where the fruit can mature slowly, thus bringing out the maximum flavour. It was in the North Midlands a hundred years ago that the dessert gooseberry reached the zenith of its popularity. There the friendly rivalry of the gooseberry shows, held in every village, created an interest in this delicious fruit which made it the most popular of all.

## CLIMATE AND SITUATION

Indifferent to cold conditions and adverse weather, the gooseberry may be classed as the fruit grower's last line of defence. It never makes the money strawberries do, but never fails when other soft fruits may. For this reason, and because the fruit will hang on the bushes until there is labour available for picking, at least a small area should be planted with gooseberries on every fruit farm and in every garden. In those districts of the north, possibly on high wind-swept ground or where excessive rain prevents the profitable fruiting of any other soft fruit, the gooseberry may be grown as a specialist crop.

## SOIL REQUIREMENTS

Gooseberries are tolerant of frost and cold winds, and for this reason may be planted as a windbreak. But soil requirement plays a larger part in the production of a profitable crop than with any other fruit. Gooseberries prefer a light, well-drained soil containing some humus. This is essential where growing dessert fruit, for without ample moisture throughout the early summer months, the fruit will not swell. A cool soil is also essential, and for this reason the plants never crop well in shallow, chalky soils which become hot in summer. A cool soil and cool conditions must be provided. But an excess of nitrogen should not be given, for this will only encourage mildew. Gooseberries should be grown 'hard' so that the wood ripens well, and since the fruit is borne on the old and new wood, as with red currants, it is more important to maintain a balance between old and new wood than to strive for the formation of an excess of new fruiting wood. This means providing both with potash and nitrogen.

Where growing large fruits for exhibition, the plants should regularly receive an application of manure water, which should be given from the time the fruits begin to set. To delay feeding, especially if the weather is warm and dry and the plants are lacking moisture, will cause the skins to burst in the same way as tomatoes.

## PRUNING AND PROPATION

Where exhibition fruit is required, the shoots should be cut back each winter to about two-thirds of their length, or to about 3 in. of the new wood, for this will direct the energies of the plant to the fruit rather than to the formation of an extension to the shoots. Where growing in cordon form, the shoots are pruned back in March to within 3 in. of their base.

The commercial grower will give the same treatment where growing for high class dessert fruit, but for culinary and canning varieties little pruning is done. Only overcrowded wood is removed, although all dead and decayed wood should be cut away each winter.

Varieties of drooping habit, such as Green Ocean or Whinham's Industry, should be cut back to an upward bud to counteract this tendency, and those varieties most prone to mildew, e.g. Howard's Lancer and Keepsake, or those of vigorous, spreading habit, should be given only limited supplies of nitrogen. Those, such as London, which make little growth require larger quantities. Gooseberries of upright habit should be cut back to an outwards bud to prevent overcrowding at the centre of the bush. To obtain the best results, the habit of each should be studied, and pruning and feeding done accordingly.

Where growing for show, where the heaviest berry in its particular colour class wins the prize, some thinning should be done in a season when there has been a heavy 'set' of fruit. Thinning should not be done until the berries have commenced to swell, however, for the birds may have already done the job. Woodpecker, London, Lord Derby, Princess Royal and Surprise are all varieties which respond to thinning and liberal feeding.

Gooseberries are always grown on a 'leg' to prevent, as far as possible, the formation of suckers. It must be said that the cuttings are never well disposed to take root and require every assistance. Only new wood should be used (easily detected as it is light in colour) and shoots about 10 in. in length are ideal. Now comes a problem which perhaps accounts for much of the failure to root; this is the non-insertion of the cuttings while the sap is still in a fresh condition at the severed end. All too often the shoots are left lying about the potting shed while the ground is prepared, or they may be sent through the post without the necessary damp moss being wrapped round the stems to retain the moisture. To encourage a high-rooting percentage it is vital to act quickly. The cuttings should be removed from the parent plants, be prepared by having all but the top three or four buds removed so as to obtain a good 'leg', and be inserted in the ground with the minimum delay.

The time to take and insert cuttings is September. First, a narrow trench is prepared in a sheltered position; behind a frame is ideal. This is made V-shape to a depth of 9 in. and 3 in. of sand mixed with a little peat is spread along the bottom. Into this the cutting is placed, first having been dipped into one of the hormone solutions or powders to encourage root formation. The soil is then pressed round the cuttings which are placed about 3 in. apart. There should be little need for artificial watering at this time of year, but the soil should always be kept moist. If cloches are available for placing over the trenches, than so much the better, for conditions can thus be controlled. Where cuttings are being raised for stock purposes, it is better to look over the bushes for the most suitable shoots before general pruning is carried out.

Besides the more usual bush form, gooseberries crop well as double and single cordons, and for the small garden, where room is restricted, this is an excellent way of growing – either in rows exactly as for cordon apples, or against a wall. A cool, partially-shaded position will suit them well.

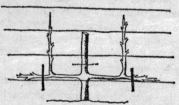

FIG. 7 *Forming a double cordon*

The single cordon is trained by cutting back lateral growth to a single bud, the leader or extension shoot being grown on. Also, new growth formed during summer should be pinched back to within 2 in. of the base or main stem in late July, after fruiting.

The double cordon is made by cutting back the main stem to buds about 9 in. from the ground, one in either direction, the shoots being trained first at an angle of 45°, then horizontally. These shoots are tied back to wires then cut back to two buds on the upper part of the shoots, the others being rubbed out. Red currants are treated in the same way.

PLANTING

Gooseberries may be planted at any time during winter, but as they come into fruit early in summer in the most favourable districts, November planting is advocated. If the soil is heavy and not too well drained, March planting is advised. Planting distances will depend upon methods of cultivation and upon variety. As with blackcurrants, it is now popular to plant closer together in the rows and to allow a greater distance between the rows. This makes cultivations easier when the plants have become large. But gooseberries do not require protection against frost, nor are they susceptible to cold winds, being planted as a hedge or windbreak, so the more orthodox planting which facilitates picking may be preferred. As the gooseberry tolerates and enjoys partial shade, it is a suitable crop to plant between young apple trees. The gooseberries are removed when about twenty years old to allow the orchard trees the maximum of room for cultivations.

After the cuttings have been rooted they should be moved to a specially prepared nursery bed, preferably where there is partial shade, and planted 3 ft. apart each way; or they may be planted into their permanent quarters the same distance apart and, after two years, alternate plants are removed and replanted 6 ft. apart. For the spreading varieties, 6–7 ft. should be allowed, and for those of more compact, upright habit, 4 ft. would be sufficient; closer planting is possible in the small garden where growth may be kept under control. Single cordons should be planted 2 ft. apart and double cordons 3 ft.

Requiring similar amounts of potash and nitrogen, strawberries are a suitable crop for growing between the rows, whilst the plants are young, but care must be taken not to damage the roots. Alpine strawberries, liking shade, do well when planted between gooseberries. The gooseberries will also provide the strawberries with protection against frost.

RED VARIETIES

BEDFORD RED. An early variety, a neat upright grower which bears large round fruit in quantity. A fine variety for the small garden.

CROWN BOB. This is a large, hairy red for mid-season. An easy grower and a heavy cropper. Makes a large spreading bush.

DAN'S MISTAKE. A fine dessert red of spreading habit raised by Dan Spencer in Derbyshire in 1850, and so named because it was a chance seedling. The berries are large, oval and of a pale red colour, mostly borne on the previous year's wood. Mid-season.

ECHO. This is a very old variety of excellent flavour. The size of the fruit is large and the season very late. Makes a bush of perfect shape.

LANCASHIRE LAD. Raised in 1824, the berries are delicious when cooked green in June and most useful when ripe for dessert later in the month. Makes a large bush and large berry.

LONDON. This is the heaviest gooseberry in cultivation bearing a round smooth fruit in mid-season. The bush makes little wood and must be done well.

LORD DERBY. Ripens late – possibly the latest red. Bearing large, oval fruit of excellent flavour. Grand for exhibition.

MAY DUKE. Raised by Messrs Pyne of Topsham, Devon, it is in the west the earliest gooseberry. Good for culinary purposes, picked green in May and delicious for dessert in June.

RIFLEMAN. Bears a large, hairy berry quite late in the season. The flavour is delicious. The crop is always heavy, but the fruit is borne at the centre of the bush making picking difficult. Late to mature.

WARRINGTON. This is the jam-maker's favourite. The colour vivid crimson, the fruit small, firm and very late.

# Gooseberry

**WHITE VARIETIES**

CARELESS. The most useful and widely grown gooseberry in cultivation; bottles and cans well, is a heavy cropper of greenish-white fruit, grows anywhere and produces a handsome berry of good flavour. Most popular of all for canning.

KEEPSAKE. A pale white, tinged green, very early and an excellent market variety, which resembles an early Careless. A very heavy cropper. Has proved excellent for canning.

LANGLEY GAGE. One of the few gooseberries to receive an Award of Merit from the Royal Horticultural Society, but on tasting this is easily understood. Bears a small, silver, transparent berry of outstanding flavour – like nectar. Of neat, upright habit.

PRINCESS ROYAL. Always in the first three at gooseberry shows, bears a huge, smooth, creamy-white berry of exceptional flavour.

WHITE EAGLE. Not so well known as Whitesmith and White Lion, but is at its best between the two and like them bears large, oblong-shaped berries of the sweetest flavour.

WHITE LION. A superb variety, very late but almost equal to Leveller in size and flavour. Extremely vigorous and hardy, it would always be the choice for a late gooseberry. Bears a heavy crop.

WHITESMITH. The first of the 'white' trio to fruit. Bears a large, downy berry of delicious flavour the length of the stem, and is most prolific. Should be in all gardens for its early fruit.

WHITE TRANSPARENT. Raised at Nantwich, Cheshire, in 1871. It makes a large but upright bush and bears a huge transparent berry, with smooth skin and a flavour both rich and sweet.


**YELLOW VARIETIES**

BEDFORD YELLOW. A most handsome berry, being of a rich golden yellow streaked with red. A mid-season variety, a heavy bearer and the fruit is large, hairy and of wonderful flavour.

BROOM GIRL. A fine market yellow, very early with fruit of medium size. The dark yellow colour, shaded olive green, gives it a most attractive appearance.

COUSEN'S SEEDLING. Popular with Kent growers. A good bearer of attractive, firm, medium-sized fruit.

EARLY SULPHUR. Very early. Bears fruit of excellent flavour and of an attractive primrose-yellow colour. Makes a large, vigorous bush.

GOLDEN GEM. A handsome, deep yellow berry, mid-season to late and of wonderful flavour. A very heavy cropper. A Whitesmith cross and introduced in 1897.

HIGH SHERIFF. A little-known variety, early and bears fruit of a rich orange-yellow colour of good flavour and oblong in shape.

LEVELLER. The favourite modern dessert gooseberry, but is only a huge cropper when done well with potash and manure and then only on certain soils. The Cox's Orange Pippin of the gooseberry world.

GREEN VARIETIES

DRILL. Late but not so late as Lancer and a useful gooseberry for a successional supply. The colour is deep green, large and of good flavour. Makes a neat, compact bush.

GREEN GEM. A variety introduced by Laxton Bros of Bedford in 1922. A good, all-round green, heavy cropping and useful – picked early for bottling and later for dessert.

GREEN OVERALL. Rather a delicious gooseberry and should be better known, for besides its unique flavour, the fruit is covered with attractive greyish down. Will form a huge berry in any soil.

GREEN WALNUT. Very dark green, of medium size and first-class flavour. Makes a small, neat bush and is excellent for town gardens.

GUNNER. Although introduced in 1820, this variety is only now coming to the front. It is of the valuable late mid-season group which closes the gaps. The sweet olive-green berries are large and of most striking appearance.

HOWARD'S LANCER. If it was not susceptible to mildew it would be just about the best gooseberry ever introduced. As it is, I know of several famous horticultural names who still give this variety as the best all-round gooseberry in cultivation, although it was introduced in 1831. It is a strong grower and regular cropper, and can be used for bottling, cooking and dessert, for which it is the latest of all to mature.

SHINER. This could be described as a white variety, shaded green. It makes a vigorous bush and a large, unique, almost square berry of great sweetness.

THATCHER. Makes a huge, oblong berry, dotted with red, very rich and sweet. The habit is spreading, vigorous and rather drooping.

**GOURD,** *see* Marrow

**GRAPE,** *see* Vine (Grape)

## GREEN MANURING

Where it is required to increase the depth of soil and its humus content as quickly as possible, usually necessary where the soil is over a rocky limestone formation, green manuring is a satisfactory method. The most rapid and inexpensive method is to fork over the surface and sow it with rape seed. This should be done early in August, so that the seed will germinate quickly and make plenty of growth before being turned into the ground in October. The soil will benefit from both the top growth and thick mat of fibrous roots which should be turned in to the depth of the spade. The roots will act as a sponge, enabling the soil to retain summer moisture during periods of drought. At the same time as the rape is dug in, give the surface a dressing of old mushroom-bed compost or decayed manure, together with some peat which will also contribute to the humus content.

HARICOT, *see* Bean, Dwarf or French

HAZEL, *see* Cobnut

## HAMBURG PARSLEY

It is a root, and so named on account of its flavour being likened to parsley when cooked. In addition its foliage, also having a similar flavour to parsley, remains green throughout winter and so may be used for flavouring soups and fish, in place of parsley. The roots are grown in exactly the same way as for parsnips or salsify, and nothing could be easier. The seedlings will also transplant more readily than any other root crop.

The plants like a long growing season, so sow the seed in March in a soil previously manured for another crop. Bring to a fine tilth, and sow thinly in rows 15 in. apart, thinning out the young plants to 9 in. A second sowing should be made in June for maturing early the following spring, to provide an all year-round supply. Throughout the summer never allow the plants to suffer from lack of moisture.

The roots may be lifted at any time during winter and early spring, with those roots from a later sowing ready early the following summer. Like parsnips, the Hamburg parsley may be cooked in numerous ways, none being more appetising than when fried in butter. The roots and foliage may also be used grated and shredded for salads throughout the year.

## HERBS

Herbs may be used about the garden in a number of ways. Some, such as the pot marigold or calendula may be planted in small beds to themselves to provide colour right through summer, whilst certain plants may be planted to form an attractive flower border giving colour from April until November. Each of the plants will prove colourful as well as having valuable culinary and medicinal properties. In most instances either their foliage or flowers will carry a distinct perfume. Ordinary soil and a position of full sun will be necessary for a border of herbs, a well drained soil being essential for all herb plants with the possible exception of those grown for the value of their roots. For the border, a number of those herbs noted for their attractive foliage may be included, the tansy, hyssop and angelica being examples as well as all those plants famed for their aromatic foliage and whose flowers are beloved by bees. Such a border will be much more a living emblem than if planted merely for colour and size of bloom. It was Eleanour Sinclair Rohde who said that 'fragrance in flowers is their music'.*

Many of the dwarf, shrubby herbs may be used on the rock garden which may be made up entirely of these plants. Westmorland limestone of strata formation is layed so as to give the appearance of having been in position since earliest days. Then, in groups about the stones, are set those plants which show a liking for a well-drained soil and a sun-baked position where the natural oil of the plants may be brought out. Here may be planted both the shrubby and prostrate thymes, which form mats of brilliant colour in shades of red and pink; the heath-like *Micrimeria corsica* with its fragrance of rosemary; the catmint and dwarf chamomiles and many more plants which grow no more than 12 in. tall. With suitable herbs may be used those rock plants which enjoy similar conditions, e.g. the fragrant androsaces, the pinks and the rock roses (*Helianthenum*) which will provide long periods of bloom and are also evergreen.

HERBS IN THE WINDOW BOX

Herbs of dwarf, compact habit may also be used to make a miniature herb garden in a window box, the aromatic fragrance of the plants permeating into the room and bringing refreshment during warm weather. Greatly in their favour is their ability to withstand long periods of dry, sunny weather without water, an important consideration where the window box has to be left unattended for any length of time. Besides the dwarf shrubby herbs, the box may include a root of parsley and of chives, and perhaps a plant of catmint. Those who enjoy the hot bitterness of the nasturtium, both of its flowers and leaves, could sow seed around the edges of the box to allow the plants to trail over the sides.

The window box may be made up either in autumn or early in spring,

* Eleanour Sinclair Rohde ran a herb farm, and between the two world wars wrote several garden books all published by the Medici Society, including *The Story of a Garden* and *Gardens of Delight*.

the box being well crocked to ensure good drainage. The soil should be freshly obtained from pastureland and should be light and friable. The herbs will benefit from a light dressing of decayed manure or of bone meal, and a small quantity of peat and coarse sand should be incorporated. The compost should be given a light dusting with lime before being placed in the box to maintain sweetness, or a handful of broken charcoal may be added for the same reason. The plants may be set closely together, for they will be kept within limits by the constant removal of the shoots for use in the kitchen. This will also prevent the plants from becoming 'leggy' as they will if allowed to make too much old wood. The nasturtiums will be removed after flowering and if the other plants are cut back in spring, they will quickly form fresh green shoots from the base.

Paths of crazy paving which so often become covered with weeds and moss growing between the stones could become transformed by planting between the stones, a number of those creeping plants which have aromatic foliage, their rich fragrance being released when the plants are walked upon. None possesses a more powerful fragrance than the Pennyroyal, *Mentha pulegium*, which has glossy green foliage and which will quickly choke out all annual weeds which form between the stones. Another valuable plant is the dwarf chamomile, *Anthemis nobilis*, which has attractive fern-like foliage and which emits a rich pungent aroma when trodden upon. The lovely creeping thymes, too, may be planted, for they will brighten up the stone with their brilliant mats of colour.

Those who have no garden, but possibly a yard which receives an abundance of sunshine, may enjoy many of the herbs by planting them in low tubs containing a similar compost as prepared for a window box. A wider variety of plants may be grown, all those herbs growing to a height of about 2 ft. being suitable. Those plants of taller habit may be planted to the centre, with the more compact plants arranged around the sides of the tub. The sages, the colourful marigolds, even the dwarf lavenders may be grown. Those plants requiring a dry soil and sun-baked conditions may be planted together and placed on the sunny side of the yard; those requiring a moist soil and cooler conditions, such as the mints, being placed in the more shaded positions. The mints are extremely valuable in this respect, and may be planted about the garden where few other herbs would grow.

One of the most pleasing uses of mint, and there are at least twenty varieties readily obtainable, is to plant a root of a variety noted for its distinctive flavouring, in various parts of the garden where the plants will be partially shaded. To walk around the garden, plucking a sprig here and there, will provide the greatest interest, and in addition is their use in the kitchen. Though herbs have almost always been given a plot of ground to themselves, they are much more attractive when used about the garden in this manner, planting between paving stones, on the rockery and about the border, for which purpose those plants of more robust habit may be used. By the side of a path the lavenders may be used or those shrubby thymes of upright habit. The rich fragrance of the plants may then be enjoyed in all parts of the garden, just as when growing in the old cottage garden, where the silver-leaved lavender is to be found growing with Madonna lilies; the old cabbage rose with the hyssop and Lad's Love, the fragrance of bloom and foliage marrying to 'refresh the spirits' as nothing else is capable of doing.

THE HERB BORDER

A border of mixed herbs, planted in a sunny position, will not only provide interest in the garden, but also the herbs will always be available for use in the kitchen and to cure simple body disorders. After all, most National Health prescriptions contain herbs of the garden in some form, and only in their colour do they differ from the brews made up from natural herbs. In the mixed herb border may be planted many of those plants whose fragrant leaves and flowers may be used in salads and drinks in addition to providing colour in the garden. The foliage of many of the plants will be beautifully serrated or may possibly be covered with minute hairs to give it a silver or woolly appearance, whilst the handsome blooms will be attractive to bees and butterflies. All those plants which have medicinal and culinary qualities should be included, except those grown for their roots and which are best grown in the kitchen garden. The plants should be arranged so that those of taller habit are planted towards the back, with the dwarf plants, the thymes to the front. The border may be edged with a row of parsley, or the plants may alternate with chives. The plants of the border should be set out in groups of three or four and formal planting should be avoided. Allow just sufficient room between the plants for the sun and air to reach them, and the result will be a live pot-pourri of delicious perfumes.

THE KNOT GARDEN

To make a herb border is probably a better method of growing herbs where garden space is limited than by growing them in small plots bordered by dwarf hedges. This was the method by which herbs were grown in medieval times, in which was known as the knot garden, each of the small plots being knotted or joined by the low hedges which were generally of lavender, the clippings of which were used to strew on the floors of the house. Such a garden laid out to a formal pattern was greatly prized by those who tended it with care throughout the year. The beds were filled with the more compact-growing herbs, together with those plants famed for their fragrant flowers, such as the violet, pink and cowslip and these were used for making wine and for sweetening.

Where space allows, a knot garden may be made on similar lines, possibly divided by a small centre path of crazy paving, between which are planted the creeping mints and thymes. Dwarf lavender may be used for the hedges, for it will withstand clipping and each plot may contain several herbs set out in formal designs. Those plants of dwarf habit may accompany them which were grown in knot gardens long ago, the violet and double primrose, pinks and forget-me-nots, and they may be planted diagonally to divide the plots into triangular sections. Into each of these, for example, may be planted the thymes, using the silver-leaved variety, Silver Queen and the Golden thyme, *T. aureus*, in separate sections with the dark green leaved thymes to provide a contrast. Each of these tiny miniature gardens may be made most attractive whilst the plants will be long living and have great value in the home.

It is felt that herb plants are far more attractive where planted in borders or small beds to themselves rather than in haphazard fashion about the vegetable garden, the exception being those plants which are grown for the herbal qualities of their roots and which may really be classed as vegetables. Most of the lovely herbs are too handsome to be relegated to the most out of the way corner of the garden, generally where they receive little sunshine and have to take a very back seat to far less valuable plants. More use may be made in the shrubbery of the taller growing, shrubby herbs such as the southernwood, lavender, hyssop, rosemary and wormwood, which grow between 3–4 ft. in height and using the upright thymes and sages to the front. In this way all these plants may be used to form a delightful shrub border. The old shrub roses may be planted at the back to form a windbreak, whilst those of less vigorous habit and the fragrant hybrid teas should be used to give colour throughout the shrubbery. Other plants, noted for the fragrance of their foliage or blooms may also be planted, most of them, including the herbs, being fully evergreen and partially fragrant the whole year round, and useful about the home in so many ways.

The shrub border will require no special soil conditions provided that the ground is well drained, whilst the plants will need little or no attention apart from the occasional trimming of unduly long shoots and the cutting out of decayed wood in spring. One point, however, is important with herbs of all groups, apart from the mints, and that is the need to plant in a sunny position, for only in such a situation will the plants continue to grow healthy year after year, and give of their full fragrance.

The herb plants should appeal just as much to modern Elizabethan gardeners as they did four centuries ago, though perhaps not for the same reasons. Today we prefer our beverages with an Eastern flavour and our tobacco from Virginia, we prefer to obtain our dried herbs from the grocer and our medicines from the chemist, and we miss much. Nothing, however, has yet been devised for providing fragrance in the garden and in the home as inexpensively and as long-lasting as the leaves and blossoms of many herbal plants, whilst diet and health could well be improved by growing as wide a selection as possible. But even by Stuart times, with the opening up of trade with the East, herb growing in England was becoming less popular, and Parkinson, gardener to Charles I, had much to say on the subject. 'The former age of our great-grand-fathers,' he wrote 'had all the hot herbs both for their meats and medicines and therewith pursued themselves in long life and much health, but this delicate age of ours doth wholly refuse them . . .' Thus the decline in the use of herbs for culinary and medicinal purposes had already begun and has continued until the present day, though the various herbal plants possess all the good qualities required by the modern gardener. They need little or no manure and once planted, very little attention. They require no staking, whilst in a well-drained soil all the plants, with but few exceptions, are completely hardy. They are also less troubled by pest and disease than most plants.

A dry soil and a dry climate will be most suitable for most herbs, and they will always be at their best following a dry summer. But whatever the weather, there will be a period in the life of each plant when it will have reached full maturity, afterwards it will begin to die back. The plant must, therefore, be harvested before this happens and the correct time cannot be measured by rule-of-thumb. Those herbs which will be used during the summer in the fresh condition, to enjoy with salads or for flavouring food and drinks will, in most instances, require no harvesting. It is only those grown for their dried foliage or petals and for their seed, which will demand care with their harvesting and drying.

Where the plants are growing under the conditions they enjoy, it will generally be possible to make two cuttings, one in midsummer, the other in autumn, but here again, much depends upon the weather. May and June, however, are often dry, sunny months, and it may be advisable to cut about 1 July to make sure of at least one good crop. The shrubby thymes and the sages should generally bear two crops.

Always select a dry day for cutting when the appropriate time arrives, which is before the flowers or leaves begin to die back when the valuable oils return to the roots or base of the plant. Should a dry period be enjoyed immediately before the herbs reach their most potent condition, it will be advisable to cut without delay, for if the plants are cut when damp, mildew may set in before they can be correctly dried, and the crop will rapidly deteriorate. Dryness from beginning to end is the secret of successful herb growing.

Cutting the shrubby herbs, for example, sage, savory and thyme, should be done with a large and sharp knife, the stems being removed about 3 in. above the base to prevent an excess of old wood from forming. When cutting savory and thyme, the whole plant may be held with one hand, while the cutting is done with the other hand, the sprigs being placed over sacking laid on the soil. Very hard, wooded plants such as southernwood or sage which have become 'leggy', will best be cut with a pair of secateurs to prevent undue pulling of the plant, with the result that the roots may be loosened. Soft-wooded plants may be cut with a pair of strong scissors. Into this category come the mints, woodruff and parsley. There are others, such as the mullein and tarragon, which will die down completely after flowering, and where it is required for the plants to seed themselves, the leaves should be removed for drying at the appropriate time and the flowers left to form seed. The stems should then be cut right back, while the annual and biennial plants are removed altogether. Those plants grown for the value of their stems such as the angelica, should be cut at regular intervals throughout summer, for it is the young stems which are required for candying and for stewing with rhubarb.

Care must be exercised with the harvesting of those plants which are grown for their seeds, such as dill and coriander. While the seed should be fully ripe before harvesting, to allow the seed pods to open will result in the seed being scattered. As they reach maturity, the pods or seed heads should be inspected daily, and removed at the first signs of any seed shedding. The seed of annual plants to be used for propagating should receive similar attention, remembering that unripened seed will be devoid of keeping qualities and will not give satisfactory germination.

The seed heads should be removed only when quite dry, or here again, mildew may occur. The heads should be cut and dropped into a cardboard box and removed at once to a dry room. There they should be placed in fine muslin bags and hung up to become thoroughly dry, after which the seed is separated by opening the pods over a fine riddle.

DRYING HERBS

After cutting, herbs should be left for an hour or so to become as dry as possible. Over-exposure to the hot rays of the sun, however, should not be allowed, or the flavour of the herbs will be lost. When drying on a large scale, either for commercial sale or for home use, a small, specially-constructed drying room will be a decidedly good acquisition. This should be built of wood, with suitable ventilation in or near the roof to permit the escape of moisture given off by the drying herbs. A small aperture at either end of the shed, or a cowl fixed in the roof will prove efficient, but if excess moisture cannot escape, efficient drying will not take place and the herbs will become mildewed and musty. Shelves should be placed around the shed, and should be made of laths with a 1 in. space between each. Where small leaves are being dried, lengths of muslin or hessian should be placed over the laths. Roof windows may be used or windows let into the sides of the shed to enable the dryer to carry out the operation with ease whilst they will provide a circulation of fresh air. Vents, made just above ground level will also ensure an efficient intake of fresh air, which will pass through the herbs and leave the house by the top vents.

Herbs may be dried in the home either by making them into bunches and suspending these from the roof of a dry shed or room (an attic is an ideal place), or they may be spread out on shelves or on trays away from the direct rays of the sun. Wherever they are drying, they should be turned daily so that fresh air can reach them. The drying should be completed as quickly as possible, for only in this way will the herbs retain their full fragrance. Especially is rapid drying necessary with those thick-leaved herbs whose leaves contain a large amount of moisture, mildew sets in if they are dried slowly. An attic or shed should be selected if possible, for the heat of the sun on the roof will enable quite high temperatures to be maintained, a temperature of 100°F. 38°C.) not being considered excessive where drying mint and parsley.

A rack for drying herbs may be made by making a number of trays about 4 ft. square, using 1-in. timber. To each tray is tacked a square of hessian canvas, and the finished trays are held into position one above another by means of four lengths of 2 in. × 2 in. timber fixed to the corners of the frames. About 12 in. should be allowed between each tray to enable the herbs to be turned and a free circulation of fresh air to reach them. A rack 6 ft. high may be inexpensively made, and will contain six trays, thus enabling a large number of herbs to be dried.

Where space is limited and only a small number of herbs are to be dried, trays of similar construction should be made to the measurements of shelves. These should stand on pieces of 2 in. timber fastened at each corner of the tray. This will keep the hessian 2 in. above the shelving, and permit fresh air to circulate around the herbs. This is vitally important for rapid drying. It should also be said that the drying room should not bebe made of stone nor of corrugated iron, for both materials tend to form condensation which will greatly hamper the drying. Where there is neither attic nor shed available, the airing cupboard will prove suitable, and especially where there is a cylinder to which is fitted an immersion heater to maintain warmth. The door of the room or cupboard should be left open to allow any moisture to escape.

STORING HERBS

When there is sufficient heat, most herbs will have dried within a week, whilst those having thick leaves will take several days longer. Where the herbs have to depend upon the natural warmth of the atmosphere they may take up to three weeks to dry, at which point they should 'crackle' and snap when touched. The leaves (or flowers) may then be rubbed from the stems between the palms of the hands, after which all unwanted material is removed. The dried leaves are placed in a fine-meshed riddle, so that soil, dust and chaff may be removed, the remaining leaves then being placed in containers for storing. Screw-topped glass jars may be used where small quantities of herbs are grown for home use, each jar being carefully labelled and placed on a shelf away from the sun. When storing larger quantities, possibly for sale, a larger container will be necessary. Wooden drums are ideal for the purpose, for wood will not absorb moisture from the atmosphere. For this reason tins should not be used, for they may cause the herbs to become damp. The herbs should be kept in a dry room, away from the direct rays of the sun, and they may be mixed as required for use in many ways in the home.

## HOREHOUND

It is the white variety, with its woolly or hairy foliage, that is grown for its medicinal properties, being used in cough mixtures. It forms a plant about 18 in. tall and is perennial, propagation being from seed. The white flowers appear in whorls, and are much visited by bees. The juice is extracted from both leaves and stems, which are also used for making a form of beer of a rich, wholesome flavour. Horehound grows well in any soil.

## HORSERADISH

A perennial which is difficult to eradicate from the garden once it is established. It is grown for its roots which provide the pungent horse-radish sauce to accompany beef. This is made by lifting and grating the fresh roots and mixing with cream.

The plant should be confined to any dull corner of the garden where it may be left down for years. A friable, well drained soil enriched with some decayed manure will be suitable and the ground should be deeply dug for the parsnip-like roots penetrate to a great depth. Plant the thongs (roots) 18 in. apart in autumn; or sow fresh seed in spring and thin to a similar distance. The roots will be ready to lift as required, the following year.

## HOTBED

A well-prepared hotbed will take the place of a heated greenhouse for raising seedling plants, or for early vegetable production. If it can be covered with a frame, so much the better, for then sowing may take place during the coldest of winter days, whilst a hotbed made in the open will enable a start to be made several weeks earlier than otherwise, to provide fresh vegetables when most in demand.

It is inexpensive to prepare, for after the hotbed has performed its task, the compost will have considerable value on the land. A hotbed will also create a natural humid atmosphere, ideal for vegetable production.

To make a hotbed for sowing in early March, obtain a bale of straw or several sacks of chaff, usually obtainable from farms merely for its carrying away. It must be made thoroughly moist, and an activator or composter, of which there are several on the market, should be sprinkled over the damp straw as it is formed in layers and made into a heap in exactly the same way as curing manure for mushroom growing. Where there is poultry or pig manure available this should be used, for it will bring about more rapid fermentation; alternatively, a small quantity of horse or farmyard manure may be added. It is important that the pig or poultry manure be quite dry and powdery when used, for wet, sticky manure will not readily heat up. The heap should be made as high as possible so that moisture is retained and the straw will more rapidly decompose. A heap may also be given small quantities of clean loam, preferably sterilised or taken from virgin land, which will help to absorb the surplus ammonia given off as the heap decomposes.

The heap should be turned after a period of eight to nine days, thoroughly shaken out, and remade into another heap, and this process should be repeated once more in a week or ten days. After allowing it another week to heat up it will then be ready for use, having turned a rich chocolate brown colour, with no unpleasant smell having a temperature of more than 100°F. (38°C.).

When making up the hotbed in a frame, the soil in the frame should be removed to a depth of 9 in., for the hotbed should be made 15–18 in. deep, and twice that depth if being made up in the open.

Soil which is removed should be placed round the outsides of the frame to help to retain the inside warmth. The compost should be trodden very firmly to preserve the heat and, as soon as it has bedded down, a 4–5 in. covering of fresh soil should be given. The bed is then ready for sowing or for accommodating pots, whichever method of raising the plants is to be followed. Correctly made, so that the compost is neither too dry nor too moist, and able to retain its heat over three or four weeks, the young plants will be ready for transplanting to a cold frame for hardening about mid-April. If no other frame is available, the plants may be partially hardened in the hotbed frame as it begins to lose heat. They may then be planted out under cloches about 1 May, or a week or so later in a sheltered garden in the south, without the protection of cloches.

Many different vegetables may be raised over a hotbed in the same frame, but better results are obtained if the plants can be moved to another cold frame, or be transplanted under cloches so that they do not become 'drawn'. If no additional glass is available, then it is advisable to delay sowing until later, so that the plants may be set out, after hardening, before they show any tendency of becoming 'drawn'. But they would have to wait until all likelihood of frost has disappeared, and this will differ over a period of almost a month in Britain, depending upon locality.

If there is no glass whatsoever it is still possible to enjoy early crops, for example, of turnips and carrots, by making use of a hotbed and allowing the plants to mature where they are sown. Even where a frame is available, an open-air hotbed should be used for raising these tender, early root crops. The bed should be prepared as described, and be made up in a sheltered corner, preferably where the plants can receive the spring sunshine. The bed should be surrounded by wooden boards or corrugated sheeting, and made 2 ft. deep to retain warmth over as long a period as possible. As a help, soil should be banked up round the hotbed. In this way it is possible to sow quick-maturing varieties in March.

HYBRIDS, *see* First Cross Hybrids

HYSSOP

A herb held to be so sacred that it was used in the Consecration of Westminster Cathedral, *Hyssopus officinalis* makes a neat evergreen bush about 2 ft. tall, and bears bluish-mauve flower spikes which are frequented by bees. It is the leaves which possess a rich aromatic fragrance. Although, like the lavender, the santolina and the rosemary, the hyssop is a valuable plant for the shrub border, it is now rarely to be seen, but in olden times it was widely grown for flavouring broths and stews. Both its leaves and dried flowers may also be used in pot-pourri.

The hyssop is native of the colder regions of central Europe and had reached England by Tudor times, for the poet Spenser writes of the 'Sharp Isope' as being good for wounds. The plants flourish in ordinary soil, and are readily propagated from slips taken during summer, and rooted as for all the shrubby herbs, in beds of sandy soil in the open. Or it may be raised from seed sown in shallow drills in spring. There are also white- and rose-flowered forms, which will come true from seed.

INDIAN CORN, *see* Corn, Sweet

# INSECTICIDES

Use insecticides as a matter of routine, for prevention is better than cure, and routine treatment will ensure clean crops. Insecticides should be used according to the suppliers' instructions, if not, severe damage to the foliage and flowers may result, whilst edible crops may be so contaminated as to cause illness when eaten. Proprietary insecticides will have been tested over a period of years and will be safe if used as directed. Read the label on the container first, and, if in doubt, find out from the local garden shop or sundriesman as to its correct interpretation before applying to the plants.

Do not use insecticides during windy weather, for damage may be caused to nearby crops, whilst splashing on the face may cause burning of the eyes and skin. Use them with care, especially those which are poisonous, and never use poisons where there are children or animals about. Most of the older remedies were highly poisonous, such as corrosive Sublimate and Lead Arsenate, but they have now been superseded by less-dangerous preparations. For Corrosive Sublimate use Calomel Dust; for Lead Arsenate use Thiol Thiocyanate as a winter wash.

After use, wash the hands and all exposed parts of the body with soap and hot water, clean the sprayer, and place all insecticides and fungicides, whether poisonous or not, under lock and key – so that they cannot be touched by children, nor by those who do not understand them.

MEASURING
    1 fluid oz. – 8 teaspoonsful
    1 fluid oz. – 2 tablespoonsful
    20 fluid oz. – 1 pint
    1 fluid oz. in $2\frac{1}{2}$ gal. – 1 teaspoonful in $2\frac{1}{2}$ points.

ABOL 'X'
It is a systemic insecticide, used to control blackfly on broad beans, rose sawfly and greenfly on roses, and greenfly on chrysanthemums. It is used at a strength of 1 fluid oz. to 2 gal. of water, and is absorbed into the tissues of the plant, remaining active for a month.

AZOBENZENE
It is used as a smoke or aerosol for the control of red spider mite in the egg stage under glass. Two fumigations should be given at an interval of 10 days.

CALCIUM CYANIDE

It is used as a soil fumigant for digging into the soil at a rate of only ⅛ oz. to every 1,000 cu. ft., and will control ants, leather-jackets and wireworm. It is used in the preparation of greenhouse borders, and gives off hydrocyanic gas on exposure. It is extremely poisonous, and great care must be taken when using it.

CALOMEL

Used as a dust on onions and brassica crops to control onion fly and brassica root fly, at a strength of 1 oz. to every 3–4 yd. in the row. It will also control club root of brassicas.

DERRIS

It is non-toxic to humans and animals, but fatal to fish. It is used in orchards, mixed with other insecticides to control plum sawfly, gooseberry sawfly, and raspberry beetle, at a strength of 1 fluid oz. to 2 gal. of water, to which is added ¼ lb. soft soap or other spreading agent. It is applied during spring or early summer, and may be incorporated into other insecticides. It may also be used as a dust. It is non-poisonous.

D.N.C. PETROLEUM

Used as a routine spray for top and hard-wooded fruits during December and January, to control capsid, red spider and winter moth caterpillar. It is a petroleum-oil emulsion, incorporating a small amount of nitrocresol to kill the eggs of aphis. The preparation should be used at a dilution of 10 per cent and applied at bud-break.

GAMMEXANE

Benzene Hexachloride (B.H.C.), it will control wireworm, earwigs, weevils (including strawberry blossom weevil), onion fly, capsids and woolly aphis, but it must not be used on or near food crops within 4 weeks of their harvesting. Use at a strength of 1 oz. dissolved in 2 gal. of water, or as a dust. Do not store near foodstuffs, as it will cause tainting.

HEPT

It will control aphids, red spider, capsids and leaf hoppers, and may be used on strawberries, and lettuce. It is used mostly in greenhouses at a strength of 1 fluid oz. to 12 gal. of water, plus a spreader, and, as the poisonous property quickly disappears, food crops may be consumed forty-eight hours after spraying. However, it should not be used on tomatoes, cucumbers or chrysanthemums, nor on yellow-fruiting gooseberries.

## LEAD ARSENATE

It will control caterpillars, and is used on top and bush fruits, but it is highly poisonous and there are other preparations which will perform as effectively. It is generally used in powder form, mixing with water at a strength of 1 oz. to 3 gal. of water.

## LINDEX

It is based on Gamma-BHC and will control greenfly and black fly, narcissus fly, apple and plum sawfly, and celery and chrysanthemum leaf miner. It should be applied at a strength of 1 fluid oz. to 2 gal. of water, seven days after petal drop in apple and plum, or as a dust. Do not use it on potatoes, blackcurrants, cucumbers, hydrangeas or vines, after flowering.

## MALATHION

An organic phosphorus insecticide, which is used in the control of mealy bug, thrips, aphis on apples and pears, peaches, apricots, and strawberries. It is used at a strength of 1 fluid oz. to 3 gal. of water, or as a dust. Use at regular fortnightly intervals for complete control.

## METALDEHYDE

It is poisonous, and it used solely to destroy slugs which may be particularly troublesome during wet weather. It is used as bait at the rate of 1 oz. mixed with 1 lb. of moist bran, and put down at regular intervals about the garden or greenhouse. It is best covered with a small box containing holes at the sides for the slugs to enter.

A more efficient method of control is to water the ground and plants with liquid Slugit, a Murphy Chemical Co preparation, which will provide immediate protection against slug attack. 1 fluid oz. of Slugit will treat 10 sq. yd.

## NAPHTHALENE

It may be used as a soil fumigant to control leatherjackets, wireworm, carrot and onion fly, and it is dug into the soil at a rate of 2 oz. per sq. yd. as it is prepared. It may also be used as a glasshouse fumigant (2 oz.

per 1,000 cu. ft.) to control red spider and thrips on cucumbers, tomatoes, carnations and vines. Here, however, it must be used with care, and it is essential to have the correct temperature and humidity, or the growing crops will be harmed.

### NICOTINE

A tobacco alkaloid, it is highly-poisonous, and for this reason has been superseded by other pesticides. It was at one time widely used to fumigate mushroom houses and greenhouses (as cones or shreds) or used as a spray at a strength of 1 fluid oz. to 12 gal. of water. It should not be used on edible crops, though may still be used on top fruits and bush fruits in spring, where a tar-oil winter wash has not proved effective. It may also be applied as a dust on flower crops.

### PETROLEUM OIL

It is used at a strength of one per cent in summer, immediately after petal drop, to control red spider on apples, pears, plums and peaches. It should not be used at greater strength, or leaf scorch will result.

### PYRETHRUM

It is non-poisonous to humans and warm-blooded animals, and may be used (during summer) as a dust, on a wide variety of crops, including cucumbers, tomatoes and lettuce, which may be attacked by capsids, leaf-hoppers, red spider, springtails, thrips and greenfly.

### SYBOL

An I.C.I. preparation, based on Gamma BHC and Derris, it will control greenfly, blackfly, caterpillars, capsids, thrips, chrysanthemum leaf miner, carrot fly, pea moth and bean weevil. To control these pests, use as a liquid at a strength of $\frac{1}{2}$ fluid oz. per gal., or as a dust.

### TAR OIL

This is an Emulsion containing a tar distillate, and it is used as a 5–10 per cent dilution on top and bush fruits only, during the dormant winter period. Tar oil will control aphis, apple sucker, winter and tortrix moth caterpillar. It will also clear the trees of moss and lichens.

### TEPP

It has similar properties to HEPT, but in more concentrated form, and it is mostly used on carnations and other flower crops under glass to control red spider, aphis, white fly, capsids and leaf hoppers. It should be used with a spreader at a strength of 1 fluid oz. dissolved in 25 gal. of water, together with 2 fluid oz. of liquid detergent.

THIOL THIOCYANATE

An all-purpose winter wash used at bud burst on top and bush fruits. It should be used at a strength of 1 pint to 4 gal. of water, and will control aphis, apple sucker, winter moth caterpillar, capsid, red spider and woolly aphis.

## KALE

There are numerous varieties of the kale, some ornamental, and most are of value as a winter vegetable. Yet they remain sadly neglected, and are rarely served in hotels and restaurants.

Their value lies in their hardiness, and the fact that they will crop well in almost all soils, provided that the soil contains a little humus and manure. For this reason they will bear through winter, under conditions which the Brussels sprout and broccoli would not tolerate. A soil which has been well manured for a previous crop, provided that it does not lack lime, and the addition of 1 oz. per sq. yd. each of superphosphate and potash, is all that is necessary to grow good plants.

The seed should be sown early in April, and the plants transplanted 2 ft. apart towards the end of May, selecting a rainy day for planting out. Plant firmly, and keep the hoe moving all summer. The soil should be trodden firmly around the plants as they grow, for this will prevent them from being blown over by autumn winds.

The handsome curled leaves (hence its country name, Curly Kale) are removed whilst young and tender, stewing them rather than boiling to bring out their delicate flavour. The leaves will become stringy and coarse if allowed to grow too large.

VARIETIES

The marrow-stemmed kale should be left for cattle, for there are numerous other varieties for the home garden.

ASPARAGUS KALE. This requires rather different treatment, the seed being sown in late July where the plants are to grow to maturity. The long shoots are ready in spring, when they are of particular value; stewed in butter they carry an asparagus flavour.

COTTAGER'S KALE. Tall-growing, extremely hardy and produces an abundance of shoots for use late winter and spring.

DRUMHEAD KALE. Makes a dwarf plant of the shape of a savoy. The curled leaves are of richest flavour.

LABRADOR KALE. Probably the hardiest of all kales, producing its low mats of curled shoots through the severest winter and spring.

MOSS CURLED KALE. Very hardy and compact, with its fronds of moss-like foliage which are very delicious when steamed.

RUSSIAN KALE. An excellent plant for late winter, producing masses of fern-like leaves; tender, and of rich flavour.

## KOHL RABI

Like the Hamburg Parsley, kohl rabi is another old favourite neglected by modern gardeners. One of its most valuable assets is that it is quick to mature, being ready to use within twelve weeks of sowing. As it is also extremely hardy and able to withstand the severest weather, three sowings should be made, the first in April, the second at the end of May, the third early in July – this last sowing for use after Christmas. Robert Thompson (see footnote on page 41), in charge of the R.H.S. Gardens at Chiswick, in his *Gardener' Assistant* published over a century ago, describes the kohl rabi as 'holding an intermediate place between the cabbage and turnip, the upper part swelling into a round, fleshy head, resembling a turnip' – a description which could not be bettered.

Kohl rabi is drought-resistant, and as it keeps free from disease it may be said to be one of the most accommodating of all vegetables. The young plants will also transplant readily. It may be cooked and served in a dozen ways, but always cook it in its skin to preserve its delicious flavour. It may be served cold in a late summer salad, or the sliced root may be fried, or steamed and served whole during winter.

The seed is sown very thinly and in shallow drills 15 in. apart, the seedlings being thinned to 8 in. in the rows. The plants should be grown quickly, so that the roots are succulent when cooked, and should be used when the size of a large orange. For this reason the ground should be well prepared, and although kohl rabi grows best in a sandy soil, it should be liberally enriched with some decayed compost. Until it is well established, water should be given whenever necessary, and although the plants will tolerate the driest of conditions, they are much more succulent when watered during such a period.

Lift them as required, but do not allow the plants to become too large.

The two best for garden culture are Vienna White and Vienna Green. The former is best for frame culture and for an early crop, the flesh being white and crisp. Vienna Green is extremely hardy, and should be sown for winter maturing.

LAMB'S LETTUCE, *see* Corn Salad

## LEEK

Both the ancient Egyptians and the Saxons held the leek in high esteem; it was an almost sacred plant, so much so that all bulbous plants were given the same name in its honour. Yet, by Elizabethan times, unlike most members of the onion family, it had sunk into obscurity. Gerard, a renowned writer on horticultural subjects of that time, said, 'It hateth the body, ingendereth naughty blood, and causeth terrible dreams'. Twenty years later Parkinson was even less favourably disposed to it, saying, 'It is in general feeding in Wales with the vulgar gentlemen' (see footnotes on page 60).

Nowadays, it is difficult to understand the opinion of these two re-nowned gardeners, for in many gardens the leek takes pride of place with the Brussels sprout as a winter vegetable, being kept for that difficult late-winter and spring period when there is always a scarcity of vegetables. Yet in Thomas Smith's *Profitable Culture of Vegetables*, first published in 1911 and still the commercial growers' textbook on vegetable growing, the author writes: 'Leeks are not greatly in demand in the south, but are appreciated in the northern counties, and in Scotland and Wales.'

### PREPARATION OF THE SOIL

Their hardiness must have to do with leeks being held in respect in the north, for they will survive the severest of winters and will thrive in all soils. But to grow them well they should be trenched, and they respond to a well-drained soil, a heavy soil being lightened by incorporating a quantity of peat, boiler ash or sand. As excessive manuring is not appreci-ated by the leek, for this crop should follow one which has previously received a liberal amount of manure.

The best method is to trench, removing soil to a depth of 10 in. – the width of a spade. Into the bottom of the trench is placed a layer of decayed garden refuse, which will continue to decay in the trench. This is covered with the friable soil into which a quantity of peat has been in-corporated, and into which 1 oz. of superphosphate and $\frac{1}{2}$ oz. sulphate of potash per yd. of trench has also been added. So that the fertiliser is not wasted it is a good idea to throw up the soil as the trench is made on either side, so that the soil together with the fertiliser, is utilised from one side only, that on the other side being used to blanch the leeks as they grow. The soil to be used for planting the leeks should also be given a 2 oz. per yd. dressing of bone meal. A friable soil in good 'heart' suits the leek well.

# Leek

## SOWING AND PLANTING

Seed is sown mid-March in shallow drills, a double row being covered by cloches to start them off, for it is essential to give the leek a long season if it is desired to grow those big succulent 'sticks'. The seed should be sown in a friable soil containing some peat and coarse sand. If the seed is kept comfortably moist it will quickly germinate, and the young plants will be ready for planting out early in July. Seed sown late, with the plants being set out at the end of July, will only result in small leeks, however well the trench has been prepared. If possible, transplant at the end of June, using a dibber to make a hole 1–2 in. deep, into which the plants are dropped. Do not fill in with soil, but water the trench after planting is completed. A double row should be made, the leeks being planted 6 in. apart, with about the same distance between the rows. When planting, allow the wide part of the leaf to fall *along* the rows, rather than across.

As the plants make growth, a small quantity of peat and soil should be placed around the plants, and never must they be allowed to suffer from lack of water. Like celery, leeks are lovers of moisture.

When the plants have made some size, towards the middle of August, corrugated paper should be fastened with an elastic band around the lower part of the plants. This will help to 'draw' the plant, at the same time blanching that part of it covered by the corrugated paper. The paper will need renewing from time to time through the season.

Feeding with a weak solution of dried blood, or with liquid manure during the autumn, will encourage the plants to attain a large size, suitable for exhibition. Though it must be said that those massive showbench leeks so often make tough, flavourless eating, and that a leek of average proportions should be the aim, as far as quality is concerned.

The plants may be dug up through the winter as required, but as they are hardy enough to stand through the severest weather, it is advisable to lift the bulk of the crop during March and early April. Neither pest nor disease troubles the leek.

Those who wish to exhibit should wash the leeks upon lifting. A leek of exhibition standard should be solid and thick, at least 8 in. in circumference; it should be well-blanched, with a clean skin, and be of a uniform thickness from top to bottom of the blanched portion, which should be from 12–14 in. long.

## VARIETIES

MARBLE PILLAR. A long-stemmed leek which may be used early. The stems measure 10 in. and when blanched are extremely tender and succulent, and of mildest flavour.

MUSSELBURGH. The new Improved strain is proving that this grand old leek can still hold its own on the show bench. The hardiest of all leeks, with the stems blanched to 15 in.

PRIZETAKER. The stems are very long and of pure white. They attain remarkable thickness, yet never lose their mild flavour.

ROYAL FAVOURITE. Raised in the Royal Gardens at Windsor, and a leek of delicious, mild flavour. The dark foliage and milky white stem make it a most handsome plant.

THE LYON. Makes a large thick stem, free from any coarseness, the leek flavour being particularly pronounced. An old favourite, which does well in all soils.

## LETTUCE

Lettuce is one of the oldest of edible plants, the earliest variety being the Roman lettuce, which records show was grown in the gardens of the Popes at Avignon during the fourteenth century. This is the lettuce we now know as Cos. Parkinson (see footnote on page 60) said that 'the white Roman lettuce must first be whited (blanched), that it may eat kindly'. The cabbage lettuce he describes as being, 'as great as the crown of a man's hat'.

When preparing the soil, old mushroom-bed compost is ideal. This not only provides the lettuce with all its food requirements, but also provides moisture-holding humus, without which lettuce will not grow well. In addition, the plants should be artificially watered and if planted in a sunny position quickly reach maturity, several crops being grown in a year.

Equally important is a well-limed soil, for one of an acid nature will, in moist weather, cause the matured plants to become slimy and limp. If peat is used to supply humus, take additional care to ensure that the soil has been well limed.

Those who possess a cold frame or cloches will be able to enjoy lettuce all the year round, it being no more a summer crop than a winter one; seed can be sown at frequent intervals throughout the year. Those who grow their plants in the back garden and who do not wish to worry with sowing seed, will be able to obtain plants from specialist growers.

By using a small part of a frame in which the seed is sown broadcast, or by sowing in shallow drills under cloches late in autumn, an early spring and summer crop may be enjoyed. By sowing in the open from spring until early autumn, lettuce may be cut from midsummer until Christmas. In favourable areas of the south-west, all sowings can be made in the open, completely unprotected, to provide an all year round supply.

## *Lettuce*

**SOWING THE SEED**

The seed is sown thinly, either in a prepared seed bed for transplanting as soon as the seedlings can be handled, or where it is to mature, some seedlings being removed and perhaps transplanted to prevent overcrowding. To provide a succession of lettuce in small numbers – which is better than making large planting at any one time – sow a pinch of seed every six weeks, selecting those varieties which are suitable for the different seasons.

Lettuce growers living in an exposed area will sow late in July for cutting from November until spring under glass, or for early spring maturing, if sowing in a favourable climate. Lettuce does not fear the cold, however intense; it is damp, foggy weather which troubles it most, causing damping off. For early summer supplies, seed should be sown under glass during February, for planting out in early April.

With lettuce it is also important to keep the plants growing from the moment that the seed is sown, watering during periods of drought, but keeping the plants under glass as dry as possible through winter. Lettuce in a soil lacking humus will quickly go to seed during warm weather, whilst those under glass will damp off if not kept as dry and as well ventilated as possible through winter.

No form of artificial nitrogen should be given to the soil, otherwise the plants will not make good hearts, and during autumn and winter will tend to be soft, so falling a victim to mildew or botrytis. Mildew may be prevented to a large extent by dusting the plants with flowers of sulphur every ten days whilst under glass.

**BRINGING ON THE PLANTS**

Where transplanting, do so following a shower, or when the ground is moist but not sticky. To plant when the soil is dry, even with the intention of watering afterwards, will almost certainly cause wilting, from which plants may take many days to recover. Plants should be moved in the early seedling stage, before forming a tap root. Should this not have been done, the home grower will find that the plants will move easier and will heart up more quickly if the tap root is removed before replanting.

Lettuces are planted on the flat, generally in rows 18 in. apart, the plants being allowed sufficient room to develop, although almost every variety will vary in habit and in space requirements. So that no ground is wasted, plants may be set out between rows of broad beans, peas or French beans, and they may be inter-cropped with radishes, or with late-maturing greens, such as cauliflower and cabbage.

Lettuce for market should be picked if possible free from moisture, otherwise they may become slimy during transit. The larger summer lettuces are generally marketed in returnable wooden crates containing two dozen, placed in rows, head downwards; winter and spring lettuce are best marketed in non-returnable crates containing thirty-six heads, for they will be much smaller.

For use in the house, lettuce should be placed in a refrigerator for an hour before required, or, where this is not possible, the plants should be carefully pulled from the soil (not cut), the roots being placed in a bowl of water which should not touch the leaves, and the bowl and lettuce being placed in a cool room until required. Lettuce purchased in a limp condition may be partially revived if placed in a cool room and sprinkled with water.

VARIETIES – HARDY WINTER AND SPRING (OUTDOOR)

ARCTIC KING. A cabbage lettuce of proved hardiness, producing large, solid heads, with few outer leaves.

BIBB LETTUCE. Of quite different type, the loosely-formed plants have rich creamy hearts, with a flavour entirely their own. An American lettuce.

HARDY WINTER WHITE. This is a cos lettuce forming large, conical heads, which make very crisp eating through winter and are completely hardy.

SUTTON'S IMPERIAL. A superb cabbage lettuce for autumn sowing, which withstands the severest weather.

WINTER MARVEL. The enormous cabbage-like heads form a large heart of wavy wax-like leaves, which make delicious eating.

VARIETIES FROM WINTER AND SPRING UNDER FRAMES AND CLOCHES

FRENCH FRAME. Very quick to mature, making a much-appreciated contribution to a Christmas salad. The leaves are very pale green, the habit compact.

MASTERPIECE. Maturing in early spring, the leaves are almost free from the usual red tinge of frame lettuce.

TOM THUMB. This lettuce cannot be too highly recommended. Indeed, it may be sown and used throughout the year and, in exposed gardens, wintered under cloches. It makes a compact, dark green head, the leaves being very crisp and icy cool.

VARIETIES FOR SUMMER SOWING

The follow varieties should be grown; they are renowned for their ability to remain firm, and not readily 'bolt' during hot weather.

GIANT CRISPHEAD. It makes a large, tightly-folded head of brilliant green and of crisp texture. It will stand for a long period without bolting.

GREEN JADE. American, and quite unlike Salad Bowl, it makes a small, tightly-closed head of rich jade-green leaves of melting crispness. It must be grown in a humus-laden soil, or it will 'bolt'.

NEW YORK. Also an American variety, very similar in size to Webb's Wonderful, and having the same excellent qualities. The leaves are of a darker green.

SALAD BOWL. This richly-flavoured lettuce is an American Gold Medal winner. It is of endive type, the plant being loose, the leaves waved and almost fern-like, crisp and cold. It will not 'bolt' during hot, dry weather, and its curled appearance and brilliant green colour makes it a particular favourite for salads.

TENNIS BALL. A deliciously-flavoured, pale-green lettuce, which makes a neat, compact head, the leaves having almost a sweet taste.

WEBB'S WONDERFUL. Unrivalled as a large family lettuce. The massive heads form tightly-packed hearts, which remain crisp and cold through the hottest weather.

COS LETTUCE

Those who enjoy the extra crispness of a Cos lettuce should grow the self-folding varieties; this particularly applies to market growers, for they save considerable time over the old method of tying every plant with raffia to blanch the hearts as in Parkinson's time (the late sixteenth and early seventeenth centuries, see footnote on page 60). These are self-folding:

JOBJOIT'S GREEN. A fine, large-leaved variety which may also be sown late in summer for autumn maturity.

PARIS WHITE. Makes a large crisp white heart.

PRINCES OF WALES. The best cos for a dry season for it is of compact habit and less liable to 'bolt' than any other.

SUGAR COS. Comes mid-way between a cos and a cabbage lettuce, with the best qualities of both. It makes an erect plant, maturing early, its leaves being deep green, crisp and sweet.

WINTER DENSITY. It is intermediate between the cos and cabbage sections, forming a large crisp head of sweetest flavour, and stands dry weather better than most.

FOR SOWING MIDSUMMER TO MATURE IN AUTUMN

Here again, those varieties should be selected which are less liable to 'bolt'.

LITTLE GEM. A cos lettuce, similar in form to the Sugar Cos, making dwarf compact heads of brightest green, and withstanding dry conditions admirably.

SUTTON'S A.1. A slightly smaller Webb's Wonderful, having the same crinkled wavy leaves, and should be grown instead of Webb's for late summer and autumn maturing.

SUTTON'S UNRIVALLED. A fine variety having smooth leaves, making a solid, white heart. Happy in either wet or dry weather.

# LIME

A term applied to the various forms of calcium, which is used to improve the texture of heavy soils and to 'sweeten' acid or sour soils. In the form of calcium carbonate (chalk) it is used on light soils of an acid nature, applied in autumn or winter at the rate of 2 lb. per sq. yd., and dug into the soil as the ground is prepared. It is also used as a 'sweetener' for the John Innes seed and potting composts, in the form of ground chalk or limestone, or as limestone flour, as used for poultry. Calcium carbonate should be used in preference to hydrated lime.

Hydrated or slaked lime (Calcium Hydroxide) is used in the preparation of all types of soil to correct acidity and to 'open up' a clay soil. It may be used in direct contact with those plants, e.g. perennial scabious, dianthus, which require ample supplies of lime in their diet. It is applied in winter or early spring at the rate of 1 lb. per sq. yd. and in the dry condition. Unhydrated or quicklime (Calcium Oxide) is used on heavy land, dug in at the rate of 1 lb. per sq. yd. as the ground is prepared in winter. The action of the moisture in the soil when in contact with the lime will cause a violent reaction, in which the lime will disintegrate in a volcanic-like eruption, at the same time breaking up the particles of clay in the soil. Humus materials may then be incorporated and the soil left in a rough condition for the frosts and wind to pulverise it further. The action of the quicklime will also bring about pest destruction. Gaslime is inexpensive and has a similar action in the soil as quicklime, but it also contains sulphur compounds which will exterminate numerous pests. However, the ground should not be cultivated for several months after an application, to allow the poisonous sulphur compounds to be washed from the soil. Use at the rate of 2 oz. per sq. yd., and do not exceed this.

# LOGANBERRY

Introduced into Britain in 1897, it bears a long, tapering fruit of deep crimson red which does not part from its plug. For canning purposes this adds to its value, for the fruit retains its shape. It is a heavy cropper in most soils and is almost immune to frost, though does not like cold winds. The fruit should be allowed to become fully ripe before using.

The Thornless Loganberry is a recent introduction which should be cultivated in every fruit garden. Bearing its fruit during late July and well into August, ripening before the main blackberry crop, it is entirely thornless, making picking and tying a pleasure rather than a trial. The fruit is a dull wine red, sweeter than its parent.

Loganberries possess a different habit from blackberries. The canes are more brittle and grow more like raspberry canes. They should be trained in fan shape rather than along the wires as with the more pliable blackberry cane. And whereas blackberries should be spaced from 12 ft. apart, depending upon individual vigour, loganberries will not require more than 9–10 ft. between each plant.

To prune, treat as raspberries, and each year after fruiting, cut back the old canes to 3 in. of ground level and tie the new season's canes to the wires for fruiting the following season. Hence the reason for the loganberry and the hybrid berries requiring even more nitrogen than the blackberry, for they have to bear new canes at the same time as fruit.

The more nitrogenous manures that can be given, the more vigorous will be new cane growth. As for blackcurrants, pig or poultry manure composted with straw will prove valuable and in April the plants will appreciate a 2 oz. per sq. yd. dressing of sulphate of ammonia, or 1–2 cwt. per acre, applied during a rainy period. With loganberries, as with blackcurrants, it is rarely possible to provide an excess of nitrogen. For this reason the two should be grown together. They also enjoy the same climate and situation – full sun and a sheltered position.


## MACE

A member of the achillea family, *A. decolorans*, this herb has the same beautifully serrated leaves possessed by all its members. It is a pleasing plant, bearing white flowers on 2 ft. stems, and is propagated by root division. The pungent leaves may be used in salads or for flavouring soups and stews.


## MANURE, LIQUID

This may be obtained as a proprietary brand and used to the manufacturer's instructions, or may be made by filling a sack with farmyard or poultry manure and immersing for three to four days in a tank filled with rainwater. The sack should be stirred around frequently so that the water comes into contact with all the manure and its complete food value is released. The liquid manure will be in concentrated form and should be diluted to requirements.

A general fertiliser may be obtained in liquid form by dissolving 1 lb.

Nitrate of Potash and 1 lb. Sodium Sulphate, $\frac{1}{2}$ lb. Superphosphate in 2 gal. of water. This should be used at a strength of 5 fluid oz. dissolved into 1 gal. of water, and at weekly intervals. It is a balanced fertiliser, containing nitrogen, phosphates and potash.

An alternative balanced fertiliser may be made up by mixing together 7 lb. Sulphate of Ammonia, 1 lb. Sulphate of Potash, and 3 lb. Superphosphate of Lime. Dissolve in 2 gal. of water and apply as above, or use in the powder form during the growing season at the rate of 2 oz. per sq. yd. Dust the surface of the ground between the plants, and hoe or rake in.

MAIZE, *see* Corn, Sweet

MANURING, *see also* Fertilisers; Green Manuring; and Sawdust

## MARJORAM

The Sweet Marjoram, *Origanum marjorana*, a native of the Mediterranean countries, is a perennial, although is not completely hardy away from the south-west. It is better grown as a half-hardy annual, sowing the seed in boxes in the heated greenhouse early in spring. The leaves should be gathered in September, 'when the sap is full in the top of them', as one old writer said.

The Pot Marjoram, *O. onites*, is a native of the same parts. It is tender and should not be planted out until May. The marjorams are cut just before the flowers are fully open and dried and used for seasoning. The fresh leaves may also be used in salads and have a sweet, aromatic taste, whilst the dried leaves are also valuable for mixing with lavender for placing amongst clothes. 'The whole plant and every part thereof is of a most pleasant taste and aromatic smell,' wrote Gerard (see footnote on pag 60).

The plants are of shrubby habit and require a well-drained soil and sheltered, sunny situation.

## MARROW

Marrows should be planted in full sun and where they may be sheltered from cold winds. They resent root disturbance, so must be grown in pots from the beginning. The most successful method is to raise the plants over a hot bed made in a frame at the end of March. Over the compost is placed 3 in. of fine soil and into this are pressed small pots touching each other. The pots are filled with John Innes sowing compost, in which peat is substituted by well-decayed manure, old mushroom-bed compost being ideal.

The seeds are pressed into the compost, their pointed ends at the top and only just covered with the compost. The seed is sown during the last days of March. The pots are given a thorough soaking and the frames placed in position, kept closed until germination has taken place, and the pots are watered when necessary. To prevent the compost from drying out too quickly, damp peat should be pressed around the pots as they are placed in the frame. During the first three weeks of April the frames should be covered with sacking at night to retain warmth.

Early in May, when the plants have formed their second pair of leaves, they will be ready for removal to a cold frame for hardening. This is done by first leaving off the glass during the daytime, then gradually at night, so that by the month end the plants will be ready to go out.

PLANTING AND SOIL PREPARATION

When manure was plentiful, one would see the marrow planted on mountains of compost, and how well they grew. Today these mountains have been reduced to minute hillocks and the plants make little headway, especially in a warm, dry summer which should suit them well. The reason is not that the plants lack nourishment, but moisture, the little mounds drying out too readily, which is fatal to the marrow, for it must be given plenty of moisture about its roots.

With the present shortage of compost, the best method is to plant on the flat, into a soil containing plenty of humus – some decayed manure, peat, spent hops, even decayed leaves or bark fibre, now readily obtainable; anything to help the soil retain moisture. If the soil is heavy or the ground low lying, make a raised bed, but work in the same quantity of humus.

Set out the plants at the end of May, allowing 3–4 ft. for the bush varieties, and 6 ft. for the trailers. Where growing under barn cloches, make the beds to fit the cloches and plant out early in May. The glass may be removed at the end of June, when the plants will have made considerable growth.

If no frame is available, the plants may be grown entirely under cloches, and although the crop will not be so early to mature, it will prove earlier than where the seed is sown in the open. Plants sown over a hotbed will be showing fruit before seed sown in the open has made its second leaves.

Those able to obtain plenty of manure could raise a reasonably early crop by making up a hotbed in the open early in April, covering with 6 in. of soil and sowing the seed under a barn cloches, the ends covered with glass to retain the warmth. An early crop will be the result of this method.

When planting out, set the plants firmly and press the small pot into the soil about 2 in. from the plant, water being given through the pot when required. Before knocking the plant from the pot, first give a thorough watering to bind the roots so that there is almost no disturbance.

When the plants have made about 18 in. of growth, pinch out the leader shoots to encourage the formation of side shoots. Under glass give daily syringings to flowers and foliage whenever the weather is warm, and those growing in the open should be kept free from weeds and watered during dry weather. A mulch of peat and decayed strawy manure will work wonders, so will regular watering with liquid manure from the time the first fruits begin to form. This will be about July from early sown seed in the south; three to four weeks later in the north.

The fruits should always be removed when they have attained a reasonable size; to allow them to remain on the plants until they have become too large will not only spoil the quality of the fruits, but will seriously reduce the crop. Keep them on the move, giving plenty of moisture and removing the fruits quickly so that others may form.

Care must be taken in removing the fruits or the plants may be damaged. Cut away the marrow where it lies rather than lifting first, for this will disturb the plant. At the same time carefully remove any dead foliage. The fruits should be handled carefully so as not to bruise them.

POLLINATING MARROWS

This is usually done by insects, especially during dry sunny periods and more in the south than the north. However, the plants will begin to fruit earlier and bear heavier crops if artificial pollination is done.

This may take place in two ways, either by dusting the male flowers and transferring the pollen to those of the female, or by removing the male flower entirely, folding back its petals and pressing it into the female flower. This should be done only on a dry day, when the pollen is dry, and only when the flowers are open and the pollen ripe.

Plants growing under glass will benefit most by this articial pollination, and no difficulty should be experienced in telling which flower is the male and which the female, for the latter has a tiny miniature marrow-like swelling of the stem immediately beneath the flower. The male is quite without this swelling.

### VARIETIES AND GOURDS

The terms, marrows, squashes, pumpkins really mean the same thing, there being only slight botanical differences between each. The squash is used as an American term for all marrows, those which should be used during summer straight from the plant, and those which will store through winter.

AVOCADELLA. This is a summer marrow of bush habit bearing small fruit, about the size of a large orange but deep green in colour, at the centre of the plant. It produces little fruit until early September. It is also known as the Argentine Marrow, and is popular in that country served cold, as it should be. By far the most delicious way of serving it is to boil it for half an hour, then allow it to become quite cold, cutting the marrow in two, removing the pulp and placing in a refrigerator for an hour. Remove half an hour before using and fill the centre with whipped cream. Add sugar and a little oil, then eat with a spoon as for melon. If served at the beginning of a meal during late summer and early autumn, straight from the plant, instead of soup or hors d'oeuvre, it will prove the most delicious appetiser imaginable. The flesh is pale pink.

Northern gardeners would be advised to grow this marrow under barn cloches or in a frame throughout the summer, watering and ventilating liberally.

BANANA ORANGE. Of trailing habit and though not one of the easiest to grow, it should be attempted in all gardens for the fruit will keep well into winter. The rich, orange-coloured flesh is firm and sweet, with the attractive flavour of ripe bananas, although it is on account of its long, lightly curved shape from which it takes its name.

BOSTON PIE PUMPKIN. This is the old American pie marrow, with orange skin and flesh, the fruits often weighing up to 8 lb. It is often known as the Sugar Pumpkin on account of its sweetness. It is of trailing habit and, like most of the winter-keeping squashes and marrows, the fruits are never at their best until late autumn when the keepers should first be used. They should be served with eggs, onions and other tasty winter vegetables. The Hubbard Squash is almost identical in habit except that its skin is deep green.

BUTTERNUT. Of trailing habit this is one of the most delicious of all marrows. The fruit keeps well into winter, the fine-textured flesh being at its best when baked. The fruits attain a length of 12 in. and are as wide as one's forearm.

CASERTA. A marrow of the bush type. Where the plants have been raised early, it will come into bearing mid-July in the south, the first of them all, yet it will continue to bear right through summer. Remove the fruits when quite small, cook for an hour and serve cold, or hot filled with one of the suggested French (dwarf) beans which have also been cooked. Serve with mayonnaise if cold; with white sauce if hot.

COURGETTE. The true French marrow which should be harvested when only 4 in. long. Regular removal at this stage will ensure a succession of fruits which are cooked in their skins, frying them in butter or margarine, like sausages, when the skins will be just as tender. They will be done and be ready to eat as soon as the skins are soft.

COCOZELLE. This is a semi-trailing variety, to be eaten during August, removed from the plant long before it attains the large proportions of which it is capable. It is particularly delicious filled with peeled tomatoes, after cooking and cooling, and served cold with salad oil or mayonnaise.

GOLD NUGGET. An American introduction, each plant bears six to eight marrows of deep golden yellow striped with white and of the size of a large orange. It makes for delicious eating and stores well. It is a bush marrow of compact habit.

GOLDEN DELICIOUS. A trailing variety bearing large globular marrows of deep orange with bright yellow, fibre-less flesh. A good winter keeper.

LITTLE GEM. A South African marrow of trailing habit, bearing small, dark green fruits of orange size and shape. After cooking, cut into halves and scoop out the succulent flesh.

MOORE'S CREAM. Of trailing habit, it may be used right through autumn and, if carefully stored, into winter. The fruits are small, oval and pale cream coloured. It is delicious baked in its skin which should be oiled, then with the pulp and seeds removed, it should be filled with cooked tomatoes, beans and mushrooms, being re-heated in its skin and served piping hot. Enjoy it with brown bread and butter.

ROTHERSIDE ORANGE. A richly-flavoured little marrow, bearing fruits the size of a large grapefruit and of the same colour. It is a trailer for summer use, and is almost like a melon. It should be cooked, then cooled in a refrigerator and served with sugar or ginger. Add cream or oil to taste, on much the same lines as for the Avocadella.

ROYAL ACORN. It will store well and makes an appetising meal around Christmas time. It forms a long fruit, though small in comparison with the ordinary vegetable marrow, the flesh remaining thick and firm in storage. It is of trailing habit, but where space is limited there is a bush form, which also keeps well and has a firm, sweet flesh.

SOUTH AFRICAN MARROW. Similar to the Avocadella, bearing a larger crop but with possibly not quite the same delicious flavour. It is easier to grow, especially in the north. It makes a neat plant though of trailing habit, the fruits being the size of a large orange when ripe, and of the same colouring. Though ready for use towards the end of August, the fruits will also keep well into winter. They should be served cold as for the Avocadella, but are delicious filled with minced meat and mushrooms, and served hot during the early winter months.

SUMMER CROOKNECK. Of a bright yellow colour with pale, cream-coloured flesh, this American squash is far more delicious than its name suggests. The fruits should be removed when 9 in. long, others suggest using when half that size. The flesh remains tender and sweet even if the marrows attain a weight of 3 lb. or more. Of semi-trailing habit.

SUTTON'S SUPERLATIVE. A bush marrow, tender and delicious when stuffed with minced meat and served hot. The fruits are of a pure bottle-green colour, the flesh deep orange and very sweet. Though it will grow to exhibition size, the fruits should be used when fairly small.

TABLE DAINTY. One of the earliest marrows to fruit, and exceedingly prolific. The fruits are small, deep green, attractively striped with a paler green. It is a summer marrow of trailing habit. It may be used either hot or cold as described, or filled with any chopped vegetables to suit one's taste.

THE TURK'S CAP MARROW. So called because it is shaped exactly like a Turk's turban, the skin being coloured orange and green. It is of trailing habit, the fruits keeping well. The flesh is rich orange and of distinct flavour. The plant seems to grow better in the south, for it must receive the maximum of sunshine.

WHITE CUSTARD MARROW. This is a bush marrow for summer use and is one of the few which should be allowed to mature fully before use. It attains the size of a small football and is delicious served hot, the pulp removed and filled with mushrooms, chopped runner beans and little Atom tomatoes.

## MEDLAR

It is rarely planted today but has ornamental value and grows well in a heavy, damp soil in which few other fruits will flourish. It does, however, require a sunny situation and protection from cold winds, thus it does better in the southern half of England. Where it is established, it blooms profusely in spring and bears heavy crops, both at the ends of the branches and on the old spurs, pruning being the same as for the apple. It is propagated by budding onto pear or hawthorn stock, and this is done in July.

As the fruits form, the trees should not lack moisture, and they will appreciate a mulch of decayed manure or garden compost to supply the necessary nitrogen and to prevent soil evaporation in summer. The fruits should not be removed until early December for, like celery, they should first be frosted. Store eye downwards on shelves in a dry airy room for about two to three weeks until they become soft, when they will make pleasant eating during the Christmas season provided that they were not removed from the tree too early. When ripe, they should be consumed without delay. The medlar is considered to be the ideal fruit to have with port.

*Left*  The original
Bramley's Seedling
apple

*Below*  Bramley's
Seedling apples

*Above*  Cox's Orange Pippin apples

*Left*  Apple 'Pearl' – of Russet-like appearance
*Below*  Apple 'James Grieve'

*Above left*  Spraying the top of an apple tree
*Left*  Brussels sprout 'Pier Gynt'

*Below*  Carrot 'Gold Spire'

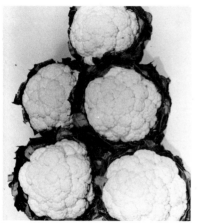

*Top*   Sweet corn, John Innes Hybrid
*Above left*   Cauliflower 'Sutton's Polaris'
*Above right*   White cucumber

Gooseberries.
*Opposite above*   A well-grown bush five years old
*Opposite centre*   White variety, Gooseberry 'Careless'
*Opposite below left*   Gooseberry 'Drill'
*Opposite below right*   Gooseberry 'Gunner'

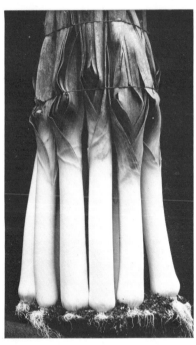

Mushroom growing.
*Opposite above*  Breaking a cylinder of pure-culture spawn into pieces suitable for inserting into the compost
*Opposite centre*  The pieces of spawn laid in staggered rows ready for planting
*Opposite below centre*  A portion of compost is lifted and a piece of spawn inserted
*Opposite below*  A one-inch layer of casing soil is placed over the compost and made firm

Mushroom development. *Left* The mushrooms break the surface *Below* Three days after their first appearance

*Left* Clusters of mushrooms almost ready for picking *Below* Mushroom 'Buttons' for market should be between 1 in. and 2 in. in diameter

*Above left*    Tree onion – useful, and strikingly ornamental
*Above right*    Potato 'Fir Apple' – pink, and of unique flavour for salads
*Below*    Plum 'Thames Cross'

*Left*  Outdoor tomato
'Sleaford Abundance'

*Left*  F.1 Hybrid tomato
'Syston Cross'

*Above*   Tomato leaves, showing Cladosporium disease

*Left* Outdoor vines growing like runner beans in Lancashire

*Below* A prize-winning display of vegetables by Wm. Robinson & Son, of Forton

VARIETIES

DUTCH or BROAD-LEAF DUTCH. It makes a large spreading top and is a valuable shade and ornamental tree, attractive in blossom and in fruit with large, broad, dark-green leaves. The fruit ripens to russet brown and measures 2 in. across. It has a reasonable flavour.

NOTTINGHAM. Also the Common or Wild Medlar, making a medium-sized straggling tree with little ornamental value, although the russet-brown fruit has better flavour than the Dutch variety.

## MELON

Several of the newer introductions mature in an average British summer and present little difficulty with their culture. They may be grown in the open but are better under glass, planting either in a frame or beneath cloches.

Seed is sown in small pots in February for melons resent root disturbance. Brisk bottom heat of 65°F. (18°C.) is necessary for quick germination. Use the John Innes sowing compost and water sparingly until germination. Keep the seedlings close to the glass and maintain a temperature of 60°F. (16°C.). Then, as soon as the pots become full of roots, move to a larger size containing a friable sandy loam into which is mixed a sprinkling of steamed bone flour and sulphate of potash. By mid-April, the plants will be ready to set out in deep boxes or larger pots, placed as close to the glass as possible and containing a compost made up of equal parts fibrous loam and decayed manure, into which has been incorporated a 1 per cent mixture of bone meal and hoof and horn meal.

Where growing outdoors, plant early May into a frame containing a mound of compost of similar ingredients. Keep the frame lights in place until the month end, then ventilate by partially raising the light during daytime. Keep the soil comfortably moist and when 6 inches high, stop the plants by removing the growing point to enable them to develop several fruit-bearing stems.

Hand pollination is necessary to set a heavy crop for melons bear male and female flowers on the same plant and the females will set better if given assistance. This is done by dusting each flower when dry with a camel hair brush; or a male flower may be removed and the petals turned back to expose the column of stamens which are inserted into the female flowers to pollinate the stigma. One male flower may be used to fertilise four females.

Do not shade the glass for melons require the maximum amount of light, and whilst the plants must not be allowed to lack moisture, especially when the fruits are swelling, over-watering in dull weather may cause root rot.

When the fruits form, place them on pieces of wood so that they will not decay as they might do if in direct contact with the soil.

VARIETIES

CHARANTAIS. Excellent for outdoor cloche and frame culture, it is a heavy bearer with the flesh thick and juicy and deep orange in colour.

CRENSHAW. Introduced by Thompson & Morgan of Ipswich, it ripens rather later than Sweetheart when the skin turns pale yellow. The thick salmon-pink flesh is improved by deep freezing whilst the flavour is outstanding.

SWEETHEART. The earliest to mature, ripening evenly and setting a heavy crop even in northern England. The flesh is deep salmon-orange with the flavour fresh and juicy.

TIGER. So named from its yellow-and-green-striped skin, the flesh, which is orange-yellow, is of exceptional flavour with high vitamin content.

# MERCURY

A useful vegetable, hardly for winter use, but the new season's leaves begin to apppear early in spring, when they may be used either for a salad or cooked like spinach, but unlike that vegetable they do not possess what is to many, an unpleasant earthy taste.

The seed is sown in spring in shallow drills 18 in. apart and in full sun and a rich soil, one containing some humus. When large enough to handle the seedlings should be thinned to 12 in. apart, and the plants kept thoroughly moist through summer.

Mercury, or Good King Harry as it is also called, is perennial and will make a large clump, the succulent leaves appearing as soon as the snow and ice has left the soil and being indispensable at a time when greens are scarce. But plant or sow it only in a soil clear of weeds, for it will occupy the ground indefinitely.

The early season's shoots should be cooked and served in the same way, when they will be crisp and tender and possess a similar flavour to that of asparagus.

This is a vegetable little grown, yet so nourishing and delicious that it should be in every garden.

# MINT

A corner of the garden which is partially shaded and where a cool, moist soil may be provided, will grow mint. But full shade should not be given, or the 'sprigs' will grow loose-jointed and will form fewer leaves.

With their creeping rootstock and bearing an abundance of leafy shoots through summer, the mints are gross feeders and require a rich, well-manured soil, and one retaining summer moisture. Their creeping habit also makes it almost impossible to eradicate perennial weeds when once the bed has been made, and hoeing will also be impossible. The ground must first be thoroughly cleaned, then humus-forming manures worked in. Hop manure is excellent for mint, also well-decayed farmyard manure, particularly cow manure. Peat may also be used, though where this is done the ground should be liberally limed, for mint does not enjoy acid conditions.

### PREPARING THE GROUND

The ground may either be prepared in trenches made 6 in. deep, the roots being spread out and covered with 2 in. of compost; or they may be planted in prepared soil on the flat, allowing 12 in. between each root. Where making up a bed for home use to accommodate a dozen or more different species and varieties, a single root of each may be obtained and planted 12 in. apart. Whether growing for market or for use in the home, overcrowding should not be allowed, or the creeping roots will rapidly exhaust the soil and will tend to choke out each other.

### PLANTING

Mint roots are sold by the bushel, and are generally received in a sack. It is most important that they do not dry out before planting, and they should be placed in a cool, shady place until required. Spread out each piece of root as one would an asparagus root, for they will not be happy if bunched together. Beds may be made up at any time between mid-October and early April, though October and November planting will enable the roots to become established before the hard frosts, and will then enable them to bear their first sprigs, as mint stems are called, early the following summer.

The first year should see only a limited number of sprigs removed, and where planting for winter and early spring forcing, no sprigs at all should be cut. For forcing, new beds should be made up each year in autumn, the roots being lifted the following November and placed in prepared soil under a frame or in deep boxes in the warm greenhouse. Early supplies may be obtained if a mild hotbed is made up in the frame, though forced mint is most in demand during early spring. Then the sun's warmth should be sufficient to force the sprigs in time to meet the early spring demand. A hotbed may be made by composting a quantity of damp straw with an activator and adding a small amount of dry poultry manure to increase more rapid fermentation. The compost should be heaped as high as possible and turned several times, at intervals of six days. It will be ready to make up into a hotbed when it has turned deep brown in colour. As the mint sprigs will grow about 9 in. tall, the same depth of soil should be removed from the frame to accommodate the compost. About 6 in. of riddled loam should be placed over the hotbed, which should have been made quite firm by treading, to enable it to retain its heat. Then when the heat of the compost has fallen to a temperature of around 65°F. (18°C.), the roots should be lifted and placed closely together at a depth of 3 in. in the soil. They should be well watered in, and the frame light should be kept in place, ventilation not being necessary at this time. Though a hotbed may be made up at any time during the winter, it will only be possible to lift the roots when the ground is not frozen. To guard against this, the roots outside should be covered with a 6 in. layer of leaves, straw or bracken in December, so that they may be lifted when required.

Semi-forcing may be done by covering the roots, which have been planted in trenches, with barn-type cloches. If covered in February, there will be sprigs for cutting several weeks before any uncovered shoots will be ready. Where forcing in boxes in a warm greenhouse, the compost should consist of one part riddled loam, one part peat or leaf mould and one part decayed manure, the roots being spread out and covered with one inch of compost. They should be kept comfortably moist and given little or no ventilation. To maintain a continuous supply through the winter, boxes should be made up each month, but where there is no greenhouse available, continuous supplies may be obtained from a hotbed followed by those from a cold frame or where covered by a cloche. Finally there will be the crop from unprotected open-ground roots.

'Sprigs' in abundance and of top quality are only obtained by giving the plants good culture. They should be given a mulch of decayed manure when they die back in autumn. Roots to be used for forcing will welcome an application of weak liquid manure given every three weeks during summer. Mint thrives on a rich diet where the soil is of a sandy nature.

Where grown well, a mint bed made in the home garden should remain healthy for four years, when it will be advisable to lift the roots, divide and replant into freshly prepared ground.

PROPAGATING

Mint may be propagated from young shoots removed in early summer and rooted 2 in. apart in a frame containing a sandy soil enriched with peat. But the culinary mints, which are prone to rust, should be propagated by lifting and dividing the roots into numerous pieces, for whereas rust, a fungus disease, attacks the stems, it does not attack the roots. There is, therefore, little likelihood of infecting fresh ground where propagating from root cuttings. Keeping the beds free of annual weeds by hand weeding will help to keep down rust, which attacks both stem and leaves, and appears as orange-coloured spores, the sprigs being unusable. As the disease may remain about the exposed crowns of the plants during winter, when lifting and dividing the roots it is advisable to place them in water heated to 112°F. (45°C.) for ten minutes before planting.

When drying mint, either for use as mint sauce or for inhaling, the leaves should be dried as quickly as possible or they will become mildewed. They should be spread out on shelves in a warm room and, when quite dry, the leaves are removed from the stems and rubbed down to almost powder form, which should show the mint as being dark green in colour. Where using in sachets for placing amongst clothes, the leaves need not be finely pulverised, but they should be quite dry.


SPECIES AND VARIETIES

There are three main forms of culinary mints: *Mentha viridis* or Spearmint, which is also Lamb Mint; *M. sylvestris*, the Hairy Mint; and *M. rotundifolia*, the Round-leaf Mint, the best form of which is Bowle's Variety. It is not troubled with rust as so many of the mints. Another form of the Round-leaf mint is the Apple Mint, readily distinguished from the other mints by its pale green shoots. These are suitable for making mint sauces.

Of the medicinal mints, used for stomach disorders, *M. arvensis*, the Cornmint, has a strong, almost oppressive smell and is used to prevent milk from curdling. The variety *piperascens*, the Japanese mint, is used for the extraction of menthol. *M. piperita* is the Peppermint, of which the black-stemmed variety has the highest peppermint content.

Possessing a most attractive fragrance is *M. citrata*, the Citrus or Lemon mint. Its deep green and yellow variegated leaves possess a refreshing and long lasting lemon fragrance, similar to that of *Pelargonium crispum* 'Variegatum', when pressed. In olden times it was likened more to the perfume of the orange, the leaves being mixed with orange juice to make a most delicious conserve. There are other forms, one possessing almost a pineapple scent and giving its name to the mint; another having the perfume of Eau de Cologne. They should be in every collection for their fragrance is rich and sweet. They add interest to the herb garden too, for by pressing the leaves whilst on the plant one may enjoy a different scent every day of the month.

Another lovely mint is the Water or Bergamot mint, *M. aquatica,* found growing wild on the banks of steams and in meadowland which is low lying. Those who may have rested on a bed of the Water mint with its pungent fragrance of bergamot will, as if in some mysterious way, have become fully refreshed within a short space of time. It is a compact, a small-leafed plant, and is sometimes called the Wild Peppermint, though it is quite a different species. ·

Forming thick mats of green, peppermint-scented leaves, studded with tiny mauve flowers, *Mentha requienii,* sometimes known as the Corsican Thyme, is a charming plant. *M. gattefossi* is of similar habit, whilst *M. pulegium* or Pennyroyal almost hugs the ground.

## MULBERRY

The Mulberry (*Moru*) requires a rich, well-drained soil and an open sunny situation, but it should be confined to those gardens south of a line drawn from Liverpool to the Wash. In the standard form, it will make a pleasant shade-giving tree, and it is rarely troubled by pest or disease. Plant between November and March, 25 ft. apart, taking care not to damage the roots, neither must they be shortened at planting time for they will bleed if cut or damaged, causing the tree to lose vigour and eventually die. Make the soil firm about the roots, and in spring mulch with decayed manure or garden compost. The trees grow to 40 ft. and have a life of several hundred years.

Standard and bush trees will require little pruning, but as the fruit is borne on spurs, nip back the young shoots to four buds in summer.

The Mulberry is propagated by cuttings 15 in. long, taken in October and inserted into trenches containing sandy compost. They should be treated at the base with hormone powder before inserting. They will have rooted by early summer. Suckers which may appear around the base of the tree should not be used, as they may be those of the wild White Mulberry (*Morus alba*), on the leaves of which silkworms feed and onto which the Black Mulberry is often grafted.

The fruit is gathered when fully ripe and deep red in colour, late in summer, either by hand or by shaking the tree, which should be done with care for the wood is brittle and breaks easily.

### DISEASE

*Mulberry Canker.* A fungus which attacks and destroys the young shoots, is the only troublesome disease. It usually attacks during cold, damp weather and mostly those trees situated in exposed gardens. Affected shoots must be removed and burnt without delay.

## MULCHING

Almost all plants will benefit from mulching – which is the term used for providing the soil around the plants with a covering of humus-forming materials, possibly fortified with a balanced fertiliser. Mulching is done for several reasons. First, it helps to keep the soil moist and cool above the roots during summer, a time of year when the plant is making most growth. Secondly, it suppresses annual weeds so that it is not necessary to disturb the ground close to the plant with a danger of root damage, whilst it cuts out much work in hoeing and forking. Thirdly, a mulch will give protection against frost, both to the roots and crown of the plant, and to those half-hardy bulbs and corms which are native of warmer climes. Fourthly, a mulch of black polythene will help the soil retain the warmth of the sun's rays and will bring about earlier cropping.

A mulch may be applied at almost any time except when frost is in the ground. Fruit and ornamental trees and shrubs will benefit from a mulch of farmyard manure in late autumn, likewise roses and herbaceous plants, when the winter rains will wash the nutrition down to the roots. Half-hardy bulbs will receive protection, and the humus content of the soil will be improved by a heavy mulch of peat applied at the same time of year.

To suppress weeds, peat may be used liberally in spring to all parts of the garden and where the plants are small, e.g. polyanthus and primrose. the peat should be worked up to the crown of the plant with the fingers, for here the plants will obtain additional benefit from the peat. It is at the crown that the new roots are formed, and the mulch will keep them cool and moist. If farmyard manure is not available, roses will benefit from a spring mulch of peat to which has been added a general rose fertiliser. Cumberland sphagnum moss peat, available in pressed packs which break down to about 10 bushels (16 packs to a ton), is a valuable source of humus and is inexpensive and easy to use. Black polythene to place between rows of strawberries to warm the soil and suppress weeds is sold in rolls 27 in. wide, which may be cut into three strips each 9 in. wide and placed along the strawberry rows.

## MUSHROOM

It is incorrect to think that mushrooms can be grown only in a heated building. With a little ingenuity they may be enjoyed throughout the year, served on toast, for filling omelettes, for stewing, pickling, for sauces, in fact with almost every meal. Like so many of these interesting vegetables, the seakale, asparagus and several more, they are inexpensive to grow, yet are expensive to buy in the shops.

## Mushroom

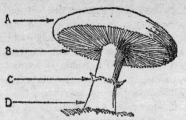

FIG. 8 *Parts of a mushroom*
A. Cap on pileus
B. Gills or lamelae
C. Veil or annulus
D. Stalk or stipe

There must be few places about the home, or even the flat, where there is insufficient room to take a box of mushroom compost; mushrooms can be grown under the stairs or in a cupboard, where they will appreciate the darkness and the warmth of the house during winter, and a garage, attic or cellar is also ideal, especially for spring and autumn crops.

About most farms or country houses too, there are buildings or rooms which are not being used for anything very special and which might be turned to good account growing mushrooms. A loft, stable, cellar or unused outhouse are all suitable places, and as no heat may be available a summer or autumn crop should be grown, a start being made during early April so that the beds would bear from early summer until October. Even garden frames, unwanted after the half-hardy plants have left them in May, can be used, the lights being covered with sacks to keep out the sunlight.

A simple method by which mushrooms may be grown between March and early November, when they are welcome growing indoors and no other place is available, is to make a trench in the garden 3 ft. wide, removing the soil to a depth of 18 in. Select a position where there is some shade but where the ground is well drained, a sandy soil being more suitable than one of a heavy nature, which may retain too much moisture.

At the bottom of the trench place a layer of stone, crushed brick, indeed anything to prevent moisture seeping up and into the compost. Then place in the trench 12 in. of prepared compost and which should be well trodden down. This is spawned and covered with clean straw, garden lights or asbestos sheeting being placed over the top. The beds are covered with virgin or sterilised loam (cased) when the spawn has 'run', the straw being replaced and also the covers. Depending upon the way the compost has been prepared, a useful crop should result.

A more simple method is to plant pure culture spawn in a lawn or field, and to rely entirely on nature to bring forth a crop during September and October. The method is to remove the turf and top soil to a depth of 8 in. filling the opening with strawy manure, inserting the spawn and replacing the turf. A dressing of common salt in July will encourage the formation of a useful crop, but this chiefly depends upon the weather, heavy picking always following a dry summer.

Mushrooms indoors enjoy those cool, dark places so frequently to be found about a farm or country property. The beds can be made directly on the floor, but the area may be greatly increased if boxes stacked on top of each other are used. Any strong boxes are suitable, and if just one or two can be taken into the home when the weather becomes colder in autumn, the supply may be kept up all the year round.

FIG. 9 *Mushroom growing in trays*

PREPARATION OF THE COMPOST

The country gardener should have little trouble in obtaining horse manure from stables where the animals are bedded on straw. Wheat straw is the best, for it breaks down more readily than that of oats or barley. Very few droppings are needed with the straw, so long as it is well soaked in urine it will ferment and heat up when made into a heap. Farmyard manure which has been exposed to the weather and has turned black and sticky will be of no use at all, so where stable manure is scarce, a reliable artificial compost may be made up by using wheat straw which has been saturated with water, and to which is added an activator to bring about fermentation, and some poultry manure, which is present on most holdings. Here the heap is made up in sandwich style, first spreading out a 9 in. layer of straw, on top of which should be sprinkled the activator. Then another layer of straw and this time some poultry manure, which must be quite dry. If in any way sticky it will not only be difficult to spread, but will not generate heat, besides tending to make the compost sticky and unsuitable for mushrooms.

Make the heap, whether using stable or artificial manure, as high and as compact as possible, and provide some protection against prevailing winds, for if the heap becomes too dry it will not heat correctly. If the heap has sufficient moisture and has been made correctly, it will be seen to be generating considerable heat after about a week. It will then be ready for turning, shaking out the straw and the materials used, and adding more water if the straw has become 'burnt' with the heat. Any water needed should be added at this stage, also 56 lb. of pink gypsum to every ton of manure. This is important for it prevents the compost becoming sticky or greasy, a condition in which the spawn will not run. The advent of gypsum was one of the turning points in successful mushroom cultivation, it eliminated what could be called 'luck'.

After another week has elapsed, the heap will be ready for turning again; the compost will be seen to be turning a brown colour and the straw should be shortening. It will require yet another turn at the interval of a week, when it should then be ready for making up into beds or boxes. Take care not to over-turn, or the compost will lose heat and nutrition. The compost should now have lost all strong smell, it should in fact carry a mushroom aroma, and when squeezed tightly, it should bind but no excess moisture should be seen. In colour it should be a rich shade of brown, in no way black or greasy, for when cold such an unsatisfactory compost would set like butter and so cut off the oxygen needed by the growing spawn.

The compost may be prepared in a cellar, in a yard or open shed. Only a small area is required for the heap is made 6 ft. tall, square and compact; a ton of manure can easily be turned in an area 12 ft. by 12 ft. When making up boxes, the compost must be thoroughly pressed down with a brick or board to a depth of 9 in. Likewise, the beds made on the floor should be beaten down with a spade. This is to conserve moisture and retain the heat.

### SPAWNING THE BEDS OR BOXES

The spawn, which should have been purchased in advance, should be inserted as soon as the temperature falls to 70°F. (21°C.). Use Pure Culture spawn which is sterilised and vigorous, and break up the cartons into pieces the size of a walnut, inserting it 1 in. beneath the top of the compost.

There is now available a new grain spawn which is either scattered over the surface of the bed, or a dessert spoonful is dropped into holes made 1 in. deep. It should be used immediately it is obtained, and for the novice it may be safer to purchase the ordinary black spawn which will keep in condition for several months. One trouble with purchasing spawn from a shop is that it may be years old and will have lost its vigour. Always ask if it is reasonably fresh, and always buy Pure Culture spawn.

Spawn may be obtained in three varieties or colours: pure white, which should be grown indoors for market; cream, which is a vigorous all-purpose variety; and brown, which is for home use. The brown is hardy, and will produce a crop under much cooler conditions than will the more temperamental white variety.

For cooking the brown variety possesses a far better flavour. than the white, having the true aroma of the field mushroom. It is rarely found in the shops for, in the same way that the public prefer white bread to the more nutritious brown loaf, so the white mushroom is most in demand. But brown mushrooms may be so easily grown at home.

After spawning, the boxes should be stood in any place out of the cold winds. and the rain, and there they remain for three weeks while the spawn permeates the compost. Should the top of the compost become dry, wet paper or sacking should be given. Then comes the time for covering the compost with soil, casing as it is called, for without this soil covering the mushrooms will not appear.

The soil should be deeply dug from a field of permanent pasture, a heavy loam being the best, and to help it to retain moisture a small quantity of peat should be mixed with it. Large stones are removed, but the soil should be left fairly rough, and it is then spread over the compost to a depth of 1 in. If sterilised soil can be obtained, so much the better, for there is then little chance of introducing any disease spores or weed seeds.

DEVELOPMENT OF THE CROP

Though mushrooms favour a dark, moist atmosphere, they do not like one that is stagnant, which can be caused by poor ventilation. Nor must the beds or boxes be given excess water which would percolate through to the compost and kill off the spawn. Water only when the casing soil requires it, when it appears to be drying out. After three weeks from the time the soil is applied the first pin-head mushrooms should appear; but if the weather is cold they may take another week. To bring on the crop, a little more water may then be given. The tiny mushrooms will not reach maturity overnight, but neither do they in the fields. They will take a full week to develop and may take twice as long in cold weather. The mushrooms should be twisted from the soil, or if growing from a main trunk, those that are mature should be broken away. Mushrooms grow in flushes, and when the beds are cleared the holes should be filled in with clean soil and all decayed stems removed. The beds should be watered, and in ten days another flush will appear. Should the weather be unduly warm, it is advisable to spray the floor and walls of the room to reduce the temperature.

If growing for sale, and mushrooms are the ideal crop for the housewife who wishes to earn an extra income on her own. The mushrooms should be removed before fully open, and will sell readily if in $\frac{1}{2}$-lb. punnets.

Mushrooms produced in the country would cost very little, only perhaps the activator, some spawn, and a little peat for the casing soil, which would cost only about 25p, for straw and poultry manure may possibly be there for the asking. If only 1 lb. of mushrooms were picked from every square foot – which is only a very average crop – then at the present price of mushrooms, a ton of manure on 100 sq. ft. would yield £20–£25 worth.

But mushroom growing is like cake making; it is perfectly easy when you know how. The secret of success lies in the correct curing of the compost, and this comes only with practice. So it is advisable to begin in a small way and then when one gains in confidence, what may have commenced as a hobby may become a profitable business and a source of great interest. And for the epicure, there would be a far more appetising diet throughout the year.

Beds may be made up in unheated buildings, or trenches as described during early spring, which would come into bearing early in May, continuing until almost the end of summer. Additional beds made up in July would come into bearing in early September and continue until the cold weather. Beds in a barn or cellar, where wall thickness would ensure greater warmth, would continue to crop almost until the year end.

To produce mushrooms right through winter, boxes, made up in July for cropping in a cellar or barn through autumn and early winter, could be transferred to a warm place in the home during late October. Under the kitchen sink or in a cupboard would suit them well, and they would continue to bear until Christmas. However, it is generally in the later winter and spring months that mushrooms are most appreciated, so fresh compost would have to be made up and boxes spawned in September. The boxes could be placed in a shed until required for taking indoors towards the year end. They would then crop until the end of spring.

Do not make the mistake of having the boxes too large to handle. It is better to use two smaller boxes, than one of such large dimensions that it will be difficult to move. The large returnable wooden fish boxes are ideal.

When filling the boxes be sure to fill the corners, pressing down the compost with a brick or a wooden block, so that it does not readily dry out. Mushrooms growing in frames must be kept shielded from the sun's rays, otherwise the compost will dry out too quickly and the caps of the mushrooms will crack, thus giving them an unsightly appearance.

CLEANLINESS

Warm, moist manure and a relatively humid atmosphere will give pests and disease every chance of becoming a nuisance. No crop, unless it be the tomato, is more prone to disease, but simple precautions will enable both pest and disease attack to be kept at a minimum.

Three weeks before the boxes or tier beds are to be made up, all wood-work and the floor and walls of the barn or shed should be sterilised with a two per cent solution of formaldehyde. This will not only kill all diseases, but will prevent 'mushroom sickness', that strange condition which will seriously reduce a crop if grown year after year in unsterilised buildings. The fumes of formaldehyde are poisonous, so it should not be used in the home. Instead, use 'Sterizal' and, as an added precaution, 'burn' the woodwork of boxes, bedboards and frames with a blow-lamp, also to kill off pests and disease.

Sterilising the casing soil or using deeply-dug virgin loam of known value will keep mycogone disease to a minimum, and dusting all beds, whether outdoors or indoors, once every week with 'Black Arrow' dust will also keep down Phorid and Sciarid flies, the grubs of which burrow into the mushrooms, making them uneatable.

## MUSHROOM SPAWN, *see* Spawn

## MUSTARD AND CRESS

It may be sown all the year round at three-weekly intervals, in shallow boxes or pans in the kitchen window or greenhouse, or through the milder months of the year outdoors. In a temperature of 48°F., the cress will be ready to cut within 3 weeks. If mustard, with its sharper flavour is also required, sow the cress 4–5 days earlier so that both will be ready together. The commercial grower uses rape seed as a substitute for both for it is cheaper and matures more quickly. Cut when about 2 in. high or as required, just above soil level, using a sharp knife.

Sow thickly in about a 1 in. depth of soil. Do not cover the seed but always keep it moist.

## NECTARINE

A smooth-skinned peach or a peach without 'bloom', it requires similar culture to the peach – a soil containing lime rubble (mortar), and a position where the summer sunshine can ripen its wood. In spring, give a liberal mulching with farmyard manure, and whilst the fruit is swelling give copious amounts of water, although watering should cease when the fruit begins to ripen. Prune as for peaches.

**VARIETIES**

EARLY RIVERS. The most reliable variety for outdoors, it is a heavy cropper, bearing in early August large brilliant red fruits of excellent flavour.

HUMBOLDT. Ripe in early September, its medium-sized fruits are deep orange flushed red, and of delicious flavour.

LORD NAPIER. A valuable early-maturing variety bearing large, pale-green fruits flushed with red.

PITMASTON ORANGE. A heavy bearer, its large orange fruits, flushed with brown, being of excellent flavour.

VICTORIA. The latest to ripen, ready in October, its large yellow fruits being flushed with red. It is a heavy bearer.

## ONION

Easy to grow from sets (bulbs), yet so many growers struggle, needlessly, to produce a heavy crop from seed – which will produce a satisfactory crop only in favourable districts. Those growing onions without a heated greenhouse in which to sow the seed early in the New Year, or where situated above a line drawn from Chester to the Wash, should rely on sets. Onions grown from sets are rarely attacked by the onion fly, and they will mature into large bulbs, even during a short summer. If they have a fault it is their tendency to 'bolt', i.e. to run to seed, if allowed to suffer from lack of moisture whilst they are swelling.

To obtain those massive, globular bulbs, such as are imported in such large quantities from Brittany each winter, a long growing season is necessary, and a deeply-dug soil containing plenty of humus. As onions, like leeks, may be grown on the same ground year after year, a specially-prepared bed should be made by deeply digging the ground, and incorporating a liberal amount of well-decayed compost in winter. At the same time, work in a 4 oz. per sq. yd. of basic slag, and 2 oz. per sq. yd. of potash just before the sets are planted. The bed should be brought to a fine tilth and allowed plenty of time to settle down before planting is done. Some specialist growers roll the bed with the garden roller before planting.

The sets are then just pressed into the soil, allowing 6 in. between the bulbs and 12 in. between the rows. The best variety to grow from sets is Stuttgarter Riesen, of which approximately 300 sets weigh 1 lb. This variety makes a large bulb which keeps well through winter. It will not readily 'bolt'.

**GROWING FROM SEED**

Where growing from seed – and an ounce of seed will produce sufficient plants for a 100-ft. row, spacing them 6 in. apart – the seed should be sown either in a cold frame or, better still, in boxes in a heated greenhouse. Sow towards the end of January, and prick out the seedlings early in March into deep boxes, where they continue to grow and are planted out, after hardening, in April. Or the seed may be sown in a frame or under cloches early in March. The Northern grower should, however, either plant sets or sow the seeds in some heat, for onions must have a long season to mature.

The young plants are transplanted to a bed prepared as described, and to check onion fly they should be dusted with soot early in May, and with four per cent calomel dust three or four weeks later.

Certain varieties may also be sown in drills in the open, or under cloches in early October. They will be sufficiently hardy to withstand an average winter, and may be transplanted early in March. This is a reliable method where neither heat nor frames are available. An additional advantage with autumn-sown onions is that they rarely suffer from fly.

By the end of August the bulbs will be almost ripe, but to persuade them to ripen off in the generally dry September weather, the tops of the bulbs should be bent over to prevent them forming seed. The bulbs should be lifted towards the month end when the ground is dry, and laid out for twelve hours in the sun to complete the drying. They are then cleaned of any loose skin and the tops removed, leaving only a small portion necessary to string them together and hang in a dry, airy shed, and use them as required.

**VARIETIES**

AILSA CRAIG. Still a fine onion for exhibition or cooking, which may be sown in autumn or spring. It makes a large globe of a rich golden-brown colour. Dobbie's Selected strain is outstanding.

JAMES' LONG KEEPING. A fine old variety, which makes a good size in the north and is not particular as to soil.

PRIZEWINNER. An outstanding exhibitor's onion forming a large globular bulb with straw-coloured skin, and of mildest flavour.

SHOWMASTER. The finest exhibitor's onion, producing large, globular bulbs weighing up to 2 lb. or more with ordinary culture. Solid and long keeping, the skin is rich golden yellow.

SUPERBA. An F. Hybrid bearing medium-sized globular bulbs of golden brown which will keep until May the following year. Early to mature, it yields heavily.

UNWIN'S EXHIBITION. Unbeatable on the show bench but, more important, it possesses a mild flavour certain to please all onion lovers. The bulbs are large, globular and uniform in shape and size.

UNWIN'S RELIANCE. This is an exceptionally reliable onion, suitable for both spring and autumn sowing, and will keep in a sound condition longer than any variety.

YELLOW GLOBE. It crops heavily, matures early and keeps well. The large globular bulbs are of deep straw-yellow and of mildest flavour.


## ONION, BUNCH

Requiring similar culture, the Chive, the Welsh and the Bunch Onion are placed under the same heading. At least one of these onions should be grown in every garden as they were in every cottage garden, to be gathered and used as required.

They may be raised from seed sown in drills in April, the young plants being transplanted in September into a soil containing some decayed manure. They will quickly grow into large clumps, and will be ready for using from the following autumn onwards. Plants may be obtained from nurserymen and, if planted in spring, they will have attained a good size by the following spring, and will be ready for use.

They may be planted in partial shade, but the soil should contain some humus, preferably leaf mould. They may be planted by the side of a path of the kitchen garden, or in a small bed where they are within easy reach of the kitchen. Insert the small bulb with its fibrous roots just beneath the soil surface, pressing it firmly. Plant the bulbs 8 in. apart, and every three years lift and divide the roots, replanting into an enriched soil. Established plants will contain up to fifty separate onions, all of which may be replanted, sold or given to one's friends. They may be split up either in the autumn or early spring.

Although each of these onions require much the same cultural treatment, the Japanese Bunch-onion is given a slightly richer soil, a little more room and a sunnier position. It makes a shallot-sized bulb, and it is this rather than the foliage which is used in the kitchen.

With the Chive it is the long grass-like leaves which are used, being cut off just above ground level and shredded into salads.

The Welsh onion is used in its entirety, being like a small leek, having a long, fairly-thick blanched stem and making little top foliage.


## ONION, POTATO

Although now rarely seen, this old form of the onion used to grow in every cottage garden in the south. And, as it is always planted in January and lifted late in July it should be confined to southern gardens. It is an interesting plant, for the onions grow to the size of golf balls beneath the surface of the ground, and are lifted in the same way as potatoes. They are the most pleasantly flavoured of all onions, being in no way strong, but sweet and succulent with the mild chive flavour. The bulbs are planted in a rich friable soil 12 in. apart, being pressed well into the soil with the tops left exposed. They like a well-drained, sandy soil. Throughout May and June feed them with liquid manure, and never allow the roots to lack moisture.

The round onions, like potatoes, will be seen growing at surface level and, to assist with ripening, the soil should be carefully scraped away with the hands during early July so that they may receive the maximum amount of sunshine to assist in their ripening. They are lifted at the month end or early in August, the soil being shaken away. After drying they are stored in an airy room, replanting some of the best bulbs in January when the frost is out of the ground. In every way a decided acquisition to any garden which permits planting before the end of February. The later the bulbs are set, the later they will be lifted, but they should be allowed a period of inactivity to form a strong root run, rather like tulips and other flowering bulbs, before they are stimulated into growth.

## ONION, SPRING

No early summer salad is complete without its spring onions. The earlier salads would contain the tops of the Welsh onion, the hardiest of all onions. Then come the chives which may be used through summer where their mildness is appreciated. For those who enjoy the stronger flavour of the spring onion, the seed should be sown in drills in early October. By sowing in autumn it will be possible to lift the plants several weeks before those sown in spring, and where growing commercially this will make all the difference in obtaining profitable returns.

It is important to keep the ground quite free of all weeds where growing onions, so make the drills wide enough to enable the hoe to be taken between the rows without damaging the plants.

The rows should be dusted with soot during the latter part of winter, for this will bring additional warmth to the soil in spring. Also give a 1 oz. per yd. dressing between the rows and, during a rainy day, of nitrate of soda, which will also encourage the plants to make some size.

Lift the plants as they swell, using the longest first. Wash away the soil and, if marketing, make into bunches of a dozen, fastening with a rubber band at top and bottom.

VARIETIES

WHITE LISBON. Most commonly used for pulling 'green', on account of its hardiness and its mild flavour.

WHITE SPANISH. Also excellent for bunching. The flavour is mild, but distinct from all other onions.

## ONION, TREE

An interesting plant which should be more widely grown. It could be grown as a substitute for all other onions, to be pickled, dried and used in stews; or chopped and used in salads. It is hardy and easy to grow. The plants produce clusters of five or six small bulblets, about the size of small shallots, at the tops of the branching stems. These bulbs may be used as required, or left to ripen, when they possess a delicate onion flavour.

The plants may be grown against a trellis by the side of a wall, or they may be planted in a bed where the stems are allowed to bend over, the bulblets taking root and forming a jungle of onions. Or the plants may be increased by removing the onions and planting exactly as for shallots, but it is advisable to plant the whole cluster together rather than to divide it up.

September is the best time to plant, 12 in. apart. They will quickly root and in spring will grow away, producing their clusters of bulbs at the end of each stem during summer, when they may be used as required.

## ONION, WELSH, *see* Onion, Bunch

## PARSLEY

*Petroselinum sativum* is one of the most widely grown of herbs, and is used for garnishing fish and for making parsley sauce. There is a profitable trade to be enjoyed by the sale of fresh parsley, with its crinkled, fern-like leaves which are well known to everyone. It requires a well-nourished soil containing plenty of humus, for parsley makes only small leaves where the plants lack summer moisture. Where growing under suitable conditions, parsley will flourish for several years, although to maintain its quality a sowing should be made every July, for the plants to be at their best the following year.

The seed, which should be thinly sown in drills 8 in. apart, will take two months to germinate and must be kept moist. Fresh seed should be used, and it is important to thin the plants in spring to about 6 in. apart to allow room for the leaves to develop. Heavy, densely-curled leaves of a rich-green colour are what are required, and they are generally marketed in wooden boxes. To prolong the life of the plants, all flower stems should be removed as they form, and to enjoy the leaves during winter, when they are most profitable, several rows should be only lightly 'pulled' during summer. If covered with cloches in December, the leaves may be obtained during mid-winter, unharmed by the hardest frosts or snow. To maintain supplies, a sowing should be made in July and another in early April. Parsley is difficult to dry, for the leaves are of a succulent nature and require high temperatures, such as a room in full sunlight. The leaves should become quite crisp before being rubbed down for storing, and this will take time.

Where it can be obtained, the True French variety should be sown. It makes large, densely-curled leaves, and is unsurpassed for flavour to make sauces. Also good is Dwarf Green, which is of compact habit and bears a very dark green leaf.

# PARSNIP

The parsnip is appreciated by some epicures, despised by others, for its flavour is pronounced, unlike that of any other root crop. When baked, the flavour will be like steamed chestnuts. It is hardy and is happy in all soils, provided that the seed is sown in ground that has been manured for a previous crop.

The plants require a long season to mature, so seed is sown early in March in a deeply-worked soil, making the drills about 16 in. apart. It is important with parsnips to thin them out at an early stage to 4 in. apart and, later, to 8 in., for the roots grow large. To grow large, exhibition-sized plants, hoe the rows in midsummer then mulch with peat and strawy manure. Or feed from late June with weak manure water. It must be said that the seed, together with that of salsify and scorzonera, is the shortest-lived of all vegetables; fresh seed must be sown each year.

The roots should be lifted through winter as required, or they may be lifted in November and stored in sand in a cellar or shed.

To grow those large, tapering roots, generally coarse and devoid of flavour, but which are needed for the show bench, it is advisable to made a row of holes 3 in. deep with an iron bar. These are filled with finely-screened soil containing a dusting of potash. Into the filled hole are placed two seeds, one of which is carefully removed when large enough to handle. Feeding with liquid manure will help to form a root of large proportions – which to satisfy the judges, should be well-shouldered, evenly tapered, smooth-skinned, and free from surplus growths and markings.

**VARIETIES**

RYDER'S EXHIBITION. This is a beautiful parsnip of mild flavour, the long, tapering root having a thin skin and milky-white flesh.

RYDER'S INTERMEDIATE. The best variety for sowing where the soil is shallow, for the roots are thick and stumpy. The flavour is excellent, the root is no way coarse.

THE STUDENT. Producing a root intermediate between the previous two varieties which is richly-flavoured and succulent.

## PEA, GARDEN OR EDIBLE

Reaching this country from the North-West Frontier of India during medieval times, it was not until the eighteenth century that the pea achieved popularity. Although the Sugar pea was known to Parkinson in the early seventeenth century (see footnote on page 60), he dismisses it in but a few lines, yet devotes several pages of the Paradisus to the culture and description of the various beans, cabbages and artichokes. Today, the pea has an all-year-round popularity, and when fresh peas are not in season the canned and frozen product is in considerable demand.

### PREPARATION OF THE GROUND

The pea enjoys a soil that has been well manured for a previous crop, but to grow well it must have liberal quantities of lime, and so the fertiliser that suits it better than any other is sewage manure collected over lime (a source of manure which, however, is being gradually discontinued by the local authorities). Where this is so, and this form of manure difficult to obtain, the ground should receive a liberal application of hydrated lime during the early winter months.

Peas should be given an open, sunny position and it is moisture-holding humus the plant likes, rather than a manure rich in nitrogen, which, if used to excess will form foliage and large deep green pods containing nothing but air and tiny peas.

Peas make their own nitrogen. If peat is used to provide humus, additional lime should be given. Spent hops are also valuable, and you should also give a 2 oz. per sq. yd. dressing of sulphate of potash, together with 1 oz. of superphosphate, to ensure early and satisfactory filling of the pods. This should be given at planting time. A light loam retentive of moisture suits the pea best, and in such a soil in a favourable district, winter sown peas will make headway.

Peas make roots which extend deeply into the soil and are valuable in that they leave behind, a soil enriched with nitrogen.

# Pea, Garden or Edible

Sowing may commence in November, an early sowing being made along-side a double row of broad beans. For this, a round pea should be used, for the wrinkled Marrowfat varieties, introduced whilst Nelson was at the height of his fame by Thomas Knight, a Herefordshire squire, tend to hold too much moisture at a time when growth is slow. The seed of the Marrowfat peas are wrinkled because a proportion of the starch content has been converted into sugar. Their introduction ushered in a new demand for a pea that for the first time could be said to be really 'sweet'. The pea of ancient times was bitter and used only for making cheap soup, hence the plant remained in obscurity for so long.

The method of sowing peas is to take out a shallow trench, 2 in. deep and the width of a spade. The soil at the bottom of the trench and that removed is dusted with potash, and the seeds are then planted separately, spacing them 2 in. apart. This allows the plants room to develop. In this way, a ½ pt. of seed (peas are always sold in the pint measure), will sow a 10 yd. row.

As mice often prove troublesome with peas, the seed should be shaken up in a tin containing red lead and paraffin before planting. Take care to wash the hands after planting and destroy the rest of the red lead, or move it to a safe place away from the children. To help with germination, sprinkle peat over the seed before the trench is filled in. It is advisable to place the covering soil through a sieve as it is replaced, so as to remove any stones which would interfere with plant growth.

As soon as the row is sown, put in the sticks right up to the trench and on either side of it. This is a better method than waiting until the plants make growth, for then there is the chance of root disturbance, and, if not staked within reasonable time, the plants will be almost impossible to stake well, with the resulting loss of crop.

Dwarf varieties will require only small sticks, but there are certain peas of exceptional quality which attain a height of 6 ft. or more. For these, very stout stakes are required which should be pressed well into the ground. After staking, fish netting should be draped over the sticks to prevent birds attacking the succulent young peas as they appear. Pigeons cause most damage.

When planting more than one row of dwarf peas, 3 ft. should be allowed between the rows and, as a general rule, the same distance should be allowed between the rows as the plants grow tall – e.g. 5 ft. should be allowed between rows of 5 ft. tall varieties.

SOWING FOR SUCCESSION

Those living in the north and who require early peas would be advised to cover a row of November- or early-March-sown peas with barn cloches, which are removed as soon as the peas reach the top. The young plants may first be supported with small twigs, the taller sticks being put into place as soon as the glass is removed. Peas sown in November should come into bearing towards the end of May, but much depends upon situation and soil, and upon the weather during the spring. A cold spring will mean that, even in sheltered gardens, late-sown peas will catch up with those sown in November. But as a rule, and given an average winter and spring, an early-maturing variety sown in November, followed by another sowing in March, will give pickings before the second earlies and main-crop varieties come into bearing. Second early and main-crop peas should be sown at fortnightly intervals during April and May, whilst early in June a sowing should be made of a quick-maturing variety to crop before the summer ends, late in August. Unlike beans, peas do not mature readily after the beginning of September, and so preference should be given to obtaining an early crop rather than a late one.

The following table gives a sound selection, from the end of May until mid-September, together with approximate sowing dates:

| *Variety* | *Height* | *When to sow* | *Maturing* |
|---|---|---|---|
| Early Bird | 3 ft. | November | Late-May |
| Early Onward | 2 ft. | March | Early-June |
| Advance Guard | 2 ft. | Early-April | Mid-July |
| Alderman | 5 ft. | Late-April | Late-July |
| Onward | 2 ft. | Late-April | Early-August |
| Kelvedon Wonder | 1½ ft. | End of May | Late-August |

FOR NOVEMBER SOWING

EARLY BIRD. This pea is round seeded and extremely hardy. It is suitable for autumn sowing in all soils. Height 3 ft.

MARKET GEM. A very hardy pea producing an abundance of short, but well-filled peas. Height 2 ft.

METEOR. Also round-seeded, very quick to mature and a heavy cropper. Height 1½ ft.

FOR EARLY-SPRING SOWING, EARLY TO MATURE

EARLY ONWARD. A wonderful pea, possessing the same compact habit of Onward, and bearing the same deep-green, blunt-nosed pods in as great profusion. Height 2 ft.

EVERBEARING. It matures just before the maincrop varieties and bears over a long period, the medium-sized pods appearing from each 'node' right to the top of the stem. 3 ft.

KELVEDON MONARCH. Like Early Onward, this is a variety of great merit. The blunt-ended pods are borne in pairs and packed with peas. Height 2½ ft.

KELVEDON TRIUMPH. Very dwarf and, for its size, a huge cropper, with extremely long pods of exhibition shape. Height 1½ ft.

KELVEDON WONDER. One of the best all-round peas, bearing early in the season; well-filled pods of darkest green. Highly resistant to fusarium wilt, it may be sown in succession throughout summer. 2 ft.

LITTLE MARVEL. A dwarf variety and a very consistent cropper in the north, the dark green pods borne in pairs and being well filled. Height 2½ ft.

TOPCROP. One of the heaviest croppers, it matures ten days later than Kelvedon Wonder, the well-filled, curved, pointed pods often being borne in pairs. Highly resistant to all pea diseases, it has delicious flavour. 2 ft.

FOR SPRING SOWING, LATE TO MATURE

ADMIRAL BEATTY. To follow Sutton's Evergreen and Alderman, the pods being large, tightly-packed and attractively curved. Height 3–4 ft.

ALDERMAN. Still a favourite exhibition pea and probably the heaviest cropper of all, with tightly-filled pods. Height 5 ft.

SUTTON'S EVERGREEN. Has recently received an Award of Merit and rightly so, for it is of strong constitution, its dark green pods being borne in pairs and tightly filled. Height 3–4 ft.

FOR LATE-SPRING SOWING, TO MATURE AUGUST

GREENSLEEVES. A vigorous grower and enormous cropper of well-filled pods 6 in. long. A pea of excellent flavour, it is highly resistant to disease. 3–4 ft. A less vigorous variety, known as Dwarf Greensleeves, is better suited to the small garden. 3 ft.

IMPROVED PEERLESS. One of the most handsome peas in cultivation and splendid for exhibition, the pods being long, pointed, slightly curved and well filled. 3–4 ft.

LORD CHANCELLOR. Forming a long, pointed, handsome pod, and being a heavy bearer, although an older variety this is still one of the best peas. Height 3 ft.

ONWARD. A superb pea of sturdy habit, requiring very little staking. The blunt-ended peas are borne in pairs and in great abundance in all soils. Height 2 ft.

FOR LATE-SPRING SOWING, TO MATURE LATE

THE GLADSTONE. A grand pea, the huge pods generally contain up to a dozen peas of excellent flavour. A valuable exhibition variety. Height 3–4 ft.

There is an art in timing peas, and as soon as the pods appear to be plumping up a sample should be removed to ascertain its maturity. To gather peas too soon, before the pods are well filled is wasteful; to wait too long, until the peas have become hard and flavourless is even more disappointing.

For exhibition, the large, pointed-podded varieties should be shown arranged around a large plate with the points towards the centre. The judges will look for freshly-gathered pods of a rich colour, and with the 'bloom' intact. They should be free from rust and well filled. All peas, whether for sale, exhibition or home use, should be well filled, and to help with this, those varieties which are late to mature should be given a mulch with decayed strawy manure which is placed along the sides of the rows, and should there be a drought it is advisable to give the plants a thorough soaking every three or four days. The pods will not fill well if lacking moisture.

### PEAS WITH A DIFFERENCE

ASPARAGUS PEA. A native of southern Europe, it is not entirely hardy in Britain and so it is better to raise the plants under glass, sowing in a frame (or in a greenhouse) early in April and transplanting the seedlings in mid-May, when they are large enough to handle. They like a sandy soil, but one containing some humus, for although they like warmth, they should not be allowed to lack moisture. The plants should be given a position of full sun and be allowed 16 in. each way, for they make spreading, bushy growth, reaching a height of only 12 in. In a warm summer the plants will be vigorous and bear a heavy crop of small, pale-green pods, which should be gathered when 2 in. long. The plants crop well when planted along the side of a path, being quite ornamental with their crimson flowers.

The pods, which are extremely succulent, should be steamed with a piece of butter, and are delicious eaten on their own with brown bread and butter, their asparagus flavour being most enjoyable, whilst they are highly nutritious.

CARLIN PEA. This tall-growing variety is grown for its winter and spring value, for the dark-coloured peas are dried in late August, to be used in winter. They possess a distinctive flavour, and after soaking the seed for twenty-four hours, they are at their best sprinkled with brown sugar and cooked slowly.

The seed is sown early in spring as described for ordinary garden peas, but they reach a height of 6–7 ft. and must be given tall, sturdy stakes. The peas are never troubled by either birds or mice, nor are they worried by rust or mildew. The plants will be smothered in short pods during July and August which should be left hanging until all are fully ripe, then the plants are pulled up and the pods detached and 'shelled'. The seeds should be allowed to dry fully in a sunny room before being boxed and stored in a dry cupboard for winter use.

PETIT POIS. For flavour, this must be one of the best vegetables. Growing to a height of 3–4 ft. the plants may be grown in the smallest gardens and bear heavy crops. Sow in April, planting the seed 4 in. apart in the trenches. At no time should the plants be allowed to suffer from lack of moisture.

The pods are gathered as soon as they are filled, and should be steamed just as they are, gathering them just before they are required. The peas will readily leave the pods after cooking and will have retained their entire flavour.

PURPLE-PODDED PEA. It is the pea's counterpart of the Blue Cocobean and is equally delicious. Like the Cocobean, its pods, flowers and foliage are of deep purple, the plants reaching a height of 6 ft. and bearing a heavy crop. It is hardy and vigorous in all soils, and bears its crop over a longer period than most peas. The peas may either be cooked fresh or dried and used during winter. They possess a rich, succulent flavour whenever they are used.

SUGAR PEA. Like a bean, for both pod and seed may be eaten together. They are stringless and are especially tender if gathered young and eaten fresh. They crop better in the south than in the north, except when a warm, sunny summer is experienced, for they then seem to do well anywhere. The seeds require the same culture as the ordinary garden peas and attain a height of only 1 ft., bearing an abundance of pods through August. Steamed whole they possess a deliciously sweet flavour, and are at their best served with young duckling.

There is also a tall-growing addition, known in France as the Mangetout pea, which grows to a height of 5 ft., making a vigorous bushy plant, which should be allowed at least double the amount of space when set in the trenches. For a large, sheltered garden this should be the choice on account of its tremendous cropping, but the dwarf sugar pea should be confined to the small garden.


## PEA, PERENNIAL OR EVERLASTING

*Lathyrus latifolius* is native of southern Europe, closely related to the native *L. sylvestris*. Since its introduction, it was to be found in every cottage garden, as it is to be to this day. Gerard (see footnote on page 60) called it Tare Everlasting or Chickling.

It is readily raised from seed sown in small pots in July, the young plants being set out in their flowering quarters the following April. They will quickly pull themselves up a trellis or over nearby trees or shrubs and will smother themselves and their hosts in flowers of purple-red during July and August. Once they take hold they are almost indestructible for, as Parkinson (see footnote on page 60) said, the root goes down to a great depth and is 'of the thickness sometimes of a man's arm'.

## PEACH

The Peach requires protection from frost when in bloom, and needs plenty of sunshine to ripen its wood, hence in the British Isles it should be grown outdoors south of the Thames or in sheltered gardens of the west. Under glass it is grown against the high wall of a leanto greenhouse and in a position of full sunlight. Fan-shaped trees should be planted in autumn, 18 ft. apart and in a soil containing lime (in the form of mortar) and enriched with slow-acting nitrogenous manures such as bone meal, given at a rate of 2 oz. per tree. This is incorporated into the soil at planting time. As with all grafted trees, make sure that the union is above soil level. Plant firmly and water well. During summer, keep the soil thoroughly moist and mulch with decaying manure or compost, for it is essential that the trees should not lack moisture whilst the fruit is swelling.

FIG. 10 A. Replacement
B. Side shoots pinched back
C. Leader shoot

Peaches are propagated by budding on to plum stocks, the Common Mussel rootstock or Pershore stock making for vigorous medium-sized trees. The peach bears its fruit on shoots of the previous season's wood. During May, new growth formed by the leaders should be cut back by about one-third, whilst the tips of the side growths should be pinched out during midsummer, pinching them back when they are about 2 in. long. A single wood bud will be retained at the base of these shoots, to grow on as a replacement for next season's fruit, the shoot which has fruited being removed at the end of the season.

In the early years of the tree, pruning should take the same lines as for the renewal system for apples; that is, whilst the tree is being built up, the shoot which will have borne fruit is allowed to grow on until it has reached about 18 in. This is then fastened to the wall and the tip pinched back to a wood bud. It is the shoot formed from this bud that will bear the next season's crop.

It frequently happens that when building up a fan-shaped peach, that the branches or arms on one side are more vigorous than those of the other side. This should not be allowed to go unchecked, otherwise the balance of the tree will be completely spoilt. As it is known that the branches of the more horizontal shoots are less vigorous than those of a more vertical position, the shoots of the weaker side should be moved to a more vertical position whilst those on the more vigorous side should be fastened back more horizontally. In this position they should remain until growth has become more even.

It is not a difficult matter to distinguish between blossom and wood buds, the latter are small and pointed, whilst blossom buds are round and fat. Where possible select a wood bud facing the wall for an extension shoot for this will ensure a straighter shoot.

Peaches and nectarines will require more space in which to bear new wood than will either plums or sweet cherries.

Peaches grown as bush trees should be drastically pruned back in early May each year to encourage a continuous supply of new growth. This will stimulate growth which is excessive and should be retarded by ringing round the roots and cutting back in alternate years after the establishment of the trees.

The chief source of worry is the tendency of the plant to 'bleed' or 'gum', but this will not prove troublesome if too much old wood is not allowed to form. This, when pruned is most likely to 'gum', so it is advisable to encourage as much new wood as possible.

All shoots appearing next to a fruit should be pinched out above the second leaf. This removal of all unwanted shoots should be spread out over a period of three to four weeks early in summer.

Root pruning will also help to restrict excessive growth and encourage fruiting. About five years after planting, remove soil to a depth of 15 in. about 3–4 ft. from the main stem and, using a sharp knife, cut away all vigorous long roots before replacing the soil and treading firmly. Netting suspended from the wall hung over the trees when in bloom will give protection from frost.

Thinning should not be done until after 'stoning'. This is a natural falling off of fruits when about the size of a walnut. Afterwards, if the plant is carrying an excess of fruits, remove others, leaving about 8 in. between each fruit to mature.

The fruit is ripe if it is slightly soft when gently pressed at the base. It should then be removed by placing beneath it, the palm of the hand and exercising gentle pressure by moving in an upwards direction. The fruit is then placed in shallow boxes or trays lined with cotton wool.

DISEASE

*Leaf-curl.* This is the most common and troublesome of peach diseases, attacking the leaves, which turn yellow and become crinkled at the edges. Later, the leaves take on a white powdery appearance, due to the spores of the fungus and, shortly after, they die back, causing loss of vigour to the plant. The disease usually appears during dull, wet weather and it will spread quickly, even attacking the young shoots. Spraying with lime sulphur just as the buds begin to burst will give almost complete control. It will also destroy the most troublesome pest, red spider.

PESTS

*Red Spider.* It is the most troublesome pest of the peach, hibernating during winter and in spring causing browning of the foliage. It is destroyed by spraying with lime sulphur at bud-break.

*Leaf-curling Aphis.* See Plum.
*Winter-moth.* See Apple.

VARIETIES

ALEXANDER. One of the earliest to ripen, it is a heavy cropper, bearing early in August medium-sized fruit of golden-yellow flushed with red.

BARRINGTON. One of the best for growing under glass in the British Isles, it is ripe towards the end of September, the large yellowish-green fruit being marked with crimson.

HALE'S EARLY. The first of the outdoor varieties to ripen, bearing large numbers of medium-sized fruits in mid-July, which ripen to a rich orange colour.

PEREGRINE. It bears a large crimson fruit which ripens early in August, and is a heavy and reliable cropper.

ROYAL GEORGE. Maturing late in August, the fruits are large, of pale yellow speckled with red. It should be grown under glass in the British Isles.

SEA EAGLE. The latest to ripen, being ready in October and it is one of the largest of all peaches, of pale yellow flushed with red.

## PEAR

Whereas the apple is European, the pear is of Asiatic origin, coming into bloom before the apple and, to crop well, requires a warmer climate. Good pear crops in Britain are grown south of an imaginary line drawn across England from Worcester to The Wash, only the hardiest pears being grown north of that line. Even in the south, the best pear-growing regions are East Anglia and Kent, and in those counties through which the Seven flows. The chalk soils, often dry and shallow, of the counties of Wiltshire, Hampshire, Oxfordshire and West Sussex, although suitable for apples, rarely produce good pears.

The pear must have its roots in a warm moist soil, a rich moist loam, and its head in sunshine. The West Country in general often produces scab, the North Midlands and further north is too cold, whilst the southern chalk brings about such a deficiency of iron that the trees make but limited growth and bear only small crops. Away from Kent, East Anglia and the Severn Valley, the pear may be considered to be the most difficult of all fruits to grow well. An English-grown apple will stand comparison with any in the world, but only rarely does the English grown pear do so.

But the pear may be cropped more satisfactorily than is so often the case if the same rules as to climate are followed as for the apple. In the colder north and in the North Midlands, there is no reason why the hardy varieties should not be planted. It is useless to plant Doyenne du Comice and Roosevelt, as delicious as they may be, with the expectation that they will crop well. But the old Jargonelle, Beurré Hardy, Catillac and Durondeau, will bear well at almost 1,000 ft above sea level and in a more sheltered position, Laxton's Superb, Dr Jules Guyot and Williams' Bon Chrétien, may be added to the list, provided that they are given the protection of a wall.

These pears are not only hardy, but also flower late, and so miss late frosts even in the colder districts. Given a sheltered garden, and preferably a wall for protection, they may be grown as far north as Lancashire and Derbyshire, and even further north in sheltered gardens.

The same consideration should be given to the planting of individual varieties as with the apple, for although the pear enjoys a warm soil, a too moist climate will cause outbreaks of scab to which the trees will eventually succumb. Both Clapp's Favourite and Pitmaston Duchess, heavy bearers which make large, vigorous trees, suffer badly from scab in the moist climate of the west.

Whereas there are numerous apples which will yield heavily in a chalky soil, there are no pears which will tolerate such a soil, likewise in the soot-laden atmosphere of our cities the apple is able to bear heavily whilst the pear will bear only spasmodic crops.

Frost pockets must be avoided, for the pear blooms earlier than the apple and even the latest of all to bloom, Catillac and Winter Nelis will not bloom sufficiently late to miss late frost, as will apples Crawley Beauty and Edward VII. The choice, then, is much more limited with pears than with apples, but as the fruit is so delicious, everything possible should be done to plant those varieties which will ensure some degree of success under prevailing conditions.

Whilst the manurial requirement of the pear is similar to that of the apple, the greatest use should always be made of farmyard manure. The greatest requirements of this fruit are moisture, supplied by the humus content of stable manure; and nitrogen; pears demand little else. If moisture and nitrogen are always available and a warm climate provided, then good crops of pears may be grown. Pears will not respond in anything like the same way as will apples to applications of inorganic fertilisers, although where the humus content of the soil is considerable, light dressings of sulphate of ammonia, to provide additional nitrogen, may be given at the rate of 2 oz. per tree in April. Fish manure and bone meal are also valuable manures – in fact, all the organics rich in nitrogen – and one of the most renowned pear growers in Cambridgeshire insists that the secret of his success is providing his trees (Conference) with a heavy annual application of either farmyard, or some other organic manure. This is best given during March, and dug into the soil round the trees, when the ground is in a suitable condition. Trees growing in grass should receive this manure by way of a heavy mulch.

It is very important to ensure that those trees growing against a wall, as do pears more than apples, receive sufficient moisture and nitrogen. Lack of both is one of the greatest causes of wall trees failing to bear heavy crops. Farmyard manure, shoddy or fish manure should be lightly forked around the trees in early winter, and this should be followed by a heavy mulch in May, before the moisture has commenced to dry out.

Pears, planted in a limestone soil, may occasionally show symptoms of lack of iron, more prevalent amongst pears than with apples. This may be cured by drilling a small hole into the main trunk of the tree, and inserting a tablet containing 1 gramme of ferrous sulphate. An older generation of gardeners hammered a large nail right through the trunk, and the effect was similar.

POLLINATION

As with apples, some pears are triploid varieties, and not only require a diploid pollinating variety flowering at the same time, but a second diploid variety which will be able to pollinate each other.

E = Early    L = Late

*The following are triploids:*

| | |
|---|---|
| Beurré d'Amanlis | (E) |
| Catillac | (L) |
| Jargonelle | (E) |
| Pitmaston Duchess | (L) |

From this it is seen that two are early flowering, and two bloom late.

With either then, it will be necessary to plant two early or late flowering diploids.

S.S. = Self-Sterile     S.F. = Self-Fertile

*These pears bloom early:*

| | |
|---|---|
| Beurré Easter | (S.S.) |
| Beurré Hardy | (S.S.) |
| Beurré Superfin | (S.F.) |
| Conference | (S.F.) |
| Durondeau | (S.F.) |
| Louise Bonne | (S.F.) |

*These pears bloom in mid-season:*

| | |
|---|---|
| Beurré Bedford | (S.F.) |
| Clapp's Favourite | (S.S.) |
| Emile d'Heyst | (S.S.) |
| Glou Morceau | (S.S.) |
| Josephine de Malines | (S.S.) |
| Thompson | (S.S.) |
| Williams' Bon Chrétien | S.F.) |

*These pears bloom late:*

| | |
|---|---|
| Dr Jules Guyot | (S.F.) |
| Doyenne du Comice | (S.S.) |
| Fertility | (S.S.) |
| Laxton's Superb | (S.F.) |
| Marie Louise | (S.F.) |
| Winter Nelis | (S.S.) |

With pears, several varieties are unable to pollinate each other, although both may be in bloom together. The very fertile diploid, Conference, is unable to pollinate the triploid Beurré d'Amanlis, though both are in bloom at exactly the same time. So do not plant them without another early-flowering pollinator, such as Beurré Hardy, or Durondeau, and expect to obtain a heavy crop, even though both are hardy and easily-grown varieties. Neither will Seckle pollinate Louise Bonne, though both are partially self-fertile and will bloom together, early to mid-season. All of which requires careful consideration before ordering your pear trees.

It should be said that though a number of varieties are self-fertile, and able to set their own pollen, they will bear a much heavier crop if planted with other varieties in bloom at the same time.

Early and mid-season flowering varieties, and mid-season and late flowering may be planted together for they will overlap, and may be relied upon to pollinate satisfactorily.

**PLANTING**

The trenches or holes to take the plants should be made before the trees are taken from where heeled in, or have been kept covered from frost, so that the roots are not unduly exposed to a drying wind. As a general rule trees for a light soil, and where of a chalky nature, should be planted from November to December. Those for a heavy, cold soil are best planted in March. Equally important is depth of planting.

Failure for the tree to bear well over a long period is so often due to either too-shallow or too-deep planting, and both contribute equally to the various cases of failure. Too-shallow planting will cause the roots to dry out during a period of prolonged drought, and especially where the soil lives over a chalky subsoil. It may also cause the trees, where Type MIX rootstock is being used, to fall over even when fully established, and especially where planted in an exposed garden.

Too-deep planting on the other hand will mean that the roots will be in the cold, less fertile subsoil, cut off from air and the sun's warmth, whilst it will mean that the scion, at which point the graft has been made on to the rootstock, will be buried and may take root. This will mean that the characteristics of the rootstock will play little part on the habit of the tree.

When buying and planting fruit trees always bear in mind that the roots are as important to the tree, more so in fact, than its shape, and for this reason the younger the tree the more readily is it transplanted. Where planting an orchard, however small, maiden trees, one year old, are not only less expensive, but are more readily established, and may be trained and pruned to the requirements of the grower, rather than to those of the nurseryman. Remember that with all trees, the younger they are the more readily will they transplant, though in this respect the exception is the pear, which will readily transplant up to twenty years of age. After the hole or trench has been made to the correct depth, so that the level of the soil will be at a point just above the top of the roots, as near as possible to the same level as the tree was planted at the nursery, a spadeful of a mixture of sand and peat should be spread about the hole, to encourage the formation of new fibrous roots as quickly as possible. To enable the roots to be spread out correctly, a small mound of soil should be made at the bottom of the hole.

The old gardeners would place a flat stone on the top of this mound to prevent the formation of a tap root. This may still have its devotees, but the shortening of any large tap root with a sharp knife just before planting should be all that is necessary, at the same time removing any damaged roots, or shortening any unduly long roots. Here again, the experienced nurseryman whose reputation is built upon the success of the trees sent out, will see that the trees are lifted as carefully as possible, with the roots in no way damaged. All too often those 'bargain parcels' arrive almost rootless and take years to become re-established.

The roots should be spread out so that each one is comfortable. Frequently trees are planted in holes which are made far too small, with the result that they are bunched up, and compete with each other for nourishment. A tree badly planted can never prove satisfactory.

When the roots have been spread out, scatter more peat and sand about them, then commence to pack the soil around them. This is best done by holding the tree straight, or at the required angle in the case of cordons, which should be fastened to the wires before the soil is filled in. By pushing in the soil with the feet – a strong pair of boots being the best guarantee of correct planting – the job may be performed by one person. As the soil is pushed into the hole it is trodden firmly about the roots so that there will be no air pockets, which would cause the roots to dry out. Tread the soil in little by little so that a thorough job is done, rather than fill up the hole and tread down afterwards. Where planting against a wall it is advisable to incorporate additional humus materials, as the soil is being placed in the hole to retain the maximum of moisture about the roots. The same may also be done where planting in a light, sandy soil. The planting of a few trees may be much more thoroughly done than where planting in an orchard, and the work should not in any way be hastily carried out. If there can be two people to do the planting, so much the better.

### HARVESTING AND STORING

Pears must be given even greater care in their picking than apples, for not only do they bruise more easily, but will rapidly deteriorate on the tree if allowed to become over-ripe, or if subjected to adverse weather, such as a period of moisture or night frosts.

Generally a pear will be ready to gather when, upon lifting with the palm of the hand and exerting no pressure on the fruit, it readily parts from the spur. This is a better method than following a text book as to the correct ripening periods of the different varieties, for so much depends upon the season and upon the situation of the tree in the garden. Given a particularly warm summer, with periods of prolonged sunshine, pears will come to maturity before their usual time, several weeks earlier in the south. But if the fruit does not readily part from the spur when lifted, if means that it is still drawing nourishment from the tree. Equally important with the pear is not to allow it to become over-ripe, for not only will its keeping qualities badly deteriorate, but also it will have lost much of its fragrance and flavour. The lifting test is more reliable than the colouring of the skin, for this depends so much on the soil, and if you wait for the fruits to attain a certain colouring they may have passed their best. In this respect, the finest of early pears, Laxton's Superb, at its best in a normal sunny season during the first days of August, must be gathered and eaten whilst still pale green, when it will part from the spurs upon lifting. To allow it to become a buttercup yellow colour, which it soon will if left on the tree, will be to lose its flavour. Similarly Williams' Bon Chrétien (the canner's Bartlett Pear) will become dry and of a disagreeable flavour if allowed to hang too long.

All pears, whether to be eaten at once or to be stored, must be removed in the palm of the hand, and carefully placed on a wooden tray, which has been lined with cotton wool. Always gather the fruit when quite dry and store in a slightly warmer place than for apples. At all times pears like warmth, a temperature of 45°F. (7°C.) suiting them best, and an airy attic room if dark and a cupboard or drawer is better than a cellar or shed, which will be colder. If placed in a cold room, pears will sweat badly and quickly lose quality. So that the fruit will not lose its bloom, the best method is to place them upright on a layer of cotton wool so that they are not quite touching. As with all stored fruit, keep each variety to itself so that the fruit may more easily be seen to reach the correct state for using.

PESTS

*Midge.* Not often troubled by the sucking insects which attack the apple, this is by far the most troublesome pest. Like the apple sawfly, the pest lays its eggs in the blossoms, the grubs following the same process as those of the sawfly. Both Laxton's Superb and Conference are amongst the most resistant varieties. The pest may be easily controlled by dusting with D.D.T. when the blossom is open, and again a month later. As D.D.T. will also control capsid, sawfly and blossom weevil, it may be considered the pear grower's great standby, as well as being effective on apples. The treatment for all pests which attack pears is the same as for those which attack the apple.

DISEASE

*Scab.* Though the symptoms are the same, scab on pears is a totally different disease from that which attacks apples. Unlike apples, most varieties of pears will not tolerate even dilute lime-sulphur sprays, but again unlike the apple, are tolerant of Bordeaux Mixture, which will control the disease if applied early in June and again when the blossoms have set. Fertility and Doyenne du Comice are frequently troubled by Pear Scab.

**VARIETIES**

CLAPP'S FAVOURITE. An American pear which suffers from scab in a damp climate, but makes a tree of vigorous, upright habit and crops heavily, the fruits being pale yellow with crimson stripes, the flesh melting and juicy. Ready late August to September.

DOYENNE D'ETE. It has so many faults that it is now rarely planted. It is a weak grower, and does best as a cordon or espalier; it is self-sterile and requires a pollinator (Conference or Beurré Hardy). It does not keep well, but for all that, it is the first to mature, and its small, round yellow fruits have an excellent flavour.

JARGONELLE. It is of straggling habit, and is a triploid variety, hence the need for pollinators, but it is extremely hardy, is highly resistant to scab, and bears a heavy crop of long tapering fruit, with its own musky flavour. Excellent pollinators are Durondeau and Williams' Bon Chrétien, the former ripening in November, the latter in September. Plant with them Laxton's Superb, and the huge Roosevelt for Christmas, and you will have a succession of fruit of outstanding quality.

LAXTON'S EARLY MARKET. Though a new variety, this has already established itself as the best pear for late July, and, like all early apples and pears, should be eaten from the tree. The medium-sized fruit, with its yellow skin, flushed with scarlet, possesses a delicious perfume. It blooms early and in an exposed garden may be troubled by late frosts.

LAXTON'S SUPERB. This is one of the best pears ever introduced, and makes superb eating if gathered in mid- or late-August, and allowed to stand forty-eight hours in a warm room before eaten. But it must be harvested just as the green skin takes on a yellow tinge; if left later, the quality will have deteriorated badly. The great value of this pear is that, although ripening early, it blooms late and so is very suitable for a northern garden. It is good in the bush form in a small garden, for it is of upright habit.

**TO RIPEN EARLY TO MID-SEPTEMBER**

BEURRE D'AMANLIS. Valuable for its hardiness, for it will bear well even in the Pennines. It makes a tree of vigorous, straggling habit, requiring plenty of room, and bears a medium-sized russeted fruit of rich perfume. Raised at Amanlis in France about 1795, it is a triploid, and should be planted with Beurré Superfin and Beurré Bedford.

DR JULES GUYOT. A valuable pear for less-favourable gardens, for it blooms late yet crops heavily, and acts as a good pollinator for most varieties. It bears a large fruit with yellow skin dotted with black, and should be eaten from the tree. At its best in the dry climate of south-east England.

GORHAM. A new American pear, very fertile, which makes a neat, upright tree. It is similar in size and colour to Williams' Bon Chrétien, the fruit retaining its pure white colour when bottled. Highly resistant to scab.

TRIOMPHE DE VIENNE. This is one of those hardy, reliable pears, now quite neglected. The fruit is not large, but is of brilliant colouring and rich flavour. The tree is of dwarf habit and bears a large crop, season after season. An excellent variety where those of more temperamental habit prove difficult.

WILLIAMS' BON CHRÉTIEN. Possibly the best all-round pear ever introduced. It makes a strong-growing, yet compact tree, and bears a heavy, but not regular crop. Introduced as long ago as 1770, by a nurseryman named Williams of Turnham Green, and half a century later into America by Enoch Bartlett, hence its canning name, the pure white flesh being of melting, buttery texture.

## TO RIPEN LATE SEPTEMBER TO MID-OCTOBER

BEURRE BEDFORD. Making a neat, upright tree, ideal as a pyramid and bearing heavy crops of glossy primrose-yellow fruits, it is a self-fertile variety, and ideal for a small garden. Raised by Messrs Laxton Bros.

BEURRE HARDY. Making a vigorous, upright tree, especially suited for orchard planting, this is a hardy variety, and a most reliable cropper. The fruit is unique in that the flesh is rose tinted and also carries a delicate rose perfume.

BEURRE SUPERFIN. This should be grown where Doyenne du Comice proves difficult, for its golden fruit possesses almost the same quality and flavour. It is quite hardy, but blooms early and may suffer from frost.

BRISTOL CROSS. Raised by Mr Spinks at Long Ashton, and has quickly become a favourite in the moist climate of the West Country. The fruit, with its bright yellow skin covered with russet, is juicy and sweet, whilst it crops heavily just before Conference.

LAXTON'S FOREMOST. A magnificent pear for late September, and a fine exhibition variety, with its clear primrose-yellow skin. It is an upright grower and crops freely, the fruit having buttery flesh, in no way gritty. Ideal for the small garden, and crops well on a west wall.

## TO RIPEN LATE OCTOBER TO END OF NOVEMBER

CONFERENCE. Most valuable as a pollinator (except with Beurré d'Amanlis) for all mid-season flowering pears, and bearing one of the most delicious of all fruits, its dark green skin being extremely russeted. It is reasonably hardy and no pear crops more regularly.

DOYENNE DU COMICE. With its deliciously-melting, cinnamon-flavoured flesh, this is the outstanding variety of all pears, but difficult to crop. It makes a spreading tree, and must be given a warm position in a soil well enriched with humus. It likes its feet in moisture, its head in sunshine. Pollinated by Bristol Cross, Beurré Bedford and Laxton's Superb.

DURONDEAU. Raised in 1811 by the Belgian of that name, it makes a compact tree, and is extremely hardy, but bears better on the western side of Britain, for it likes plenty of moisture. If gathered at the end of September, the handsome, golden fruit with its crimson cheek, will keep until the end of November.

EMILE D'HEYST. Extremely hardy and suitable for a northern garden, but should be grown in bush form, on account of its spreading, weeping form. The Lane's Prince Albert of the pear world. The richly-flavoured fruit with its strong rose perfume should be eaten from the tree late in October, as it does not store well.

LAXTON'S RECORD. One of the best November pears, which should be grown where some of the others prove difficult. The medium-sized fruit has a yellow skin, flushed with crimson and russet. The flesh is juicy and melting, with a powerful aromatic perfume.

LOUISE BONNE. This pear is a strong grower, making a large, well-formed tree, and is a heavy cropper in the warmer districts, especially in the south-west. The green fruit, with its crimson flesh being of outstanding flavour. Grown at least 300 years ago.

PITMASTON DUCHESS. The large golden russeted fruit, is of exceptional flavour and is a favourite for exhibition, but it is a shy bearer, and a too vigorous grower for a small garden. It also takes longer to come into bearing than most pears. It is a triploid variety.

SECKLE. A late-maturing dessert pear discovered in a wood near Philadelphia early in the nineteenth century. It is a weak grower, but bears heavily in light soils, the delicious, brownish-red fruits being spotted with white.

### TO RIPEN IN DECEMBER TO JANUARY

GLOU MORCEAU. To ripen correctly, it must be given a warm, sunny position, and although blooming very late, and being quite hardy, it does better in the south, where it acts as a good companion and pollinator for Comice. The fruit is extremely juicy, and free from grit, and should be eaten early December.

PACKHAM'S TRIUMPH. A New Zealand introduction with a great future; already it has proved itself on a commercial scale in Britain, the fruit keeping in perfect condition from mid-October until late in December. It is a vigorous grower, and a free bearer, the fruit being similar in both appearance and flavour to Comice, and without that pear's difficulties in culture.

ROOSEVELT. This is the largest of all pears, and the most handsome fruit in cultivation, the smooth golden-yellow skin being tinted with salmon pink. It is a vigorous, but erect grower and free bearer, the fruit being at its best in December.

SANTA CLAUS. For eating in the New Year, this is one of the best pears. The fruits are almost as large as Roosevelt, of delicious flavour, and with an attractive, dull-crimson russeted skin. The tree is of vigorous, but upright habit, and is a free bearer, proving with its resistance to scab, extremely useful in districts of moist climate.

WINTER NELIS. Exactly the same remarks may be used for this variety as for Glou Morceau, as to its culture. It makes only a small fruit, but its flavour is outstanding, rich and melting, having the perfumes of the rose, and it will store until February.

TO RIPEN FEBRUARY TO APRIL

BERGAMOTTE D'ESPEREN. The best variety raised by Major Esperen, it should be given the warmth of a wall to ripen and mature its fruit, which, with its pale yellow skin, remains rich and sweet until March.

BEURRE EASTER. The richly musk-scented fruit will store in perfect condition until Easter. It is hardy, and a heavy cropper, but requires careful culture throughout.

CATILLAC. A late bloomer, vigorous grower, and extremely hardy, cropping heavily and requiring plenty of room. The huge, crimson-brown fruit should not be harvested until November, and carefully stored will keep until May. It is used chiefly for stewing, but will make pleasant eating during spring. It is a triploid, and should be planted with Beurré Hardy and Dr Jules Guyot, for pollination. At least 300 years old.

JOSEPHINE DE MALINES. It bears a heavy crop of small, though deliciously-flavoured fruits, at their best during February. It is a hardy variety, but prefers the warmth of a south or west wall if planted in northern counties. It is a regular bearer, but is of rather weeping habit, not always easy to manage. Raised in Belgium by Major Esperen, John Scott describes it as being 'juicy and sugary, with the (balsamic) perfume of the hyacinth . . . one of our most delicious pears.'*

*Hardy varieties in order of ripening:*

| | |
|---|---|
| Jargonelle | Beurré d'Amanlis |
| Laxton's Superb | Durondeau |
| Beurré d'Amanlis | Emile d'Heyst |
| Dr Jules Guyot | Catillac |
| Williams' Bon Chrétien | Josephine de Malines |

* John Scott founded the Royal Nurseries, Merriot, Somerset, where he grew the largest selection of apples and pears in England. His *Orchardist* was published in 1860 by H. M. Pollett, London.

# Pear

*Pears of spreading or weeping habit:*

Beurré d'Amanlis  
Catillac  
Emile d'Heyst  
Josephine de Malines

*Varieties of dwarf habit:*

Beurré Bedford  
Beurré Superfin  
Dr Jules Guyot  
Laxton's Foremost  
Laxton's Superb  
Williams' Bon Chrétien

*Varieties requiring warm conditions:*

Bergamot d'Esperen  
Doyenne du Comice  
Glou Morceau  
Marie Louise  
Winter Nelis

*Pears maturing July to August:*

Jargonelle  
Laxton's Early Market  
Laxton's Superb

*Pears maturing September:*

Beurré d'Amanlis  
Dr Jules Guyot  
Gorham  
Triomphe de Vienne  
Williams' Bon Chrétien

*Pears maturing October:*

Beurré Bedford  
Beurré Hardy  
Beurré Superfin  
Bristol Cross  
Laxton's Foremost

*Pears maturing November:*

Conference  
Doyenné du Comice  
Durondeau  
Emile d'Heyst  
Laxton's Record  
Louise Bonne  
Pitmaston Duchess

*Pears maturing December to February:*

Glou Morceau  
Packham's Triumph  
Roosevelt  
Santa Claus  
Winter Nelis

*Pears maturing March to May:*

Bergamotte d'Esperen  
Beurré Easter  
Catillac  
Josephine de Malines

# PESTS

## AMERICAN BLIGHT, *see* Woolly Aphis

### APHIS (GREENFLY)
The green aphis and rosy aphis are amongst the most destructive of pests which attack apples, peaches, plums, gooseberries, currants. The eggs of both aphis winter on the plants and these can be killed by a tar-oil wash applied in December. If allowed to hatch, the aphis will feed on the young shoots, then on the leaves causing them to curl, then on the buds and young fruits. In spring and at monthly intervals until late in summer, spray with Abol X or Sybol but do not use these on chrysanthemums, or an insecticide based on gamma-BHC on currants.

### APPLE BLOSSOM WEEVIL
A grey or black insect which winters in the bark of apple trees, emerging in early spring to feed on the flower buds and there lays its eggs. In April the grub hatches out and feeds on the stamens and style. It ejects a sticky substance which prevents the petals from opening. The buds do not open, but turn brown and fall off. If tar-oil or other winter washes do not give control, spray at bud break stage with Murphy Spring Spray containing BHC and DDT.

### APPLE SUCKER
The insect resembles a greenfly and lays its eggs on the spurs in autumn. In spring the insects hatch out to feed on the buds, causing them to turn brown and fall away. The eggs are readily destroyed in winter by a Tar-oil or Thiol Thiocyanate wash as routine. Or spray in the green bud stage with Lindex or liquid Malathion.

### BLACKFLY
The most troublesome pest of broad beans, it also attacks chrysanthemums. It is discouraged by pinching out the tops of the plants, or spraying with liquid derris from early May until late July.

### CABBAGE CATERPILLAR
The caterpillar of the Cabbage White butterfly which, if allowed to go unchecked, will destroy large numbers of plants in a few days. It lays

its eggs on the leaves of cabbage, cauliflower, broccoli, etc., and in a few days they hatch out to small creamy-white grubs which devour the leaves and penetrate to the centre of cabbage and cauliflower, making them almost unsaleable. To control, dust the plants with derris once a fortnight from early June until mid-September.

#### CABBAGE ROOT FLY

The small grey moth lays its eggs in the soil in spring and the tiny white maggots attack the roots of young brassica plants, causing them to turn yellow and wilt. To prevent an attack, dust the roots with calomel before planting or, if this has been omitted, spray the ground around the plants with Lindex solution. As a further precaution, work Aldrin dust into the soil when made ready for the plants.

#### CAPSID

It attacks apples and currants; chrysanthemums and dahlias, causing distorted leaves and flower buds; plant growth, too is often stunted and sparse. For apples and currants, spray in January with DNOC, or tar-oil; or with Thiol at bud-break. With dahlias and chrysanthemums, spray with Lindex as routine from early summer. Under glass, control with Lindane smokes.

#### CARROT FLY

It has a long, tapering body and large, spreading wings; it lays its eggs in the soil. The yellow larvae burrow down to the roots, devouring them and the carrot itself, which, upon lifting, may have noticeable marks of tunnelling about the surface. It attacks turnips, swedes, carrots and turnips, its presence may be detected by the foliage turning yellow. To prevent an attack, either treat the seed with a combined dressing, or dust the rows with Lindex when sowing. In June, dust again with Lindex, for as it burrows to a considerable depth, the pest is difficult to eradicate.

#### CELERY FLY

It lays its eggs amongst the foliage, between early June and mid-August, the larva attacking the leaves, causing them to blister and decay. All affected foliage should be removed and burnt; to prevent an attack, treat the soil with Aldrin dust before planting. Spraying the foliage with Quassia in June will prevent the flies from laying their eggs.

**CHERRY FRUIT MOTH**

The small green caterpillars enter the buds as they open and later bore
into the fruits making them unsaleable and unfit to eat; or they are reduced
to a slimy mass. Later, they fall to the ground and with them the caterpillars to form chrysalids. The moths emerge early in July to lay their
eggs on the leaves. To prevent an attack, spray with tar-oil when dormant
and dust the trees with derris when the blossom begins to open.

**CHERRY SLUGWORM**

The green slug is the larva of a sawfly. It emerges from the eggs which
are laid in the tissues of the leaves of cherry and pear tree. It immediately
begins to eat the surface tissues of the leaves, causing them to turn brown,
and trees may be completely defoliated. The larva then falls to the ground
and winters in a cocoon, until the sawfly emerges early in July to begin
again its cycle of destruction. As routine, the trees should be dusted with
derris. This should be done every fortnight from early July until the end
of August.

**CLEARWING MOTH**

Concentrating its activities on the redcurrant, the moth lays her eggs
along the branches; upon hatching, the grubs tunnel into the stems, feeding
on ths sap and causing the branches to decay and die back. When once
the grub enters the stems control is difficult, but routine spraying with
tar-oil in winter should ensure trouble-free plants.

**CODLING MOTH**

It begins its attack on apples in early July, soon after the sawfly has left
the trees. The moth is grey and is active at night, laying its eggs on fruit
or foliage; the eggs are scarcely visible to the naked eye. The tiny white
caterpillar eats its way into the fruit, quickly making the fruit uneatable
with its tunnelling. Its presence may be detected by a heap of brown
substance at the entrance to the hole. It winters as a larva, turning to a
chrysalis in spring. To prevent an attack, spray with wettable DDT early
July and again at the month end.

**COLORADO BEETLE**

It is rare in Britain, but is so destructive to potato crops that it is a
notifiable pest. It has orange-and-black striped wings and when fully
grown measures about ½ in. in length. It winters in the soil, working its
way to the surface in spring. Its eggs are orange and the grubs are also

orange; where in numbers, they will quickly wipe out a whole plantation. As a precaution, treat the soil with Aldrin dust before planting.

### FLEA BEETLE

It is often mistaken for the Colorado Beetle, for it is black and shiny, with two bright yellow stripes down the outer edge of its back. It mostly attacks turnips and swedes, and all brassica crops, devouring the leaves and often severing the plants at soil level. An attack will be prevented by treating the soil with Aldrin dust before planting, and the plants should be dusted with Sybol or Lindex when planted out or as soon as the seedlings appear.

### LEAF HOPPER (CUCKOO SPIT)

The pest will be seen jumping from leaf to leaf on roses and many other flowering plants, and badly mottled leaves due to its sucking the sap will denote its presence. It inhabits crevices of walls during winter, coming out in spring, when a severe attack will defoliate a plant. The insects are greenish-yellow, spotted with black, and they should be removed by hand where observed. An attack may be prevented by spraying (or dusting) with Sybol or with Lindex in May, and repeating at monthly intervals. An alternative is to dust with malathion.

### LEAF MINER

It attacks chiefly the three Cs – chrysanthemums, cinerarias and celery, and it is a tiny grey insect which lays its eggs on the underside of the leaves. When the grubs hatch out, they work their way between the upper and lower surface of the leaves, making thick white lines or tunnels which are clearly visible. Spraying with Lindex or liquid malathion once every two weeks from the time the plants are in their first pots or planted out will give control.

### LEATHER JACKET

The brownish-grey grub of the daddy long-legs, which is often to be found in turf. It causes the grass to die back in patches and it will attack plants just below soil level, often severing the stems, as do slugs and wood-lice. It is eradicated by treating the soil with Aldrin.

### MEALY BUG

A white, wax-like insect, like a small beetle, which produces white masses, like cottonwool, on the stems of vine, peach and apricot. It is also found on greenhouse plants, especially cacti. Vine rods should be regularly scraped to prevent the pest sheltering in the paper-like bark, and plants on which its presence is noted should be painted with methylated or surgical spirit. Vines, peaches and apricots should be sprayed with winterwash whilst dormant (December).

ONION FLY

The flies lay their eggs in the necks of onions and shallots when these are planted out in spring. Small white grubs hatch out, which tunnel into the onions, eating out the centre, with the result that the leaves turn yellow and the plants die back. An attack may be prevented by dusting the ground with calomel before planting or sowing seed; or dip the bulbs into a thin paste made of calomel dust and water before planting out.

PEA MOTH

The most troublesome of all pea pests, the white larvae being responsible for 'maggoty' peas, they will devour large plantations where not kept in check. They may be eradicated by treating the soil before planting with Gammexane or Aldrin dust, or by spraying the plants with Sybol at fortnightly intervals from the time they come into bloom until the pods have formed.

PEAR-LEAF BLISTER MITE

The mite attacks the young leaves of the pear in spring, causing reddish-brown blisters to appear in which the eggs are laid. Mites, invisible to the naked eye, hatch out and later; they winter in the bud scales, and attack the young leaves as they appear in spring. Spraying with lime-sulphur early in spring as the buds open will prevent an attack.

PEAR MIDGE

The small grey midge lays its eggs in the blossom of the pear tree during late spring. Upon hatching, the white maggots eat into the fruitlets as they form, reducing them to a slimy mass. As the fruits fall, so do the grubs, to remain in the soil over winter and to pupate as midges the following spring. Dusting the trees with derris when the blossom begins to open will give control.

RASPBERRY BEETLE

It is the most troublesome of all raspberry pests, and also attacks the loganberry and blackberry. The beetle is greyish-brown, about $\frac{1}{8}$ in. long, and the female lays her eggs in the flowers. The greyish-white grubs feed on the fruits, making them unfit for use. To control, dust the flowers with derris as soon as they open, and again when the fruit begins to set. This should be done as routine each year.

RASPBERRY MOTH

The pest winters in the soil at the base of the canes, emerging from a cocoon in spring as a silvery-brown moth with yellow spots on the wings. They lay their eggs in the blossoms, and the small caterpillars hatching out feed on the young fruits, causing them to die before reaching maturity. To control, soak the soil around (and the canes themselves) with tar-oil in January and dust the blooms with Derris as they open.

RED SPIDER

A minute red insect with spider-like legs, which attacks apples, plums, damsons, peaches, apricots, tomatoes and cucumbers under glass, and flowering plants in greenhouses and frames, especially carnations and violets. The pests cluster together on the underside of the leaves, sucking the sap and reducing the vitality of the plant whilst the leaves turn brown and wither. Spray apples, plums and damsons with DNOC during the dormant stage, and peaches and apricots and other plants in the open with liquid derris or malathion, or with lime-sulphur at bud-break. Tomatoes, cucumbers and carnations under glass should be fumigated with an azobenzene smoke which is repeated after 10 days. Dry conditions, indoors and out, encourage red spider attacks.

ROOTAPHIS, *see* Woolly Aphis

SAWFLY

In its various forms, this pest appears on apples, plums and gooseberries when in bloom, feeding on the pollen. It is less than $\frac{1}{2}$ in. long and attacks the flower buds in spring, boring a hole through the sepals and calyx where the female deposits her egg. From this, a white caterpillar will emerge after about 10 days. It tunnels its way into the bud, causing a yellow liquid to drip from the hole made by the adult and the bud turns brown and dies. The larva then falls to the ground (late in June), where it winters in a cocoon just below the surface of the soil. To prevent an attack, spray the trees with Lindex solution; apples at petal fall; plums 8–10 days after; or with derris mixed with a speader.

SCALE

Like white scales, the insects attack peaches and apricots, figs, roses, vines, cacti and ornamental trees and shrubs, and are to be found clustering about the stems, where they suck the sap and lower the ability of the plant to combat disease. Spry with tar-oil wash in December or spray with malathion in early spring.

TARSONEMID MITE

A troublesome strawberry pest. The mites begin to lay their eggs in the heart of the plants when growth commences in March and, as a precaution all plants should be given a 20-minute immersion in hot water at 110°F. (43°C.). It must however, be noted that at 113°F. (45°C.) the plants will be killed, hence the need to take careful note of the temperature. Dusting the plants with flowers of sulphur at the end of March (also as a precaution against mildew) will give partial control; likewise spraying them with a two per cent lime-sulphur solution.

TORTRIX MOTH

Shakespeare's 'worm i' the bud', the caterpillars attack roses, apples and pears, causing the leaves to curl up at the edges and hold the flower petals in a rain-proof canopy, made by spinning silken threads beneath which they will feast for hours, preventing the flower from opening and causing defoliation, weakening the plant and eventually causing its death. They turn to chrysalids in June, and to moths by mid-July. This is one of the most destructive of garden pests and an attack must be prevented by routine spraying with Abol X or Sybol, applied early in May each year and at monthly intervals throughout summer. Or dust with Lindex every 14 days, although not on vines or blackcurrants.

VINE WEEVIL

The larva, with its fat, cream-coloured body, attacks the roots of vines; also of auriculas and chrysanthemums, whilst the weevil itself hides beneath the surface of the soil by day, attacking the stems of the plants at night. The pest is exterminated by soaking the soil in spring with Lindex solution, and pot-grown plants will be kept free if a small amount of Jaypeat Compound is placed in each pot before being filled with compost. Alternatively, add Gammexane dust to the potting compost, and this will keep the soil free from the pest.

WINTER MOTH

They measure about 1 in. long and are green in colour. They feed first on the buds and blossom of fruit trees, then on the leaves and fruits, sometimes defoliating the trees. Towards the end of June they fall to the ground to pupate, the moths emerging in winter. The females are wingless and crawl up the trunk of the trees to lay their eggs on the branches, to recommence the life cycle. Grease banding the trees in October will prevent the females from reaching the branches. As an additional precaution, spray with tar-oil or Thiol Thiocynate in January.

WOOLLY APHIS

Also known as Root Aphis or American Blight, it chiefly affects apples, producing masses of a grey-woolly substance around the branches. Here, beneath their woolly covering, the pests winter, and lay their eggs in spring. The insects cause swellings to appear on the branches on which they feed beneath the woolly covering. Later, the swellings split and become a ready entrance for fungus diseases. The pest may be eradicated by spraying the trees in the green-bud stage with a malathion preparation, and an outbreak will usually be prevented by the routine spraying with tar-oil wash or Thiol Thiocyanate in December. However, as the pest is carried from tree to tree by the wind, an outbreak may occur at any time and the trees should be inspected regularly.

The pest also attacks auriculas, especially those growing in pots. They cluster around the neck of the plants, like tiny pieces of cotton wool. If unchecked, the plants will turn yellow and die back, and a stunted flower stem will usually reveal the presence of the pest. It is exterminated by painting the neck with either methylated or surgical spirit, and treating the soil with Sybol in dust or liquid form, one teaspoonful to a gallon of water.

PLUM (AND GAGE)

For a northern garden, or one troubled by frosts, it will be wiser to plant late-flowering apples, damsons, and the very latest flowering of the plums, for, as a rule, the plum is the first of all these fruits to blossom early in April. For this reason, plums planted commercially are the most unreliable of fruits; they either escape frosts, and crop so abundantly that the price of fresh fruit is uneconomical to the grower, or they may be badly damaged by frosts, when there will be little fruit available. Where frost proves troublesome, as where the land is low lying, or perhaps close to a river, then all but the very latest flowering plums should be avoided, and these should be given the protection of a walled garden. Plums do not require such a large amount of sunshine as pears, and provided that they are given frost protection, they will ripen well on a west wall, thus leaving the southerly positions for the pears, with the apples being planted in the more open and exposed parts of the garden.

GROWING AGAINST A WALL

Plums do better as bush trees than as standards, and in the fan-shaped form rather than the horizontal form. Where planting in a small garden, apples should be planted as cordons, pears as espaliers, and plums as fan-shaped trees against a wall. This is not only the most reliable method, but the most economical, for a wall plum, well supplied with moisture and nitrogen, will soon cover an area 10 ft. high and a similar distance in width.

Varieties to plant will depend upon aspect and district, some plums being more hardy than others, and the selection should be made accordingly, planting the late-flowering plums and gages in a more open situation, the more tender and choice varieties against a wall. So many walls are clothed in uninteresting ivy, when they might be growing delicious fruit, but with wall trees it must be remembered that they must never lack moisture. Lack of humus and moisture at the roots is the cause of so many giving disappointing crops. A wall, especially where it receives some sun, will bring out the flavour to its maximum, but if the trees are not supplied with abundant summer moisture, the fruit will remain small, and the flesh dry.

The plum will come quickly into bearing as a fan-tree and is not troubled by biennial bearing as are many apples, neither does it require the same attention to pruning as the apple or pear. It bears the bulk of its fruit on the new wood, and apart from the removal of any dead wood, the pruners are better left in the garden shed. Excessive pruning, especially in the dormant period, will cause untold harm by 'bleeding', from which stone fruits suffer. The Government's Silver Leaf Disease Order, demands that all dead and decayed wood is removed and burnt by 15 July each year, and this, together with any shortening of unduly long shoots, should be done early in spring, as the trees come into life after their winter rest. At this time any cuts will quickly heal.

POLLINATION

As with apples, usually the most richly flavoured plums and gages require a pollinator, especially where the connoisseur's plum, Coe's Golden Drop, has been used as a parent, for its blossoms are sterile and will not pollinate each other. About half the most popular plums possess self-sterile blossom and require a pollinator, whilst the rest are self-fertile and will, unlike apples and pears, bear a heavy crop entirely without pollinator. A number, however, are only partly self-fertile, and will set heavier crops with a pollinator flowering at the same time. Again, plum pollination is less complicated, in that the blossom period covers only eighteen to twenty days, and except for the very latest to bloom – such as Marjorie's Seedling and Pond's Seedling – most will overlap, and so the flowering periods may generally be simplified into 'Early' and 'Late' for pollinating purposes. The early-flowering, self-fertile varieties will pollinate the early-flowering sterile varieties, and the same with those which bloom late. It is, therefore, a more simple matter than when considering apples, pears, and cherries, where many varieties do not prove suitable pollinators, although in bloom at the same time. Of all plums only the following in no way overlap, or only by a day or so, and those of group (a) should not be relied upon to pollinate those of (b) and vice versa:

| *Early (a)* | *Late (b)* |
|---|---|
| Bryanston Gage | Belle de Louvain |
| Count Althann's Gage | Czar |
| Jefferson | Late Transparent Gage |
| Monarch | Marjorie's Seedling |
| President | Oullin's Gage |
| Warwickshire Drooper | Pershore |

All plums and gages remain in bloom, unless damaged by frost, for exactly 10 days, a shorter period than any other fruit, and those of group (a), the first to bloom, will have almost finished when those of group (b), the last to bloom, commence to flower.

It should be said that President is incompatible as a pollinator to Cambridge Gage, though both are in bloom at the same time.

Unfortunately many gardeners, after giving careful consideration to the selection of suitable vareties for various soils and climates, do not take the pollination factor into consideration, it being pure luck if the self-fertile varieties are planted, and where self-sterile varieties fail to set their fruit; this is blamed on the soil, climate, or even upon the nurseryman. The following plums are self-fertile to their own pollen:

| *Early* | *Mid-season* | *Late* |
|---|---|---|
| Denniston's Superb | Victoria | Belle de Louvain |
| Early Transparent | Reine Claude de Bavay. | Czar |
| Monarch | | Golden Transparent |
| Warwickshire Drooper | | Laxton's Gage |
| | | Ouillin's Golden Gage |
| | | Pershore |

Any of these varieties should be planted with a self-sterile variety in bloom at the same time.

## Plum (and Gage)

Plums self-sterile to their own pollen:

| Early | Mid-season | Late |
|---|---|---|
| Black Diamond | Bryanston Gage | Kirke's Blue |
| Coe's Golden Drop | Transparent Gage | Pond's Seedling |
| Count Althann's Gage | | |
| Jefferson Gage | | |
| President | | |

### SOIL CONDITIONS

Strange as it may seem, whereas by far the greater number of apples and pears planted in Britain during this century are for dessert rather than for culinary use, the opposite is the case with plums; the greater percentage, such as Czar, Yellow Pershore, and Belle de Louvain, being planted for the canning and jam industries. The result is, that if we wish to enjoy those richer-flavoured plums and gages, we must grow them ourselves. But before making a selection, soil must be considered with some care.

Plums like a heavy loam, and John Scott in his *Orchardist*, the commercial growers' bible, published in 1860, says 'plums succeed best in strong, clay soils, mixed with a proportion of loam. On such soils the plum reaches the highest perfection in the shortest possible time.' A soil retentive of moisture is the secret of success with plums, and one continually enriched with nitrogen, preferably of an organic nature.

Light soils should have large quantities of shoddy, or strawy farmyard manure incorporated at planting time, especially where planting wall trees. A liberal mulch of an organic manure, rich in nitrogen, should always be given in April each year. Where this is unobtainable, give 1 oz. of sulphate of ammonia to each tree at the same time, and immediately after any pruning has been done. Watering should be done whenever necessary during a dry summer, especially with wall trees and with recently-planted trees in the open.

Though several varieties, such as Pond's Seedling and the old Green Gage, will crop well and remain healthy on a chalk-laden soil, most other varieties soon, like pears, show signs of chlorosis and never bear well. When there is a reasonable depth to the soil this may be largely overcome by working in plenty of organic manure. Where there is almost a complete absence of lime in the soil, the two most tolerant varieties are Czar and Victoria, for as long as the soil is heavy yet not waterlogged, they will bear well. Shoddy and composted straw should be added where the soil proves heavy and sticky. Czar, the most accommodating of fruit trees, will also bear abundantly in a light, sandy soil containing a very small percentage of loam.

One may ask what weight of fruit is to be expected from a twenty-year bush tree, growing in an average soil, and being constantly mulched with organic nitrogenous manures? Taking good years with the bad, and a wide selection, the average should be about 40 lb. per tree, with Victoria, Czar and Pershore, as high as 50–60 lb. and with Coe's Golden Drop and Kirke's Blue as low as 8–10 lb. per tree, but still worth growing for their delicious fruit. It should be said, however, that where given favourable conditions, the shy bearers will crop more heavily, whereas there may not be a marked difference with the others; for instance, when planted against a sunny wall in a southern garden, with their roots well supplied with moisture and nitrogen.

PROPAGATION AND ROOTSTOCKS

The choice of rootstock is not large, and generally bush and fan-trained trees are grown on what is known as the Common Plum and Brompton Stock, and standard trees for large gardens or orchards on the Myrobalan stock. The latter is generally used for the heavy-cropping varieties, such as Czar and Monarch. Owing to the incidence of gumming and the chances of introducing disease, plums are budded rather than grafted. Budding is done in July, for plums and cherries, the bud being removed with a strip of bark, cut out with the pruning knife. This is then fixed against the wood of the selected stock, into which a cut in the bark has been made 6 in. from the base. The bark on both sides of the cut is carefully lifted from the cambium layer, and into this the bud is fixed. It is held in position by tying with raffia, leaving only the actual bud exposed. In from four to five weeks the union should have taken place, when the raffia is removed. The following March the stock is cut back to within 1 in. of the bud, which will grow away to form a tree.

The gages and plums in the artificial forms are mostly budded on to the Common Plum or Brompton stocks, but the varieties President, Czar and Marjorie's Seedling are incompatible with the Common Plum stock and so are usually budded onto the Myrobalan. The Common Plum makes a robust tree, is resistant to Silver Leaf, and so is always used for Victoria and Pond's Seedling, whilst it is generally used for the less-vigorous varieties such as Coe's Golden Drop.

For a small garden, the Brompton stock is probably the best, for the trees gow sturdily, but come quickly into bearing; they also send up few suckers, an important consideration for the amateur, for they will require but little attention apart from the occasional removal in spring of any dead wood.

At one time the Common Mussel stock was widely used, but the trees on this stock require copious amounts of water and tend to sucker badly. With this stock the trees come more quickly into bearing than on any other, but like Type MIX with apples, they bear abundantly for a time, then lose vigour.

## Plum (and Gage)

It should be said that several of the gages, especially Oullin's Golden and Count Althann's, are incompatible with the Myrobalan stock; whilst several others, such as Yellow Pershore, crop well and are generally planted on their own roots, but being slow to form suckers they cannot be used for propagating other plums on a commercial scale.

Spring is the safest time to carry out any pruning of plums, just when the buds are beginning to burst, for it is at this time that the wounds quickly heal over and almost no 'bleeding' occurs. This not only reduces the vigour of the tree but provides an entrance for the dreaded Silver Leaf disease, the fungus deriving its nourishment from the cells of the tree, thereby greatly decreasing its constitution. Early-autumn pruning, which may be carried out on early fruiting varieties when the crop has been cleared, is permissible, but all cutting should be done between the end of April and mid-September, for during the winter the cuts will remain 'open' for dangerously long periods.

In any case, plums require very little pruning, for the trees will form their fruit buds along the whole length of the younger branches, and especially with standard trees where established; thinning of overcrowded growth either in May or September, depending upon lateness of crop, will be all that is required. A well-grown plum tree will be able to carry a much larger proportion of wood than will any other fruit tree, and drastic reduction, even of neglected trees, must never be performed as with apples and to a lesser extent, pears.

When renovating a neglected tree, it may be advisable to cut away with the pruning saw one or two large and partially-decayed branches. If so, this should be done during May, a time when the large cut will heal rapidly, and so that the energies of the tree may be concentrated to the remaining wood. With plums it is even more important to cut out any wood close to the stem from which it is being removed, so that the wound will heal rapidly and completely. But before making any cuts, see if the tree can be renewed in vigour by removing some of the small, thin wood which plums make in quantity, and possibly root pruning will be more satisfactory than the cutting back of any large branches.

### REMOVAL OF SUCKERS

One of the greatest troubles with plums is the continual formation of suckers at the roots, and these, if left, will utilise much of the nourishment needed for the proper functioning of the tree. They should be removed whenever the roots of the tree are pruned, and must be cut away right to their source, otherwise they will grow again. It is first necessary to remove the soil from around the tree to expose the roots, but it will be found that the suckers generally arise from a point in the roots just below the point where the scion has been grafted on to the rootstock.

This calls for the utmost care in removing the soil right up to the scion and then in cutting out the sucker shoot with a sharp knife. For bush or standard trees it is advisable to ring round half the tree one year and to complete the removal of suckers and vigorous roots the following year. It is essential to pack the soil well round the roots when the work has been done, or there will be the chance of the tree becoming uprooted by strong winds.

TREATMENT OF FAN-TRAINED TREES

In renovating fan-trained trees, in which form the plum crops abundantly, more pruning will be necessary and this should take the form of pinching back shoots in mid-summer and in removing all unwanted new wood. A number of young growths may be pinched back between mid-June and mid-July to form a new spur system, and these will need to be cut further back, in the same way as described for apples, but early in September rather than in winter. By degrees the old spurs may be drastically reduced to make way for the new ones. In conjunction with the shoot thinning of wall trees, root pruning should be given every three or four years. This will prevent excessive wood growth.

FIG. 11 *Forming a fan-shaped tree*

The formation of a bush and standard form of plum tree takes the same lines as described for apples and pears. Planted in the maiden form they may be formed as required, the yearly pruning consisting of pinching back the new wood to form fruiting buds.

FORMING THE FAN-TRAINED TREE

Both plums and cherries crop abundantly in this form, all varieties

245

proving suitable, though naturally some are more vigorous than others and will require more frequent pruning at the roots. The method of forming the fan is to cut back the maiden to an upward bud. This should leave on the lower portion of the stem two buds, which will break and form the arms. Unsuitably placed buds should be removed, and any not breaking must be nicked or notched as previously described for the formation of espaliers.

After the previous season's growth, they are pruned back to 18 in. and the leader or central shoot is cut back to two buds. It is from these buds that the fan-shaped tree is formed.

Canes are used for tying in the shoots so that they may be trained to the required shape. As growth continues, each shoot may be cut back the following spring to two more buds, which will complete the shape of the tree, although canes will be needed until the shoots have taken on the required form.

Cultural treatment will henceforth consist of cutting back a third of the new wood formed by the branches each May, and the pinching back of all side growths. The shoots will continue to break, and where there is room a number may be tied in to continue the fan-like shape.

HARVESTING AND STORING

Unlike pears, plums should be allowed to remain on the trees until ripe; the longer they will hang, the better will be their flavour. As plums are more numerous than pears, the best test as to whether they are ready for gathering is to remove one and taste it. It should be pleasantly soft, juicy and in no way dry, and the stone should readily part from the flesh. It should also possess a rich flavour.

Few gardeners realise that certain varieties will keep as readily as most pears if removed by their stalk, so as not to damage the 'bloom', and if placed in a dry, airy room. The older generation of fruit growers would wrap the fruit in pieces of newspaper, for they said it kept better this way, but this should not be necessary. Those that will store for several weeks include Coe's Golden Drop; Laxton's Cropper; Laxton's Delicious, bred from Golden Drop and hence its similar qualities; and the grand old variety, Angelina Burdett. Golden Drop will keep up to nine months in store.

DISEASES

*Brown Rot.* It causes:

(a) Spur Blight, the infection of the new leaves which are attacked by spores, which later travel down the spurs and on to the branches, causing decay and loss of fruit.

(b) Blossom Wilt, which is the same infection, only it is the blossom that is mainly attacked, causing it to fall away before the fruit is set. Both Blossom Wilt and Spur Blight may be controlled by spraying with a one per cent lime-sulphur solution just before the blossom opens. A wash with petroleum-oil solution in February will give additional control, and the two should also keep down red spider and destroy the eggs of the leaf-curling aphis. This spraying programme, given once every three years, or whenever necessary, should be sufficient to keep the plum orchard in a healthy condition, with a derris spray immediately after petal fall.

(c) Fruit Rot, where the fungus disease attacks the individual fruits, causing them to mummify on the trees. There is no known cure but luckily the trouble is not common.

*Canker.* The varieties Victoria and Czar seem most prone to attack, which concentrates on the main stem of plums, causing the troubled area to become decayed. Should the trouble extend completely round the stem, the tree will die back and be of no further use. Myrobalan B stock has proved very resistant.

*Silver Leaf.* This fungus is the most dreaded of all plum diseases, entering through a cut or break, which is the primary reason why all pruning should be done in May. From June to September the plum exudes a gummy substance wherever a cut has occurred and this will tend to keep out the fungus. Where breakages occur at other times of the year, the wound should be treated with white lead paint as a precaution against the fungus making entry. The fungus lives on the dead wood, which must be removed throughout the life of the tree. A Ministry of Agriculture Order actually makes this compulsory by mid-July of each year, when all dead wood must be removed and burnt.

PESTS

*Leaf-Curling Aphis.* This greenfly causes damage to the leaves and young fruit in much the same manner as the red spider. The eggs are laid on the branches in late autumn and hatch out in early spring. A tar-oil wash given during December or January will kill off all eggs and control is therefore not difficult.

*Plum Maggot.* This may prove troublesome in some seasons, the eggs being laid on the young fruit, from whence the grubs work their way into the centre. Fruits will either fall prematurely or will be uneatable if they mature. The best method of control is to soak the trunks of the trees with Mortegg during winter.

*Sawfly.* The Plum Sawfly lays its eggs in the flowers where the hatched grubs remain until the fruit begins to form, when they begin their tunnelling in much the same way as in apples and pears. Effective control may be made by spraying with Lindex, 1 oz. to 2 gallons of water, immediately after petal fall.

VARIETIES (PLUMS)

RIPE LATE JULY AND EARLY AUGUST

BLACK PRINCE. Ripe before the last days of July, it makes a small tree, yet is a huge cropper, the small, black, velvety fruit having the true damson flavour, and being delicious for tarts and for bottling. Highly resistant to Silver Leaf Disease.

BLUE TIT. Raised by Messrs Laxton Bros, and follows Czar. It bears a blue fruit with the true greengage flavour, and is one of the best early plums for dessert. Makes a small, compact tree and is very fertile.

CZAR. Makes a fine orchard tree with its vigorous habit, yet it is compact and a most reliable cropper. Its blossom appears late and is very resistant to frost, and so it bears heavily in cold gardens, and especially in heavy soils. The fruit is of a bright shade of purple, of medium size, and is useful both for cooking and for dessert. Introduced and raised by Thomas Rivers in 1875, it is ready for use at the beginning of August.

EARLY LAXTON. The first plum to ripen, towards the end of July. The small, golden-yellow fruit carries a rosy-red flush, and is sweet and juicy. It blooms early and is pollinated by River's Early Prolific or Laxton's Cropper. It makes a small tree, and is valuable for a small garden.

RIVERS' EARLY PROLIFIC. Making a small, but spreading tree, this is a good companion to Early Laxton, for it is grown chiefly for cooking, the small purple fruit possessing a rich damson-like flavour. Pollinated by the early-flowering gage, Denniston's Superb, it rarely misses a crop.

RIPE MID-AUGUST TO MONTH END

GOLDFINCH. To ripen in mid-August this is possibly the best of all plums. Raised by Laxton Bros, it has Early Transparent Gage blood, and is equally as delicious, the golden-yellow fruit being sweet and juicy. It makes a compact tree, and bears consistently heavy crops.

LAXTON'S BOUNTIFUL. Has Victoria as a parent, and bears a similar fruit, but of not quite so good flavour. It bottles better than any early plum, and should also be used for jam rather than for dessert. It makes a large, vigorous tree and bears enormous crops.

PERSHORE (YELLOW). Used almost entirely for canning, bottling and jam, it was found in a Worcestershire garden, and is widely grown in that county. It makes a bright yellow fruit with firm flesh. It is valuable for a frosty garden, for it is very late flowering.

UTILITY. One of the most handsome plums and a fine all-round variety, raised by Laxton Bros, and introduced forty years ago. It bears a large exhibition plum of bright purple-red. Early flowering, it may be pollinated by most of the early blooming plums, especially Denniston's Superb. Matures between Goldfinch and Victoria.

VICTORIA. Found in a Sussex cottage garden more than a century ago, and the most widely-grown plum of all. Extremely vigorous, it is the most self-fertile of all plums; it is frost resistant, crops well in all forms, and is used for every purpose. Its only weak point is that it is often troubled by Silver Leaf Disease. Ripe at the end of August. Like Czar, it crops well in clay soils.

RIPE EARLY TO MID- SEPTEMBER

ANGELINA BURDETT. Known to early eighteenth-century gardeners, and much too good to become extinct, yet there is only one nursery where it is still propagated. The large fruit is of deep purple, speckled with brown. It is ripe at the very beginning of September, but will hang for a fortnight. It will also keep for a fortnight after removing, and as it is extremely hardy, and is a regular bearer, it should be in every garden.

BELLE DE LOUVAIN. Of Belgian origin, it makes a large tree, and is slow to come into bearing, but for bottling and cooking, it is most valuable, also for a frosty garden on account of its late blooming.

JEFFERSON. Almost like a gage in its flavour and rich dessert quality, the pale-green flesh being sweet and juicy. Raised in the U.S.A., it blooms early and requires an early-flowering pollinator such as Denniston's Superb. It makes a compact, upright tree, ideal for a small garden, but should be planted in the more favourable districts. The fruit is pale green, flushed with pink.

KIRKE'S BLUE. To follow immediately after Jefferson, this is an equally delicious plum for dessert, its large violet fruits, being sweet and juicy. Introduced by Joseph Kirke of the Old Brompton Road, London, about 1825, it is a shy bearer in the north. Czar and Marjorie's Seedling are the two best pollinators.

LAXTON'S CROPPER. This is an excellent all-purpose plum for September, the large black fruit hanging for several weeks when ripe. It is a strong grower, and bears a heavy crop in all districts. Will store well.

POND'S SEEDLING. It makes a large tree and is valuable for cold gardens, in that it blooms late. The rose-crimson fruit is large and handsome, and if not of the very best dessert quality, it is good. Crops well in a chalk-laden soil.

THAMES CROSS. A new plum raised at Long Ashton. It bears abundantly in the West Country, where it makes a large tree and bears large, pure golden-yellow fruit. Has Coe's Golden Drop as a parent, and the flavour is similar.

WARWICKSHIRE DROOPER. Making a large, vigorous tree with drooping branches, this is an excellent all-purpose plum, where room is available. May be described as a later and improved Pershore. The yellow fruit is shaded with scarlet and grey.

RIPE IN LATE SEPTEMBER AND EARLY OCTOBER

COE'S GOLDEN DROP. It blooms very early and should be given the protection of a warm wall, whilst it also likes a soil containing plenty of nitrogenous humus. It bears a large fruit of quite exceptional flavour, pale yellow, speckled with crimson. At its best in early October, the fruit will keep until the month end, its rich apricot flavour, and almost treacle sweetness, being the most delicious of all plums. It makes a spreading tree, requires an early-flowering pollinator, and is a shy bearer. Raised 200 years ago by Coe of Bury St Edmunds, this is the Cox's Orange or Comice of the plum world. Denniston's Superb is the best pollinator.

LAXTON'S DELICIOUS. This is one of the finest of dessert plums, the deep-yellow fruit, flushed with red, being juicy and deliciously sweet. It has Coe's Golden Drop as a parent, but is a much better cropper, especially as a wall tree. Like its parent the fruit may be kept several weeks, if harvested about the third week of September. A vigorous grower, it blooms late, Oullin's Golden Gage or Majorie's Seedling being suitable pollinators.

LAXTON'S OLYMPIA. Making a large, spreading tree, it blooms late and ripens its fruit about 1 October. The coal-black fruit is of medium size, is sweet, and possesses a flavour all its own, similar to preserved plums from the Mediterranean. It bears a very heavy crop.

MARJORIE'S SEEDLING. Extremely fertile and of vigorous upright habit, it makes a large tree. It is the last to come into bloom, and the latest to ripen its large, crimson-purple fruit. Ready for gathering at the end of September, the fruit will hang until the end of October, when it may be used for all purposes. Raised in Staffordshire, it is most suitable for a cold northerly garden.

MONARCH. Similar in all respects to Marjorie's Seedling, the tree habit and quality and colour of the fruit being the same, it must be considered inferior to Marjorie's Seedling, in that it blooms very early, and is frequently damaged by frost, neither does the fruit hang so well.

PRESIDENT. Raised by Thomas Rivers and an excellent dessert plum, being large, rich purple, with its deep-yellow flesh juicy and sweet. Makes a large, spreading tree. It blooms early and requires a pollinator.

SEVERN CROSS. Raised by Mr Spinks at Long Ashton, this is the latest of all dessert plums, for it hangs well into October, and is valuable where a succession of fruit being golden-yellow, flushed and spotted with pink, extremely juicy and of good flavour.

## Plum (and Gage)

**Extremely hardy plums:**
Angelina Burdett
Czar
Early Prolific
Laxton's Delicious
Pershore
Pond's Seedling
Victoria

**Long-hanging plums:**
Angelina Burdett
Laxton's Delicious
Marjorie's Seedling
Pond's Seedling
Severn Cross

**Plums of vigorous, spreading habit:**
Coe's Golden Drop
Czar
Laxton's Bountiful
Laxton's Olympia
President
Warwickshire Drooper
White Magnum Bonum

**Plums of dwarf, compact habit:**
Black Prince
Early Laxton
Goldfinch
Jefferson
Kirke's Blue

With plums, pollination may be divided into two sections, those that bloom early to mid-season, and those in bloom mid-season to late.

S.S. = Self-Sterile          S.F. = Self-Fertile

| Early-flowering: | | Late-flowering: | |
|---|---|---|---|
| Black Prince | (S.S.) | Angelina Burdett | (S.F.) |
| Blue Tit | (S.F.) | Belle de Louvain | (S.S.) |
| Bryanston Gage | (S.S.) | Cambridge Gage | (S.S.) |
| Coe's Golden Drop | (S.S.) | Count Althann's Gage | (S.S.) |
| Denniston's Superb | (S.F.) | Czar | (S.F.) |
| Early Gage | (S.S.) | Giant Prune | (S.F.) |
| Early Laxton | (S.S.) | Golden Transparent | (S.F.) |
| Early Prolific | (P.S.F.) | Kirke's Blue | (S.S.) |
| Early Transparent | (S.F.) | Late Transparent | (S.S.) |
| Greengage | (S.S.) | Laxton's Delicious | S.S. |
| Jefferson | (S.S.) | Laxton's Gage | (S.F.) |
| Monarch | (S.F.) | Marjorie's Seedling | (S.F.) |
| President | (S.S.) | Oullin's Golden Gage | (S.F.) |
| Thames Cross | (S.F.) | Pershore | (S.F.) |
| Victoria | (S.F.) | Pond's Seedling | (S.S.) |
| Warwickshire Drooper | (S.F.) | Reine Claude de Bavay | (S.F.) |
| | | Severn Cross | (P.S.F.) |
| | | White Magnum Bonum | (S.F.) |

NOTE: Plums Czar, Golden Transparent, Laxton's Gage and Oullin's

Golden Gage, all late-flowering, may all be considered self-fertile varieties.

*Most suitable varieties for a chalk soil:*

| | |
|---|---|
| Greengage | Pond's Seedling |
| Marjorie's Seedling | River's Early Prolific |

Though the self-fertile varieties will set fruit with their own pollen, they will set much heavier crops when planted with varieties in bloom at the same period.

PLUMS AND GAGES TO RIPEN JULY TO AUGUST

| | |
|---|---|
| Black Prince | Laxton's Bountiful |
| Blue Tit | Laxton's Gage |
| Czar | Oullin's Golden Gage |
| Denniston's Superb | River's Early Prolific |
| Early Gage | Utility |
| Early Laxton | Victoria |
| Early Transparent | Yellow Pershore |
| Goldfinch | |

VARIETIES (GAGES)

TO RIPEN EARLY TO MID-AUGUST

DENNISTON'S SUPERB. Really a gage-plum hybrid, but possesses the true gage flavour, and is extremely hardy and fertile. Like James Grieve amongst apples, this plum acts as a pollinator for more plums than any other variety. It was raised in New York in 1835, it blooms early mid-season, and can set heavy crops without a pollinator. It is of vigorous habit in all soils, and ripens its fruit, green flushed with crimson, by mid-August. One of the best of all plums or gages, whichever it may be considered.

EARLY GAGE. Raised by Laxton Bros, this is the first of the gages to ripen, at the beginning of August. The tree is vigorous and healthy, and when pollinated (Denniston's Superb) bears heavily, the amber-yellow fruit possessing a rich, but delicate flavour.

EARLY TRANSPARENT. Raised by Thomas Rivers, it makes a dwarf tree and is able to set a heavy crop with its own pollen. It blooms early and ripens its fruit during mid-August, when the pale apricot skin is so thin as to show the stone. The richly-flavoured fruit possesses a distinct fragrance when ripe.

OULLIN'S GOLDED GAGE. It ripens in mid-August and is a remarkably fine dessert variety. Like Denniston's Superb, it seems to be a hybrid raised in France a century ago. It is valuable in that it is one of the latest gages to bloom, and though good for dessert, it is one of the best for bottling and jam.

TO RIPEN LATE AUGUST TO EARLY SEPTEMBER

CAMBRIDGE GAGE. Raised and used by Chivers of Cambridge, it bears a fruit similar to the true Greengage, but is hardier and is a heavier cropper. Flowering late, it is a valuable variety for the North Midlands.

LATE TRANSPARENT. Making a small, dwarf tree, and setting a heavy crop with its own pollen, it possesses similar characteristics to Early Transparent, though it blooms later, Laxton's Gage being a pollinator. The bright-yellow fruit is speckled with red, the flavour being rich, almost peach-like.

LAXTON'S GAGE. The result of Greengage × Victoria, it makes a large, spreading tree and blooms quite late. It is a useful variety for Midland gardens. The yellowish-green fruit, which possesses a rich flavour is ripe at the end of August. It is a heavy bearer in most soils.

TO RIPEN MID-SEPTEMBER TO EARLY OCTOBER

BRYANSTON GAGE. The fruit is ripe mid-September, being pale green, speckled with crimson, and with a russeting nearest the sun. It makes a large, spreading tree, is early-flowering, and with Victoria as a pollinator, which is essential, it crops well. Its flavour equals the greengage, yet it is little known. It was found in a Dorsetshire garden at the beginning of the nineteenth century.

COUNT ALTHANN'S GAGE. One of the most richly-flavoured of all the gages, it makes a large, but compact tree, blooms late and ripens its fruit towards the end of September. Introduced from Belgium a century ago, the fruit is unusual for a gage in that it is dark crimson, speckled with brown. Should be eaten as soon as ripe. It must have a pollinator, but it crops heavily.

GOLDEN TRANSPARENT. Like all the Transparents, raised by Thomas Rivers, it makes a dwarf tree, is self-fertile and blooms late. The fruit, which is possibly the most delicious of all gages or plums, ripens early October, the last of the gages to mature.

GREENGAGE. At its best during September, depending upon the locality, when its greenish-yellow fruit is rich and melting, and faintly aromatic. Known to early eighteenth-century gardeners, it is a shy bearer unless pollinated with Victoria, and should be grown in a sheltered garden. It was introduced from France in 1720 by Sir William Gage, and grown in the garden of Hengrave Hall, Suffolk.

REINE CLAUDE DE BAVAY. A first-rate plum of exquisite flavour, ripe about 1 October, it will hang for several weeks. It makes a neat, compact tree. and is self-fertile, blooming very late. The richly-flavoured fruit is large. and almost orange in colour, speckled with white. The best gage for a small garden.

## POTATO

Apart from its food value, the potato has another important quality. This is in its ability to crop reasonably well, provided that it is well manured, in 'dirty' land, land which has been allowed to become infested with weeds which are often difficult to eradicate. Due to the process of lifting and general cultivations, the soil goes through a rigorous cleaning, the land being so well broken up that it is possible for all perennial weeds to be eliminated. The ground also being heavily manured, it will be in perfect condition to grow a crop of peas or beans the following year.

For the home garden, the potato is also valuable for crop rotation, from which all plants derive benefit. Also, land of a peaty nature, low-lying, which would be unsuitable for most other crops, will, if suitably prepared, grow good potatoes. In fact, potatoes, like strawberries, favour a soil which is slightly acid, one with a pH value of about 6.5. For this reason, a soil which has recently been limed, or one of an alkaline nature will produce a potato liable to scab, and a crop much reduced in weight.

Should the soil be heavy, containing a high percentage of clay (which, in a wet summer would cause water logging), it would bring about a rotting of the tubers and trouble from fungus diseases. A clay soil should be made more friable by digging in liberal amounts of strawy manure. A soil of a light, sandy nature should, in addition to quantities of well-decayed manure given at planting time, be given copious supplies of moisture-holding materials, leaf mould, wood bark, and especially peat, which suits the potato best of all humus materials.

In autumn the ground should be deeply dug over and cleaned as well as possible, but the soil should be left in a rough condition, so that it may be subjected to frost over the winter months.

### STARTING THE TUBERS

There is no doubt that sprouted tubers will greatly increase the yield and especially in the case of early potatoes, will ensure the earliest possible crop depending upon soil and situation. And as early in the New Year as possible should be chosen for commencing the sprouting. A frost-proofed room is an essential, but first obtain the tubers from a reliable source. A stone of potato seed, certified grown in Ireland or Scotland (that grown on high ground in the north of England is equally as good) will yield from 100–200 lb. of potatoes if grown well. Sound seed tubers of even size must be used.

The method of sprouting is to place 1 in. of damp peat into a shallow wooden box and place the tubers into this, stood on the ends which were attached to the roots. Do not cut the tubers and dip them in lime as was at one time considered of value. Potatoes do not like lime, which only encourages scab. Place the boxes in as light a place as possible, but away from strong sunlight.

The value of sprouting is obtained during those late springs when the ground is too cold and wet to plant. The planting is best delayed until soil conditions are more suitable, and yet the tubers continue to grow unharmed. If, at planting time, the tubers contain more than two 'sprouts', all shoots should be rubbed off other than the two strongest.

With sprouted potatoes a crop at least three weeks earlier than with unsprouted seed may be expected, whilst a 20 per cent heavier crop is to be expected, due to the longer growing period.

PLANTING THE SETS

Early potatoes should be planted as soon as climate and soil conditions permit. This may be February in sheltered gardens in the south-west, as late as early April in the exposed north. Later March or early April will prove most suitable for the second earlies and maincrop. Though the soil will have been broken down to a fine tilth by the frost and will contain quantities of humus, it will not yet be in a condition to grow potatoes of exhibition quality, and of a flavour which will satisfy the connoisseur of good food.

First, the trench should be opened up to a depth of 8 in., making it the width of a spade, the trenches being 2 ft. apart, to allow for earthing up. At the bottom of the trench and to a depth of 2 in. is placed some well-decayed farmyard manure, which is covered with peat, and on to this the tubers are placed 2 ft. apart. The trenches for the early crop need be no more than 18 in. apart. Do not plant too close, for if so, the top growth, the haulm, will become drawn. It will not obtain its correct quota of air and light, and fungus diseases will be prevalent. Nor should one be in a hurry to get the tubers into the ground. Wait until the soil is friable and beginning to warm up. Remember the old adage, 'plant late potatoes early and early potatoes late'!

After planting the tubers, taking care not to break off the sprouts, cover with more peat or some friable soil which has been placed through a riddle. Then, into the soil which will be used to fill up the trench, add 2 oz. per yd. of a mixture of superphosphate to encourage maturity, and sulphate of potash. This not only increases the yield, but also builds up a plant which will show considerable resistance to disease. The mixture should be in the proportion of two-thirds superphosphate to third potash. Nitrogen in artificial forms cannot be recommended, for in a wet season it not only makes excessive top growth of a 'soft' nature, liable to disease attacks, but the mature tubers tend to become dark-fleshed when cooked. The manure should contain sufficient nitrogen without the aid of artificial stimulants. It is better to add the fertiliser to the soil for covering rather than bringing it into direct contact with the tubers.

If the land is low-lying or of a heavy nature, the tubers are best planted in ridges. The soil is taken out in 'V' fashion. A drill 6 in. deep is made at the top of the ridge, and here the tubers are planted as described.

It is important, when planting, to select a position where the plants may enjoy full sun, for they are never happy in shade, or even partial shade. So that the plants will obtain the maximum of sunshine, the rows should always be made from north to south, when both sides of the rows may receive the same amount of sunlight.

EARLY CROPS

To obtain the early crop in the quickest possible time after planting, a position should be selected where the land has a southerly slope. Even in an exposed garden this will ensure maturity a full fortnight before those not enjoying such a favourable position. A light, sandy soil is essential for an early crop. A mild hotbed should be made up by composting a quantity of straw with an activator. To this is added a small amount of poultry manure, some farmyard manure and a liberal amount of decayed leaves. When this has thoroughly composted, a quantity should be spread to a depth of 4 in. along the rows, and the sprouted tubers are placed on this warm compost. As soon as the sprouts appear above the ground, soil should be drawn over them, and, to provide additional protection, early peas should be sown between every double row of potatoes.

Earlier crops may be enjoyed by making up a gentle hotbed from the same compost heap. The method is to remove soil to the exact measurements of the frame lights. This is done to a depth of 6 in., which is filled with compost. On top is placed 4 in. of soil, frame boards being built around. The sprouted tubers are gently pressed into this soil, peat being placed over and around them. The tubers are set 9 in. apart, 4 in. of soil being placed over them, followed by the lights. Heat is preserved by heaping soil around the outsides of the frames, and covering the lights with sacking or mats. This will also exclude all frost. In this way, the tubers may be planted about 1 March, and will yield a much-appreciated crop towards the end of May.

Watering when the weather becomes warm in spring is a matter of importance, and to help to conserve moisture it is advisable to give a covering of moist peat and compost as soon as the shoots appear.

HARVESTING THE CROP

As the foliage appears above the soil, earthing up should be done at regular intervals, and as a precaution against blight the foliage should be sprayed with Bordeaux Mixture early in July, and again at the month end.

A reliable indication as to when the crop is ready for lifting is when the foliage begins to die down, although for show purposes or for eating in the home it may be desirable to lift before. Lift carefully with a fork, taking care to place it well away from the centre of the plant so as not to damage the tubers. When requiring tubers for exhibition, a safer method is to remove the soil with the hands, so that the tubers cannot be damaged. They are then immediately placed in a deep bucket or barrow lined with a sack, which is also used for covering the potatoes to exclude light. Always lift when the soil is dry and friable, for the potatoes will not keep if washed, which will be necessary if the soil clings to them. Potatoes lifted early for use or for exhibition will not, of course, be stored, although it is advisable to keep them in the dark, under the stairs or in a cellar being ideal. Those growing limited quantities of main crop for home consumption will also find the potatoes will keep well placed on a layer of straw in any frost-proof building, but they must be kept away from light if they are not to turn green. The drier the potatoes when lifted the better they will keep.

'New' potatoes may be enjoyed all the year round, and are never more appreciated than at Christmas time – for which a number are placed beforehand in metal biscuit tins containing dry peat, and buried 12 in. deep in the garden, with a large stone marking their position.

EXHIBITING

No vegetable has a more satisfying appearance than a dish of potatoes of uniform size, and measuring up to show standards. The Royal Horticultural Society in their *Show Handbook*, written 'For the Guidance of Exhibitors and Judges', give a maximum of 20 points for a perfect dish of potatoes, made up as follows:

| | |
|---|---|
| Condition | 4 points |
| Size | 4 points |
| Shape | 4 points |
| Eyes | 4 points |
| Uniformity | 4 points |

Potatoes conforming to these standards should be 'medium-sized, shapely, clean, clear-skinned tubers. Eyes few and shallow'.

257

When preparing tubers for exhibition, do not scrub them, or their skin will be damaged. It is preferable to wipe the tubers very carefully with a damp cloth, but much depends upon the condition of the soil at lifting time. If dry and friable almost all the soil will fall off without in any way harming the 'bloom' of the potato.

## VARIETIES
### FIRST EARLIES

DI VERNON. Those who enjoy a waxy-fleshed potato with a slight earthy flavour will find this variety very appetising. It is a handsome tuber, creamy-white, shaded with mauve, and a heavy bearer.

ECLIPSE. One of the last of the earlies to mature, but extremely heavy cropping, the small white-fleshed, kidney-shaped tubers cooking well.

EPICURE. An old favourite difficult to better for flavour. It matures early, and has the ability to withstand frost better than any other variety.

HOME GUARD. Now very popular, its oval tubers being of uniform size make it good for exhibition.

PENTLAND BEAUTY. A 'red' potato which is oval and pink-skinned, with shallow eyes and short haulm. It is the heaviest cropper of all the early varieties. Raised at the Pentlandfield Station in Scotland, and introduced in 1962.

SHARPE'S EXPRESS. This is the best early for heavy soils. A heavy bearer, the kidney-shaped tubers have a pale golden flesh; it is richly flavoured.

ULSTER CHIEFTAIN. Early to mature, cooking to a floury texture with a rich flavour, but it likes a warm soil, clear of all weeds. It is a very heavy cropper.

### SECOND EARLIES

Extremely valuable for bridging the gap between the early-maturing and maincrop varieties.

CATRIONA. This is a handsome, second early variety which does well on poor land, though is not of particularly good flavour. Introduced by Mr Archibald Finlay in 1920, it is flat kidney shaped, of a pale cream colour with a bright purple eye, a well-grown sample being very striking. Though a heavy cropper, it is susceptible to dry rot.

CRAIG'S ROYAL. Good for exhibition and good for eating. The well-shaped, white kidney tubers have an attractive red splash round the eyes.

DUNBAR ROVER. A reliable cropper for a light soil. The tubers are white and oval, the flesh purest white, a delicious variety for baking. It is immune to Wart Disease.

SUTTON'S OLYMPIC. One of the finest potatoes in existence. Though maturing early it will keep through winter and makes delicious eating. The tubers are round and pink skinned, similar to King Edward. It crops heavily in all parts of Britain, grown well yielding from 200–250 lb. from a stone of seed.

ULSTER ENSIGN. Raised in Ulster by Mr John Clarke. It is classed as a second early, and is a tremendous cropper. It is of rounded kidney shape, cream coloured with a pink eye. It does not keep well but makes for delicious eating.

MAINCROP VARIETIES

ANGUS BEAUTY. A new maincrop variety, and early to mature. The tubers are kidney-shaped, white, splashed with mauve. It is a strong grower, bearing a heavy crop and makes pleasant eating.

ARRAN BANNER. A potato almost devoid of flavour, with tubers that lack attractiveness, it yields heavily and is grown by farmers to feed to stock.

ARRAN COMRADE. A round potato, late to mature. The colour is white with a faint netting, a most handsome tuber. It was raised by Donald MacKelvie on his Isle of Arran croft, and introduced in 1920. This to my mind is the finest of the Arrans, in that it also makes delicious eating cooked in its jacket.

ARRAN VICTORY. This is the only coloured variety to reach us from Arran, and it is outstanding both for flavour and in its cropping powers. It is a round purple variety, and in Ireland it is now grown everywhere, to the exclusion of numerous old favourites – and the Irish know a good potato when they see one!

DR McINTOSH. Producing the largest number of uniform tubers per plant than any variety, it is late to mature and bears a long, kidney-shaped tuber with extremely shallow eyes. A heavy cropper, showing strong resistance to blight and being of good flavour, it may be classed as one of the finest all-round varieties ever introduced.

DUNBAR STANDARD. This potato is also becoming popular for exhibition; it is of white, kidney shape, with very shallow eyes. It is of good flavour when cooked but tends to break up badly. Its foliage grows tall and upright, making earthing up easy.

GOLDEN WONDER. A hundred years old and unsurpassed for quality and flavour – which might be described as being somewhere between that of a chestnut and an artichoke. It is, however, a light cropper unless grown in a soil which suits it, and it must be grown well.

KERR'S PINK. A hardy variety, late to mature and though an old one still a firm favourite. It does well in a heavy soil and in moist western districts. The tubers are round and pale pink. It keeps well and is of excellent flavour.

KING EDWARD VII. Raised in Northumberland at the beginning of the century, this pink-skinned, kidney-shaped variety possesses delicious flavour, and may be classed as the Bramley's Seedling amongst potatoes for baking. A red-skinned form called Red King, is also proving equally delicious. Both keep well right through winter and spring.

PENTLAND CROWN. Introduced in 1958, it has now replaced the older Majestic as the most prolific maincrop variety, for it crops heavily in all soils and stores well. The white, kidney-shaped potatoes have excellent flavour.

RED SKIN. Like all the red- and pink-skinned varieties, this bakes to an appetising floury texture, and although the skin is deeply coloured, the flesh is very white. It is now becoming extremely popular for exhibition as well as for cooking.

STORMONT DAWN. A new potato introduced in 1942, of outstanding quality, many growers selecting it as their maincrop variety. A heavy cropper, 13 cwt. having been obtained from 56 lb. of seed from a mid-May planting. It will keep well right up to Easter and longer, and is said to be the best potato of all for baking. It possesses a delicious flavour, but then it has Golden Wonder for a parent!

STORMONT 480. Raised in Northern Ireland and introduced in 1958, it crops heavily, the flattish tubers being shaded with pink to give it an appearance of the King Edward.

THE BISHOP. Described as the greatest exhibition potato ever introduced, but like all those of handsome appearance or of distinctive flavour, it is a shy cropper. It is the Cox's Orange of the vegetable world, it must be done well. It is a long, kidney-shaped potato, pure white and almost free of eyes. An additional value is, it does not readily turn green when exposed to light.

SALAD POTATOES

Most early-maturing potatoes are suitable for serving cold with salad, particularly Di Vernon and Epicure. Another of high quality is the Pink Fir Apple Potato. It is planted early in April, as for the ordinary early potatoes, the roots being ready for lifting as required from July. The tubers are long and pink-skinned, similar to those shown of the original Spanish potato in Parkinson's *Paradisus* (see footnote on page 60). They have a pale lemon flesh after cooking, and when quite cold their flavour is delicious. They have a waxy texture, enjoyed by some though not by all. Edward and Lorna Bunyard in *The Epicure's Companion** describe them as being 'too pasty' for their tastes.

* Published by J. M. Dent & Sons Ltd. in 1937.

PESTS AND DISEASES
PESTS

*Eelworm.* Where land is infested with this pest it should be rested from potatoes for four years, so that the eelworms will have nothing on which to feed and will die out. Where they attack the potato, the foliage turns yellow and looks sickly. There is no known cure other than to rest the land.

DISEASES

*Blight.* This is a most dangerous disease if it is allowed to take hold. The foliage is covered in brown spots which not only destroy the foliage but also the tubers. It is easily prevented by spraying the foliage once every fortnight from 1 July with Bordeaux Mixture.

*Scab.* This often makes its presence felt where land is of a chalky nature or where the soil has been treated with lime. The tubers become infected with ugly scabs, but whilst of no use for marketing or for exhibition, may be cooked and eaten. The only means of guarding against the trouble, should it become prevalent, is to plant no potatoes for four years in the same ground.

PRUNING, *see* Fruit Trees, Pruning

PUMPKIN, *see* Marrow

QUINCE

It requires a moist, heavy soil when it will live to a great age, requiring little attention and growing dwarf and twisted. But the fruit will only ripen well in a warm garden.

It is propagated by stools or suckers which are removed from around the plant with a sharp spade and grown on as standards, planting about 18 ft. apart in a sunny position. Apart from the removal of dead wood, it will require little pruning over the years, but will appreciate a yearly mulch of decayed manure and humus such as clearings from ditches.

The highly flavoured fruit is gathered at the end of October when quite dry and stored on a layer of cotton wool in a dry, frost free room until fully ripened, the flesh then being deep golden-yellow. If carefully stored, they will keep until Christmas.

VARIETIES

MEECH'S PROLIFIC. An American variety, noted for its earliness and regular cropping, the smooth-skinned fruit ripening to pale yellow and of delicious flavour.

PORTUGAL. The best for all purposes, bearing heavily, the large oblong fruits ripening early and to deep orange whilst the flavour is outstanding. Introduced to Lord Burghley's garden in 1610 by John Tradescant.

# RADISH

A salad is enhanced by the appearance of sparkling red radishes, but it was as hors d'oeuvre that they were most used in Tudor days, 'as a stimulent before meat, giving an appetite thereunto'. We are also told that 'gardeners (of the time) used great fences of reeds tied together, which seemeth to be like a mat upright, to defend them (radishes) from the cold winds and to bring them forward the earlier'. The radish still receives attention from the market grower, an early crop being sown on a gentle hotbed in a frame in March, or from the month end onwards, and at regular intervals throughout summer. Those large, coarse roots often sold in shops, which are hot and bitter when eaten, and often quite stringy and difficult to digest, have been allowed to remain too long in the beds so that they will become large enough to catch the public's eye. When in bunches, and to have them sweet and succulent, the turnip-rooted varieties should be no larger than a five penny piece, and those of tapering form being no thicker than the little finger. Gathered in this condition they will be juicy and nut-like. But they must be grown quickly. A radish – no matter what its size and shape – will be hard, bitter, and stringy if it takes too long to mature.

They are best sown broadcast in a raised bed. This should be made up during winter, with quantities of humus incorporated so that, if the summer is warm and dry, the plants will not lack moisture. Old mushroom-bed compost is ideal for radishes, but a mixture of peat and well-decayed farmyard manure is equally valuable. Work in deeply, then allow the soil to become pulverised by frost. In March the bed should be raked to a fine tilth and all stones removed. The seed is sown thinly and as soon as the soil is friable, being merely raked in. Never at any time must the seed be allowed to lack moisture.

Seed may be sown on a hotbed during February, the roots being ready for gathering in about five weeks. Both home and commercial growers should sow at regular intervals so as to keep up a continuous supply.

**VARIETIES**

**FOR FORCING**

SAXA. A radish of rapid maturity, making a round brilliant scarlet root. The flesh is crisp and white.

WOOD'S EARLY FRAME. For those who prefer a long radish. It produces a long carmine-pink root.

**FOR OUTDOORS**

CHERRY BELLE. Useful both outdoors and for forcing, it matures early and forms a round cherry-like root of brilliant cherry-red, with crisp, white flesh.

FRENCH BREAKFAST. A market favourite, it forms a long cylindrical root of brilliant red, tipped white, striking when bunched. The flesh is white and full of flavour.

ICICLE. It forms a long tapering root of ivory-white and is deliciously sweet.

SCARLET GLOBE. It makes a large, round root of deepest scarlet, with crisp white flesh which is mild and sweet.

SPARKLER. Forming a round cherry-like root, half scarlet, half white with crisp, sweet flesh, it matures in three weeks from sowing.

**FOR WINTER USE**

BLACK WINTER. Few have heard of it let alone grown it, although it was a vegetable well known to Tudor and Stuart gardeners. Parkinson (see footnote on page 60) describes its qualities and sums up its culture when he says, 'the Black Radishes are most used in the winter and must be sown after mid-summer; if sown earlier they would run up to stalk and seed'. They do, and sowing should take place towards the end of July, the seed being sown in drills 12 in. apart in a soil which has been well manured for a previous crop.

It makes a round root almost like a small turnip, and is black-skinned, the flesh being white and succulent if grown well, in no way stringy. Sliced or grated into a salad, the flesh has a distinct nutty flavour, without any of that fieriness found so often in summer radishes.

The seedlings should be thinned out to 6 in. apart in the rows, kept free of weeds, and well watered through summer. Late October the roots are lifted and stored in dry sand in a cellar or cool shed, to be used in winter. They are delicious as hors d'oeuvre, sliced and served with salad oil. Seed is readily obtained and costs only a few pence per ounce. There is also a long form, also quite black, and also grown by Tudor gardeners. It requires the same culture, but if the soil is heavy or stony it is not as satisfactory as the round variety.

China Rose. Those who are put off from growing a winter radish by the appearance of the black variety should try China Rose. It requires the same culture, the seed being sown in July in drills, and lifted and stored in the same way. It is like a large French Breakfast, of blunt tubular form, thickening towards the base. The colour is vivid cerise-red with the flesh white, cool and crisp. It is most attractive sliced with the black radish and used in hors d'oeuvre or salads. It is also delicious for winter sandwiches served with land cress, or with cheese and brown bread.

## RAMPION

It is *Campanula rapunculus*, which grows nearly 3 ft. tall and is a biennial. Seed is sown in early summer for the plants to bloom the following year. It is an attractive plant for the flower border, its leaves being glossy, whilst it bears small bell-shaped flowers of clearest blue. Its leaves are pleasant in salads or in stews, and its roots may also be boiled, or grated and used raw in salads. If required to be cooked, the plants are lifted in autumn and kept in boxes of sand to use through winter.

## RASPBERRY

The raspberry has a shorter season than the strawberry, but crops heavily for the amount of ground it occupies, and has a flavour all its own. It enjoys a soil which is capable of retaining moisture and, unlike the strawberry, which will crop well in a light soil provided that the potash content is satisfactory, the raspberry prefers a heavy loam, able to hold moisture throughout summer. Raspberries will produce little new cane and a poor seedy sample of fruit in too dry a soil. One of the most profitable plantations in England is situated along the banks of a stream.

Before planting time, as much decayed compost as can be obtained should be worked into the soil. Pig, poultry and farmyard manure is ideal, and this can be augmented by a quantity of decayed straw or garden refuse. Bracken treated with an activator, to which has been added poultry or pig manure, will make an ideal compost. Work in as much humus as possible, for it must be remembered that the plants have to produce not only a heavy crop of fruit, but also an abundance of new cane to provide for next season's crop. This calls for a soil rich in nitrogenous humus. Care must also be taken to select a frost-free position, especially for those varieties which tend to suffer in this way. Malling Promise is a variety that seems prone to frost attack, whereas Newburgh is resistant. Indeed the raspberry may quite easily be grown in a frosty area where strawberries are known to suffer badly, provided that the later-flowering (and fruiting) varieties are grown. Here, Norfolk Giant,

Newburgh and Malling Jewel are suitable. Raspberries will benefit from a light application of sulphate of potash after planting, but do not require such concentrated amounts as the strawberry or gooseberry; bonfire ashes raked into the prepared bed should be sufficient in most soils.

### PLANTING

Plant when the soil is in a friable condition. If sticky, heel in the canes and protect with straw until conditions improve. Always purchase clean stock certified by the Ministry of Agriculture as being free from the 'mosaic' virus disease. A raspberry cane will produce a profitable crop for at least twelve years if clean stock is obtained and soil conditions are to its liking. Norfolk Giant and Newburgh, both highly-resistant to frost damage, are equally immune to virus attacks.

The canes should be planted about 18 in. apart in the rows, depending on the vigour of the variety. Malling Promise, which is particularly vigorous, should be allowed an extra 6 in., and as much as 6 ft. should be allowed between the rows, with an extra 1 ft. for the vigorous varieties.

Plant neither too shallow nor too deep. The latter is a common failure when planting raspberries, for many rely on deep planting to support the cane. Two in. below the surface of the soil is the required depth. Deeper than 3 in. may mean that new growth is never seen; the old gardeners certainly knew what they were talking about in this matter. The same rules apply to blackberries too.

When the canes have been planted and made firm, they should be cut back to 12 in. from soil level. This is to encourage vigorous new shoots to appear during the first season. Those who believe they can obtain a fruit crop the first summer and still build up a strong plant will be disappointed.

### STAKING AND TYING

Staking need not be done until the new shoots are appearing and have reached 18 in. in height, which will be about June, following autumn planting. Possibly the best time for the work would be April, so as to relieve the busy picking and hoeing season of May to August. There are numerous methods of staking raspberries:

(a) The canes are tied to 6 ft. posts, which are made doubly secure by fastening a length of strong wire to the top of each post along the row. The canes should be planted one on either side of a post, and spaced about 3 ft. apart to enable cultivation to be done with a mechanical hoe – not only up the rows, but also between the posts, thereby reducing hand hoeing to a minimum.

(b) The canes are fastened to a series of wires with posts placed at intervals of about 7–8 ft. The wires will provide additional strength and a saving of posts will be achieved.

(c) The wires may be run down either side of the canes to form a 'box'. This method is very common, but unless particularly well made, with very stout wire, the canes will come out of the 'box'. Again, at least 6–7 ft. posts will be needed, with the wire taken down the rows at 12 in. intervals almost to the top of the stakes. Where shorter stakes are used and the wire is not taken right to the top, many of the taller canes may be badly broken during a spell of windy weather.

(d) There is also the rope method. Here the canes are fastened together in arches, held in position by strong stakes. By this method it is not necessary to fasten the individual canes to the wires, and there is less fear of breakage by wind. It has been found that bending the canes partially checks the flow of sap to their tops, and thus ensures even ripening and swelling of the fruit right down the canes.

Where canes are being planted against a wall or wattle-hurdles, they may be held in place by wires fastened at intervals. Correct staking and tying is the most important part of raspberry culture; badly staked rows mean not only broken canes but make cultivation and picking difficult.

MULCHING

During the summer the canes will benefit from a monthly mulch, first given in early June. This will keep the roots cool and will help the soil to retain the moisture content necessary for the production of a large, juicy berry, and the formation of the necessary new growth. Raspberries detest a light dry soil, and although liberal amounts of compost will greatly help in this respect, it is only half the battle. A regular summer mulch will complete operations. Lawn mowings are ideal and a quantity of granulated peat placed down the rows in late May will prove greatly beneficial. Where there are no grass mowings, partially composted straw or well-rotted farmyard manure will be equally good. Provided that plenty of manure has been used in the preparation of the soil, peat and grass mowings are most useful, as they can more easily be worked into the soil.

PRUNING

In October, after fruiting has ended, the old wood which has borne a crop of fruit the past summer should be cut out at ground level. If too much of the old wood is allowed to remain, it will only tend to introduce disease. The new season's shoots should be carefully tied to the wire, if this has not already been done, and all weak growth cut out, leaving about six to eight new canes to each 'stool', depending upon the vigour of the variety. Weeds should be removed from the rows and the summer mulches forked in, taking care not to fork too near the stools. A dressing of well-rotted manure round the base of the canes will complete the work. All wood cut out must be burnt immediately.

FIG. 12 *Cutting out the old canes*

The season of fruiting will also play its part in pruning operations. Where autumn fruit is desired, the canes should be cut back to within 6 in. of the ground in early March, as autumn-fruiting varieties bear their fruit on the new summer's growth and not on the canes formed during the previous year. They will need liberal applications of farmyard manure to form the fruit by autumn. Commencing with the early Malling Promise, and ending with the extremely late November Abundance, it is possible to obtain a succession of fruit over a period of five months.

PROPAGATION OF CANES

For those wishing to increase their stock for the home garden on only a small scale, it will be possible to obtain the necessary canes from the fruiting plantation by lifting the stools where they are thick in the row. The canes are divided by pulling them apart from the stool. Only canes of completely healthy appearance should be used; any canes showing blight, wilt or virus must be left entirely alone. Nor should new plantations be made where old canes have previously been fruiting for several years – this applies to all soft fruits, especially strawberries and raspberries. Where canes are required for sale a different method of propagation is used, for it is impossible to grow both for fruit and for canes, except where growing on a considerable scale. Where a profusion of canes is required, stool beds are planted. No staking is done and the canes are set out 12 in. apart, in rows 3 ft. apart. To encourage an abundance of new growth the canes are cut back frequently. They should be mulched in the normal way throughout the summer. When being dispatched for sale, they must on no account be allowed to suffer from drying winds; they must be taken under cover as soon as lifted and counted, and tied up in sacking at the earliest possible moment.

# Raspberry

**EARLY VARIETIES**

LLOYD GEORGE. When first introduced, it was the best of all raspberries; as important to the raspberry-grower as Royal Sovereign was to the strawberry-grower. But, like that grand variety, it suffered from every conceivable disease, until it became necessary to introduce New Zealand stock into Great Britain. The new stock – free of virus and extremely vigorous – has again allowed it, if not now standing supreme, to produce a heavy crop of top-class fruit. Though the flavour of the fruit is not equal to that of Malling Exploit, it is of a good, even size, firm and of a bright red colour.

MALLING EXPLOIT. A variety for the garden, and popular with the Scottish growers on account of its suitability for jam making and freezing. Early fruiting, it produces plenty of cane, and in gardens is best grown up wires against a wall. In the north it has proved a heavier yielder than Malling Jewel, and its flavour is first-rate; equally important, the fruits remain vivid scarlet for a considerable time after picking, and do not become soft. They are also large, and suitable for growers of dessert raspberries for sale in punnets.

MALLING JEWEL. This would be first choice for early fruiting in a frosty district, because the blooms open later than those of the other earlies. It makes a tall, smooth, upright cane, which turns an attractive purple in late August. The large, conical fruits, abundantly produced, are rich-crimson and pleasantly sweet, but without aromatic flavour. Besides being a heavy bearer, it is excellent for freezing and canning.

MALLING PROMISE. This was the first of the many excellent varieties from East Malling, introduced by Norman Grubb in 1946. It has Newburgh for a parent and is, with Royal Scot, the first to ripen its fruit. It bears a heavy crop of huge, conical berries, which tend to become soft, especially in a rainy season, so they are used for dessert rather than for processing. This variety is popular in Scotland, although the canes are apt to suffer slight damage during a prolonged period of severe frost.

RED CROSS. This drought-resisting variety was introduced by George Pyne of Topsham, Devon. It is extremely resistant to disease, and is a vigorous and heavy cropper of large, juicy fruit. One of the best varieties yet raised, but it is now difficult to obtain completely virus-free stocks.

ROYAL SCOT. One of the best of all raspberries, introduced from Scotland, and having strong cane growth. The first raspberry of all to ripen, it carries its berries evenly along the small branches, so they are easy to pick. They 'plug' well and remain firm on the canes for some time, even in wet weather. The fruit is large, deep salmon-red when ripe, and has a delicious flavour. For the garden this variety is outstanding, but the commercial grower prefers one which, like Malling Notable, will ripen all its fruit together and can be cleared from a plantation in three pickings; Royal Scot requires six.

# *Raspberry*

MALLING ENTERPRISE. Sister to Malling Jewel and a valuable variety, although it will not make new cane growth unless it is grown in a heavy loam containing plenty of moisture-holding humus. On heavy land and in frosty areas it is the best of all varieties. The canes are smooth and turn a rich crimson in early autumn; the berries are large, firm and sweet.

MALLING NOTABLE. Extending its fruiting into mid-season, Malling Notable follows closely on the heels of Malling Jewel, but is not so good. Cane growth is not strong, and the canes have a habit of bending over. The fruit is large, juicy, of a dull crimson colour and 'plugs' easily. It is not such a heavy a cropper as Malling Jewel, although the fruit is outstanding in quality. Not suitable for the amateur's garden, because all its fruit is ready at once.

MILTON. A top-class, mid-season raspberry for the amateur, raised at the Geneva (New York) Experimental Station. It crops well during a wet season. It bears a large berry which ripens to a deep pink and hangs well, and does not become soft and sticky in wet weather, or when fully ripe. It produces plenty of cane and an abundance of sweetly aromatic fruit; it is a lovely berry for eating from the cane.

NEWBURGH. An American introduction which enjoys the damp conditions of the West. In certain districts of the south-east its vigour has been reduced by cane midge, but where this is not prevalent and clean stocks can be obtained it is an outstanding variety, favoured by exhibitors on account of its huge fruits which 'plug' easily and remain dry for some time; indeed, it is apt to be rather too dry and tends to crumble. West of the Pennines, it yields better than any other variety.

PYNE'S ROYAL. Raised at Messrs Pyne's Nurseries in 1907, this variety has withstood the test of time and must be the oldest still in commerce. It bears a magnificent crop, and is a grand sight, the fruit is sweet, large and juicy, and makes wonderful jam. A fine exhibition raspberry, as with the new Malling introductions and Newburgh. If it has a fault, it is its shyness at producing new cane growth.

ST WALFRIED. A Dutch introduction, and a good one. It is an August-fruiting variety, bearing quite unique, long-shaped fruit of vivid red colour, and very juicy. It 'plugs' well, remains firm when picked, and is now a recognised commercial raspberry.

TAYLOR. Well suited to a heavy loam and, like Newburgh, of American origin. The canes grow tall, are light brown in colour, and are completely free of prickles, so the fruit is easily picked and the canes can be fastened to the wires without trouble. The fruits are large, pleasantly aromatic and not too sweet. Like the American Red Rich autumn strawberry, the fresh acid flavour is a pleasant change from those of the sweet varieties raised in Britain.

LATE VARIETIES

MALLING LANDMARK. This is the latest summer variety, fruiting later than Norfolk Giant, and although useful in this respect the vigour of the plant and the quality of the fruit are nothing like so outstanding as the earlier-fruiting Malling varieties. The fruit is soft and difficult to plug, but is of good flavour.

NORFOLK GIANT. Not only is this long-established variety valuable for its immunity from disease, but also it opens its flower late and so escapes damage in the most frosty areas. Fruiting late, it is also useful for carrying on until the autumn varieties are ready. It is the best raspberry for bottling, canning and quick-freezing, and although, as a dessert fruit for garden cultivation, it leaves much to be desired, its other useful qualities will ensure its value for many years.

YELLOW VARIETIES

There are a number of yellow-fruiting varieties which should be grown on a small scale in the garden for providing fruit for the house. The two best varieties given here are good for bottling, make delicious jam, and possess a delicate flavour for dessert.

AMBER QUEEN. This delightful raspberry was raised by Mr Harraway of Warminster, Wiltshire, and is most distinctive. The canes are strong and abundantly produced; the fruit is large, juicy and of a most attractive shade of orange-yellow, tinted red.

YELLOW ANTWERP. This is perhaps the best pure yellow variety, the large berries being rich, golden yellow, very sweet and juicy. It is a heavy and reliable cropper.

AUTUMN-FRUITING VARIETIES

These are a most useful group, producing fruit on the new season's cane, which should be cut down early in spring. The varieties follow the late summer-fruiting raspberries, and in favourable districts will bear until the frosts.

HAILSHAM. An old favourite, hardy, vigorous and free cropping. The rich crimson fruit is deliciously flavoured and ready for eating in October.

LORD LAMBOURNE. The berries are of a rich golden-apricot colour, borne in great profusion, and the foliage of the canes is bottle-green, making a most wonderful sight in late October.

NOVEMBER ABUNDANCE. The latest of raspberries, often cropping until early December. It is one of the few to hold an Award of Merit, and bears rich red fruit of excellent flavour.

ZEVA. A Swiss introduction, it crops from late summer until November, and makes sufficiently sturdy cane growth that it may be grown without support. It bears heavily, making a large berry 1 in. long, dark red in colour, and of delicious flavour.

This is a hybrid raspberry and is a fruit of great interest. The canes grow in clusters from the rootstock, like a blackcurrant, but the habit is compact, making it an ideal fruit for a small garden. It may be planted against a low wall or in the border. The plant should be treated as a raspberry, cutting back the canes to 8 in. of ground level after planting in November, and eliminating the old canes after fruiting.

The fruit is similar to a raspberry in appearance, but grows more like a mulberry when fully ripe and possesses much of the mulberry flavour. The fruit is borne, like that of the blackberry, in long, arching sprays, which ripen from late in July until early October and are delicious for tarts and jam making.

## REDCURRANT

The most satisfactory way of growing this crop is in double cordon formation, planted against a wall where the fruit can be protected by netting draped from hooks. The plants will remain in bearing for twenty years or so, and will be little troubled by pest or disease, although birds remain a constant worry to the large grower, often as much as half the crop being taken as the berries are reaching maturity. Small pieces of tin foil fastened to canes and placed at regular intervals about the bushes will be of help in scaring off the birds, and fish netting should be used for covering wherever possible. It is also advisable to pick the fruit the moment that it is ripe. To delay a single day will be to lose a large amount to birds. The red currant has not so long a season as the blackcurrant, nor can it hold its fruit as well, and adverse weather when the crop is ready for picking may also cause considerable losses.

### PRUNING AND PROPAGATION

Little pruning is required, for the fruit is borne on the old as well as on the new wood but, as with gooseberries, unduly old and all decayed wood must be cut away to prevent the bush from becoming overcrowded and to maintain its health. Upon planting, all shoots must be cut back to a bud about 3 in. from their base, and this will form the main stem. This should be done during early April, and the following year the new shoots should also be cut back to a bud within 3 in. of the point at which the shoots were formed. Such action will build up a shapely plant and encourage the formation of a good head. Afterwards, the occasional shortening back of an unduly vigorous shoot or the removal of old or overcrowded wood is all that is necessary.

The cordon is formed by growing on the main stem or shoot and cutting back all side shoots, whilst the double cordon is formed by cutting back the main stem to a bud about 8 in. above soil level. Two buds, one on either side of the stem, are trained in an outward direction as described for gooseberry cordons. Cordons against a wall, or alongside a path, should be planted 2 ft. apart and securely fastened to strong wires, whilst double cordons are allowed about 3 ft. 6 in.

FIG. 13 *Pruning a red currant*

To increase the stock, 15 in. shoots of the new season's wood should be removed early in October and, as the plants are grown on a leg, all except the upper four buds should be removed. The shoots are then inserted 3 in. deep and 6 in. apart into a trench of peat and sand, and made quite firm to encourage rapid rooting. Like gooseberries, red currants are slower to root than blackcurrants, and they should be given assistance by inserting the rooting end of the cuttings in hormone powder. The shoot is allowed to remain in the row for either one or two years, after which it is planted in its permanent quarters and the head formed as described.

SOIL REQUIREMENTS

Both red and white currants enjoy the same manurial conditions as the gooseberry, and they should always be planted near each other if both crops are required. The plants must be given a deeply-dug soil which, preferably, should be of a light nature. It must be free from perennial weeds and should contain some humus. This need not be of such a heavy nitrogenous nature as for blackcurrants, for an excess of nitrogen will encourage an excess of plant growth to the detriment of fruit.

A balance between fruit production and plant growth should be maintained. Like gooseberries, these currants enjoy plenty of potash in the soil, given in the form of wood ash which has been stored dry. This is raked into the top soil after planting, and again each spring. Where growing commercially give each plant a 2 oz. dressing of sulphate of potash in April and harrow or rake it into the soil. To supply humus, work in seaweed, hop manure, decayed leaves and garden compost, or peat, possibly augmented with some shoddy or farmyard manure. Both red and white currants like humus, and where this is lacking the fruit will remain small, seedy and devoid of juice, neither will the plants make much new growth. It is vital to provide the plants with plenty of humus where growing against a wall, in which position a shortage of moisture often causes failure to crop well. Like all soft fruits, red and white currants appreciate an early summer mulch of strawy manure, seaweed or peat which will help to maintain moisture in the soil.

PLANTING

Planting may take place at any time during the winter months, but preferably between October and December, which will allow the plants time to settle down before frosts. Being of compact habit, with the possible exception of Laxton's No 1, the plants may be set out 3–4 ft. apart each way, allowing 5 ft. for Laxton's. Before planting, any roots should be removed which may have formed on the leg, otherwise these are liable to form suckers, which must be removed with a sharp knife.

With red and white currants it is important to select a sheltered position, for they detest cold winds almost as much as blackcurrants. Nor only will a strong wind cause bud dropping, but it will also damage the plants by breaking off the brittle wood. For this reason these currants always crop better in the warmer districts of the south, or in a walled garden. Where the garden or ground is exposed, then grow gooseberries instead, or the hardier Fay's Prolific or Red Lake.

Where growing only a few plants, a weekly application of liquid manure, as for dessert gooseberries, will make a great difference in the fruit, almost doubling the size, but as with gooseberries commence this feeding as soon as the fruit begins to set, otherwise if left until the berries are swelling the additional moisture may cause the skin to burst.

Used as fresh fruit, red and white currants in combination make a pleasing decoration, and with their rich fragrance and rather tart flavour they will greatly improve a dish of raspberries, in the same way as the acid Red Rich strawberry improves the particularly sweet varieties.

# Redcurrant

EARLIEST OF FOURLANDS. Introduced by Messrs Bath's of Wisbech, this follows Laxton's No 1 by a few days. Bud burst is early, so it should be confined to a sheltered garden. It makes a large bush, but the habit is upright and compact. It bears a long truss and large scarlet fruit.

FAY'S PROLIFIC. An American variety raised in New York State in 1865. It is a valuable currant for a northern garden in that it comes late into bloom. It also makes a small, compact bush and fruits freely.

LAXTON'S No 1. The report of the National Fruit Trials (1920–50) sums up the growing of red currants with this remark: 'Laxton's No 1 is un-doubtedly the outstanding red currant for commercial purposes.' Also 'for all purposes'. It is a strong grower, a reliable cropper in all districts, and is the first red currant on the market. The berries are firm and of a good rich colour, although not so large as those of Red Lake.

## MID-SEASON VARIETIES

HOUGHTON CASTLE. Raised at Houghton Castle, Hexham, and in-troduced in 1920. Bud burst is late, and so it is a useful variety for a northern garden. It makes a large, spreading bush and crops heavily, the big, deep-crimson fruit being richly flavoured.

LAXTONS PERFECTION. Only in the moist climate of the South West and in a sheltered garden does this variety, introduced by Laxton Bros in 1910, give of its best. It makes a tall, upright bush, the fruit trusses being long and heavily-laden with bright red berries of exhibition quality. It may be described as a late mid-season variety, as it retains its fruit well into August.

RED LAKE. Introduced into Britain from the Minnesota Experimental Station, it has gained an Award of Merit. It makes a neat, compact bush of upright habit, and may be classed as an early mid-season variety. The fruit is borne in long trusses, the berries being of dessert quality, large, bright scarlet and juicy, with a glossy, tough skin. The fruit stands up to adverse weather and will transport long distances. If only one variety is to be grown, this should be it.

## LATE VARIETIES

RABY CASTLE. Raised in Northumberland, like Houghton Castle, it is useful for a northern garden in that it blooms late. It makes a small, neat bush and bears a heavy crop, but the fruit is small unless grown well.

WILSON'S LONG BUNCH. The latest of all, hence its value in prolonging the season, but a good, late red currant is badly needed. It forms a bush of very spreading habit, but it is late into bloom and misses all frosts. The pale, cerise-pink berries are borne in long trusses, hence its name.

# RHUBARB

With its ability to produce a large quantity of fruit over a long period and from only a very small space, no amateur's garden should be without its supply of roots. They may be lifted and forced in a greenhouse or cellar to provide an early New-Year crop, or covered and semi-forced for a spring crop, to be followed by fruit for early summer use pulled from naturally-grown roots. Rhubarb will be indispensable for the first six months of the year, and for the market grower there is always a ready sale for forced rhubarb sold locally.

## SOIL AND CULTIVATION

Before the young roots are planted the land must be well cultivated. A heavy loam, well-drained and yet moist, is the ideal, although where considerable quantities of manure and compost are available, rhubarb may be grown on almost any soil. But a deeply-cultivated, well-manured soil will encourage a heavy crop of thick, succulent stems. Deep trenching, and at the same time working in as much farmyard manure or home-made compost as possible, will provide the required humus. Old mushroom-bed manure is also ideal, as it is for all other soft fruit crops.

Peat is also useful for working into the soil, but this should be supplemented with manure or shoddy. Remember that the larger the leaf the more vigorous will be the crown the following season, so everything must be done to encourage as much leaf growth as possible – and this means heavy nitrogenous manuring.

Rhubarb also loves bone meal and 4 oz. per sq. yd. applied when the land is made ready will be greatly beneficial. Should the land be heavy, the same quantity of basic slag should be substituted for the bone meal, and a 1 oz. per sq. yd. dressing of sulphate of potash every other spring will not be found excessive. Very early varieties, which are to be covered in the open, will respond to a 2 oz. per sq. yd. application of sodium nitrate as soon as the new growth appears. Rhubarb will also appreciate 4 cwt. of lime per acre, applied each winter.

All weeds must be removed before the roots are planted out, but the soil should first be allowed to settle down for several days. The earlier, less-vigorous varieties are planted out in rows 3 ft. apart each way, and the later varieties should be allowed an extra 6 in. each way. This distance will allow the roots to reach a good size, and allow room for covering and pulling. For the first season, lettuce or strawberries may be planted between the rows, but where the strawberry is to be allowed to crop a second season, the rhubarb roots should be allowed an extra 6 in. between the rows.

The roots should be set out when the soil is friable. They must be firmly trodden in, and the soil should be brought up to the level of the crown bud.

PLANTING

The young crowns or eyes, or roots, as they are variously called in different localities, are planted out during winter. November and early December is the best time, for this allows the roots to become established before the frosty weather, so that they will produce a number of stems during the first summer. If it is proposed to commence rhubarb growing in this way, the roots may be purchased as offsets containing a bud with a piece of root attached. If few or no stalks are removed during the first season, the roots will have made plenty of growth by the following summer, and will be sturdy enough to be semi-forced, or forced in heat the subsequent winter. Where growing for sale it will perhaps be better to concentrate on two varieties, an early and a mid-season, both of which may be forced to extend the season. When required for home use only, then a single root of several varieties may be grown.

Where it is intended to force the roots, no stems should be removed for two years. Provided applications of fertilisers, manure and peat mulches have been given each winter and spring to build up a sturdy root, the third season will show a good-sized clump, which may then be semi- or cold-forced in early spring, or forced in heat the following winter.

METHODS OF FORCING

Those without heat may grow rhubarb of the same quality as that grown in heat, and in view of the high costs of fuel, cold-forcing is more economical. One method is to force alternate rows in alternate years by removing the crowns in late February, dressing with a mulch of manure and covering each with an earthenware pot or even a small tea chest. Between the pots or chests, straw is heaped to help retain the sun's warmth. Wattle hurdles are erected to keep off cold winds, and as much brushwood as can be found is placed inside the hurdling for additional protection. The plantation is given no further attention apart from the removal of the straw as soon as new growth is observed, and a dressing of sodium nitrate is applied at the rate of $\frac{1}{2}$ oz. per sq. yd. The straw is then replaced and left until the stems are seen to be pushing up the chest and pot lids, when they will be found ready for pulling and bunching. This early rhubarb will be a rich, pink colour, and although it is several weeks later than heat-forced rhubarb, it will be in equal demand by the housewife who is more rhubarb-minded in late spring and early summer than during the winter days, when boiled puddings tend to dominate the table.

Rhubarb may be cold-forced in a number of other ways. Where it is intended to use lights, the roots are planted in beds rather than in rows. This will mean planting them closer, and leaving a path between each bed. Turf may be placed around the beds to add warmth, and to raise the glass so that the stems are allowed to develop to their correct length. Old bricks or stones are suitable but are less warm. The lights are placed over the beds, which are given exactly the same treatment as previously described. To keep off bright light and to conserve as much warmth as possible, straw and sacks should be placed over the lights and held down by lengths of wood.

When it is intended to force the roots in a building, a cellar or stable is ideal. A quantity of hot, well-rotted compost must be available to stimulate growth. This may be prepared by rotting straw with an activator such as Adco 'M', and additional heat can be gained by adding to the compost a small quantity of dry poultry manure, some oak and beech leaves, and any available farmyard manure. The whole is turned several times until it reaches a thoroughly decomposed condition and is generating a large amount of heat. The compost should be ready for taking indoors during early February.

Meanwhile the roots are lifted and left exposed to the elements for two or three weeks. The more severe the weather, the more will they benefit. Early in February the compost is spread out on the floor of the room to a depth of 6 in., and several inches of soil is placed on top. Over the whole the roots are placed close together, and a quantity of peat and fine soil is then tightly firmed around the clumps, filling in all cavities. The bed is given a thorough watering and all windows are darkened to encourage the stems to grow long and straight, and to be of a good colour. The same procedure is used when the roots are forced in heat, only in this case the manure bed is generally dispensed with, the roots being taken indoors in December. It must be remembered that those roots intended for forcing should not have been pulled the previous summer. All growth must be allowed to die down in the autumn before the dead leaves are cleared away, and the roots lifted early in December to weather.

Where growing for semi-forcing in the open, if the roots are pulled only moderately and the covers removed after three to four weeks' pulling, they can be gently forced the following spring. There must however be no pulling the preceding summer, and the roots must be manured in the autumn.

Those roots forced over a hotbed or in heat should be removed as soon as all pulling has ended, and replanted in beds which have been well replenished with manure and fertiliser. There they must be left for at least eighteen months, until they have recovered from their more severe forcing. No pulling should be done until such time as they have fully recovered. Ultimately they may be forced again, but this time only cool-forced in the nursery beds.

Rhubarb is increased by division of the crowns or by seed sowing; though a true stock may only be obtained by division.

The clumps are lifted in October and November, and the roots are cut into pieces, each containing an eye or bud. A three-year clump may be divided into as many as six or more offsets.

Dust the divisions with hydrated lime to keep them as clean as possible; many growers do this when making new plantations with their own roots. The divisions are made with a sharp spade or knife, and care must be taken to handle the roots as gently as possible. Provided that the bud is undamaged, even though there is virtually no root adjoining, the plant will grow in the spring, although it may take longer to build up into a sturdy forcing clump.

The raising of plants from seed will save money but they will take three years to come into bearing. The two most reliable varieties for the reproduction of seedling fruit are Myatt's Victoria and Glaskin's Perpetual. All varieties except The Sutton – a seedless variety raised by Messrs Sutton's of Reading – bear seedpods late in summer. Unless it is desired to save the seed, these seed stems must be cut off at ground level as soon as they form, in order to direct the strength used in the formation of seeds to the roots. This is essential if forcing is contemplated.

If the seed (which must not be more than two years old) is sown in boxes in a heated greenhouse or frame in September, the seedlings can be moved to the open ground in late March; alternatively, sow seed direct into the frames in late March, or even into drills in the open ground. Provided that the seed is kept moist it will readily germinate, and the plants will be large enough to transplant by June. They should then be planted in beds 1 ft. apart. The following spring every alternate plant is removed, and planted elsewhere. The ground must be well manured and thoroughly cleaned before the seedlings are transplanted. No pulling must be done for the first two seasons, after which the roots will be ready to produce a crop, and be suitable for forcing, in their third year. Those living in the south can save much valuable time by sowing the seed in frames, or even in the open, in September. In this way almost a full year will be saved in producing a crop.

EARLY SUPERB. This is an excellent variety which received a Highly Commended award at the 1949 Royal Horticultural Society's Rhubarb

Trials. It is a heavy cropper, and reaches maturity before Royal Albert. It forces well in heat or under lights.

HAWKE'S CHAMPAGNE. Another very early variety, it bears stems of the brightest crimson and forces excellently.

PARAGON. Where soil is of a clay nature, this should do well. It bears long sticks of bright scarlet colour which have a brisk flavour when cooked.

RED SUNSHINE. A new Australian variety, very early to mature and bearing huge sticks of a rich crimson colour, sweeter than most rhubarbs. It forces well.

ROYAL ALBERT. This must be just about the best rhubarb for cool-forcing in the garden, as it is very hardy, very early and produces a stem of the brightest scarlet.

TIMPERLEY EARLY. A fine new early of Cheshire origin. It forces well and bears long, stout stems of an excellent colour when ripe.


SECOND EARLY VARIETIES

CANADA RED. A Canadian introduction excellent for cool forcing. The large stalks are a brilliant crimson colour, freely produced over a long period.

DAWE'S CHALLENGE. Of Norfolk origin, raised at Messrs Dawe's Nurseries. It follows Myatt's Linnaeus and Stott's Monarch, and as an all-round variety is unrivalled under all conditions.

MYATT'S LINNAEUS. This is a grand variety to follow the earlier rhubarb. It is an exceedingly strong grower and forces well, besides making large stems when grown in the open ground.

STOTT'S MONARCH. This fine rhubarb matures at about the same time as Linnaeus. It is a very strong grower, a heavy cropper, and the stems – which mature green in colour – are deliciously sweet with an attractive pine flavour.

SUTTON'S RED. A most handsome rhubarb which crops heavily and is perhaps the best variety for bottling and canning.


LATE-MATURING VARIETIES

DAWE'S CHAMPION. Another fine rhubarb raised by Messrs Dawe's, in Norfolk. This variety matures just before The Sutton and Victoria, and closes the gap following Stott's Monarch and Sutton's Red. It is a heavy cropper, and does well in all districts, providing the most colourful stick of all the rhubarbs.

GLASKIN'S PERPETUAL. As the name implies, this is a continuous cropper, producing green stems, shaded red. It is an excellent garden rhubarb.

MYATT'S VICTORIA. This is the last of the rhubarbs to mature, and it must be the most popular variety for open ground pulling. It is excellent for canners, as it makes a strong stem and crops heavily.

THE SUTTON. This is one of the few rhubarbs to receive an Award of Merit. It is not so late as Victoria; it forces well, and makes an immense stem of the most brilliant crimson. As it does not seed, it crops over a longer period than most varieties.

## RUE

*Ruta graveolens* could be used to advantage in the border, for it has attractive serrated leaves of a blue-green colour and bears pale yellow flowers on 20 in. stems, at which distance the plants should be set out. The leaves, eaten raw in salads, are an excellent tonic and, like Wormwood, they will keep away insects. For this reason, in olden times the leaves were used in prisons and work-houses, strewn over the floor. The leaves possess the same bitterness as those of Wormwood but have a refreshing aroma, like that of hay in the stack. Plants may be raised from seed or from cuttings, and will grow well in ordinary soil.

## SAGE

Since ancient times *Salvia officinalis*, the Common Sage, has been used in stuffing for the richer meats and game, and perhaps more dried sage is marketed than any other herb. But it is important to obtain a broad-leaf strain.

It may be readily raised from seed sown in drills during summer, but so many strains have a narrow leaf. These will be greatly inferior to the broad-leaf sage, of which there is also an attractive variegated-leaf form, and one bearing a red-tinted leaf, which is used for making cough mixture and to help a sore throat. An infusion of sage, 1 oz. of the dried leaves to 1 pint of boiling water, and taken cold, is an excellent help to the digestion and for those who suffer from anaemia. It may also be used as a hair tonic.

The plant likes a sandy soil, but being shallow-rooting it will appreciate a mulch of well-decayed manure given in autumn. To keep the plants tidy, and to prevent them from forming an excess of old wood, cut in June and again at the end of summer, and for market make up liberal sized bunches. For this purpose, and for supplying sage for packeting dry, only the broad-leaf form will be required, and a stock may generally be obtained only from cuttings. These will root quickly in frames or in the open in a sandy soil. When planting, space 2 ft. apart, for they form large bushes and require the maximum amount of sunlight and air.


## SALSIFY

Also known as the vegetable oyster, it is so called on account of its unique flavour. It is easy to grow and causes little trouble with its cooking. It is said to turn a dirty brown when cooked, but the change in colour can be prevented if it is covered in lemon juice, when it will retain its creamy colour. This will also enhance its flavour.

Salsify is consumed in large amounts in France and Italy during mid-winter and could be a regular member of the winter diet in Britain. In cooking, the roots should not be peeled, for in this way they lose flavour. First scrub them clean, then boil them with lemon juice for about an hour. Then scrub the roots again with a brush, cut into slices and serve with meat and thick gravy, or with white sauce, and it will be a great improvement on the carrot. Fried in butter after boiling, it is equally delicious, and is also very nutritious.

As the roots grow like thick pencils and about the same length, they must be given a deeply-worked soil, preferably one which has been well manured for a previous crop, for fresh or excessive manure will cause the roots to fork, like carrots. It is not particular as to soil, provided that it is well-drained, but the roots must never lack moisture. Like the parsnip, the salsify is slow-growing, so it should be sown thinly in shallow drills 16 in. apart in March, thinning out any seedlings if necessary to 6 in. apart. Keep the soil free from weeds and the roots moist, otherwise in a dry summer the plants will run to seed. Kept moist, they will continue to grow until autumn, but as the roots are perfectly hardy and the flavour is enhanced after frost, lift when required. When grown for sale the roots are fastened together in bundles of twelve.

Take great care in lifting the roots, for if broken they will 'bleed' and lose their flavour.

The best variety is the improved form of Sandwich Island Mammoth.


## SAVORY, SUMMER

An annual form, the plant being very much like thyme, and with a similar flavour. Seed is sown in spring, and the stems, which grow 12 in. tall, are removed together at the end of summer, tied into bunches and dried. It should be used in all mixed dried herbs for stuffing – for which purpose it is superior to the Winter Savory. Parkinson (see footnote on page 60) tells us that the herb may be 'boiled with peas to make pottage'. The plant likes a dry soil and a sunny position.

## SAVORY, WINTER

The perennial form, propagated from cuttings or by root division. The leaves, which are small, are dried and mixed with other herbs, and possess the refreshing pungency of thyme. It likes a sandy soil and full sun, when it will grow about 20 in. high and the same distance across. The shoots are cut in June and again late in summer to prevent the plants becoming woody. Parkinson (see footnote on page 60) tells us that when used with meat, the Winter Savory is 'effectual to expelleth the wind', for which purpose it was widely planted during Stuart times.

## SAVOY

It may be said to be the hardiest member of the cabbage family – indeed it should not be used until the New Year, after the plants have been subjected to severe frosts, when they are crisp and tender when cooked. Their crinkled and deeply-veined leaves enable the winter rains to drain away so that, unlike the winter cabbage, the hearts never become soggy.

The savoy requires the same culture as the winter cabbage, a rich soil, well-limed and not lacking in humus. The seed is sown at the end of April, the plants being transplanted towards the end of May, preferably when the ground is moist. Plant 18 in. apart each way, and keep the surface of the soil well broken up through summer.

VARIETIES

EARL DWARF GEM. A splendid dwarf variety, making compact, small round heads of top quality.

IRISH GIANT. A handsome late drumhead variety, making a succulent, compact head the outer leaves being deeply ravined and crinkled.

OMEGA. The last to mature, hence its value, for it will hold through the severest weather, and will be ready for use in early spring when the Brussels sprouts are finishing.

TOM THUMB. The variety to grow in a small garden, being of almost miniature habit, the heads being solid, the crinkled leaves a deep green. As it matures quickly two sowings may be made, one in March to use during December, another late in April to use in the New Year.

# SAWDUST

When organic manures were readily obtainable, sawdust was rarely used in the garden, possibly only as a winter mulch, to give protection against frost. With a scarcity of organic manures, sawdust is in greater demand. Like any other organic manure, it has to be brought into condition (composted) before it is able to provide humus. This may be done by mixing it with a quantity of dry poultry manure and moist peat, and building up the materials into a heap. This will enable considerable heat to be generated due to bacterial action, which will break down the sawdust more rapidly. Poultry keepers may use peat and sawdust on the floor of the poultry house, and as this will be already mixed it may be composted without the addition of other materials. Although sawdust in itself will have little food value, where used with peat and poultry (or farmyard) manure it will open up a heavy soil, and add valuable moisture-holding capacity to light land, thus greatly improving the fertility of the soil.

Where only limited supplies of poultry manure are available, add 14 lb. of nitro-chalk or 7 lb. sulphate of ammonia to every 1 cwt. of sawdust, making the sawdust moist before mixing, so that chemical reaction can take place. When the sawdust has been partially composted, straw, saturated with water or liquid manure, can be added, and after further composting the materials will be in a suitable condition to dig into the soil. It should be said that sawdust obtained from hardwood trees will take longer to compost than from soft woods, but being free from resin, will be of better quality to use on the land.

# SCARLET RUNNERS, *see* Beans, Runner

# SCORZONERA

It was Louis XIV who suffered so much from indigestion that he ordered this root to be grown in large quantities in the Royal Gardens. For those who also suffer from this trouble, this is a useful vegetable with a flavour quite as pronounced as that of the salsify. Like that vegetable it will also 'bleed' and lose its flavour if it is carelessly lifted or cut. In the campaign for kitchen cleanliness it has fallen from the favour it enjoyed during the eighteenth century, its almost-black skin adversely affecting its good qualities. The plant requires the same culture as the salsify, a long growing season and a deep, friable soil. It may be lifted at any time during winter, or left in the ground to be used in early spring, when there is usually a shortage of vegetables.

The best variety is the Giant Russian.

# SEAKALE

Long known to English gardeners for Gerard (see footnote on page 60) tells us that he found it growing on the seashore on several parts of the Essex coast, and he goes on to mention that it will grow well in a sandy soil. Yet it remains unknown to most of our generation, and is to be found growing in few gardens. Thomas Smith in the *Profitable Culture of Vegetables*\* describes it as being 'easy to grow, simple and inexpensive to force, free from pests and diseases, and wholesome to consume'.

Like celery, it enjoys a deep, rich soil, preferably of a sandy nature but, provided that it is friable, almost any soil will do. Again like celery, the more robust the stems are the more tender it will be, so the aim must be to grow it well. Being a maritime plant, it is always at its best growing in the salt-laden atmosphere of the coast. It must be given salt, generally in the form of kainit, which should be worked into the soil when the beds are being prepared in autumn. Give 2 oz. per sq. yd., and as much manure and humus materials as possible, for although seakale enjoys a sandy soil it must have ample supplies of humus to maintain moisture. At planting time, 2 oz. per sq. yd. of superphosphate should also be raked in.

Taking more than 2 years to mature from seed, seakale is almost always grown from thongs which are sent out by specialist growers in early March, tied in bundles. These thongs are removed from the main root before it is forced, the top of each being cut level, the bottom slanting, so that the bundles can be made up with each thong in the same direction. As the first roots are generally forced about the end of November, any thongs which have been removed should be bundled and placed in slightly damp sand, away from frost, where they remain until used in March. Thus having once formed a bed, it should not be necessary to have to purchase more thongs.

PREPARING THE SOIL

The bed should be 5 ft. wide, to allow for hand weeding and lifting without damaging the plants. A slightly-raised bed will prevent excess moisture standing about the roots during periods of heavy rain. Then as soon as the soil has lost all traces of frost towards the end of March, the thongs are planted with the straight end upwards. Space them 16 in. apart in the rows, with the top about 1 in. below soil level. Keep the hoe moving throughout summer, and never allow the plants to lack moisture. A peat mulch between the rows will be appreciated, and will suppress weeds, whilst an application of manure water once each week will help to build up a thick, sturdy root.

Towards the end of October the foliage will be found to be dying

\* Published by Longmans Green, 1911.

down, and it should be removed. The roots are then lifted and trimmed, and stored in damp sand in a shed or cellar, to be used for forcing when required.

FORCING THE ROOTS

Provided that complete darkness is maintained the roots may be forced almost anywhere, in deep boxes in a cellar or shed, in the manner described for chicory, or in the open where indoor space is limited. Another method is to make up a small 'pit' against a garage wall which provides some shelter. On three sides, 3 ft. wide corrugated sheets are let into the ground to a depth of 8 in., and held in place with stakes. A small hotbed is then made up to a depth of 12 in. Over this is placed 6 in. of fine soil, into which the roots are planted 4 in. apart, with the crowns level with the surface. They are watered in, straw is placed over the top, and heavy sacking and corrugated sheeting is placed over the bed (held on stout stakes) to maintain absolute darkness. Where there is a dark shed or outbuilding available, a similar bed could be made up indoors, where conditions would be darker and warmer. Here the corrugated sheeting would not be required, but a surround of bricks could be put in position to hold the bed together and maintain the heat in the compost.

The shoots will be ready for removing when 8 in. long, which will take from 2–4 weeks, depending upon the temperature of the hotbed and the atmosphere. After the roots have been forced they should be destroyed, a new bed being formed from the thongs which will have been removed before the roots are forced.

Lily White and Ivory White are both similar varieties and satisfactory in every way, but whether they are tender and sweet depends upon how they are grown through the summer.

# SHALLOT

This crop presents no difficulties in its cultivation. For pickling, to provide a welcome addition to the winter meats, a small bed should be grown. The bulbs require a rich soil containing some decayed manure, the ground being prepared during winter when the surface will be broken up to a fine tilth by the frosts. In March the soil should be dressed with 2 oz. per sq. yd. of potash, and rolled to ensure a firm bed.

The shallots are set out as soon as the soil is right, sometime in March, the small bulbs being pressed into the surface, in no way covering the bulbs. Plant 9 in. apart each way, and all the attention necessary is to keep the bed free from weeds and the surface stirred up, so that air and moisture can reach the roots.

Towards the end of August the necks should be bent over to encourage ripening, the clusters of small bulbs being lifted and dried at the end of September. To bring out the maximum amount of flavour they should be stored in a dry room for a month, but no longer, before being pickled.

The best variety is the Giant Red-Skinned. Where possible use Dutch bulbs, which will have been specially grown for seed purposes, and will have enjoyed a long ripening season.

## SPAWN, MUSHROOM

The old type of mushroom spawn was collected as compressed, decomposed manure where horse droppings had collected over the years, such as in mill-tracks under cover. It was known as 'virgin' spawn, pieces being inserted into a prepared hotbed, but the crops were most unreliable. It was not until the advent of 'pure culture' spawn of a vigorous strain and made under controlled conditions that commercial mushroom growing became a profitable occupation. Mushroom spawn is obtainable in brown, cream or white varieties, the white, like white bread, being the most popular variety.

Pure culture spawn is made by washing and shedding composted horse manure and after packing into quart-size bottles, is sterilised and inoculated. As soon as it is fully impregnated, the bottles are removed to an inoculation room to impregnate growing material contained in another series of bottles. It is this second generation spawn which is marketed in either dry or moist (partially-dry) condition. Dry spawn should be used by the beginner, for it will keep indefinitely and may be used when required. Also, it will take little harm if the compost is more moist than desirable.

Spawn may be made to grow on a vegetable medium such as on tobacco stems, which are rich in nitrogen, a necessary food for growing spawn; also on grain, rye being most popular, for the grains are light and, weight for weight, there are twice as many per carton in comparison with wheat – and thus more mycelium. Grain spawn, which is moist and must be used at once, is inserted into the mushroom bed by means of a spoon, a small hole 1 in. deep being made with the fingers of one hand whilst spawn is inserted with the other.

Before using the cylinders of manure spawn, they are broken into pieces of the size of a walnut, which are inserted into the compost at intervals of 8 in. One carton of spawn is sufficient for 50 sq. ft. of mushroom bed.

# SPINACH

This plant is not a universal favourite, nor is it very successful in the garden, for the summer spinach so readily runs to seed, whilst plants of the winter variety just as readily decay should the weather be damp and foggy. But those who do appreciate the health-giving qualities of this vegetable may wish to grow it, and for summer use it is best grown from a succession of sowings, beginning with the first about mid-March. To prevent the plants from running to seed, select a position of dappled shade, and provide a humus-laden soil. The plants should be grown as coolly as possible. And, as it is required to obtain an abundance of leaf, and in the quickest possible time, work into the soil some nitrogenous manure, supplemented by a $\frac{1}{2}$ oz. per sq. yd. dressing of nitrate of soda when the plants have made some growth.

The seed is sown in shallow drills 12 in. apart, the plants being thinned to 9 in. in the rows. It is the round-leaf varieties which should be used for summer, sowings being made every three weeks until mid-July, whereafter sowings are made of the winter or prickly spinach varieties, continuing until mid-September.

So that winter spinach does not decay, seed should be sown on a raised bed, of sufficient width to take five rows, each 12 in. apart, so that picking may be done from either side of the bed.

The leaves should be gathered before they become too coarse, and as soon as the plants run to seed they should be grubbed up. Where growing commercially, the plants are cut off at soil level and packed like early summer lettuce.

### SUMMER VARIETIES

MONSTROUS VIROFLAY. Strangely named, but a most valuable round-leaf variety making a large plant. Excellent for canning and deep freeze.

NOBEL. The heaviest cropper of all the summer varieties, the leaves being large and fleshy.

### WINTER VARIETIES

HOLLANDIA. The long, deep-green leaves are arrow-shaped, and most attractive in the garden. A most prolific variety.

STANDWELL. Named for its hardiness and for an abundance of large, succulent leaves.

# SQUASH, *see* Marrow

# STRAWBERRY, ALPINE

These richly-flavoured strawberries should be in every amateur's garden. The fruit makes delicious jam and adds a special fragrance when mixed with the ordinary strawberries. Also, as they enjoy a certain amount of shade, the plants may be used for those more sunless corners about the garden where the ordinary varieties would not ripen well. Again, where space is strictly limited, for an edging to a border or for growing in pots or window boxes, the runnerless alpines (increased by division like a primrose) will prove suitable. They like a moist soil, thoroughly enriched with humus, so as much decayed manure, peat and leaf mould as possible should be worked in. The plants will then continue to fruit throughout late summer and autumn. The alpine strawberry, not to be confused with the autumn-fruiting perpetual, is *Fragaria vesca*, known to continental gardens at the beginning of the sixteenth century, and in-introduced into England two centuries later.

They were, then, at once acclaimed for the quality of their fruit, and today, although they are not widely grown commercially, they find a ready sale to top-class restaurants for mixing with the less-delicately-flavoured, late-summer strawberries. Although the fruit is small, the size may be enlarged by thinning and by liberal feeding. The main flush of fruit is obtained during July and August, but the plants continue to yield until the end of autumn.

Propagation is by division, or by runners where these are formed, but the most vigorous plants are obtained from seed. All the alpines grow readily in this way. The best method is to sow the seed in autumn in boxes containing the John Innes sowing compost. The boxes are placed in cold frames until the seedlings are planted out in early April, allowing 20 in. between the plants. They will bear well for two years, and should then be divided, or fresh plants should be raised from seed.

## VARIETIES

BARON SOLEMACHER. Forming no runners and easily raised from seed, the tall-growing plants bear most handsome, long red berries of rich flavour when ripe. If thinned and liberally fed, the fruits grow quite large.

BELLE DE MEAUX. Raised in France about 1880, this alpine forms runners. The crimson fruit is wedge-shaped, but quite small and of excellent flavour. Like all alpines the fruit should not be picked until completely ripe.

DELIGHT. This is a creamy-white form of Baron Solemacher, the fruit possessing a distinct perfume as well as being very sweet. Served with the bright red Solemacher, they make a pleasing decoration and improve the flavour of fresh dessert fruit.

# STRAWBERRY, LARGE FRUITING

The most popular fruit, for it comes quickly into bearing and, for the area of ground it occupies – about 1 sq. ft. per plant – no fruit crops more heavily.

Strawberry growing has been revolutionised by the 'Cambridge' introductions of Mr Boyes, and by those raised in Scotland by Messrs Reid and Carmichael. In pre-war days, there were three main commercial varieties: Madame Lefebvre, the earliest of the three to mature; Huxley Giant, a heavy cropper of rather coarse fruit; and Royal Sovereign, raised by Laxton Bros in 1892, which had Noble and King of the Earlies for its parents. Both parents were also raised by Thomas Laxton, the latter containing the 'blood' of the celebrated Black Prince, a wonderful variety. Of the three old favourites, Royal Sovereign has for long been troubled by virus, but is as yet unsurpassed for the quality of its fruit, whilst Huxley and Lefebvre are still grown chiefly for their hardiness and resistance to disease. But they all cropped at about the same time, which meant that there was an abundance of fruit for a period of only four weeks, and if frosts or wet weather ruined the crop, then the outlook for the strawberry grower was poor indeed.

Now all this has changed, and by growing for succession, even where no glass protection is used, there will be fruit from early May until November. This ensures not only a long period of income for the commercial grower, but also that at least a part of the crop will avoid adverse weather conditions. For the amateur, the long fruiting period will also add interest to the garden. Even greater interest may be enjoyed if a number of the alpine strawberries, and those varieties which will most satisfy the connoisseur of choice fruit, are also grown.

PREPARING THE SOIL

Strawberries like a light, loamy soil, well-supplied with humus. Such a soil warms quickly with the early spring sunshine, and is generally well drained. Neither will it become too compact with constant treading during the picking season, as will a heavy soil, and so prevent oxygen reaching the roots. Plants growing in a heavy, badly-drained soil may suffer considerable losses from Red Core root disease, especially when a wet winter is followed by a cold spring. Where the soil tends to be heavy, the three best varieties to grow, being highly-resistant to Red Core root rot, are the Cambridge introductions: Vigour, Sentry and Rival. These crop heavily in a stiff loam, whilst they may be said to be the most reliable varieties for wet districts.

A clean and well-manured soil is vital for a heavy crop. Planting into ground infested by perennial weeds, impossible to eradicate after planting, will never grow good crops. Preferably, strawberries should be planted into ground which has previously grown a crop of potatoes, for then the soil will be well pulverised and free from weeds. It is best to follow rotational cropping, allowing the land a rest for two years after every four year, or two year, crop.

But first make the ground clean, then work in some humus. This may take the form of decayed farmyard manure, and as much as twenty tons to the acre where the land is light and lacking in humus. The amateur will dig in what manures are available, material from the compost heap, straw decomposed by an activator, to which may be added either pig or poultry manure, decayed leaves, shoddy, spent hops or peat. These materials may also be used on a commercial scale. Seaweed is valuable, but everything depends upon situation, for to minimise transport expenses, humus-forming materials should be obtained as near home as possible. Those who live in the North will find shoddy, many times richer in nitrogen than farmyard manure, readily obtainable. Use it at the rate of two tons to the acre, and augment by peat and a 1 oz. per sq. yd. dressing of potash.

Strawberries must have nitrogen, phosphorus, and potash, for they absorb these minerals from the soil in almost equal quantities. Fish meal and animal manures contain all three ingredients, and they should be used where possible. If shoddy is available, then it must be augmented by bone meal, or steamed bone flour and sulphate of potash, 1 cwt. per acre, or 2 oz. per sq. yd. when planting in the garden. Remember that the lighter the soil, the more potash a plant will require. So, with a retentive loam, half the quantity may be given; and, in a sandy soil, half as much again. In place of sulphate of potash for the private garden, wood ash stored under cover has valuable potash content, but the ash will need to be used liberally. Potash should be raked, or harrowed into the top soil just before planting is done, the other materials being worked into the soil when the ground is cleaned.

It is important, when preparing the ground, to incorporate plenty of humus-forming materials. This will open up a clay soil, and will retain moisture in a light one. Strawberries must have an abundance of moisture during spring and summer to help to swell the fruit, yet the ground should be sufficiently well-drained for excess moisture to seep away during winter. As strawberries crop best in a slightly acid soil, one with a pH value of 6.0–6.5 is desirable, and peat, also slightly acid, is the best form of humus. In peat, the plants will form masses of fibrous roots, which enable them to obtain the maximum nourishment from the soil. Use peat in quantity for it is cheap, whether growing commercially or in the home garden. Strawberries should not be planted on newly-dug turf land, unless it has previously been treated for wireworm, for strawberry roots suffer more from this pest than any other fruit.

Apart from the use of sulphate of potash, strawberries do not take kindly to artificial manures, and with their greater use during the past decade it is worth noting that the yield of commercial plantations has diminished. On the continent today, and in Britain until 1940, strawberry ground received up to 50 tons of farmyard manure to the acre, or its equivalent in shoddy. On the continent still, and in Britain until 1940, an acre of strawberries would yield between five and six tons per acre, Royal Sovereign being the most popular variety. Today in Britain the average yield is between two and three tons, but in County Wexford and County Mayo in Ireland, where the old manuring methods are still practised, the yield is double. Plenty of humus and organic manure is the secret of success with this crop.

PLANTING

There is as much controversy today as there ever was over planting methods. Growers are divided between planting 18 in. apart in beds 5–6 ft. wide, so that picking can be done from both sides, and planting in rows 3 ft. apart and allowing 18 in. between the plants in the rows. Both methods will take about 10,000 plants to the acre, but whereas those growing in beds are allowed to form runners, which are left undisturbed to bear fruit, those planted in rows have the runners removed to form a separate plantation. Clean ground is vital to successful fruiting under the bed system, for perennial weeds could choke out the young plants. In a dry season, plants in beds crop more heavily than plants in rows, whilst the dense foliage provides protection from rains with little loss of fruit through splashing. So strawing or mulching is unnecessary for plants in the bed system.

If the soil is heavy or low-lying, it is advisable to plant either on raised beds or along the top of shallow furrows to guard against Red Core. There is, however, some risk of frost damage with plants growing on ridges and, where the land (or garden) is troubled by late frosts, it will be better to plant on raised beds. Here the plants, growing close together, provide mutual protection from frost and from cold winds. And, as there is risk of mildew amongst plants on the bed system, only those varieties which are resistant should be grown in this way. Non-resistant varieties require a greater circulation of air.

Gardeners of old would plant in October and disbud during the first season, to build up a sturdy plant to fruit heavily in the following season. This meant that the plants occupied the ground almost eighteen months before fruiting. But, provided that they are given good cultural treatment, and are planted during August and September for early-fruiting varieties, and up to the end of October for those which fruit late in the season, the plants can be allowed to fruit during their first summer, although there may be some loss of stamina.

A number of varieties produce better-quality fruit in their first season from such a planting. It is, however, important to plant the earliest-fruiting varieties before the end of August, and where it is not possible to do any planting until the beginning of the year, then all varieties except the autumn-fruiting perpetuals should be disbudded in their first season. Where the land is heavy, it is advisable to plant early-September, whilst the soil is still warm, and rooting will then be accomplished before winter. Plants set out later may be lifted from the soil by hard frosts, and may be damaged. In any case, it is advisable to tread all plants early in March, so that the roots may have full contact with the soil when they commence to grow.

As planting should never be done when the ground is wet and sticky, late-summer and early-autumn planting is to be preferred, though a light, sandy soil may be planted at any time.

Planting is done with a wide-nosed trowel, so that a good-sized hole may be made, and the roots spread out. Roots placed into the soil bunched together will never perform their function, and the plants will remain stunted and bear only a light crop. Make the plants firm by treading.

Always plant 'runners', as strawberry plants are called, which have been removed from one-year-old parent plants. The most vigorous are those which have formed first, those nearest the parent, whilst runners from 'maiden' or one-year plants are more vigorous than from older plants.

It is advisable to obtain Certified Plants; that is, from those plantations which have been subject to Ministry of Agriculture inspection for clean and virus-free stocks. Suppliers of runners usually concentrate on producing either runner or fruit, never both, from the same plantation. The removal of runners, as soon as they appear, from the fruiting plants, enables these plants to concentrate their energies into the bearing of heavy crops, whilst exactly the reverse is the case with those plants grown for the production of runners. Here the plants are deblossomed rigorously, so that their energies are directed into the formation of sturdy runners. Where growing commercially, a plant cannot be expected to bear a heavy crop, in addition to producing large numbers of runners, without loss of stamina.

When planting, take care not to allow the roots to become dry, otherwise the plants may take a long time to recover and to form new fibrous roots. The best method is to place the plants either in boxes of damp peat, or in moss upon arrival, and they should be kept in this whilst being planted. With large-scale planting – and 10,000 plants will be required for one acre of ground – it is advisable to take delivery in two consignments, to allow time for planting the first lot before the second batch arrives. Planting should also be done as quickly as possible, but adverse weather may hold up operations, and this should be allowed for when asking for delivery of the second batch. Always use a strong garden line for planting, taking care to space out the rows to sufficient width, to allow either a hand or mechanical hoe to be taken between the plants in early spring, to aerate the soil and to kill annual weeds.

Do not plant too deeply. Strawberries, as most soft fruits, are surface-rooting plants, hence the frequent necessity to top dress and mulch. It is also important to exercise care when hoeing, for it is not advisable to work too near the plants. The shallow-rooting quality of strawberries enables them to be grown in fairly shallow soils, provided that they are enriched with humus-forming manures to prevent drying out during a period of drought.

Early in April, especially following a long, cold winter, the plants should be given a light top dressing with sulphate of ammonia to stimulate them into growth. This should be applied during a period of rainy weather so that it is washed into the soil. The commercial grower should use 1 cwt. per acre; the amateur gardener 1 oz. per yd. where growing in rows, or 2 oz. per sq. yd. in beds.

If April is moist and warm, the plants will, by the month end, have commenced to form bloom and also runners. Where growing chiefly for fruit, the runners must be removed. The first fortnight of May is the most worrying period of the year for the strawberry grower, for a hard frost will, in a single night, blacken the blossom and spoil any chance of a good crop. This is why both amateur and commercial growers are advised to plant at least one of those varieties which come late into bloom, for if only early varieties are grown, in one out of every three seasons, the crop may be partially damaged. The grower is relieved when he knows the blossom has set its fruit without being damaged by the frost, for this goes far towards ensuring a heavy crop.

After the blossom has set fruit, the plants should be mulched. Peat, spread thickly between the plants and up to the crowns, will help the soil to retain its moisture whilst the fruit is maturing, and at the same time will suppress annual weeds. A peat mulch will also protect the fruit from soil splashing quite as well as the more-popular straw, and wherever possible it should be used in preference. Straw is not so practical; it harbours slugs and mice, and tends to remove some of the nitrogen from the soil as it is trodden in. And, whereas the peat, after the crop has been picked, may be worked into the soil, the straw must be tediously gathered up and either burnt or composted.

Amateurs growing only a few plants could use thick layers of newspaper for keeping the fruits clean as an alternative to strawberry mats. The paper must be used thickly, and is placed between the rows, up to the crown of the plants. Mats of bamboo or plastic are also economical and long-lasting, but a combination of peat, and newspaper – the former useful in so many ways about the garden and greenhouse – will prove satisfactory.

But whatever material is chosen, it must be in position by the time that the fruits are beginning to swell and are still green, for when once they attain some size they will ripen quickly. Where only one or two plants of several varieties are being grown, maturing in succession, broken crocks or glass may be used to prevent splashing and these will also conserve moisture. They will in addition hasten ripening by reflecting the rays of the sun on to the fruits.

WATERING AND FEEDING

Whilst the fruits are swelling, artificial watering will be necessary during a dry period. Strawberries must be given an abundance of moisture at this time, and the months of May and June, when the early mid-season crops are maturing, are usually the driest months of the year. Strawberries lacking sufficient moisture will bear only small, seedy fruit, lacking in flavour, and it may be necessary, where the soil is of a sandy nature or where the plants are growing in the dry regions of East Anglia, to water until the completion of the crop. This, however, should be modified whilst picking is taking place for, of all soft fruits, strawberries and raspberries in particular, should be marketed or picked for home use only when quite dry, otherwise the fruit will rapidly deteriorate.

Regular spraying of the beds will keep down Red Spider attacks, whilst watering with dilute liquid manure water, obtainable in concentrated form in bottles, and clean and easy to use, will help form exhibition-sized fruit of good flavour. Liquid manure will also help to build up a plant which will bear a heavy crop during the next year or so. An excellent method of irrigation is by the use of rotational sprinklers, placed at intervals about the plantation, and fed from a hose.

As soon as the fruits become swollen they will colour rapidly, and the plants should be looked over daily, possibly twice daily if the weather is warm and sunny. After fruiting, the ground should be cleared of straw, if this has been used, and the rows or beds should be given a dressing of a mixture of peat and decayed manure. The hoe should be kept moving if planting has been done in rows.

What to do with the foliage, as it begins to die back in early autumn, is also a matter of controversy. Some burn it off together with the straw, a drastic method, whilst others take a grass cutter along the rows and in this way remove the top foliage, a more satisfactory method especially as it may then be dug into the soil for humus.

The first runners will be ready for removal from the beginning of July. Maiden or one-year plants produce the best runners. The amateur should remove those required to make a new bed and destroy any others throughout summer. How long to allow a bed to remain in bearing must be determined by the condition of the land, the health and vigour of the plants, and their cropping powers during the previous season. Some growers plant in August and plough in the plants as soon as they have fruited the following summer, but plants grown in a well-cultivated soil will bear for two, three and even four seasons without deterioration of the fruit. Runners removed from maidens are used to form a second plantation, and, in turn, these plants yield runners. So, whilst bed (ii) is in its first year of cropping, bed (i) is in its second season and ready for removal. In this way, there is always a bed fruiting in its first year and another cropping for a second year, no runners being removed from second-season plants.

For a second-year plantation, a 2 oz. per sq. yd. dressing with sulphate of potash should be given in early March, followed by 1 oz. per sq. yd. of sulphate of ammonia in early April. Future beds will be healthier if the ground is rested from strawberries after every four years.

STRAWBERRIES UNDER GLASS

With the high cost of heating, few can afford the luxury of a crop of strawberries grown in a heated greenhouse. But today there are several varieties which will naturally fruit under glass without heat, at much the same time as those grown in heat did, in pre-war days. So, unless they are intended for a special purpose, such as an exhibition or banquet, strawberries are now rarely grown in heat. Excellent profits, however, may be obtained from open-ground plants given glass protection, and there are two forms of glass for forcing, Dutch lights and cloches.

The commercial grower generally uses lights, the amateur uses cloches, but each is efficient. Under glass the fruit will be clean and no splash protection need be given, but unless correctly ventilated the plants may suffer from mildew and the fruits from botrytis, a disease which causes them to rot away before ripening. To ripen fruit under glass in a satisfactory condition calls for skill, and many go wrong by covering the plants too soon. When winter comes the strawberry plant, like the grower himself (who has had six strenuous months, often picking from daybreak until dusk), is ready for a break, and it should be given a period of cold and rest to become revitalised. However early a crop is desired, no plants should be covered before mid-February, preferably towards the end of the month, after having first been given a dressing with potash. It is not only necessary to plant mildew-resistant varieties under glass culture, but also those varieties which do not make an excess of leaf. Strawberries are hardy plants, and demand the maximum of ventilation, and, in this respect, the less foliage the plants make the better.

It will be necessary to decide upon the type of glass to be used before planting, for it is essential to be able to cover the maximum number of plants to make the glass economical. Dutch or ordinary garden lights may be supported on 9-in boards, or on old railway sleepers. Under lights, set out the plants 15 in. apart each way. By this method it may be possible to plant four rows of a compact variety.

As the plants need as long a period of growth as possible if they are to bear fruit early in May, the beds should be made up in August. The soil must be deeply worked and enriched, and only top-quality plants should be used. Where barn-type cloches are used, make a double row 9 in. apart allowing 18 in. in the rows. A single row with the plants 15 in. apart may be covered with the ordinary tent cloche. It is more economical if used again in autumn and early winter to cover the perpetuals. It may also be used to protect the ripening fruit of a late variety, such as Cambridge Rearguard, during a period of adverse weather.

Suitable varieties for commercial culture under glass are:

| | |
|---|---|
| Cambridge Epicure | Cambridge Rival |
| Cambridge Premier | Cambridge Vigour |
| Cambridge Regent | Royal Sovereign |

Additional varieties for the connoisseur are:

| | |
|---|---|
| Aurora | Reine de Précoces |
| Regina | Wadenswill 4 |

All these varieties are early-maturing, resistant to mildew, of compact habit and ideal for cloching. The rows should be made from north to south to make for even ripening of the fruit.

COVERING THE FRUIT

Before the plants are covered they should have had a thorough soaking, especially following a period of hard frost, which leaves the soil dry and powdery. Also dust the plants with flowers of sulphur to guard against mildew. This treatment should be repeated at fortnightly intervals. By mid-March the sun's rays will be warmer, and on suitable occasions ventilation should be given during the day time. If a cold wind is blowing allow the glass to remain over the plants, otherwise in a few minutes it will undo all the previous good work of protection. In an exposed position, take care to ensure that the lights are prevented from being blown about and broken. They are best held in position by strong telephone wire extended over the glass.

At the time when ventilation is given, the plants will often require a soaking, though on the mild, moist days often experienced during late March, the coverings may be left off for several hours to obtain moisture naturally. When possible, all moisture should be given before noon to enable the surplus to dry off the flower trusses before nightfall. Until mid-March it is advisable to withhold water, otherwise hard frosts may damage the plants as they make new foliage.

By 1 April, the plants will be coming into bloom, and to help with fertilisation, remove the glass on suitable occasions. This will ensure that the plants receive all the ventilation necessary. Unless a cold wind is blowing, the glass protection should be removed entirely during the day, up to the time when the fruit begins to ripen. At this stage the glass should be kept in place to give protection and hasten ripening. The glass should be used, not for forcing purposes, but rather to guard the fruit against adverse weather and frosts, so that picking may commence early in May. There is little demand for the fruit until then, and it is during the last three weeks of May, when the weather becomes more summer-like, and until the first of the outdoor fruit is ripe, that protected strawberries make the highest prices.

Both first- and second-year plants may be covered but, to build up a vigorous growth for second year cloching, they must be heavily mulched as soon as fruiting has ended, and fed with dilute manure water throughout summer. After covering for two years it is advisable to destroy the plants.

GROWING IN TUBS

Where space is limited, fresh strawberries may be grown in tubs or barrels, into which holes 1 in. in diameter and 18 in. apart have been drilled to take the plants. The tubs should be filled with a suitable compost, and a small courtyard or verandah could possibly accommodate several tubs or barrels, and succession of fruit enjoyed. Tubs are preferable, for if planted in the usual way all the plants may be given abundant moisture. This is essential if the plants around the sides are to fruit well.

The half-barrel or tub should also be drilled with drainage holes, over which are placed, first large crocks then a layer of turf. The tub is then filled to within 1 in. of the rim with turf loam, which has been enriched with some decayed manure, some peat, a small amount of coarse sand and a handful of bone meal to each tub. They should be mixed well together and allowed to settle down before planting takes place in autumn, or in March for the perpetuals. If placed in a position protected from cold winds, an early June crop may be enjoyed. The compost must never be allowed to lack moisture. If May is a dry month, which it often is, give the compost a thorough soaking twice each week, so that the moisture will percolate to those plants situated at the base of the tub. It should not, however, run out at the bottom. Liquid manure water will also help large, richly-flavoured fruits to form.

Strawberries may also be grown in large pots. They require the same compost as in tubs, but additional moisture, for compost in pots dries out rapidly during early summer and watering may be necessary twice daily. Pot-grown plants may be purchased early in March; they will be more expensive than runners, but will bear fruit the same season and may also be retained in their pots to fruit the following year.

## VARIETIES

The strawberry grower today has a wide range of varieties suitable for all districts and soils and for spreading the season over a period. Experiments have proved that several varieties are suitable for freezing and canning and so, for whatever trade the grower is catering, he has a wide choice. Not all those described here are suitable for the commercial grower, but as the connoisseur of fruit must be satisfied, amateur varieties are also given. By following the choice of the professional grower exclusively we miss much that appeals to the highest tastes, and many old varieties now neglected should be saved from dying out completely. The varieties are described in order of fruiting, the descriptions being as detailed as several years' experience of their cultivation allows.

## VERY EARLY VARIETIES

AURORA. An excellent French variety for cloching, but its large crimson fruit ripens so quickly that the plants should be picked over twice a day, and the fruit marketed locally if possible. Very like Reine des Précoces, in that its glossy, deep-green leaves and large crimson berries are of handsome appearance, the fruits being of delicious flavour. Crops well in all soils.

CAMBRIDGE BRILLIANT. A variety which crops well in lime-laden soils and bears large, brilliant scarlet fruit of similar shape to Royal Sovereign. Good either for cloching or for open-air culture, it makes a compact plant and forms short, heavily-laden fruit trusses.

CAMBRIDGE EARLY PINE. One of the earliest of the Cambridge varieties, too leafy for cloches, but resistant to mildew. The medium-sized fruit is round, of a bright scarlet colour and with a smooth, glossy skin from which moisture quickly drains. In a wet season, or in an area of excess moisture, this is of great value. Although not one of the heaviest croppers, it is extremely consistent in light soils, and the blossom is very resistant to frost.

CAMBRIDGE FORERUNNER. Extensively grown in the moist western side of Britain, where it has proved valuable for cloching and, although early, it bears its dark crimson fruit over several weeks. The fruit should be marketed locally. This variety has not proved such a heavy cropper away from the west as was first indicated.

CAMBRIDGE PREMIER. Resistant to mildew and red core root disease, it crops heavily and may be said to bridge the earliest varieties with the second earlies. It forces well, and is valuable for cloching, making a compact plant, while it crops well on all soils. The large, bright-orange, wedge-shaped fruit is firm and travels well, although the amateur may find a variety of richer flavour. Not as frost-resistant as Cambridge Regent, and where not given protection it should be grown in the south for an early crop. If this variety has a fault, it is that the tip of the berry sometimes remains green when the rest has fully ripened.

CAMBRIDGE PRIZEWINNER. One of the best flavoured of early strawberries, the fruit travels well and retains its colour. It is a consistent cropper, does well in the West Country and is becoming more and more popular in Kent and East Anglia, where it bears heavily in most soils. An exhibition variety, the fruit being round and even in shape.

CAMBRIDGE PROFUSION. To crop well it needs a light, well-drained soil and, as it is susceptible to Red Core, it must not be grown on land where the trouble is known to be present. It is early, and useful for cloching as it makes little foliage, whilst being resistant to mildew. The round berries possess food flavour.

CAMBRIDGE REGENT. A prolific cropper, and for gardens in the Midlands and North it is possibly the best early strawberry, for its blossom is highly resistant to frost. The fruits mature 10 to 14 days before Royal Sovereign and, although it bears heavy crops in a light, sandy soil, it is at its best in a stiff loam. It is such a heavy cropper that it must be grown well. The large, orange-scarlet, wedge-shaped fruits possess good texture and quality. It is not suitable for cloching, as it is susceptible to mildew.

DEUTSCH EVERN. A German variety generally used for cloching. It bears heavily, with fruit of good texture but of small size, like Perle de Prague. Cambridge Brilliant or Regent would seem to be better commercial varieties.

HATIVE DE CAEN. A very hardy, frost resistant variety which crops as well in the North as it does in Holland. It makes a large, leafy plant and matures very early, the deep pink fruit possessing a rich perfume and exceptional flavour.

MADAME LEFEBVRE. This variety has now been replaced by a number of the Cambridge and continental introductions. It makes a large, bushy plant and bears a cerise-pink berry of rather soft texture.

PRECOCE MUSQUEE. The earliest strawberry par excellence for the connoisseur. With its rich perfume and delicate musky flavour, it is very similar to the old Black Prince and should be grown in every garden. The fruit is large and does not travel well.

REGINA. A favourite with the Germans and Russians for their early crops. The fruits are large, deep crimson and of exceptional flavour. The blossom is frost-resistant, and in soils containing plenty of humus it bears a heavy crop over a long period.

REINE DES PRECOCES. Excellent under cloches, but where grown in the open it should be confined to the south-west or to a sheltered garden.

Very resistant to mildew and botrytis, it bears a heavy crop of scarlet fruits. With its glossy, bottle-green foliage, this is a handsome variety in the garden.

SURPRISE DES HALLES. Almost as hardy as Hâtive de Caen, the blossom being untroubled by light frost even though the trusses are held above the foliage. It bears a huge crop of deep crimson berries, which should be marketed before fully ripe.

WADENSWILL. Where the fruit can be placed on ice for an hour to bring out its unique fragrance, it has no peer amongst soft fruits. The berries are small, almost round, and are deliciously sweet. Raised in Switzerland this is, as one would expect, a hardy, frost-resistant variety.

SECOND EARLY VARIETIES

CAMBRIDGE EARLY. Introduced in 1937, when it found favour owing to its resistance to Red Core root disease and to its reliable cropping in a heavy soil. Its round, medium-sized fruit ripens a few days before Royal Sovereign, and travels well. Does not crop well on a light soil.

CAMBRIDGE FAVOURITE. Well named, for this variety is a favourite with commercial growers. The large, light-red fruit keeps and travels well, whilst it remains in bearing longer than any summer strawberry. It is a strawberry which has put money into growers pockets, being in no way troubled by frost, mildew, botrytis or drought. It is the best of all strawberries for a light, sandy soil.

CAMBRIDGE RIVAL. Year by year the good qualities of this variety have earned it increasing popularity, and in Wales and the West it is more widely grown than any strawberry. Like Regent, it prefers a heavy loam in which it crops heavily, the fruit trusses being held well off the ground – which makes for easy picking and ensures clean fruit. The berries are of conical shape and of a bright crimson with glossy skin, like Early Pine, and whilst making a large plant it does well under cloches. An extremely heavy cropper, the fruit possesses outstanding flavour. A panel selected from 120 members of the Royal Horticultural Society Fruit Committee, selected it as being the most delicious strawberry, superior even to Royal Sovereign.

CAMBRIDGE VIGOUR. At trials of the East Malling Research Station, this proved the heaviest cropper, bearing almost double the crop of Royal Sovereign. It is possibly the best strawberry yet introduced, for it is a strong grower, is highly resistant to Red Core and crops well even in a lime-laden soil. The medium-sized fruit is deep glossy crimson, very like that of Early Pine, but it is a heavier cropper and the fruit travels well. Early autumn-planted maidens crop well in the first season, whilst the plants also bear well up to four years old, though the fruits mature later than on maidens.

MID-SEASON VARIETIES

BLACK PRINCE. Raised in 1822, and if it can be found, it should be grown in every amateur's garden. The small, glossy, crimson berries are like old port wine, almost treacle sweet. This variety forces well and crops well under cloches, the fruit making the most delicious of all strawberry jam.

CAMBRIDGE ARISTOCRAT. One of the most delicious of strawberries, the fruit having crimson flesh of a sweetness and flavour comparable to the alpines. The plants are resistant to Red Core and mildew, and bear heavily, the fruit being ready a few days after Sovereign. For jam, it is the equal of the older and less robust Little Scarlet, whilst for the essence market this is the favourite.

CAMBRIDGE SENTRY. An excellent variety, cropping well in a heavy soil and valuable for its resistance to mildew and botrytis in a moist district. The fruit trusses are held erect above the foliage, making it unnecessary to protect it against splashing. The fruit, which is wedge-shaped, remains dry under the wettest conditions, and retains its bright crimson colour after canning and freezing, being sweet and of good flavour.

HAUTBOIS. This is only for the amateur or connoisseur, for the fruits are too small for commercial use. It is the *Fragaria elatior* from which the modern strawberry was evolved, and it holds its fruit high above the foliage. Plants are obtainable in Ireland and bear large leaves and small, deep crimson-purple berries, which are particularly sweet and carry a delicious musky flavour.

HUXLEY GIANT. Of robust constitution, this variety, introduced in 1912, crops heavily in all soils, is not troubled by Red Core or frost, and travels well. Its round, crimson fruit is the most irregular both in shape and in ripening of all strawberries, yet it is of such vigour that the plants crop well for several years.

PERLE DE PRAGUE. May be said to be early mid-season. It was introduced by Mr Jessel of Dunwood, Hampshire, in 1938 and, owing to its resistance to Red Core it was (and still is) widely planted in Hampshire. It bears a tremendous crop of good-flavoured fruit, but of so small a size that it rarely commands top prices. Its texture is soft, and where possible it should be marketed locally.

ROYAL SOVEREIGN. Raised by Thomas Laxton and introduced in 1892, it has never been surpassed for quality and appearance. The brilliant scarlet, wedge-shaped fruit always commands a ready sale, even during glut periods. It prefers a light soil, but one enriched with humus, and the virus-free Malling 48 strain should be grown. But like the choicest of fruits, Sovereign suffers more from virus, mildew and botrytis than any strawberry, so is best grown in isolation and on the drier eastern side of Britain. The original Laxton strain possesses much more flavour than the East Malling strain.

RED GAUNTLET. A valuable strawberry, being resistant to Red Core and a heavy cropper, the large scarlet fruits possessing excellent flavour. It is a compact grower with small foliage, and its trusses are held well above the foliage.

### LATE MID-SEASON VARIETIES

CAROLINA. An old variety, grown in the days when Black Prince was the best strawberry. The foliage is deep green, the fruits of brightest scarlet, wedge-shaped and carrying a distinct pine flavour. This variety may be obtained in Ireland and is included here on account of its delicious flavour.

FENLAND WONDER. An interesting variety, for it was found fruiting in the wild state on a church wall at Emneth in Norfolk in 1952, and was thought to be such a fine late strawberry that it has become widely planted in the Wisbech district. Maturing about the same time as Climax (now no longer grown) it would appear to be the answer to the Climax grower's prayer, for the fruit is equally large and, whilst retaining its colour, travels better than any variety. It is one of the sweetest and best flavoured of strawberries and crops heavily over a long period.

SPANGSBJERG YDUN. A Danish variety introduced by Messrs L. and W. Howard of Maldon, Essex, where it has cropped heavily. It is immune to frost and bears well and over a long period in the dry climate of Essex.

SURPRISE. Raised by Mr D. Carmichael of Carluke, Lancashire, and first released in 1954, this vigorous variety has shown resistance to Red Core, and although bred from the same parents as Climax, with a similar fruiting season, has shown none of its troubles. It crops heavily, the fruit being round, very sweet and of a bright scarlet colour. It also 'plugs' well. But its most important virtue is its resistance to Red Core in a district where whole plantations of less-resistant varieties have been wiped out.

TALISMAN. Raised by Mr R. D. Reid at the West of Scotland Institute. It crops heavily, transports well, and its long, conical-shaped fruit is of good texture. It is highly resistant to Red Core. It is also excellent for canning, freezing and for jam, and commands top prices for dessert.

TEMPLAR. A variety bearing large conical fruits of pale red, turning to dark red when ripe. It is resistant to Red Core and is a heavy bearer with its trusses held upright above the foliage.

### VERY LATE-FRUITING VARIETIES ·

CAMBRIDGE LATE PINE. Those who prefer a sugar-sweet fruit with a slight pine flavour will prefer this variety to Rearguard, but both should be marketed locally. Late Pine bears large, round, bright-crimson fruit similar to the older Waterloo. It bottles and cans well, and is a popular variety for dessert trade for holiday resorts.

CAMBRIDGE QUEEN. Though the plant is resistant to frost, drought and mildew, the richly-flavoured fruit tends to be soft and requires eating as soon as picked. It makes a neat, compact plant, crops heavily, the wedge-shaped fruit being of a bright salmon-red colour.

CAMBRIDGE REARGUARD. Although its fruit turns a deep crimson colour if transported a distance and possesses rather a sharp taste like the American Red Rich, it crops well in all soils. As it is sometimes troubled by mildew, it is at its best in the drier climate of the Eastern Counties. The fruit is large and wedge-shaped.

EVEREST. A seedling raised by Mr Carmichael of Carluke and holding its trusses high above the foliage. Where late frosts persist, this, like each of the late-fruiting varieties, will come through unharmed. It is suitable for low-lying land in the North, cropping heavily, its round, crimson fruit being of top quality.

SPAT AUS LEOPOLDSCHALL. A German variety, and the latest of all the summer strawberries. It is at its best during the latter part of August when the holiday season is at its height; hence the value of all the strawberries in this section. It is a heavy cropper even in heavy soils, and is resistant to mildew and botrytis.


AUTUMN-FRUITING STRAWBERRIES

These, the Remontants, may be divided into two types or groups:

(a) Those which bear the whole of their crop during the latter part of the year, from August until possibly December.

(b) Those which yield two distinct flushes of fruit, the first in early summer, the second in late autumn. These are now known as the two-crop strawberries, and are especially valuable for the amateur's garden, where space is limited.

Those who have to contend with a lime-laden soil and find that their strawberry plants suffer from serious iron deficiency may be able to enjoy autumn fruit from the late-crop varieties by planting in early spring. The plants are removed at the year end after fruiting, and the runners grown on to fruit the following year.

Whilst the true autumn-fruiting varieties may be planted in spring, the two-crop varieties should be planted early in autumn, to enable them to become established before the winter and so bear a crop in the early summer. In this way they occupy the ground only nine months, or they may be grown on for a second year if given good cultivation. It is also possible to prolong the season of the autumn-fruiting varieties by making a planting both in spring and in autumn. Those planted in autumn are then allowed to set fruit on the first flowering trusses which appear during

May. The fruit will be ready about 1 July. Where only late-summer and autumn fruit are required, those planted in spring should be disbudded until 1 June. There will thus be a succession of fruit from mid-summer until almost the year end.

If the bulk of the crop is required in autumn, it is necessary to disbud until the end of May. These are perpetual-fruiting strawberries, and will continue to bear in flushes, like mushrooms, right through summer and autumn, but where heavy pickings are required in autumn, when the crop is most profitable, the plants must not be permitted to waste their energies during the early-summer period. The two-crop varieties will bear fruit in two main flushes and, unless a particularly heavy crop is required in autumn, disbudding is not necessary.

To extend the season, almost until the year end in favourable districts, cloches or frames should be used, and this will mean making up the beds to suit the type of glass chosen. By far the best method so far tried is to use the barn type cloche. A double row of plants is set out, spacing the rows 12 in. apart. They make large plants, and too close planting will cause botrytis and congestion with the runners.

METHODS OF CROPPING

From an early April planting, one method is to allow the parent plants to bear fruit in addition to runners. The runners will begin to form by mid-summer, and are left in position and allowed to root, but all blossom is removed. The plants fruit from late in August and the beds, which will be a mass of runners by mid-October, are then covered with the cloches. If situated in a warm, sunny district, the plants will continue to fruit almost until Christmas, when they may be dug up and destroyed, leaving the runners to bear the following season; alternatively the parent plants may be potted and placed either indoors or in a warm greenhouse to bear fruit for the festive season.

The following spring the runners are thinned out, keeping the beds 3 ft. 6 in. wide, and a fresh bed is made up. There are then two beds to bear a crop the following season, at the end of which the original bed is dug in. Where growing under cloches the plants must be given as much fresh air as possible by removing the covers whenever favourable, for it must not be thought that the Remontants are in any way tender. Where severe weather is experienced and in a district where late frosts persist, these strawberries will fruit abundantly when the summer-fruiting varieties often fail. It is an excess of moisture rather than cold weather which causes trouble with the Remontants. In a cold, dry climate where the plants receive a fair share of sunshine, covered plants will fruit until early December and will crop until early November without protection. In a cold, wet district the fruit may be troubled by botrytis after the end of October, whether covered or not, but where this occurs only those varieties which show resistance to the trouble should be grown.

Whilst the cloches must be protected from strong winds, the plants should be given an open, sunny position. Growing too close to a hedge or wall will not only deprive the plants of much necessary moisture but also of air and sunlight, so necessary to combat botrytis and to ripen the autumn fruit. Whereas the alpines will fruit well in almost full shade, and the summer maincrop strawberries may be given partial shade, the Remontants must have a position of full sun. They also require a rich soil and clean land, for the plants may occupy the ground for two years. Where growing on the runners in the original beds, the soil must be rich with humus and plant food if heavy crops are to be enjoyed. Plenty of moisture-holding materials are essential, so dig in decayed manure in any form, as well as spent hops, peat, shoddy or leaf mould. And do not neglect to provide the plants with potash, 2 oz. per square yard on light land, and with phosphates, preferably in the form of bone meal and at the same rate, where the soil is on the heavy side.

Allow the soil to settle down before planting, for they like a firm bed. Early in June, after the last disbudding and when the plants have made some new growth, it is advisable to provide them with a mulch of peat and decayed manure. This not only helps to retain summer moisture in the soil but also will suppress annual weeds, thus making weeding unnecessary when the runners are beginning to form. Peat is also an excellent medium for the rooting of runners. In summer the plants must never be allowed to lack moisture, for it is during the period of the warmest weather that the fruit is being formed, and bearing such huge crops, it is essential that the plants receive all the moisture they require.

As the fruits mature, the peat mulch will act as a guard against soil splashing, but straw is not recommended, for it will interfere with the formation and rooting of runners. Instead, mats may be used around the parent plants, or better still, inexpensive special wire elevators for the heavy fruit trusses, which may be obtained from Messrs Chase of Shepperton. These are pressed into the ground around the plants and removed at the end of the crop. The elevators not only prevent dirty fruit but allow the maximum of air and sunshine to reach the trusses, hastening ripening and doing much to prevent botrytis, more troublesome with the autumn than with the summer crops.

A number of varieties will form early runners, and these may be allowed to fruit late in autumn and grown on for a second season. Late runners should be de-blossomed and the beds thinned out in early autumn, new beds being made up. The smallest runners will bear a heavy crop the following autumn, and none should be discarded. Also, those formed later in the season will come into fruit later the following season, and so every runner should be carefully used, not only for making new beds but to prolong the crop. In this way the amateur may allow the two-crop varieties to fruit early, possibly covering with cloches to encourage this and by the use of runners in various stages of maturity and by de-blossoming, the plants may be persuaded to give fruit from May until December, even though pickings will be light. There will be little difference, however, in the final weight of the crop if the plants are allowed to fruit perpetually or are encouraged to give the bulk of their fruit in autumn, the varieties La Sana Rivale, Triomphe and St Claude, giving around 1 lb. of fruit per plant in a single season under both methods.

After fruiting the plants will die back completely, no foliage whatsoever being seen above ground. It is, therefore, important to discontinue cultivations and planting from Christmas until 1 April, otherwise the roots may be damaged and the plants may take a long time to recover.

It has been said that the public will have tired of strawberries by the end of August, but the large sales now enjoyed by frozen fruit throughout the year would dispel this idea, and those who have grown the autumn-fruiting varieties, which realise very remunerative prices, have learnt that well-grown strawberries sell at any time and make a welcome change during the late-autumn period.

## VARIETIES

ADA HERTZBERG. A German variety which is of value to the northern garden, in that it ripens its fruit into winter. The crop is large; the pillar-box red berries possessing excellent market texture.

CHARLES SIMMEN. On account of its huge cropping powers and its handsome heart-shaped fruit, which is brilliant orange and richly flavoured, this is the finest of all strawberries; but only for the amateur, for it forms no runners and has to be increased by the slow process of crown division. This should be done as soon as new growth commences in April. Like St Claude, it crops over a long period and is highly resistant to botrytis in the dampest districts.

GABRIEL D'ARBONVILLE. Like Charles Simmen, this variety produces no runners and must be increased by division of the crowns. It bears a large, glossy, crimson fruit of exceptional flavour, and possesses a delicate fragrance. A fine variety where space is limited, for it makes only a very small plant.

GENTO. Raised by Hummel's of Stuttgart, it begins to crop in June, when the fruits are small, and continues until early October, the fruits increasing in size each week. The large, wedge-shaped berries are red fleshed and are of excellent flavour.

HAMPSHIRE MAID. It may be said to bridge the gap between the late-summer and autumn-fruiting varieties, but it is suitable only for light land. It bears sweet, conical fruits on upright trusses over a long period, but will only crop heavily if kept well watered through summer and autumn.

KUNTNER'S TRIUMPH. Pineapple Triumph it is often called, because of the distinct pine flavour of its rounded fruits. It is an Austrian variety which prefers a light soil, and like Red Rich it forms copious runners. The fruit colours well into late autumn and travels well.

LA SANS RIVALE. This is the heaviest-cropping strawberry, producing up to 2 lb. of fruit per plant if given individual attention, and 1 lb. or more when grown commercially. It makes but little foliage and holds its fruit trusses well above the ground. If the plants are de-blossomed until 1 June it comes into bearing 1 September, reaching a peak throughout October. The fruits are large, wedge-shaped, sweet and of a vivid scarlet colour. They are of firm texture and transport well.

LIBERATION D'ORLEANS. A two-crop variety of outstanding quality which crops heavily. At its best in a heavy, humus-laden soil, the fruit possesses exceptional flavour and has a similar shape and colour to the Royal Sovereign, which makes it popular with the salesman.

RECORD. Though a two-crop variety, it crops as heavily in autumn as the true autumn-fruiting varieties. It makes a huge, bushy plant, the largest of all strawberries and bears its trusses well above the foliage. The large, oval fruits are deep crimson and travel well. It crops well in a cold, clay soil and should be planted in the north.

RED RICH. An American introduction, this is a genuine two-crop variety bearing the first flush in early summer, followed by a heavier crop in early autumn. The crimson fruits are very large and of poor appearance, soft in texture and possessing a sharp, acid flavour, pleasing to those who favour a refreshing fruit. It makes a large number of runners, which should be thinned where growing in beds.

ST CLAUDE. This variety has a longer season than any strawberry, maturing its first fruit in August and, in the south, continuing until November. The conical fruits are firm, rather hard in fact, and travel well. The size of the fruit is retained throughout the crop, the skin being glossy and of a dark crimson colour, sweet and with a rich fragrance. The dark green plants remain healthy whilst the fruit strongly resists botrytis.

ST FIACRE. One of the first French Remontants, and worth growing on account of its exceptional flavour. The plants are of hardy constitution and form plenty of runners, whilst they fruit continuously from mid-July until early November, the fruit being of a good texture.

TRIOMPHE. The blunt, bright salmon-pink fruit is exceptionally sweet and rich, but its texture is soft and it should be marketed locally. It is also more suitable for the drier districts, for it suffers from botrytis in a damp climate, or where planted in a clay soil. It crops heavily, but the plants have an untidy habit with the fruit trusses sitting on the ground.

VICTOIRE. A two-crop variety, continuing to crop very late indeed. It

307

cloches well, but suffers from botrytis unless great care is taken with ventilation. It does however hold its trusses above the foliage. Its richly-flavoured, cerise-red fruits are the largest of all strawberries.

CLIMBING FORM

Herr Hummal's amazing remontant, Sojana, introduced into Britain in 1957, has given satisfaction. By forming long runners, it may be grown against a wall or trellis upon which it will grow to 6 ft. or more in height, or it may be grown along the ground like a rambler rose and covered with continuous cloches. It may also be grown in pots and trained up long canes arranged fan-wise. It should be given shelter from cold winds, and as it crops from early August until late November it requires a well-nourished soil and must never lack moisture. If growing in pots, insert them in the ground to half the height of the pots to prevent them from being blown over and to conserve moisture. A sunny position is also essential for them to bear well in autumn. They also require a permanent position for they are perennial, dying back in winter to come into growth again in spring, when the soil should receive a liberal dressing with de-cayed manure. Set out the plants 3 ft. apart in late autumn.

As much as 14 lb. of fruit may be obtained in one season from a single plant and its runners if fed well and kept moist at the roots. The fruit is bright red with the flavour of alpine strawberries and hangs in trusses of three or four. It is produced all the way up the stems. Where growing upright, regular attention to tying is important. There is no tedious weeding, no disbudding, no strawing to keep the fruit clean, no trouble from slugs, and its upright habit makes it possible to produce strawberries in a restricted area, or where there is no garden at all.

SWEDE

It requires the same cultural treatment as the turnip, and should be sown in spring for summer use, and in late July for autumn and winter use. Sowing at this time, the plants will not run to seed and though they will make roots little larger than a cricket ball, they may be stored in sand and will be tender and sweet and delicately flavoured. For larger roots, sow 1 in. deep in May, in drills 15 in. apart and thin out to 10 in. apart in the rows. Extremely hardy, they may be lifted and used when required.

Purple Top Improved is the best variety for successional sowing, form-ing large rounded roots with deep golden flesh of pleasant flavour.

## SWEET CECILY

The handsome fern-like leaves of *Myrrhis odorata* have a strong aniseed taste, one or two added to a salad proving most tasty. The roots may also be cooked and eaten in small quantities. It grows like horseradish, forming a large root and large leaves, and the whole plant dies down in winter. The seeds, which may be removed in early autumn, possess an aroma which may be likened to furniture polish – for which purpose they were indeed crushed and used in olden times. The roots should be planted into a rich soil and in a part of the kitchen garden where other root crops are grown. If the ground is undisturbed in autumn, the seeds will sow themselves.

## TOMATO, OUTDOOR

A warm friable soil is essential for an early and heavy crop, and the ground should be trenched for best results. Soil to a depth of 15 in. should be removed, and into the trench is placed as much humus as it is possible to obtain. Farmyard manure may not be available in quantity, but at least some may be acquired, and this should be incorporated into a compost heap. This is made up by composting straw with an activator, to which is added a quantity of dry poultry manure to assist in fermentation. If the heap is stacked high to allow it to heat up quickly and turned at weekly intervals for three weeks, a useful compost will be the result.

Long straw will help greatly with the aeration of the soil, a free circulation of air being necessary for a sturdy rooting system. Some growers place uncomposted straw at the bottom of a trench and stand this on end as an aid to air circulation. This is a successful method, but it is preferable to use composted straw. Uncomposted straw will use up vital nitrogen from the soil whilst in the process of rotting down, and it should first be treated with sulphate of ammonia, which costs only a few pence per pound. Where it is required that the straw be stood on end in the trench, the sulphate of ammonia can be sprinkled over the straw when in position, and allowed to begin decomposition before the top soil is added.

Horticultural peat and spent hops or hop manure of a proprietary brand, will also add to the humus content of the soil, and should be used where possible. Chopped seaweed is also an excellent organic fertiliser, and is used in large quantities by the tomato growers of the Channel Isles. Shoddy (cloth waste) is also most valuable, especially when used in conjunction with partially-composted straw. In all but the lightest soils, peat should be used in quantity, and again for mulching the plants when the fruits begin to form. Should it not be possible to compost a quantity of straw, it will be advisable to place lawn mowings and chopped garden refuse at the bottom of the trench.

The use of lawn mowings as a means of providing 'green' humus is not popular but experiments carried out at the Cheshunt Research Station have shown that where up to 40 tons to the acre was added, yields increased considerably.

Another 'green' product that normally runs to waste is pea and bean haulm, which may be obtained for the asking in the country. This is a valuable source of nitrogen and will give excellent results in the crop yields of all vegetables. But although bean haulm may not be available to the town gardener, lawn mowings are, and during the summer months they should be stored for use in autumn when the new trenches are made. The country gardener should collect all the pea and bean haulm during the summer months, and have this available for incorporation into the compost heap in preference to using it in the uncomposted state. Where the soil is heavy, ashes which have been weathered and well mixed into the top soil will help to encourage a strong rooting system.

It is suggested that a trench be taken out rather than to double dig a portion of the garden and incorporate the humus that way, so that the manures may be kept in as concentrated an area as possible.

A trench will help to keep the land free from tomato 'sickness' where a yearly crop is being cultivated, for the exact position of the trench will have been marked and that for the following year's crop may be made some distance away. This is more satisfactory than using up a larger area of ground for the same crop year after year, with no exact knowledge of where last season's crop was set out.

Where 'new' land is being used to grow tomatoes – and this will be the case where one is taking up residence in a newly-built house – the turf should be removed and placed grass downwards at the bottom of the trench. The mass of tiny fibrous roots of the turf will also be a source of additional humus, and for this reason many growers use turf for lining the trenches in a glasshouse. Turf will even improve with stacking, and will be more valuable where mixed with farmyard or poultry manures.

When once the humus content of the trenches is established, and this will decompose either in a compost heap or in the trenches themselves over winter, the base fertilisers should be added. The humus materials should have been covered over with 2 in. of soil and trodden firmly. This treading will prevent any air pockets, but where straw is present in quantity, it will not prevent circulation of the air. Early in spring the base fertilisers may be mixed with the top soil and added to the trenches, or forked into the land where trenches are not being used.

Additional supplies of nitrogen can be provided by dried blood, meat and hoof meal, which are concentrated and slow-acting, and enable the plants to take in the valuable food over the whole of their cropping period. These prepared organic manures when used with artificially-composted straw or 'green' manures have produced excellent crops when horse manure cannot be obtained. Tomato plants starved of nitrogen show a tendency to become thin and lanky, with a yellow blotching of the leaves, and also an uneven ripening of the fruit. Thus nitrogen is most important. However, where ample supplies of horse, poultry and pig manures are being used the addition of prepared nitrogen manures must be within limits, otherwise a 'soft' plant and delayed ripening of the fruit will result.

Another requirement of the tomato is potash. Here, poultry manure which has been stored dry before using in the compost heap contains almost ten times the potash concentration of farmyard manure, and where guano or poultry droppings have been used in this way almost no extra potash will be needed. Where farmyard manure only is being used, and only on a small scale, it will be necessary to give potash additions. Sufficient may be given in the form of wood ash, which, like poultry manure, has been stored dry. Wood ash contains about the same quantity of potash as does poultry manure. The inorganic sulphate of potash may be used sparingly instead, and this substance contains about eight times the concentration of pure potash. Where organic manures are not in concentrated form, a 4 oz. per sq. yd. dressing of hoof meal (5 parts) and sulphate of potash (1 part) will provide the necessary requirements.

Potash is released more readily to the plant where phosphates are available in the soil. Other than this, the result of using phosphates is neither for better nor for worse, although where a compound rich in phosphate is being used as a soil dressing (superphosphate and bone meal are the most efficient) less potash will be necessary.

RAISING THE PLANTS

Anyone who does not possess a heated greenhouse must either purchase plants, well hardened off, for planting out early in May under cloches, or early in June when growing in the open, or must sow the seed over a hotbed in a closed frame.

The hotbed should be made up to a depth of 8 in. early in April or a week earlier if situated in a favourable area. Over the hotbed, which has been well trodden to conserve heat and moisture, is placed a 1 in. covering of sterilised soil made up to the formula of the John Innes compost.

After covering the compost the seed is individually sown, spacing it 2 in. apart and just covering it with soil. It is watered and the light is placed over the frame. Excessive moisture should not be given, and as soon as germination has taken place the seedlings should be given ventilation on all suitable occasions.

As soon as the seedlings have formed their first pair of leaves they should be moved to small pots containing the John Innes potting compost.

By the end of May, after hardening, the plants will be ready to be set out in the open in the south, or under cloches in the colder parts. If no cloches are available the plants should remain in the frame until about 6 June. Do not plant out too soon even where glass covering is available, for until mid-June the nights remain cold and there are few insects about to pollinate the first trusses which are so important. If these lower trusses fail to set, the crop will not only be lighter but will also be later.

The plants are set out from 3–4 ft. apart each way and, of course, in a position of full sun; if possible, too, they should be planted where there is protection from prevailing winds. Plant firmly and water well, henceforth keeping the soil comfortably moist. Bud-drop will result if the soil is too dry. Plants which are growing in large pots where they are to crop will require attention to their watering, for the soil will dry out more quickly.

Plants in the open ground must also be watered with care, for otherwise the soil will be thrown up onto the foliage or lower flower trusses, with the possible result that fungus spores may cause damage, and such troublesome diseases as botrytis and Buckeye Rot may be the outcome. The bush tomatoes are more liable to suffer in this respect, owing to their dwarf habit, and many growers place a layer of clean straw under each plant about three weeks after they have been set out in the open ground. This not only prevents splashing of the foliage and trusses which are formed only a few inches from the soil level, but the straw acts as a mulch preventing the soil from drying out too readily. A thick layer of horticultural peat may also be used in place of the straw, although for bush varieties I favour straw. In any case, nothing should be placed around the plants until they are well established, for a mulch will tend to prevent the warmth of the sun penetrating to the soil. This will have a detrimental effect on early plant growth. If the plants are set out towards the end of May, then mid-June will be sufficiently early for the straw to be placed in position.

Heavy splashing of the soil will cause it to 'pan' and form a crust through which the requisite oxygen is unable to penetrate to the roots of the plants, causing possible die-back. Should a crust form on the top of the soil – which it may do as the season advances however carefully the waterings have been given – this may be broken up by pushing a cane into the soil at regular intervals, taking care to keep away from the stem of the plants or damage may result.

POLLINATING THE FLOWERS

There is another aid in the setting of the trusses. This is the practice of pollination by carefully brushing each flower with a small camel hair brush, or even with a few hen's feathers tied tightly together at the end of a small stick. This procedure should take place around mid-day, when the flowers are open. It can only be done when all moisture is off the flowers, and so it is advisable to withhold overhead syringing until after hand pollinating has been done. This is done each day during the early part of the summer. A dozen plants can be pollinated in a few minutes, and syringing can then follow.

Outdoor plants cannot be pollinated when they are wet from rain or mist and an appropriate time must be awaited. Plants grown under frames or cloches whilst forming their first trusses will be under a greater degree of control. As the season advances daily brushing of the plants will not be necessary, two or three times a week being ample, but plants in the open will usually receive all the pollinating they require from the work of bees and other insects. Where large numbers of plants are being grown and time is at a premium, the plants may be reasonably pollinated by merely shaking the supports to which the plants are fastened. This will produce a dusting effect on a small scale and is quite useful where plants are growing indoors.

BRINGING ON THE CROP

Those varieties with dwarf habit, Atom, The Amateur and Tiny Tim will require neither 'stopping' nor the removal of side shoots. They 'stop' themselves and will restrict themselves to only a certain number of shoots.

Those of taller habit should be 'stopped' at the fourth truss, so that they will ripen their fruit before autumn. Most of the ornamental tomatoes will make tall bushy plants and so are better supported by pea sticks and allowed to grow at will. The ability of these plants to look after themselves makes them valuable to the gardener with only limited time at his disposal.

FIG. 14 *Side growths to be removed*

Those orthodox yellow-fruiting varieties should have the side growths removed with a sharp knife or even with the fingers, whenever they are observed growing from a leaf joint.

The question of a mulch placed round the plants is important. A light dressing of peat and strawy manure given early in July will help to preserve moisture in the soil and will keep down annual weeds, thus making hoeing and hand weeding, with the danger of damaging the roots, unnecessary.

Over the mulch a layer of clean straw should be placed to prevent soil splashing, and on which the fruits may rest without damage, although if the trusses are supported by twigs this will be a decided help in ripening and keeping the fruit free from blemishes. As an aid to ripening a light dressing of sulphate of potash, 2 oz. per sq. yd., could be given just before the mulch, and from the end of July until mid-September a weekly application of dilute manure water will maintain the nourishment required by the later-maturing fruit.

Defoliation also calls for attention as the crop is ripening. No leaves should be removed until they have completed their part in the health of the plant, for foliage is just as important as root action, the two going hand-in-hand.

First, it is permissible and a good idea to cut back the lower leaves when once the plant is established. This will prevent any attack of botrytis owing to the splashing of the bottom foliage with soil particles through careless watering, or due to heavy rain. It also allows for a free circulation of air, also a safeguard against botrytis or mildew. This is particularly advisable with bush varieties, especially in a season of dull, damp weather where these particular varieties tend to form more foliage than is necessary. It is preferable to cut back the leaves just half-way, otherwise complete defoliation may be too drastic.

As the season advances and the plants appear to be making too much foliage due to a wet, sunless summer, it is permissible to thin out the leaves when the plant has formed five trusses. Again, it is advisable to cut back only half of each leaf. Much will depend upon the season, and should the hours of sunshine be above average, it is better not to defoliate, and many growers even allow one or two side shoots to make more growth than usual before they are cut out. This will provide the plants with additional leafage for converting carbon dioxide, and also provide some protection for the plants where intense sunlight tends to dry up the foliage. So much depends upon the weather and the type of tomato being grown that no definite instructions on defoliation can be given. The removal of the leaves simply for the sake of doing so is wrong; in fact, no gardening operation of any kind should be performed unless there is a reason for doing so.

As the crop draws to its close the sun's warmth becomes weaker, and a certain amount of fruit remains to be ripened. Then more defoliation may be done, for now the plant no longer needs the starches and sugars to produce its crop of fruit. The work is completed, and all that remains is for the final ripening of the fruit.

## RED VARIETIES

ATOM. A distinct 'break' in outdoor tomatoes, being of almost prostrate habit and making little foliage, the plant needs neither staking nor stopping. When once the fruit has formed, it ripens quickly with the minimum amount of sunshine. Owing to its low habit it is the best of all tomatoes for an exposed garden, and may be brought into fruit by early July if planted under barn-type cloches.

Owing to the rapid maturing of the plant, seed should not be sown until towards the end of April, for the plants must be kept growing without check, as it will not be possible to set them out before the second week of June, except where glass is being used, and they can then be planted out early in May. These tomatoes need a well-manured soil and, when the trusses form, they should be kept above the soil by stout twigs, wood wool or moss being placed around the plants to prevent splashing. Cloches should be removed when the first ripe fruit is ready, and they may then be placed on their sides around the plants to give protection from winds.

Atom is not a large fruit, being about the size of a large golf ball and just what the housewife likes. It ripens without any traces of 'greenback', and apart from feeding with liquid manure each week, requires almost no other attention.

SLEAFORD ABUNDANCE. An F.1 Hybrid, it grows only 12 in. tall with little foliage, and forms large trusses of well-coloured, medium-sized fruit of excellent flavour.

SUGARPLUM. Excellent for growing in pots on a terrace or verandah, or in the garden room, it is a tall-growing variety bearing long, heavily-packed trusses of small, dark-red fruits which are excellent in salads and, being sweet and juicy, are loved by children.

THE AMATEUR. This has established itself with both amateur and market grower alike, not only for its quick powers of maturity, but also because of the high quality of its fruit, equal to that of most indoor varieties. Like Atom, it requires no stopping and it is a heavy cropper. Growing to a height of only 15 in. well-grown plants in a normal summer will yield up to 10 lb. of fruit, and I have even picked 14 lb. from clocked plants before mid-September. The first fruit matures a fortnight later than Atom, and has won praise by its excellent flavour and firmness. The habit is slightly more upright than that of Atom, and it makes more foliage.

WITHAM CROSS. A variety of merit. Resistant to all forms of cladosporium, it gives a heavy yield of non-greenback fruit and is one of the first to mature.

## Tomato, Outdoor

The yellow-skinned varieties are not as popular as they might be. Their fruit is never quite so prolific, yet the flavour is rich, and they possess a smooth sweetness, absent in the reds. The following are recommended for outdoor culture.

AMERICAN WHITE. This is included under yellow tomatoes, for the fruit has a pale yellow shading. It is a novelty of handsome appearance when mixed with red and yellow varieties in a salad. It is a heavy cropper of large, well-shaped fruits, and does well both outdoors and in a cold house. The flavour is outstanding.

GOLDEN JUBILEE. Bearing a large fruit of brightest yellow with the flesh almost the colour of an orange, this is a new and splendid variety. The habit of the plant is stiff and short jointed.

MID-DAY SUN. A Stonor introduction, being a heavy cropper, specially in the South. The deep canary-yellow fruits are of medium size and particularly well shaped.

THE CHERRY TOMATO. The vivid scarlet fruits are about the size of a large cherry, having a rich flavour and borne in long clusters right through summer and autumn. They are used whole in salads, and eaten in this way their full flavour is retained.

THE GRAPE TOMATO. A new and unusual introduction, the fruit being borne in long sprays like grapes, which they resemble in size. They are very sweet and juicy, delicious in salads, and are more like a fruit than a tomato in this respect.

THE PEAR TOMATO. Also tall-growing, but requiring the same treatment as given to the more orthodox varieties. The fruit is crimson and in shape exactly like small pears. The flavour is outstanding the plants being most prolific. This is a splendid tomato for bottling.

TINY TIM. This is a Currant Tomato, which makes a small bushy plant about 20 in. high, being a dwarf counter-part to the ordinary Currant Tomato which attains a height of 3–4 ft. or more. Like Atom, it is very suitable for growing in pots on the veranda or terrace of a town flat, where its fruit will be particularly welcome through summer, and the plants requiring the minimum of attention. With the Currant Tomato, the side shoots should not be removed for they will later bear fruit, and here size does not matter. The tall variety is best grown up stout pea sticks.

YELLOW PERFECTION. An Unwin introduction, having deeply cut fern-like foliage like that of a potato plant. The plant is a vigorous grower and comes quickly into bearing, the lower trusses setting their fruit to a remarkable degree. The fruit is of the size of that of The Amateur, and is an attractive golden-yellow colour.

There are also other interesting tomatoes of great ornamental value in a salad and which make delicious eating, being more like ripe, red gooseberries than tomatoes, and sweet and juicy.

# TOMATO, UNDER GLASS

Clean conditions and the maximum amount of light is necessary to grow a satisfactory crop, hence the reason for the successful cropping of plants growing in a Dutch-type greenhouse.

To guard against Tomato Mosaic, caused by the Tobacco Mosaic and the most dreaded of all tomato diseases, it is advisable to sow Anti-Virus Seed. This is seed which has been heat-treated for virus control and then tested to ensure its freedom from seed-borne infection. Heat-treating will add an extra pound sterling per ounce to the cost of the seed, and germination will usually take longer. But it is worth it.

Where growing in a heated greenhouse, sow the seed early in January in a temperature of 60°F. (16°C). After germination, this may be reduced to 55°F. (13°C.) in which temperature the young plants will grow after moving to individual pots.

Where planting in prepared beds, work into the soil a considerable quantity of well-decayed manure, then take out several trenches 12 in. deep and 9 in. wide. Into the trenches is placed moist wheat straw to a depth of 6 in. and stood on end. This is covered with a layer of soil and is allowed 3 weeks to settle down before filling in the trenches so that they are level with surrounding ground. The straw is to allow the maximum amount of air to reach the roots of the plants.

Plant 3 ft. apart and keep comfortably moist at the roots and free from draughts. A buoyant, sweet atmosphere should be maintained. The plants may be trained up 6 ft. canes or up twine suspended from the roof of the house, and the plants should not have their growing point removed until they reach the top or have formed five to six trusses.

It may be found more suitable to grow the plants in large pots rather than in the border, and these plants will be treated in a similar way. Firm planting is essential and, as the tomato is shallow-rooting, no further cultivation should be done apart from a top dressing with decayed manure given when the first fruits are setting.

Shortly after the plants have been set out they will begin to form side shoots at the point where each leaf joins the main stem. As soon as large enough to handle, the side growths must be removed with finger and thumb or with a sharp knife, taking care not to harm the main stem.

When the first flowers open, dust them with a camel-hair brush to help them to set fruit, and increase the humidity of the house by damping down on all warm days. After the plants have formed their fifth truss, remove the top 2 in. of the main stem so that they will concentrate their energies in the setting and ripening of the trusses – which is all they can manage in an average summer. Throughout the life of the plants ensure that they do not lack moisture, for alternating periods of dryness and moisture will cause the fruit to crack. Lack of moisture will also cause the plants to be stunted, and they will be unable to form the number of trusses they may be expected to do. As the fruit begins to swell, each truss should be supported by tying with raffia to the cane, and any side shoots must be removed almost daily. Plants set out in their fruiting quarters by mid-April will normally begin to ripen their first fruit by mid-July. To enable the upper-most trusses to ripen, it may be necessary to defoliate the plants so that all their energies may be directed to this end. Defoliation should be done gradually, beginning early in September, from which time the plants will require less water.

VARIETIES

AILSA CRAIG. For long a valuable commercial variety, it bears a large crop of evenly-sized fruit, of good colour and superb flavour.

ALL ROUND MILDEW RESISTANT. Where the disease is troublesome (often in a low forcing-type house) this variety should be grown. The fruits are bright red, of even size and good flavour.

ASTRA. The large trusses grow at one side of the plant only and they have short, sturdy stems. It is a heavy cropper in a cold or heated green-house, the fruits being of excellent shape and fleshy.

CRAIGELLA. It has Ailsa Craig as one parent and is virtually free from green-back. An early cropper, the trusses are borne to the top of the plants, the fruits being of medium size and of good colour and flavour.

DOBIES' PEACH. It forms large trusses of up to 20 or more fruits or even shape and yellowish-orange colouring, with low acid content.

KELVEDON CROSS. An F.1 Hybrid, it is one of the best all-round toma-toes, a heavy cropper in a cold and a warm greenhouse, ripening early and uniformly. The attractive globular fruits have excellent flavour.

M.M. An F.1 Hybrid, it is similar to Moneymaker but bears larger trusses. The fruit is well coloured without 'greenback', and it is highly re-sistant to Cladosporium. It does well in a cold or slightly heated greenhouse.

MONEYMAKER. A heavy cropper for a cold or heated greenhouse, bearing large trusses of evenly-sized fruits of excellent colour and flavour.

RED ENSIGN. It comes into bearing quickly and is equally good in a cold or heated greenhouse. From an early sowing in a heated house, it will begin cropping early June. It is resistant to Cladosporium, and its well-shaped fruits are free from greenback.

SYSTON CROSS. An F.1 Hybrid, it has shown greater resistance to Cladosporium than any other. Grown in a warm house, it may be ex-pected to form 10 trusses, the fruits being blood-red with an upright calyx and without any coarseness or uneven ripening.

WARE CROSS. One of the first of the F.1 Hybrids, its parents being E.S.1., as the seed bearer, and Potentate – both old commercial favourites. It is one of the earliest to mature, the fruits being round and even in size. Sown early, it may be allowed to form ten trusses in a heated house and is the most profitable of all tomatoes.

TUBS, *see* Fruit Trees in Pots and Tubs

# TURNIP

For an early crop, sow Early White or Red Top Milan in a frame over a gentle hotbed towards the end of February, admitting plenty of air as soon as the seed has germinated. The best method is to broadcast the seed, thinning to 6 in. apart, and keeping it well supplied with water. The roots will be ready for pulling early in May, when scarcity of vegetables will make them greatly appreciated. The roots should be pulled as soon as they reach tennis ball size.

A sowing should also be made in early April between peas, to mature at the end of June, lifting the roots before they become too large. They must be given a rich, deeply-dug soil and a firm seed bed. Thin to 6 in. as soon as large enough to handle and never allow the plants to suffer from lack of moisture, otherwise they will grow coarse and woody.

For winter, sow in July, as described for a spring sowing. It is not advisable to sow before this time, otherwise the roots will become too large. Completely hardy, they are lifted as required. For winter, sow Golden Ball, with its sweet yellow flesh, which may be allowed to stand until the New Year.

For exhibition the roots should be medium-sized, solid and clear-skinned, small roots going against the merits of the exhibit. But it is the small sweet, tender roots which are appreciated as food.

VARIETIES

EARLY SNOWBALL. Outstanding for early maturing outdoors, it makes a shining white globe and is excellent for exhibition and cooking.

EARLY WHITE MILAN. One of the best for early maturing, bearing medium-sized roots of purest white, tender, and delicately flavoured.

GOLDEN BALL. The most delicious variety when cooked, being round and with deep yellow flesh which is sweet and juicy. The best for keeping.

RED TOP MILAN. Half reddish-purple, half white and flattened top and bottom, it is tender and of good flavour and may be used as an alternative to Early White Milan.

**VEGETABLE OYSTER,** *see* Salsify

**VINE (GRAPE)**

The vine is hardier than the fig. South of a line drawn from Chester to Norwich, and in the west from Cornwall to Rothesay, it will grow and crop well against a warm wall, and in the open, too, trained horizontally along wires.

It requires a sunny situation, where the fruit can ripen, also the wood or canes, without which there will be little fruit the following year. It also requires a deep, loamy soil, preferably over a limestone subsoil, and, where lime is not present, mortar should be incorporated. And it requires Nitrate or Sulphate of Potash, at the rate of 1 oz. per sq. yd., applied to the soil in spring. Nitrogenous manures, except the slowly-acting ones, should be avoided, for they encourage soft growth and tend to cause outbreaks of mildew. Plant in October, 6–7 ft. apart.

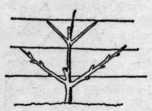

FIG. 15 *Starting a horizontal vine at an angle of 45°*

Under glass, vines may be planted in the border, or in a specially-prepared border outside the greenhouse, the shoots being taken inside through an opening made at the base, from where the canes are trained up the roof. The soil should be prepared to a depth of 3 ft. with a 6 in. layer of bricks or stones placed at the bottom and rammed firm as for figs. Alternatively, use boiler ash (clinker) or mortar. The soil should be a friable loam, to which is added a liberal sprinkling of bone meal and some mortar. Plant firmly.

Grapes may be grown in a cold greenhouse, but where heat is available, a more reliable crop can be expected. A winter temperature of 42°F. 5°C.) should be maintained, and this is gradually increased to 60°F. (16°C.) in spring when the flowers appear. Artificial heating is discontinued with the natural warmth of early summer, when ample ventilation is provided.

When the buds begin to 'break', a moist atmosphere should be provided to encourage them to do so, the vines being syringed frequently and the floor of the house made damp. Syringing stops as soon as the fruits begin to colour and, if the weather is dull and cool, gentle artificial warmth should be made available.

PRUNING

A vine is capable of making considerable growth during a season, a young shoot often reaching a length of 20 ft. or more. If this is cut back to half its growth, it is then called a rod, and on this grapes are borne the following year. Every eye may develop a shoot which will be capable of bearing a bunch or two of grapes, but, at the same time, buds appearing on the older wood or rods are also capable of bearing fruit. There should, however, be a preponderance of new wood, then those eyes formed on the old rods will not find sufficient vigour to fruit. A vine, however well grown, cannot be expected to bear fruit in plenty on both the new and old wood so one has the choice of:

FIG. 16 *Vine*
A. Foliage bud
B. Fruit bud

(a) Allowing one or two new shoots to make growth and restricting all other new growth. This is known as the long rod system.

(b) Allowing the plant to bear a larger number of growths, but keeping these shortened.

(c) Cutting back all new wood to the main stem to form the spur system.

THE LONG ROD SYSTEM

With the vine, all pruning must be performed in winter, during the dormant period before the sap begins to rise. New Year's Day is chosen by the specialist growers to begin pruning, but all work should end by the first days of February. With a new vine indoors, it is best to form two main stems or rods, which are trained in an outward direction and are allowed to grow at will during their first year. During this time they will make around 20 ft. of growth, and at the year end one of them, the weakest, is cut back to two eyes at the base. As with fruiting trees, the important point to keep constantly in mind is the close connection between root activity and the formation of new wood, which means that the plant should be allowed to make as much leaf as can be properly maintained.

The remaining shoot should be tied to the roof, for it is on this that next season's crop will be borne, and the stronger of the two buds should be trained to bear next season's wood and crop. The original may, in turn, be cut back to two eyes, the stronger of which should be retained for growing on.

To prevent overcrowding all laterals must be cut back to two buds, one to bear the fruit and the other, which should be stopped at two leaves, to provide the nourishment. If in excess, some foliage should be removed.

### THE SPUR SYSTEM

Not nearly so commonly used, is the short spur system. From the rod which has been allowed to grow away unchecked during the first year, alternate buds are selected on each side of the stem to produce short laterals in the following season. These bear fruit and are stopped one joint beyond. The shoots are then cut back to two buds in winter. The rod is not removed, but fruit and leaf growth forms from one of the two eyes in the following year.

FIG. 17 *Vine pruned to one bud for new season's lateral*

But the most popular method is now the established spur system. A newly-planted vine is cut back to two eyes or buds, which are trained up the roof in opposite directions. For the first year they are allowed to grow at will. The following winter they are shortened to half their length, and all laterals are cut back to two buds, one of which, as we have seen, will produce fruit, the other leaf. This will eventually build up a system of spurs similar to those of the spur-bearing apples.

All fruit bearing laterals should be stopped at the first joint after the bunch has formed and all non-fruiting laterals must be pinched back to 2 in. Unwanted laterals should be removed completely.

# Vine (Grape)

The one drawback to the established spur system is that old vines are frequently found to be a mass of spurs, far too many for the formation of a yield of quality fruit. Where this is the case a number of the spurs should be cut right away, using a sharp knife, for on an average one lateral shoot to every foot length of rod is sufficient. All laterals should be cut back to the first good eye or bud from the main rod.

With an established vine it frequently happens that, with the commencement of a new season, the buds at the lower portion of the rods refuse to make any growth, whilst those at the rods are most vigorous. To even out this growth, the rods should be lowered from the roof for several weeks before being tied back again. This will persuade the lower buds to break and, at the same time, retard those at the top.

During the first season the vine should not be allowed to bear any fruit, and each lateral should be allowed to bear only a single bunch during the following two seasons.

The pinching of laterals during summer should be done over a period of several days, so as not to cause any check to the growing plant (which too-vigorous defoliation may do). Then, later all lateral growths formed from the shortened non-fruiting lateral must be pinched back as soon as they have made one leaf, so as to concentrate the plant's energies into the forming of fruit.

Although occasionally a vine is seen growing in the open against a sunny wall in the usual vertical position of the greenhouse, it is rarely seen in the horizontal form which suits it better. It requires the same treatment as for espalier pears. First a young plant is cut back during winter to the three lowest buds about 15 in. from the ground, the cut being made immediately above a bud growing in an upwards direction. This is to form a leader shoot. The buds beneath should be trained, one on one side and one on the other, first in an upright position, then, when growth becomes vigorous, the rods may be tied to wires in a horizontal position. At the end of the season these rods should be shortened back, also the leader shoot. The following season other rods, spaced 18 in. above, should be trained in the same way. Each rod or arm is treated in the same way, as for the indoor spur method. All buds on the lower side of the arms or rods should be rubbed out.

Vines grown in the open in the vertical position may either be grown against a wall, or trained up stakes or wires like runner beans. In this way, they would follow the single rod and spur system, all laterals being pinched back as described.

## PROPAGATION

Vines are propagated by (a) cuttings; (b) budding; (c) grafting; and (d) layering, but the easiest method is to take cuttings. For outdoor vines, plump, well-ripened canes are removed early in spring and cut into 15 in.

lengths. They are inserted 4 in. deep in trenches of prepared soil and made firm. To encourage rooting, they may be treated with hormone powder before inserting into the soil. In summer they must be kept comfortably moist, and by late autumn they should be well rooted. They may then be moved to their fruiting quarters, or potted and grown on in a frame for 12 months, pinching out the side shoots and removing the tendrils. They must not be allowed to bear fruit until their fourth year, but should be encouraged to use their energy in producing plenty of strong canes.

Where heat is available, the canes are removed in January and cut into pieces 3 in. long, each containing a plump bud or 'eye' from which the new shoot will form. The cuttings are inserted into individual pots or squares of turf containing a sandy compost, and kept comfortably moist in a temperature of 65°F. (18°C), when they will root in 6 months and be ready to move into larger pots to grow on, those growing in small squares of turf being planted as they are.

BRINGING ON THE CROP

When the fruit has set it must be decided how many bunches the vine is able to bring to maturity, and this depends upon its age and size. The bunch should be of pleasing shape and the grapes as large as possible, well covered in 'bloom'. Where there is overcrowding, nip out the grapes and their stalks with a pair of pointed scissors, also any damaged fruits. At this time, those grapes growing under glass should be given ample ventilation, or they will become soft and will decay before reaching maturity. When ready to cut, a bunch of Black Hamburgh should be dark crimson and globular, whilst Angevine Oberlin will be rich yellow, like a Leveller gooseberry.

PESTS

*Mealy Bug* frequently attacks the vine and the shiny, wax-like bugs are difficult to control, because pesticides run off them easily. Its chief breeding ground is the bark which should be removed whenever it becomes loose but taking care not to damage the under skin. Peeling is done at pruning time in January when the main stems should be gently scrubbed with soap and water. This should keep the pest at bay.

DISEASES

Mildew attacks the leaves and stems in a dull wet summer and occasionally those plants growing in a cold greenhouse. Dusting the stems and foliage with green flowers of sulphur in spring when the weather is dry should prevent any serious outbreak.

VARIETIES

A number of French-raised hybrids have proved to be heavy croppers and capable of ripening their fruit outdoors in the British Isles. Outstanding is Seibel 13047, which is hardy and bears rose-coloured fruit of excellent flavour. Two yellow varieties are Buckland Sweetwater and Angevine Oberlin, both hardy and prolific, whilst Black Hamburg and Noir Hâtif de Marseilles are outstanding black varieties for indoor or outdoor culture.

## WATER CRESS

A plant native to marshy ground in the British Isles and N. Europe, it has been consumed by man from earliest times for its nutritional value and pleasantly bitter taste. It has hollow stems and grows about 12 in. tall, its dark green leaves being rich in vitamins.

It requires running water to grow it successfully, the plants being set out 3–4 in. apart in a bed made 5 ft. wide to facilitate cutting the cress from both sides of the bed. Early summer is the best time to make up the beds so that the plants will become established by winter. In the warmer parts of Britain, the plants will continue to grow and may be cut all the year round. In the north, cover the beds with polythene 'frames' raised 15 in. above the plants to give winter protection.

The bed should be made of fresh loam, into which a little decayed manure is mixed.

To grow water cress without running water, prepare a trench 3 ft. wide and 12 in. deep, and at the bottom place 4 in. of decayed manure and, over it, 2 in. of loam. Top up with a 2-in. covering of sand. Plant the roots well down and 4 in. apart. At all times, keep the plants saturated with water.

## WALNUT

Both the Black Walnut, *Juglans nigra*, and *J. regia*, the Common Walnut, are fairly quick growing, and as specimen trees provide valuable shade for the open garden. They will eventually reach a height of 100 ft. and have grey-green compound leaves which are sweetly resinous when crushed. *J. nigra* has deeply-furrowed bark. No pruning should be done unless any branches are damaged by wind, for unnecessary cutting will cause the trees to 'bleed', like cherries.

Plant young trees, for as they grow older, they transplant less easily. They may be propagated from nuts sown 2 in. deep, and choice fruiting varieties are grafted on to seeding plants.

## WORCESTER BERRY

It has the blackcurrant and the gooseberry as parents, and possesses the characteristics of both. It makes a tall shrub, growing up to 6 ft. tall where the soil is enriched with humus. Its long sturdy branches are covered in thorns like the gooseberry, but its fruit is borne in long sprigs, or trusses, like a blackcurrant. Again, the fruit combines the characteristics of the two parents, best described as being crimson-black, about the size of Laxton's Giant currant, but with the true gooseberry flavour. It makes an excellent plant for a windbreak, although it grows and crops better where not too exposed.

# NOTES

# NOTES

# NOTES

# NOTES

# NOTES

# NOTES

# NOTES

# NOTES

# NOTES